CONSENT

This book considers the concept of consent in different contexts with the aim of exploring the nuances of what consent means to different people and in different situations. While it is generally agreed that consent is a fluid concept, legal and social attempts to explain its meaning often centre on overly simplistic, narrow and binary definitions, viewing consent as something that occurs at a specific point in time.

This book examines the nuances of consent and how it is enacted and re-enacted in different settings (including online spaces) and across time. Consent is most often connected to the idea of sexual assault and is often viewed as a straight-forward concept and one that can be easily explained. Yet there is confusion among the public, as well as among academics and professionals as to what consent truly is and even the degree to which individuals conceptualise and act on their own ideas about consent within their own lives.

Topics covered include: consent in digital and online interactions, consent in education, consent in legal settings and the legal boundaries of consent, and consent in sexual situations including sex under the influence of substances, BDSM, and kinky sex. This book will appeal to students and scholars interested in issues of consent from the social sciences, gender theory, feminist studies, law, psychology, public health, and sexuality studies.

Laurie James-Hawkins is the Social Science Faculty Dean for Undergraduate Education, a Senior Lecturer (Associate Professor) in Sociology, and Deputy Director for the Centre for Intimate and Sexual Citizenship (CISC) at the University of Essex. She is a Sociologist of health and gender, and her research interests include sexual consent, reproductive health, contraception, abortion, gender, sexuality, and hookup culture among emerging adults. In the last several years she has been studying the impact of alcohol on university student definitions of sexual consent. Her recent publications include "Just one shot? The contextual effects of matched and unmatched intoxication on perceptions of consent in ambiguous alcohol-fuelled sexual encounters."

Róisín Ryan-Flood is Professor of Sociology and Director of the Centre for Intimate and Sexual Citizenship (CISC) at the University of Essex. Her research interests include gender, sexuality, kinship, digital intimacies, and feminist epistemology. She is the author of *Lesbian Motherhood: Gender, Sexuality and Citizenship* (2009), and co-editor of *Secrecy and Silence in the Research Process* (2010) and *Transnationalising Reproduction* (2018). She is also co-editor of the journal *Sexualities: Studies in Culture and Society*.

TRANSFORMATIONS

Series Editors
Dr Rachael Eastham, Lancaster University, UK; Email: r.eastham1@lancaster.ac.uk
Dr Patricia Prieto-Blanco, Lancaster University, UK; Email: p.prieto-blanco@-lancaster.ac.uk
Dr Laura Clancy, Lancaster University, UK; Email: l.clancy2@lancaster.ac.uk

For proposal submissions please contact the Series Editors or the Commissioning Editor Emily Briggs at Emily.Briggs@tandf.co.uk.

For over two decades the Routledge Transformations book series has housed interdisciplinary feminist research on crucial, global issues. From Sara Ahmed examining the relationship between strangers, embodiment and community; to Stephanie Lawler's stories of mothers and daughters; and collections from feminist thinkers tracing the shifts in feminism over time; Transformations has published over 25 distinct texts that contribute to the rich histories of feminist theorising.

Transformations seeks to reinvigorate its commitment to inclusion and feminist praxis by expanding and diversifying its pool of authors. We especially welcome proposals from transformative voices emerging from activism intersecting with academic research, voices from the global majority world, and voices that highlight how an intersectional focus contributes to the decolonisation of academy and popular feminism.

Books in the series:

Power, Knowledge and Feminist Scholarship
An Ethnography of Academia
Maria do Mar Pereira

Difficult Conversations
A Feminist Dialogue
Edited by Róisín Ryan-Flood, Isabel Crowhurst and Laurie James-Hawkins

Consent
Gender, Power and Subjectivity
Edited by Laurie James-Hawkins and Róisín Ryan-Flood

For more information visit series page: https://www.routledge.com/Transformations/book-series/SE0360

CONSENT

Gender, Power and Subjectivity

Edited by Laurie James-Hawkins and Róisín Ryan-Flood

Routledge
Taylor & Francis Group

LONDON AND NEW YORK

Designed cover image: 'Femme's Guide to the Universe' [quilt] 2020 by Sarah-Joy Ford.

First published 2024
by Routledge
4 Park Square, Milton Park, Abingdon, Oxon OX14 4RN

and by Routledge
605 Third Avenue, New York, NY 10158

Routledge is an imprint of the Taylor & Francis Group, an informa business

British Library Cataloguing-in-Publication Data
A catalogue record for this book is available from the British Library

Library of Congress Cataloging-in-Publication Data
Names: James-Hawkins, Laurie, editor. | Ryan-Flood, Róisín, editor.
Title: Consent : gender, power and subjectivity / edited by Laurie James-Hawkins, Róisín Ryan-Flood.
Description: Abingdon, Oxon ; New York, NY : Routledge, 2024. |
Series: Transformations | Includes bibliographical references and index.
Identifiers: LCCN 2023028190 (print) | LCCN 2023028191 (ebook) |
ISBN 9781032415758 (hardback) | ISBN 9781032415741 (paperback) |
ISBN 9781003358756 (ebook)
Subjects: LCSH: Sexual consent--Case studies. | Women--Social conditions--Case studies. | Sexual minorities--Social conditions--Case studies.
Classification: LCC HQ32 .C656 2024 (print) | LCC HQ32 (ebook) |
DDC 176/.4--dc23/eng/20230802
LC record available at https://lccn.loc.gov/2023028190
LC ebook record available at https://lccn.loc.gov/2023028191

ISBN: 978-1-032-41575-8 (hbk)
ISBN: 978-1-032-41574-1 (pbk)
ISBN: 978-1-003-35875-6 (ebk)

DOI: 10.4324/9781003358756

Typeset in Sabon
by Taylor & Francis Books

CONTENTS

ILLUSTRATIONS

Figures

Tables

ACKNOWLEDGEMENTS

A project such as this book takes a tremendous amount of time, effort and the support of many people. We would like to thank the many authors who contributed to the chapters in this book. They were wonderful to work with and have made this book what it is. We also thank the Department of Sociology and the Centre for Intimate and Sexual Citizenship (CISC) at the University of Essex who provided support for this book. We also could not have completed this project without the fabulous contribution of Agnes Skamballis who prepared the final manuscript. We thank Sarah-Joy Ford for allowing us to use her beautiful artwork on the cover of this book. Her work speaks to many of the issues we address in this volume, and we could not be more pleased to include art related to feminism, sexuality and consent on the book cover. Our thanks also to Klein Imaging who produced the photo of Sarah's art. Sarah's piece is based on photographer Phyllis Christopher's image of Shar Rednour. We would also like to thank Phyllis and Shar for inspiring this piece and agreeing to Sarah's artwork appearing on the cover. Rosalind Gill provided a brilliant and generous intellectual engagement with this volume in her foreword, for which we are very grateful.

Laurie would like to thank her husband Brian, children Emily and Mira, and her father Larry, all of whom have supported her ambitions and work. I also thank my mother, Cherie, who would have been tremendously excited about the work being done by her daughter on behalf of women and girls everywhere and who would have loved this book. Thanks also to Stefanie Mollborn who was the best PhD advisor, and who remains a trusted colleague and friend. My thanks to Dr. Veronica Lamarche with whom I have built a wonderful research agenda on consent. Finally, my thanks to my dear friend Dr. Cara Booker who is always there when I need someone.

Róisín would like to thank her son, Daniel, for his patience and encouragement while completing this book. His presence brings joy to my life every day.

As ever, my family in Ireland – particularly my parents Ann and Seán – provide steadfast support that keeps me grounded. My dear friends Christina Bodin, Kellie Burns, Rosalind Gill, Tamara Herath, Giovanni Porfido, Embla Säfmark and Julie Shanahan continue to be a source of laughter and inspiration in life.

CONTRIBUTORS

Kellie Burns is a Senior Lecturer at The University of Sydney. As a historical sociologist she is interested in the intersections of gender, sexuality, health and schooling. She is particularly interested in the role of schools as public health spaces across the late nineteen and early twentieth centuries, examining how ideas about childhood, disease and health were constructed alongside the norms of gender, sexuality, race and class. Her recent publications include: Hayes, H. M. R., Burns, K., & Egan, S. (2022). 'Becoming "good men": Teaching consent and masculinity in a single-sex boys' school.' *Sex education* (ahead-of-print), 1–14. Davies, C., & Burns, K. (2022). 'HPV vaccination literacy in sexualities education.' *Sex Education*, (ahead-of-print), 1–9.

EJ-Francis Caris-Hamer is a doctoral student at the University of Essex within the Department of Sociology, United Kingdom. Ze has been a qualified teacher since 2003, working both in the 11–19 and Higher Education sector. EJ's research interests include Queer Theory and application, Feminist Theory, Sexuality, Gender, Criminology, Education, and the Relationships and Sex curriculum. Ze is currently researching the barriers to Queer inclusion within the 11–19 Education Sector. Recent publications include an edited chapter 'Beyond the binary boxes: Challenging the status quo in "diverse educators".'

Cristyn Davies is a Research Fellow in the Specialty of Child and Adolescent Health, Faculty of Medicine and Health, University of Sydney. She is co-chair of the Human Rights Council of Australia, and ambassador for Twenty10 Incorporating the Gay and Lesbian Counselling Service NSW. Cristyn has expertise in gender and sexuality; child and adolescent health; sexual and reproductive health; health education and comprehensive sexuality education, adolescent vaccination; knowledge translation and implementation science.

Cristyn is widely published and is committed to using evidence-based research to close the gap between research and its translation into policy and practice.

Brooke A. de Heer is an Assistant Professor in the Department of Criminology and Criminal Justice at Northern Arizona University. Her research agenda focuses on issues of gender and power in sexual violence, with an emphasis on validating marginalised peoples' experiences with sexual violence and working to dismantle systems of oppression that create disparate health outcomes. She is the co-author of the book *Campus Sexual Violence: A State of Institutionalized Sexual Terrorism* and has been published in *Feminist Criminology, Violence Against Women, Sociology Compass, Journal of Interpersonal Violence*, and *Violence and Victims*.

Aoife Duffy is a lecturer in international human rights law and author of *Torture and Human Rights in Northern Ireland*. Aoife has published interdisciplinary scholarship on human rights, international law, and transitional justice.

Suzanne Egan is a lecturer in the School of Social Sciences, Western Sydney University, Australia. Suzanne's research focuses on feminist theory, sexual violence, trauma studies, with more recent work with colleagues in decolonising educational practices. Recent publications include: Egan (2020) *Putting Feminism to Work: Theorising Sexual Violence, Trauma and Subjectivity* (monograph); Egan, S., & Mikitas. N., (2023). 'Developing ethical pedagogical practices: Exploring violence prevention work with academics,' in E. Pritchard., & D. Edwards (Eds) *Sexual Misconduct in Academia. Informing an Ethics of Care in the University*; Hayes, H. M. R., Burns, K., & Egan, S. (2022). 'Becoming "good men": Teaching consent and masculinity in a single-sex boys' school.' *Sex education* (ahead-of-print), 1–14.

Alexandra Fanghanel, PhD is Associate Professor of Criminology at the University of Greenwich, UK. She is co-lead of the Gender, Deviance and Society Research Group. She researches public space, securitisation, and sexuality. Her recent book, *Disrupting Rape Culture: Public Space, Sexuality and Revolt* was published in paperback in 2020.

Pantea Farvid, PhD, is an Associate Professor of Applied Psychology at The School of Public Engagement, at The New School, in New York City. She is the founder and director of The SexTech Lab there, researching and teaching in the area of the critical psychology of gender and sexuality, psychology for social change/justice, and technologically mediated intimacies. Current projects she is working on include research projects on mobile dating during the pandemic and the experiences of young nonbinary folks, as well as book projects on undoing sexual racism and the psychology of heterosexuality.

Alexandra Grolimund is a PhD (human rights and research methods) candidate in the School of Law at the University of Essex, where she teaches criminal law, human rights and criminology. Her research interests include socio-legal studies of sexuality, human rights, queer history and sadomasochism.

Kerry H. Robinson is a Professor of Sociology in the School of Social Sciences at Western Sydney University, Australia. Kerry's research interests and expertise are in gender and sexuality studies; gender and sexuality among diverse young people; sexual harassment; gender and sexuality-based violence prevention; childhood, young people, and sexual citizenship; and sexuality education. Kerry is currently chief investigator on several national competitive grants, including an ANROWS-funded project #Speakingout@work, sexual harassment of LGBTQ young people in the workplace and workplace training. Recent publications include *Feminists Researching Gendered Childhoods: Generative Entanglements* (2019); *Trans Reproductive and Sexual Health* (2023).

Hannah Margaret Ruth Hayes is a PhD Candidate at the University of Sydney in the Department of Gender and Cultural Studies. Her research interests include consent, masculinities and relationships and sexualities education. Recent publications include: Hayes, H. M. R., Burns, K., & Egan, S. (2022). 'Becoming "good men": Teaching consent and masculinity in a single-sex boys' school.' *Sex education* (ahead-of-print), 1–14.

Carli Hoffacker is a second-year doctoral student in Counselling Psychology at Indiana University, with an intended PhD minor in human sexuality through the Kinsey Institute for Research in Sex, Gender, and Reproduction. Carli holds a BA with honours in Psychology and Spanish, as well as an area certificate in Clinical Psychological Science from IU. Prior to beginning her PhD, Carli worked as a clinical research coordinator at the University of Pennsylvania Centre for Mental Health, conducting qualitative and mixed-methods research in public health and community mental health. Her current research interests centre around perpetration of sexual coercion, and factors influencing the perception of sexual enticement behaviours as coercive or benign.

Kristen N. Jozkowski, is the William L. Yarber Endowed Professor in Sexual Health in the Department of Applied Health Science and a Senior Scientist with the Kinsey Institute for Research in Sex, Gender, and Reproduction at Indiana University. Her research focuses on sexual consent and sexual refusal communication and abortion attitudes. Her work has been supported by both federal and private agencies such as the National Institute of Alcohol Abuse and Alcoholism and the American Psychological Foundation. She holds a PhD in Health Behaviour and doctoral minors in mixed research methods and human sexuality from Indiana University.

Melissa Kang (MBBS MCH PhD) is a medical practitioner and academic specialising in adolescent health. She is Associate Professor and Co-Head of the

General Practice Clinical School at The University of Sydney and Adjunct Associate Professor in Public Health at The University of Technology Sydney. Her research focuses on access to health care and adolescent sexual health. She was the medical consultant for 23 years for a help column in the Australian teenage girls' magazine *Dolly*. She has published four books for adolescents including *Welcome to Consent* and *Welcome to Sex*.

Veronica Lamarche is a relationship scientist and senior lecturer in psychology at the University of Essex where she leads the Relationship Science Lab. Dr. Lamarche joined the University of Essex as a lecturer in 2017 after completing her PhD in Social-Personality Psychology at the University at Buffalo. Prior to that she completed her BA (honours) in Psychology and Business at the University of Waterloo. Dr. Lamarche's work examines how people balance trust and dependence in their romantic partnerships during periods of vulnerability and uncertainty.

Patricia Lewis is a Professor of Management, specialising in gender and entrepreneurship and more recently gender and leadership in the Kent Business School, University of Kent, UK. Her current research uses Postfeminism as a critical concept to investigate the gendered aspects of entrepreneurship and leadership. She has published widely in a range of journals including *British Journal of Management, Gender, Work & Organization, Gender in Management: An International Journal, Human Relations, International Small Business Journal, Organization, Organization Studies*. She was Joint-Editor-in-Chief of Gender, Work and Organization from mid-2017 to the end of 2020. She was elected to the British Academy of Management College of Fellows in 2022.

Mark McCormack is a Professor of Sociology and his research examines how social trends related to gender and sexuality map onto everyday experiences of individuals. A core focus has been documenting how the decrease in homophobia in Britain and the United States influences the experiences of young people, including an expansion of socially acceptable gendered behaviours for male youth and improvement in life experiences of gay and bisexual youth. His work also explores drag cultures, consumption of pornography, the interface of sexuality with illicit drug use, and the social impact of COVID-19, focusing on sexual practices and sexual cultures.

Claire Meehan (she/her) is a Senior Lecturer in Criminology. She is a feminist scholar who conducts co-constructed research with young people to gain insights into their understandings and experiences of sexual media. Some of her most recent publications include: *Talking with Girls about Porn* (2023), "There must be a willy waiver": Young women's use of humour as safety work when reacting to unsolicited dick pics; "If someone's freaky everyone loves it": Young women's responses and reactions to non-consensually shared intimate images of other young women; and "It's like mental rape I guess": young New Zealanders' responses to image based sexual abuse (2022).

Sarah Molisso is a doctoral researcher in the Sociology department at City, University of London. Her PhD working title is 'South Korean online feminisms: The dissemination of feminist ideas in webtoons on Instagram'. Alongside her research, Sarah currently works on Operation Soteria Bluestone, a Home Office funded project which aims to transform the policing response to rape and serious sexual offences in England and Wales. She has co-authored the paper, 'A procedural justice theory approach to police engagement with victim-survivors of rape and sexual assault: Initial findings of the 'Project Bluestone' Pilot Study' (2022).

Rebekah Nathan is a second-year clinical psychology MA student at Teachers College, Columbia University. Concurrently with her masters she is completing a 'Sexuality, Women, and Gender' certification. Her research focus is the influence of pornography on the formation of women's sexual identities. She previously conducted research for Dr. Barry Farber's Affirmation and Disclosure Lab at Teachers College, and is currently a member of Dr. Panteá Farvid's SexTech Lab at The New School. Current projects she is working on include: the Gender Matters Symposium 'Trappings, Tropes, Implications of the Tradwife Movement: the Influencer Positionality,' and the psychology of heterosexuality.

Patricia Palacios Zuloaga is a Chilean lawyer and lecturer in law at the University of Essex Law School. She holds degrees from the University of Chile, Harvard Law School and NYU School of Law. She teaches and researches in the fields of international human rights, women's rights, LGBTIQ+ rights and Latin America. Her recent work has focussed on reformulating the understanding of impact of the Inter-American Court of Human Rights and on strategic litigation of abortion rights in Latin America.

Jordan Pascoe is Associate Professor of Philosophy, Women and Gender Studies, and Critical Race and Ethnicity Studies at Manhattan College in New York City. She is the co-director of the Society for the Philosophy of Sex and Love. She is the author of *Kant's Theory of Labour*, an intersectional analysis of labour, sexuality, enslavement and domesticity in the philosophy of Immanuel Kant. Her research engages philosophy and sexual justice, the social epistemology of disasters, and the politics of reproductive labour.

Laura Pascoe (MS, PhD, CD) is a certified childbirth doula and co-founder of the Doula Support Foundation, a Canadian-based nonprofit that increases access to doula services to low-income families. In addition to doula-ing, Laura works as an internationally experienced practitioner, educator, and researcher advancing evidence-based strategies to prevent violence and advance gender equality and sexual and reproductive health and rights. Her work primarily focuses on engaging and mobilizing men and boys as co-beneficiaries, stakeholders, and allies in creating a caring, just, and equal world for all.

Helen Rand is a Senior Lecturer in the Law and Criminology Department at the University of Greenwich. She completed her doctorate in April 2020, from the Sociology Department at The University of Essex. Her PhD was titled 'Digital sex markets: Entrepreneurship and consumption within an uncertain legal framework.' More broadly her research explores the inter-relationship between socio-legal structures and constructions of genders and sexualities. She is currently working on a project exploring students' perceptions of legal frameworks and how they relate to their lived realities of sexual consent. She has published in *Feminist Review and Sexualities*. She tweets @HelenRand1.

Victoria Rawlings is a Senior Lecturer and ARC DECRA Fellow in the University of Sydney School of Education and Social Work. She works alongside school communities with teacher and student co-researchers to explore and influence institutional cultures of gender and sexuality. She also conducts research on cultures of gender and sexuality in education more broadly and in other spaces, previously conducting research on LGBTQ+ self-harm and suicide in the United Kingdom, the gendered culture of Australian Football umpiring and the lived experiences of queer scientists. Recent publication: Rawlings, V., & Loveday, J. (2021). '"A threat to the social order": A "problem frame" analysis of the Safe Schools Coalition Australia programme within print media.' *Discourse: Studies in the Cultural Politics of Education, 43*(6), 851–865.

Juliana Riccardi is a senior undergraduate student pursuing a BA in psychology at Eugene Lang College of Liberal Arts, at The New School, in New York City. She is an active member of Dr. Panteá Farvid's SexTech Lab and Dr. McWelling Todman's Psychopathology Lab. Her research interests lie in the psychology of interpersonal relationships especially in relation to gender and intimacy, as well as clinical psychology and psychopathology. Current projects she is working on include: the Gender Matters Symposium 'Trappings, Tropes, Implications of the Tradwife Movement: the Influencer Positionality,' writing on the psychology of heterosexuality, and a study on the effects of SSRIs on boredom.

Chrissie Rogers is a Professor of Sociology at the University of Kent. As a Leverhulme Trust research fellow, Chrissie has been researching learning disability, mental health, and criminal justice processes. She is also leading the evaluation strand working on the 'Believe in Us' project, with Heart n Soul, funded by the Health Foundation, Common Ambition stream. Chrissie graduated from the University of Essex in 2005 with a PhD in Sociology (ESRC), after which she was awarded an ESRC post-doctoral fellowship at the

University of Cambridge. Chrissie is currently writing, *Disability, Families and Criminal Justice*. She has previously published *Parenting and Inclusive Education, Intellectual Disability and Being Human: A Care Ethics Model*. Chrissie has written on mothering/parenting, learning disability, ethics of care, intimacy, education, criminal justice and qualitative methods.

Jessica Simpson is a Lecturer in Sociology in the School of Humanities and Social Sciences at the University of Greenwich. Dr. Simpson obtained her PhD in Sociology from City, University of London in 2020. Her doctoral thesis was a longitudinal and comparative study following students working in the sex industry and mainstream employment through Higher Education and into the graduate labour market in the UK. She is currently working on Participatory Action Research with strippers seeking to challenge the punitive licensing and banning of strip clubs across the UK.

Samantha Wallace is an assistant teaching professor of English at Babson College. She specialises in feminist theory and contemporary fiction and media, with a focus on representations of sexual and gender-based violence. Her current book project argues for the value of uncertainty to feminist theory as a way of acknowledging the complexities of representations of sexual and gender-based violence. Recently published work includes 'In defense of not-knowing: Uncertainty and contemporary narratives of sexual violence' and 'Circulating spaces and circulating podcasts: Digital methods as a means of integrating world literature and the public humanities.' Forthcoming 'Literatures of consent' and 'What happened in the cane? A rereading of Jean Toomer's "Fern".'

Abigail Whitmer is a senior undergraduate student studying psychology, political science, and gender studies at Eugene Lang College of Liberal Arts at The New School and a member of Dr. Panteá Farvid's SexTech Lab. Her studies and research have a focus on gender, sexuality, the interactions between politics and psychology, and resisting the hegemonic subjugation of progress in these areas.

Liam Wignall is a senior lecturer in Psychology at the University of Brighton. His work broadly focuses on the internet's impact on sexuality, focusing on how kinky gay and bisexual men use the internet to generate social identities, connect with others for kink practices, and forge online and offline communities, publishing on this in his book *Kinky in the Digital Age* and co-leading an edited collection, *The Power of BDSM*. His work also explores sexual consent in kink and young adult populations, the kink subculture pup play, non-exclusive sexualities, and crossovers between drug consumption and sexual practices.

FOREWORD

Rosalind Gill

This is an extraordinary book: thrilling, exhilarating and important. When I began reading it, I had no idea that it would have such a profound effect upon me. Like many other feminists, I thought I understood what consent means and how vital it is. I expected the book to affirm a trajectory from a singular 'no means no' perspective to one that promotes enthusiastic and ongoing consent in dynamic situations, and to offer new case-studies, up to date and varied examples. I hoped also that it might generate novel concepts or tools to think with. I knew it would be a good read. But I was unprepared for just how good.

From Jordan Pascoe's brilliant opening essay onwards, this book – in the best way – provokes and disturbs and interrogates many of the taken-for-granted ideas I had about consent and left me buzzing and excited for what we can do together with this careful yet radical thinking, and where collectively we might take this next. This is a book that is more than the sum of its parts, that really builds across the corpus of chapters, and that ends leaving you (me) in a different place from where you (I) started. It opens things up rather than closing them down. It starts a conversation; it galvanises new thoughts, ideas, directions for action, practice and policy. It is at once nuanced and specific but also expansive, bold and generative. It is an invitation to do nothing less than rethink what consent means, why it matters and how we might use it to create a better, more socially just world.

Questioning Consent

Perhaps more than anything else this is a book that asks questions. After the (still-ongoing) devastating reverberations of #MeToo – the breaking news stories, the painful personal accounts, the harrowing testimonies, and all the films, books, music and other creative engagements – consent has a new visibility in cultural life like never before. Yet this, the authors suggest, is precisely why it needs to be interrogated and reconsidered; why the time is not just right but urgent for a volume like this. Laurie James-Hawkins and Róisín Ryan-Flood refuse to be satisfied with common-sense notions of consent; they want contributors to the book and readers of it to ask challenging questions and to start 'difficult conversations' – to use a phrase from their other work. Let's not assume that consent is 'self-evident and straightforward' they argue; instead let's interrogate 'the definitions, boundaries and applications of consent'. They ask us to think about: How does context impact what consent means? How do different educational and legal institutions conceptualise consent and with what consequences? 'How do wider social formations of power affect someone's ability to "give" consent?' Who is excluded from common conceptions of consent? And why has consent as a concept become so attached to the (sexual) body, and to conceptions of a seemingly autonomous, rational, unified subject who is able to 'exercise' consent?

Troubling Sexual and Embodied Consent

For many people, thinking about consent means thinking about sex in conditions where parties are not equal – that is to say, across human life, striated as it is by deep and enduring relations of power and inequality. Free associating on the word 'consent' usually generates meanings such as 'sexual consent', 'age of consent', 'consenting adults', and so on. The book begins with these conceptions, but it also aims to trouble them and to move beyond them. As James-Hawkins and Ryan-Flood put it: 'we purposefully and intentionally move beyond that narrow definition of consent to think more broadly about our rights as human beings and the myriad ways in which we consent to other people and to institutions and social structures within different contexts in our lives'. The volume represents exciting new work about consent in different sexual contexts – research that explores how alcohol complicates understandings of consent (James-Hawkins and Lamarche, Jozkowski); how LGBTQ+ populations may conceptualise sexual consent differently from cisheteronormative society (de Beer); and how consent is embedded in kink practice (Wignall and McCormack).

Going beyond purely sexual consent the book also invites us to think about broader experiences of embodiment in the context of consent, coercion and control. Here the reproductive body comes to the fore in a series of powerful chapters that situate the right to abortion within a discourse of a woman's consent to continue or discontinue a pregnancy (Duffy); that look at the violent denial of consent involved in rape and forced sterilisation (Palacios Zuloaga); and that consider issues of informed consent during childbirth (L. Pascoe).

Digital Culture and Consent

Another important contribution the book makes is in exploring how new digital and imaging technologies and practices are changing how we understand, think about and practice consent in diverse contexts. Sarah Molisso looks at spycamming in South Korea – the practice of (men) filming women without their knowledge or consent, often in private spaces such as bathrooms – showing how this violates their rights, autonomy and privacy, but also foregrounding women's creative resistance to this. Claire Meehan explores the non-consensual digital sharing of sexual images of young women, problematising existing risk-based and abstinence-focussed education and suggesting new ways forward. Pantea Farvid, in turn, is interested in women's intimate camming work for private audiences – a contrasting example because it is chosen not coerced – and the ways these are shaped by broader constellations of classed, racialised and gendered power. Róisín Ryan-Flood's chapter offers a novel and original analysis of the ways in which the rights of egg and sperm donors and recipients are being transformed by cheap, direct-to-consumer genetic testing services such as 23andMe alongside social media that facilitate relatively easy tracing of individuals – raising new and challenging questions about upholding and balancing the rights of different parties involved. How can we build ethical frameworks for all these new, complicated and dynamic situations, where the technologies run ahead of humans' capacities to imagine complex dilemmas, let alone design legislation or build thoughtful, nuanced and sensitive sets of principles on which to base policy?

Thinking Interdisciplinarily

A strength in taking this ambitious project forward is the interdisciplinarity presented here. This is a book that draws on multiple different disciplinary traditions and approaches, and this is vital for the work proposed. The volume offers us contributions from literary and cultural studies (Wallace), education (Burns, Rawlings and Hayes), youth studies (Davies and Kang), psychology (Farvid), law and legal studies (Fanghanel, Zuloaga), criminology (Rand, Rogers), philosophy (J. Pascoe), nursing and midwifery (L. Pascoe), management and business studies (Lewis) and sociology (Caris-Hamer, Molisso). These disciplinary lenses are enhanced by more specific foci and areas of interest – including media, health, and bio-ethics – as well as by a reflexive interest in what powerful disciplinary discourses themselves 'do' in the world (what they produce or enact) – for example, political representations of human trafficking (Rand) or legal depictions of sexual play 'gone wrong' (Fanghanel). The work presented here also draws on knowledge produced through different methods: interviews, literary analysis, philosophical argumentation, and participatory action research. Together this multiplicity of engagements, sites, analytical frames, reflexivity, and different takes on the 'same' concept offer us rich illuminations of the complexity of what consent is and 'what it could be' (J. Pascoe).

Intersectional Engagements

The volume is thoroughly intersectional in its attentiveness to identities, loca-
tions and differences that are ineluctably freighted by power. Not surprisingly
gender is central to many of the analyses presented here, which often foreground fraught issues of consent between women and men, or the relations
between women and institutions shaped by misogyny including medicine, education and the law. Gender is also central to EJ-Francis Caris-Hamer's chapter
which looks at young people changing their names and pronouns in a school
context. Class, race (Farvid), sexuality (de Heer) and disability (Rogers) are
also discussed in relation to consent, underscoring a conception of the social
world as characterised by what Patricia Hill Collins calls a 'matrix of domination'. This operates not only in relation to stable identity positions but also in
relation to practices – as Alexandra Grolimund illustrates in her discussion of
the 'Spanner' case, showing how BDSM practices were systematically presented
as criminal acts in this notorious trial, despite the demonstrable explicit consent
given by participants.

Consent and Power

Questions of power animate this collection, extending and adding to an existing
body of work that many of the authors discuss. The book takes discussions of
consent beyond what me might call 'power-blindness' (in homage to critiques of
colour blindness) – a very common form of discourse, often well-intentioned,
that in its liberal individualism and tendency to treat people 'as if' they are
equally positioned in relation to power and consent, ends up reproducing the
very injustice it is ostensibly designed to challenge. Yet in even apparently
consensual heterosexual encounters, women and men are differently positioned,
with women's agency located 'in their ability to refuse or accept a man's sexual
advances' – and not in conditions of their own choosing, as James-Hawkins
and Ryan-Flood make clear – not least because of the force of cultural scripts
around femininity. Jordan Pascoe argues that 'consent is part of the superstructure of sexual injustice' priming a 'yes or no' response, 'but often silencing
other articulations of boundaries, desires, preferences and limits'. Pascoe also
locates consent as a 'key apparatus of white supremacy', constructed on the
privileging of white female subjects at the expense of others who become
expendable, disposable, disrespectable. This does not 'just happen' to be the
case; it is constitutive of the concept of consent and of white womanhood, it is
contended. Such arguments trouble liberal juridical conceptions of consent and
provoke important broader conversations.

Further 'trouble' (to be welcomed) comes in the forms of critiques of disciplinary power – medicine, the law, the media – and also in the framing of
questions about who gets to make decisions – seen for example in Caris
Hamer's exploration of who decides if new names and pronouns are adopted in

the institutional context of the school – and why it is that gender-congruent changes are accepted more readily than names that signal gender transition? In turn, Chrissie Rogers' chapter skewers some of the fundamental assumptions about sexual consent from a different direction. She asks how the experiences of people with autism or learning difficulties may pose a challenge to the fictive subject that lies at the heart of many social and legal conceptions of consent – the autonomous, rational, freely choosing subject. This chapter brings vital engagement from a wider set of debates in disability studies around power, consent, entitlement, dependence and independence, pleasure, playfulness and vulnerability.

Not In My Name: Consent and Everything Else

Finally, the volume is crucial for the way it radically opens up the idea of what is the 'proper domain' for discussions of consent. As we have seen already debates about consent are largely centred on sexual practice, increasingly extending to issues of embodiment too. But why these parameters and boundaries? What would happen if we started to think about consent in far wider terms, and beyond the individual? Patricia Lewis initiates this thought experiment with a fascinating chapter about women's consent to long-hours working culture. If long hours are normatively demanded of professional women who want to 'get on' in the workplace, in what sense can they be said to have freely consented? Push this further and we are faced with a stimulating multitude of questions: who, after all, has consented to bullying, to poverty, to unaffordable housing or impossible fuel bills, to exclusion or dispossession, to racism or disablism?

The slogan 'not in my name' has been used repeatedly by social movements often opposing war – perhaps most famously against the attacks by the US and its allies against Iraq and Afghanistan. Participants in protests such as the February 2003 demonstration in London, the largest in UK history, invoked an explicit refusal to consent to attacks by governments on civilian populations – yet it is relatively rare to see consent mobilised in this way. What would it mean if we expanded the notion of consent to include a far wider range of domains, actors, institutions and structures, and how would it change the way we think about it?

This book raises such questions. It extends our understanding of consent. It keeps the issue of power to the fore. It opens up new ways of thinking and engaging. It asks us to imagine how the world could be otherwise. It is an important contribution and an inclusive and generative one that I hope will prompt urgently needed discussion.

References

Collins, P. H. (1990). Black feminist thought in the matrix of domination. *Black feminist thought: Knowledge, consciousness, and the politics of empowerment*, 138(1990), 221–238.

Ryan-Flood, R., Crowhurst, I., & James-Hawkins, L. (Eds.). (2023). *Difficult conversations: a feminist dialogue*. Taylor & Francis.

INTRODUCTION

Laurie James-Hawkins and Róisín Ryan-Flood

In 2017 the #MeToo campaign went viral and the world was suddenly intensely focused on the notion of sexual consent. As we began to delve into what sexual consent actually means in our research, we realised that the fundamental issue at hand goes beyond just sexual consent. Questions arose such as: What does it mean to consent? Who has the right to consent and to what are they allowed to consent? Where are the legal and ethical boundaries set regarding consent – to sex, to childbirth, to sex work, to long working hours, or to pronouns one chooses to use? We used this notion of complicating the idea of consent as a starting point for a symposium hosted by the Centre for Intimate and Sexual Citizenship (CISC) at the University of Essex. The resulting day-long event was the basis for this edited volume. In this book, we explore the idea of consent as a cultural concept.

Consent is most often connected to the idea of sexual assault and is often viewed as both a straight-forward concept and one that can be easily explained. One either consents or one does not. Yet there is confusion among the public, as well as among academics and professionals as to what consent truly is, how to define it, and even the degree to which individuals are able to conceptualise and act on their own ideas about consent within their own lives. Thus, rather than view the idea of consent as self-evident and straightforward, this collection interrogates the definitions, boundaries and applications of consent. We examine the nuances of consent, how it may work, or not work, in different contexts and situations, and how it operates both within and outside of sexual relationships and encounters, including in legislative and online settings. We address a number of questions: How does context impact what consent means to an individual? How do educational and legal institutions conceptualise different types of consent? How do individuals conceptualise, define and apply consent? How do wider social formations of power affect someone's ability to "give" consent? What does consent mean in online settings?

DOI: 10.4324/9781003358756-1

With #MeToo entering the popular vernacular, people from all walks of life and in multiple academic disciplines have begun to theorise what it means to "consent" with no clear definitions emerging. While it is generally agreed among academics that consent is a fluid concept, legal and social attempts to explain the meaning of consent often centre on overly simplistic, narrow and binary definitions that view consent as something that occurs at a specific point in time rather than an ongoing negotiation between two actors. In addition, most definitions of consent assume that all actors have equal power to enact consent – a notion that we question in this volume. While several chapters do focus on sexual consent, we purposefully and intentionally move beyond that narrow definition of consent to think more broadly about our rights as human beings and the myriad ways in which we consent to other people and to institutions and social structures within different contexts in our lives. Rather than simply focus on consent in in-person sexual situations, this collection examines the concept of consent from a variety of disciplinary and practical perspectives to address how our vision of what consent means may need to adjust to how we enact consent in the real world, whether in face to face or in online settings. Fundamentally, in this volume we question the notion of consent as it currently stands, embedded inextricably within power differentials that enable some groups (e.g., cisgender heterosexual white men) to use consent to reproduce the existing power structure in our society.

The Power to Consent

Consent is a complex and multi-layered concept (Halley, 2016). While there is an assumed shared understanding of consent as a concept when it comes to sex (Beres, 2007; Beres, 2014; Gotell, 2007), in reality, not everyone has the same working definition of what constitutes consent to sexual activity (Beres, 2014; Halley, 2016), much less what it means to consent in other situations to any activity that impacts us as human beings. In fact, feminist scholars have long questioned the ways in which the notion of consent in and of itself may be reproducing power differences that already exist within society (Halley, 2016; Masters, 2018; MacKinnon, 1997, 2016; Varon and Peña, 2021). Society currently premises shared understandings of consent on individualistic and equal power among all people, regardless of their gender, race, class, or membership in any subordinate group (Loick, 2020; Masters, 2018; Varon and Peña, 2021). This assumption of an underlying equality is flawed however, and makes the assumption that all individuals are "autonomous, rationally calculating, and free" (Gill and Arthurs, 2006: 445), when in reality many groups are socially and normatively constrained in the choices and options available to them when they are asked to consent to an event or action that impacts them (Burkett and Hamilton, 2012). An intersectional analysis is therefore required in order to address consent in all its complexity.

In this volume we ask if our current definitions of consent are adequate and question if those who are at a power disadvantage really have the ability to freely consent. Can women, LGBT+, disabled, racial minorities and others at a power disadvantage truly be considered free actors? The idea of being able to freely consent is rooted in the notion of individualism and suggests that all actors are equal (Gill and Arthurs, 2006), while feminist work suggests that not all people have the same capacity to give consent (Burkett and Hamilton, 2012; Gill and Arthurs, 2006; Graybill, 2017; Masters, 2018). However, these arguments go beyond intentional wielding of power by more powerful groups to pinpoint social structure itself as reproducing power in ways that constrain choices even when social actors are not aware of these constraints (Powell, 2008). This suggests that the freedom to consent "will always be saturated with normative ideas and power relations" (Linander et al., 2021, p. 111). For example, in the most common deployment of "consent" as a concept – sexual relationships – gender roles frame men as the aggressor, as the agentic actor in the situation, while women are the gatekeepers, the passive body who must agree to or refuse sex (Powell, 2008). In this situation women are simultaneously supposed to be agentic in their ability to refuse or accept a man's sexual advances, but also are supposed to enact appropriate femininity in remaining fundamentally passive in sexual situations (Hindes and Fileborn, 2020; Powell, 2008). This notion is supported in myriad ways in western culture including in literature (Philadelphoff-Puren, 2005), media (Hindes and Fileborn, 2020), and in day-to-day interactions with those around us. Yet while consent is implicated in situations of power and its misuse, it can also be a source of pleasure and playfulness, depending on the ways in which social or sexual actors engage with it as consenting adults.

Consent: Moving Beyond Sex

While consent is something that permeates most of our interactions with others, recent efforts to expose widespread sexual victimisation across different sectors and industries (e.g., entertainment, academia, government, health) and redefine consent and assault, such as the #MeToo movement, have focused on consent as an issue only in sexual situations. However, scholars also have interrogated the notion of consent in other areas including digital consent (Carmi, 2021), Artificial Intelligence (Varon and Peña, 2021), the ethics of informed consent in research (Kovacs and Jain, 2020; Masters, 2018), consent to medical imaging (Frost 2021), and human trafficking (Doezema, 2002). Clearly consent is an issue that impacts many areas of our lives and as such we need to interrogate it from different perspectives and in different contexts. While consent continues to be discussed most often in terms of consent to sexual activity, it is our hope that this volume will both problematise the fundamental assumptions about what consent is, as well as stretching our imaginations to envision the hidden areas in which we give consent but do not think about our experiences as based on ideas of consent.

Organisation of the Book

This book is divided into five parts: "Cultural Representations of Consent"; "Shifting Meanings of Consent"; "Women's Bodies and the Narrative of Consent"; "Consent in a Digital World"; and "Legal and Political Representations of Consent". In the first part, authors explore the different ways in which culture make representations of what consent is. The first chapter by Jordan Pascoe argues that current conceptions of consent are premised on a racialised and gendered world in which consent is defined by suggesting that some bodies are entitled to consent (i. e., white men, some women), while others are not (i.e. most women, racial minorities). She states that we must use an intersectional lens if we are to define what it means to consent. Chapter 2 by Samantha Wallace examines the ways in which literature can use notions of consent to reinforce the gendered inequality that perpetuates sexual violence, or to highlight the ways in which consent is so much more than simply agreement. She argues that portrayals of sex and consent in literature can offer a look at the issues that arise when consent is equivalent to what is "said" and how this is experienced at different levels. Next, Alexandra Grolimund questions how law uses consent to bolster societal notions of BDSM as equivalent to criminal behaviour even in the face of explicit verbal consent. She draws on the infamous "Spanner" case as a case study to examine the ways in which activism can illuminate the perceptions and motivations of BDSM practitioners. In the final chapter in this part, EJ-Francis Caris-Hamer examines who holds the right to consent to a young person changing their preferred pronouns or name within an institutional setting. Ze explores the ways in which trans gendered changes in pronouns and names are policed through requiring parental consent, while gender congruent name changes are not.

The second part of the book examines how consent is defined in different contexts, and how different definitions of consent can include and exclude groups of people. In the first chapter in this part, Chapter 5, Brooke de Heer examines the role of consent to sex amongst LGBT+ populations. She examines how queer people are often left out of discussions about consent and discusses the ways in which queer individuals may conceptualise consent in ways that are different to the larger societal discourse of consent. Chapter 6 by Kristen Jozkowski and Carli Hoffacker examines the literature on alcohol and sexual consent, interrogating how definitions of consent are fluid when alcohol is part of the equation. The chapter explores the ways in which socio-cultural norms impact definitions of consent and whether it is even possible to define "consensual, drunk sex". In Chapter 7, Laurie James-Hawkins and Veronica Lamarche explore how alcohol is used as a way to justify both that consent is present and that consent is absent in a sexual encounter. They explore how this ambiguity can open the door to definitions of consent that are subject to the individual perspectives of an individual judge. The final chapter in this part by Cristyn Davies, Kerry H. Robinson and Melissa Kang in conjunction with the Wellbeing, Health & Youth Commission, describes a process by which shared understandings of consent can be developed with the participation of youth. They argue that intersectionality is fundamental to these shared understandings and definitions.

In the third part of the book, authors look at how women's bodies are controlled using common narratives of consent that do not take into account power differentials within society. Thus, in the first chapter Aoife Duffy frames abortion rights through the lens of a human right to consent to either continuing or discontinuing a pregnancy. She argues that attempts to control women's reproductive outcomes are a violation of their human rights and their right to self-determination. In Chapter 10 Patricia Palacios Zuloaga discusses the male lens through which law is framed. She applies this to international human rights in considering legal cases of rape and forced sterilisation of women. The next chapter, by Laura Pascoe, explores women's autonomy during labour and birth from the view of doulas and midwives. She suggests that informed consent during birth to procedures such as a caesarean section is critical and a right that must be defended if we are to grant women authority over their own bodies. Finally, Chapter 12 by Patricia Lewis interrogates the ways in which women's autonomy is impinged upon by the demands of long working hours within industry. She discusses how the idea that one can "never say no" intersects with gendered norms to make discussions about consent to long working hours skewed to the detriment of women in leadership positions.

Part IV of the book looks at how consent functions in new ways within the digital world. In Chapter 13 Claire Meehan looks at digital sharing of sexual images, an issue that disproportionately affects young women. She argues that despite attempts to legally regulate such abuse, little headway has been made due to the heavily gendered, risk-based and abstinence only focus of consent education, suggesting that consent education must be reimagined within a rights-based framework. This is followed by Liam Wignall and Mark McCormack's chapter, which interrogates the ways in which consent is embedded within kink practice. They focus on how consent is negotiated through online platforms and what this means for assumptions about "safe, sane and consensual" kink practices. Sarah Molisso, in Chapter 15, discusses the spy cam epidemic in South Korea, exploring how hidden filming of women violates their rights and autonomy. She suggests that online forms of resistance have worked to subvert misogyny and help women to regain lost autonomy. The final chapter in this part by Panteá Farvid, Rebekah Nathan, Juliana Riccardi and Abigail Whitmer explores the practice of camming or streaming sexual performances for a live audience. They connect this form of technologically mediated sex work to in person sex work and explore the ways in which these performances are shaped by broader power structures at the intersection of race, class, and gender.

Finally, Part V of this volume examines legal and political representations of consent. In Chapter 17, Alexandra Fanghanel looks at how sex games "gone wrong" have been treated within legal settings. She explores how the concept of consent is represented within court settings. The next chapter by Kellie Burns,

Suzanne Egan, Hannah Hayes, and Victoria Rawlings discuss how discussions of consent within sex education are both politically and socially charged. They explore the ways in which consent, gender and power have been represented in the news media and used in politics to further the agendas of specific groups. Helen Rand and Jessica Simpson in Chapter 19, examine the ways in which political representations of international human trafficking and commercial sex work is premised on the idea of consent, and the impact this has for sex workers. They interrogate what we can learn about the politics of consent through using a sex work lens. In Chapter 20 Chrissie Rogers examines the impact of criminal justice policies about sexual consent on those with autism and/or learning disabilities. She describes the ways in which the criminal justice system can struggle with issues of consent when dealing with people who could be considered non-autonomous and considers the ways in which the legal system has treated those who are not necessarily capable of recognising social and sexual cues. Lastly, the final chapter in this section, by Róisín Ryan-Flood, examines donor conception families and how people are using DNA testing or social media to bypass the laws of anonymity and trace their donors, or donor relatives without their consent. She explores whose consent is needed – that of the child, the recipient parents, or the donor parent when it comes to overriding the anonymity of donors. Her chapter illustrates how contemporary technologies raise complex questions about rights and consent in relation to donor conception.

Together the chapters in this volume address important issues related to consent and how the concept of consent is used in a myriad of ways and contexts, far beyond the realm of just consenting to sex. They make powerful arguments for the importance of attention to difference, inequalities and temporality. The collected chapters explore complex contexts and difficult dilemmas. They highlight the significance of consent to all our daily lives and how it is never simply given, but always a continuous negotiation situated within wider power dynamics. We hope that you will find the following chapters as thought-provoking as we do.

References

Beres, M. A. (2007). "'Spontaneous' sexual consent: An analysis of sexual consent literature." *Feminism & Psychology* 17(1): 93–108.
Beres, M. A. (2014). "Rethinking the concept of consent for anti-sexual violence activism and education." *Feminism & Psychology* 24(3): 373–389.
Burkett, M. and K. Hamilton (2012). "Postfeminist sexual agency: Young women's negotiations of sexual consent." *Sexualities* 15(7): 815–833.
Carmi, E. (2021). "A feminist critique to digital consent." *Seminar.net*, 17(2): 1–21.
Doezema, J. (2002). "Who gets to choose? Coercion, consent, and the UN Trafficking Protocol." *Gender & Development* 10(1): 20–27.
Frost, E. A. (2021). "Ultrasound, gender, and consent: An apparent feminist analysis of medical imaging rhetorics." *Technical Communication Quarterly* 30(1): 48–62.
Gill, R. and J. Arthurs (2006). "Editors' introduction: new femininities?" *Feminist Media Studies* 6(4): 443–451.

Gotell, L. (2007). "The discursive disappearance of sexualized violence: Feminist law reform, judicial resistance and neo-liberal sexual citizenship." *Feminism, Law and Social Change:(Re) Action and Resistance*: 127–163.

Graybill, R. (2017). "Critiquing the discourse of consent." *Journal of Feminist Studies in Religion* 33(1): 175–176.

Halley, J. (2016). "Currents: Feminist key concepts and controversies." *Signs: Journal of Women in Culture and Society* 42(1): 357–379.

Hindes, S. and B. Fileborn (2020). "'Girl power gone wrong':# MeToo, Aziz Ansari, and media reporting of (grey area) sexual violence." *Feminist Media Studies* 20(5): 639–656.

Kovacs, A. and T. Jain (2020). "Informed consent-said who? A feminist perspective on principles of consent in the age of embodied data." *A Feminist Perspective on Principles of Consent in the Age of Embodied Data* (November 2020).

Linander, I., Goicolea, I., Wiklund, M., Gotfredsen, A., & Strömbäck, M. (2021). "Power and subjectivity: Making sense of sexual consent among adults living in Sweden." *NORA-Nordic Journal of Feminist and Gender Research* 29(2), 110–123.

Loick, D. (2020). "'… as if it were a thing.' A feminist critique of consent." *Constellations* 27(3): 412–422.

MacKinnon, C. (1997). "Rape: On coercion and consent." *Writing on the Body: Female Embodiment and Feminist Theory*: 42–58.

MacKinnon, C. A. (2016). "Rape redefined." *Harvard Law & Policy Review* 10: 431.

Masters, A. E. (2018). "Feminist theory reveals a need for justice over autonomy in research ethics." *Voices in Bioethics* 4.

Philadelphoff-Puren, N. (2005). "Contextualising consent: The problem of rape and romance." *Australian Feminist Studies* 20(46): 31–42.

Powell, A. (2008). "Amor fati? Gender habitus and young people's negotiation of (hetero) sexual consent." *Journal of Sociology* 44(2): 167–184.

Varon, J. and P. Peña (2021). "Artificial intelligence and consent: A feminist anti-colonial critique." *Internet Policy Review* 10(4): 1–25.

PART I

Cultural Representations of Consent

1

THE WHITENESS OF CONSENT

Jordan Pascoe

One of the central lessons of the #MeToo movement is the importance of sexual consent: the need for more consent, and for better consent. Legal jurisdictions, college campuses, and workplaces have taken up this charge, instituting, refining, and enforcing consent policies. We are getting better at consent, and better at recognizing non-consent as a serious violation, as well as an insidious form of injustice.

This chapter asks what is at stake in getting "better" at consent by pushing on consent's lineage, and its limits. In some ways, asking "what is consent?" is harder for us now, precisely because of how deeply consent has come to shape not just our sense of sexual morality, but our conceptions of gender, autonomy, and power. When our concepts and our social practices are intertwined, institutional and legal definitions may not reflect social practices or everyday use (Haslanger 2012, p. 368). In the case of consent, where so much analysis centres on legal and institutional definitions, this gap is particularly pernicious, undermining our ability to understand how consent and social practices organize one another, and how they, in turn, subvert institutional and legal definitions. This chapter explores these questions, naming the limits and premises of sexual consent to make space for us to more carefully engage the question of what consent is – and what it could be.

In asking "what is consent?", I adapt a set of tools Sally Haslanger has developed to scrutinize the concepts that organize our world. Haslanger identifies three ways to scrutinize socially charged concepts (2012, pp. 367–371). In the case of consent, we can distinguish between *manifest* consent, or how consent is explicitly and publicly defined, and *operative* consent, or how it is implicitly understood and practiced on the ground. Thus, if a state law or college policy defines mutual, affirmative consent, but enforces the policy primarily by tracking whether a clear "no" or act of resistance signified non-consent, then

DOI: 10.4324/9781003358756-3

we have a disconnect between how consent is manifestly defined, and how it operates on the ground. And likewise, if we include in our definition of consent a right to terminate a sexual encounter at any time, but in practice, women feel unable to do so without a really good reason, then consent is not operating *in practice* in alignment with our manifest definitions. If revising and refining our manifest definitions does not produce shifts in how things operate on the ground, then we need to pay attention to the limited power of manifest definitions in socially charged circumstances.

While manifest and operative definitions can help us understand what something like consent *is*, and how it works, then a third approach, what Haslanger calls the *ameliorative* approach (2012, p. 376), asks: what *should* consent do? Ameliorative revisions have historically refined consent and rape law, moving us from a resistance model of rape towards one in which "no means no", and now in the direction of mutual, affirmative consent. This work of ameliorating consent has been a central project for feminist, LGBTQ +, disability, and campus activism, as well as global movements against sexual violence, and it has positioned sexual consent as a key tool for sexual and gender justice. This chapter engages the gaps between manifest and operative definitions of consent to identify some difficulties with which those seeking to ameliorate consent must grapple. My argument points to the limits of such ameliorative projects, and to the necessity of thinking beyond consent.

Consent and Sexual Injustice

During his trial, Harvey Weinstein's defense lawyer Donna Rotunno made the case for the value of sexual consent: "If I was a man in today's world, before I was engaging in sexual behaviour with any woman today, I would ask them to sign a consent form" (Honderich 2020). It is striking that such a defence of consent came from Weinstein's camp, even as feminists called for more sexual consent as a remedy for the forms of injustice the MeToo movement had exposed. Despite the epistemic divisions that characterized the MeToo era, there was consensus on this point: consent was supposed to protect everyone: women, from sexual violation of various stripes, and men, from unfounded accusations of sexual assault and harassment.

Consent was often deployed as a defence by men accused of MeToo violations. Weinstein famously insisted, throughout his trial, that "all sexual encounters were consensual" (Levenson 2020); Les Moonves, the CEO of CBS, responded to claims that he had bullied and coerced women into sexual encounters by insisting that he always stopped when women said no (Farrow 2018). Louis C.K. proudly asserted that he always asked for consent before masturbating in front of women – but failed to pay attention to whether that consent was granted (C.K. 2017). These cases reveal the degree to which, as Kate Manne has argued (2022), sexual consent still operates through an assumption of male entitlement to consent. Thus, even as feminists ameliorate consent, agitating for refinements to its manifest definitions, it often operates as a defence of male sexual entitlement – which is, after all, how consent was originally constructed.

In its earliest legal iterations, sexual consent could only be denied through "resistance to the utmost of her abilities": the presumption of male entitlement to consent was so strong that only a measurement of the degree of resistance on the part of the victim – skin under fingernails, bruises, tearing – was sufficient to establish that a man was not, in fact, entitled to consent. The resistance standard assumed that only violent or earnest resistance could make a woman's refusal legible to men; her physical resistance made sex forcible, making it possible for him to know he was raping her. The "no means no" standard asserted that women's *words* were sufficient to produce this knowledge — as long as that word was "no". It created, in Susan Estrich's words, a new "reasonable man" standard: "reasonable men should be held to know that no means no" (1987, p. 92). In doing do, it expanded the definition of rape beyond forcible sex, to include non-consensual sex. But at the same time, it left presumptive consent intact; it assumed that women were saying yes to sex just unless they weren't.

Consent is thus best understood as a *reform* of rape law and rape culture, one that produced critical and targeted transformation, but that tacitly endorsed existing understandings of sex, gender, violation, and power (Dotson 2014). Consent required, really, only one significant shift in epistemic practices: the resistance standard assumed that men could only know that a woman did not want to have sex with him if she resisted "to the utmost of her ability" (Estrich 1987, p. 33); consent replaces resistance with spoken refusal. But in doing so, it doesn't reject the underlying assumption that sex is something men are entitled to just unless a woman can make her refusal legible to him. Rather, it enforces the established structure of sex and sexual availability, understanding sex as what men take it to be, and women as the gatekeepers of sexual access.

So it is perhaps not surprising that despite widespread consent education, many women retain the habit of thinking that refusing consent will be dangerous, that even consent to other activities – accepting a drink, a date, a drive, an invitation to his dorm room or apartment – produces male entitlement to consent. This shows that the *operative* definition of consent has remained remarkably resilient, even in the face of decades of feminist work to ameliorate consent. The murkier cases of #MeToo gave us occasional glimpses of the ways in which consent is *part of* the superstructure of sexual injustice: though consent was designed to make refusals of sex legible, consent has scripted women's participation in sex, ensuring that men were primed (one hopes) to hear that "yes" or "no", but often silencing other articulations of boundaries, desires, preferences, and limits. As the #MeToo movement illustrated, again and again, sexual violations often involve the coercion of consent, the silencing of other kinds of sexual speech acts, and the pervasive habit of believing that one ought not to terminate a sexual encounter once it is begun or expected (a belief premised on the assumption that a heterosexual encounter properly concludes with male orgasm). The #MeToo movement revealed the way that, even as feminists, LGBTQIA+, and disability scholars and activists have engaged in a variety of practices to ameliorate consent, our celebrations of "active" or "affirmative" consent can blind us to the ways that consent operates not as an articulation of one's own desires or preferences, but as an agreement to the desires or preferences of another.

This gendered analysis may seem poorly attuned to the new, gender-neutral consent policies proliferating across legal jurisdictions and college campuses. But these manifest definitions tend to obscure both how rooted the legal framework of consent remains in heterosexual assumptions about defilement, penetration, and male orgasm, and how the discipline of consent reproduces gender as a pattern of proposal and acceptance. In these ways, consent operates as a normative gender project that shapes what women can know, want, and ask for, even as it expects so little from men that it teaches them to be poor listeners, poor knowers, and poor moral agents (Pascoe 2022); it operates to norm and enforce both male entitlement to sex and compulsory heterosexuality. Thus, projects that seek to ameliorate consent, to generate better, more egalitarian, inclusive, and gender-neutral variants of consent, must grapple with the gender discipline embedded in the structure of consent, and with the ways that these norms are extended through consent as it is revised to become inclusive in gender-neutral forms. This tension is reflected in our current reckoning with sexual injustice, which arrived at the end of a decade that saw the legalization of same sex marriage, and the mainstream acceptance of terms like "transgender" "cisgender" and "nonbinary." Yet #MeToo was pointedly heterosexual, refocusing our attention on systemic sexual and gender injustices under patriarchy: as a project of transitional justice (Wexler et al. 2019), #MeToo allowed us to find the power dynamics of hetero-sex problematic at precisely the moment at which their peculiar heterosexuality became legible for us.

My goal, in making these arguments, is neither to reduce consent to compulsory heterosexuality in an exclusionary key, nor to undercut the power of consent as a tool for combatting sexual and other violations and injustices. The inclusive project of ameliorating consent – reflected in this volume – has transformed our understanding of permissible sex, of the law's role in combatting rape culture, and of the myriad violations that shape our interactions with one another, from hospitals and doctor's offices to the workplace and the family.

But as consent has become a hegemonic discourse which shapes the terrain of both sexual violation and sexual injustice, we have sometimes lost the critical distance to ask: what *is* consent? What kind of mechanism is it? How is it constructed? What does it assume? What legacies and inheritances are smuggled in with consent? What possibilities does it open up – and what does it foreclose? Is consent *sufficient* for crafting a vision of sexual justice? How do we ensure that competing visions of sexual justice will not simply be *reduced to consent*?

In asking these questions, I seek to engage consent with the kind of scrutiny that we often bring to other inherited concepts, to see what assumptions and habits are embedded in both the ideal and praxis of consent, which need to be grappled with in any project aiming to ameliorate consent, or to make it more inclusive. In doing so, my aim is to open spaces for other ways of knowing about sexual justice, by identifying *how* consent operates as a distinct and peculiar way of knowing.

Consent and the Racial Contract

Sexual consent has its roots – like so many modern ideas – in the Enlightenment, when consent was constructed as the foundational political right of the modern era: the basis for the social contract, which reconfigured political power as subject to the *consent* of citizens. The right to consent – or refuse – distinguished citizens from slaves, and "civilized" men from "savages". In this sense, as Charles Mills (1997) has argued, it is not only a *social*, but a *racial* contract, one which embedded a prior epistemological agreement about who had the right to consent in the first place. This explains, Mills argues, how the very ideals of equality and consent that shaped modern political conceptions of freedom and equality simultaneously justified enslavement, settler colonialism, imperialism, and patriarchy: these ideals were never meant to be universal. Thus the social contract, premised on the right to consent, is also a domination contract: those without the right to consent can – and must – be subject to domination.

Sexual consent has long worked in the same ways (Pateman and Mills 2007; Freedman 2013). Sexual consent emerges as a legal right against the backdrop of slavery and coloniality: the right to consent to sex – and the legal definition of rape – coalesce in historical conditions in which only *some* women could consent, and in which racial and colonial domination were premised upon exclusions in the emergent right to sexual consent. In the US, the right to consent was inscribed in rape law as a *white* woman's right during the era of enslavement (Freedman 2013, p. 28). Ann Stoler has traced the ways that, in colonial settings around the globe, the arrival of white women necessitated an "embourgoisement" of colonial settlements, including the establishment and enforcement of laws against sexual violation (1989, p. 640): without white women, there *were* no problems of sexual violation, since "native" women were considered sexually accessible. From colonial Indonesia (Stoler 1989) to the Cape (Scully 1995) to the American South (Freedman 2013), the right of white women, of upper-class women, of "respectable" women to consent was made legible against the inability of *other* women – enslaved women, "savage," "native" or "oriental" women, sex workers, poor or low-class women – to consent. Chattel slavery explicitly operated through sexual exploitation and the rights of white men to the bodies (and reproductive capacities) of enslaved women; the enforcement of this entitlement became a critical dimension of enforcing the racial and colonial order in the wake of legal slavery (Freedman 2013; Scully 1995; Sharpe 2016).

This history reveals sexual consent as an exclusionary right, one that was never supposed to be universal: the right of white women to consent – or refuse – sex is *premised upon* men's sexual access to other women, enforced through slavery, coloniality, sex work, and other forms of domination (Freedman 2013; Stoler 2010). Within this matrix, the right to sexual consent was constructed as a key part of white women's agency – and of their virtue. From the Jim Crow South to the early 19th century Cape, as white men raped Black women with impunity as a mechanism for enforcing white supremacy, white women's sexual agency was often *only* legible when threatened by a Black man (Freedman 2013, pp. 100–101; Scully 1995). Accusations of raping white women served as one of the most reliable justifications for violence against Black and other men of colour, who were punished, imprisoned, and lynched for sex – both real and imagined – with white women; in both US and global colonial contexts, these imagined threats justified legal innovations that stripped Black and colonized men of their right to move in public spaces (Thornberry 2016 p. 876; Stoler 2010, p. 59). The pervasiveness of these mythologized threats ensured that 19th and early 20th century courts interpreted any sexual contact — even when it was explicitly consensual — between white women and Black men as rape; white women, under social pressure, were often complicit in this (Freedman 2013, p. 93). White women's right to consent was explicitly a right to consent *to white men*; "rape" is historically constructed as a violation of *white* women's bodies, and thus, of whiteness itself. White women's right to consent is thus an apparatus of whiteness, a form of agency required to make the violation of white women by non-white men legible and monstrous.

The problem, then, is not only that sexual consent is historically constructed as white, but that whiteness, and in particular, white womanhood, is constructed through sexual consent. This is not just history: this complicity echoes in majority white universities, where a disproportionate percentage of the sexual assault complaints pursued by these institutions are against minorities, leading critics to call attention to the disparate impact of campus sexual assault and gender discrimination policies on men of colour – even as studies show that Black men tend to be more careful about consent, to seek it explicitly, and to be wary of drunken hookup culture, attuned as they are to the long history of rape as a tool of criminalizing Black men (Hirsch and Kahn 2020, p. 74; Wade 2017, p. 95). As one student puts it,

> "as a Black man, it feels like a threat to my life in the most basic way to be intoxicated if I hook up…. With white girls, they get impatient. They're like, 'Go ahead. Just *do* it already. Stop Asking!' And that raises my anxiety. Because you can't begin to understand what happens if I just 'go ahead'."
> *(Orenstein 2020, p. 157)*

These fears illustrate the ways that the exclusions built into consent continue to operate and reverberate, ensuring that Black men have good reason both to be particularly attuned to consent – and to take consent with a grain of salt, knowing the history of Black men lynched and imprisoned for having consensual sex with white women. They also reveal the persistent ways that white women understand the right to consent as a key feature of their agency – "just *do* it already" – without attending to the intersectional matrix of domination and exclusion through which their sense of sexual agency is constructed. Thus, in contemporary contexts, sexual consent remains a key apparatus of *white* womanhood – and so projects that seek to ameliorate or universalize sexual consent are complicit in treating the structure of white womanhood as a model for womanhood *per se*, without grappling with the ways that consent was never constructed to be universal.

The Whiteness of Consent

What does the whiteness of consent reveal about contemporary projects to ameliorate consent? It may seem strange to critique consent, at this moment, when it finally seems to be becoming a widely held tool for sexual and social justice; it may seem strange to draw on this history, when sexual consent has been one of the central victories of the past 50 years of feminism. But this history can help us to see the ways that the whiteness of consent remains *part of* the "moral magic" of consent, or its ability to transform an impermissible activity or use of another person into a permissible one.

First, like whiteness, sexual consent operates through a "rational" market of access and exclusion, in ways that mirror Enlightenment conceptions of property (Harris 1993). It locates rationality in the ability – and willingness – to consent (for white women) and in the capacity (of white men) to respect that consent. And by extension, it constructs *irrationality* as the inability to consent (for women of colour) and the inability to respect consent (for men of colour).

Second, this "rational" market of access ensures that consent is designed to legitimize relations of inequality. Though we tend to believe that (manifest) consent is an equalizing force, that it is "empowering," creating opportunities for the less powerful person in a sexual situation to assert themselves, in practice, (operative) consent is often the mechanism through which a powerful person makes their will felt by someone less powerful. This isn't a malfunction of consent: it's how consent is built. Consent is structured to treat all persons *as if* they were equal, *as if* the rights and duties that consent transforms were symmetrically distributed. In many cases, consent operates to make otherwise unequal, coercive relationships permissible (Pateman and Mills 2007).

Third, this enforcement of inequality is concealed by arguments about virtue: virtue consists in the ability to refuse, so that it, like other graces of womanhood, was explicitly white, ensuring that non-white women could not be virtuous, since they had no enforceable right to refusal. This justified men in assuming that the duty to "respect women" by respecting their consent referred only to white women, and then only to so-called *virtuous* white women. We saw variations of this assumption at work in defenses against accusations of sexual violation during the #MeToo movement, when men from Donald Trump to Brett Kavanaugh insisted that they "respect women" and trotted out daughters, colleagues, and friends, to repeat this claim, or sign joint letters assuring us that the perpetrator in question indeed "respected women" in the sense that he respected *them*. The claim to "respect women" *in general* – to respect women who are *respectable* – was deployed to excuse his treatment of a particular woman, who is, implicitly, *not* deserving of his respect. The duty to "respect women" – a variant of the duty to ask for and respect consent – names a male virtue premised on the assumption that respecting women will not disrupt male entitlement, since it refers, circularly, only to those women deserving of respect. It is premised, in other words, on the epistemological contract (Mills 1997) that ensures access to women who are not, by the terms of that contract, deserving of respect. This, in turn, makes the respectful treatment of one's wife, or daughters, or mother, consistent with predatory behaviour in other spheres; it allows men to fetishize virginity or purity in one part of their lives while nourishing an addiction to gonzo porn in another.

Fourth, consent legitimizes and obscures these inequalities and exclusions by configuring the right to consent as an *individual* right. Consent is cast as a necessary feature of (white) women's autonomy and agency, the right to be respected as an individual with rights to her own person, to be heard when one speaks, to see one's words – namely, one's *refusal* – gain uptake in the world. What is distinctive to white women, then, is this right to refusal: like other liberal arguments, my freedom consists primarily in my right to say no. (And in light of this right of refusal, my "yes" – which registers as definitive only when granted to white men – becomes a sign of the value of white men, of their specialness as "proper" men, as men capable of respecting refusal.) Consent prepares white women to understand our agency as organized through rightful refusal and virtuous giving (Manne 2017), and to learn how to *carefully* give and refuse within the rules of the system (which means not asking too many questions about what happens to other women, as well as granting himpathy (Manne 2017) and white empathy where it is due). It is the mechanism through which we come to understand what we must give as *ours to give* (e.g., virginity as sacred gift, the "power" of being wanted/being sexy), to be deserving of respect. Consent here is an individual right, proof of autonomy and the right to oneself.

Historically, white women's sexual consent – and their right to sexual refusal – is racially structured so as not to disrupt white men's entitlement to sex. White women's right to refusal is not disruptive precisely because of a sexual economy in which white men are always already entitled to other women's bodies: to the bodies of their slaves or those subjugated in colonial struggle, of prostitutes and others commodified in a racialized sexual economy. This history constructs consent as the sort of right that characterizes liberal white feminism: an individual right that depends implicitly on men's ongoing entitlement to the labour or bodies of other women, just as white women's right to prioritize careers and work outside the home by outsourcing reproductive labour hinges on the development of a racialized global care chain that ensures that men's entitlement to that labour remains undisrupted. The right to consent – and the sexual autonomy that follow from it – depends upon the outsourcing of normative sexual violation to women of colour, and poor women, ensuring that white male entitlement to sex is undisturbed by this right.

This is not just a historical problem, but one that white feminism is reproducing in new forms, whether in the ways that MeToo persistently centred the sexual harassment of wealthy, and often famous, white women, while failing to develop sustained and systemic resources for working-class women who face compounded variations of these threats (Alcoff 2021), or in the strict rules and laws surrounding sexual consent *on campus*, which ensure that women protected by institutions have the right to consent, but do not extend to women not protected by the institution. This is particularly charged in a post-*Roe* era, in which wealthy women have access to abortion and poor women do not, crystalizing the ways that the right to consent is not only the right to consent to sex, but to pregnancy and all that follows from it. Conservatives like Erica Bachiochi (2021) frame this as creating an opportunity for a new sexual culture in which men *must* respect women's right to consent in a charged atmosphere in which sex might, once again, lead to a pregnancy from which there is no escape. But Bachiachi's argument is premised on the claim that, thanks to feminism and its reforms, women *now have the power* to insist upon that right to consent, without grappling with the ways that this power has always been exclusionary and premised upon the inability of other women to do so.

Thinking Otherwise: Beyond Consent

Consent is a critical and valuable reform, but if it is complicit in the structures of whiteness in the ways I am suggesting, then it is one we ought to wield carefully, with close scrutiny of what we smuggle in with consent. And even as consent is poised as *the* solution to a range of violations, it is important to remember that, as Christine Emba put it, consent is just the floor: it was never supposed to be the ceiling (2022). As feminists, activists, and sex educators alike have sought to ameliorate and open the possibilities of what consent can be, we have sometimes claimed that a wider range of sexual communicative practices – sharing desires, negotiating our ends, imagining together what sex could be – are forms of consent. But when we reduce all practices of sexual justice to consent, we mire them in the limits of consent. We make them part of the floor, instead of recognizing them as critical infrastructure that rests upon that floor, reaching up towards the ceiling.

There are many examples of this. One is the forms of communication many of us became practiced in through the Covid-19 pandemic. During the worst seasons of the pandemic, we had to engage in deep negotiations to see one another. It was insufficient to ask for consent, to say "can I come inside? Can I take my mask off?" or to offer an invitation, "will you come for Christmas?" Instead, we found ourselves engaged in deep practices of negotiation: how will we see each other? In what space and context and with what rules of engagement? If you see me, who else will you see, and how? How careful are you being, and what is "careful" to you? How accountable am I to you, when I am away from you? What am I willing to give up for this relationship? How will I live with myself if I get it wrong, and if my choices have implications not just for you but for your family, your network? These questions reveal this not as a project of consent, but as one of negotiation, the work of creating inter-subjective ends (Alcoff 2018; Pascoe 2022). These intersubjective ends are not arrived at intersubjectively – but through a process of end-setting, sharing, negotiating, and remapping. They track the ways that, as Michelle Anderson (2004) has argued, sexual negotiations cannot and should not be reduced to sexual consent but understood as a form of communication through which participants construct sex and sexual possibilities for themselves.

The practices of negotiation that many of us engaged in during the Covid-19 pandemic are also oriented around questions of accountability, shared risks, and the labour of constructing shared values and limits. These are crucial practices for sexual justice, particularly in a post-*Roe* world. But they require us to understand our sexual engagements – like our social engagements during Covid – as more than a question of individual rights. They require us to recognize our actions as impacting others in ways we cannot foresee, to understand engagement as a collective assumption of risk, and to reflect on how our actions impact the inequitable distribution of vulnerability. These are seeds of a non-carceral accountability, which asks us to think of our engagements with others as questions of vulnerability, accountability, and solidarity, rather than of agency and autonomy.

I point to this pandemic example because it offers the hope that many of us have *already* practiced forms of engagement beyond consent, that we have collectively crafted new tools that might inform new approaches to sexual justice. Of course, these tools, too, are flawed: our accountability to one another during Covid was always shaped and limited by unequal entitlements rooted in white supremacy and misogyny, by designations of "essential" or "key" labour that designated some as disposable, and premised the health and safety of others on that designation of disposability. We will need more resources to challenge these entrenched patterns. We need intersectional forms of solidarity that shift our priorities in feminist movement (Alcoff 2021; Srinivasan 2021), movements that insist upon the sexual subjectivity of the most marginalized and vulnerable (Kempadoo and Doezema 2018; Kukla 2021), and aspirational visions of sexual and reproductive justice that envision worlds that have never yet existed (Ross et al. 2017; brown 2019). We need to look beyond Western frameworks (Nzegwu 2010) and to harness erotic imaginaries that refuse to think within the boundaries of consent (Lorde 2012). And we need to centre transformational and non-carceral visions of sexual justice and accountability that refuse the narrow framework of individual rights (Burke 2021; Chen et al. 2011; Kaba 2021). My point is simply that if we turn to these tools and imagine them to be variants of consent, then we will fail to recognize the radical possibilities that they offer, and we will wield them as if they could be made consistent with our existing and intersecting systems of domination.

References

Alcoff, L.M, 2021. The radical future of# MeToo: The effects of an intersectional analysis. *Social Philosophy Today*.

Alcoff, L.M., 2018. *Rape and Resistance*. John Wiley & Sons.

Anderson, M.J., 2004. Negotiating sex. *Southern California Law Review*, 78, p.1401.

Burke, T., 2021. *Unbound: My Story of Liberation and the Birth of the Me Too Movement*. Hachette UK.

Bachiochi, E., 2021. *The Rights of Women: Reclaiming a Lost Vision*. University of Notre Dame Press.

brown, A. 2019. *Pleasure Activism: The Politics of Feeling Good*. AK Press.

C.K. L., 2017. These stories are true. *New York Times*, 10 November.

Chen, C.I., Dulani, J. and Piepzna-Samarasinha, L.L. eds., 2011. *The Revolution Starts at Home: Confronting Intimate Violence Within Activist Communities*. South End Press.

Dotson, K., 2014. Conceptualizing epistemic oppression. *Social Epistemology*, 28(2), pp.115–138.

Emba, C., 2022. *Rethinking Sex: A Provocation*. National Geographic Books.

Estrich, S., 1987. *Real Rape*. Harvard University Press.

Farrow, R. 2018. Leslie Moonves steps down from CBS. *The New Yorker*, 9 September.

Freedman, E.B., 2013. *Redefining Rape*. Harvard University Press.

Harris, C.I., 1993. Whiteness as property. *Harvard Law Review*, 106(8), pp. 1707–1791.

Haslanger, S., 2012. *Resisting Reality: Social Construction and Social Critique*. Oxford University Press.

Hirsch, J.S. and Khan, S., 2020. *Sexual Citizens: A Landmark Study of Sex, Power, and Assault on Campus*. WW Norton & Company.

Honderich, H., 2020. Harvey Weinstein trial: Could written sexual consent stand up in court? *BBC News* (online), 12 February.

Kaba, M., 2021. *We do this' til we free us: Abolitionist Organizing and Transforming Justice* (Vol. 1). Haymarket Books.

Kempadoo, K. and Doezema, J. eds., 2018. *Global Sex Workers: Rights, Resistance, and Redefinition*. Routledge.

Kukla, Q.R., 2021. A nonideal theory of sexual consent. *Ethics*, 131(2), pp.270–292.

Levenson, M. 2020. Who's who in the Harvey Weinstein trial. *New York Times* (online) 19 February.

Lorde, A., 2012. *Sister Outsider: Essays and Speeches*. Crossing Press.

Manne, K., 2017. *Down Girl: The Logic of Misogyny*. Oxford University Press.

Manne, K., 2020. *Entitled: How Male Privilege Hurts Women*. Crown Publishing Group.

Mills, C.W., 1997. The racial contract. In *The Racial Contract*. Cornell University Press.

Nzegwu, N., 2010. Osunality, or African sensuality: Going beyond eroticism. *JENdA: A Journal of Culture and African Women Studies* (16).

Orenstein, P., 2020. *Boys & Sex: Young Men on Hook-ups, Love, Porn, Consent and Navigating the New Masculinity*. Souvenir Press.

Pascoe, Jordan. 2022. *Kant's Theory of Labour*. Cambridge University Press.

Pateman, C., and Mills, C.W. 2007. *Contract and Domination*. Polity.

Ross, L., Derkas, E., Peoples, W., Roberts, L. and Bridgewater, P. eds., 2017. *Radical Reproductive Justice: Foundation, Theory, Practice, Critique*. Feminist Press at CUNY.

Scully, P., 1995. Rape, race, and colonial culture: The sexual politics of identity in the nineteenth-century Cape Colony, South Africa. *The American Historical Review*, 100(2), pp.335–359.

Sharpe, C., 2016. *In the Wake: On Blackness and Being*. Duke University Press.

Srinivasan, A., 2021. *The Right to Sex: Feminism in the Twenty-first Century*. Farrar, Straus and Giroux.

Stoler, A.L., 1989. Making empire respectable: The politics of race and sexual morality in 20th-century colonial cultures. *American Ethnologist*, 16(4), pp.634–660.

Stoler, A.L., 2010. *Carnal Knowledge and Imperial Power*. University of California Press.

Thornberry, E., 2016. Rape, race, and respectability in a South African port city: East London, 1870–1927. *Journal of Urban History*, 42(5), pp.863–880.

Wade, L., 2017. *American Hookup: The New Culture of Sex on Campus*. WW Norton & Company.

Wexler, L., Robbennolt, J.K. and Murphy, C., 2019. #MeToo, Time's up, and Theories of Justice. *University of Illinois Law Review*, p.45.

2

LITERATURES OF CONSENT

Samantha Wallace

Literature has participated in the broader, global imperative to bring issues of sexual and gender-based violence into the public sphere and into popular discourse, in part, because narrative—the telling of an experience—has always been foundational to anti-rape activism. In the wake of #MeToo and turbulent changes to Title IX policy precipitated by changes in governmental leadership in the US, consent is at the forefront of public discourse, including within contemporary literature.[1] Because most sexual assault occurs within the context of intimate personal relationships, the expectation of consent should be in the foundation of the experience, and current practices of consent in the US highlight the necessity of continued, emphatic verbal communication. Yet, the prevalence of acquaintance-based sexual violence, the predominant form of sexual and/or gender-based violence, speaks to both the necessity and failure of consent as a concept and a practice. Fiction, with its ability to dramatize characters' nuanced, unspoken interiority, provides a window into broader cultural meditations about what might be lost when we rely on a concept and a practice founded solely around what must be said. As this chapter argues, these registers of experience are fundamental to understanding the context in which a word of consent can be given or withheld.

In the first part of this chapter, I trace the evolution of media representations of sexual and gender-based violence in the US alongside the trajectory of US anti-rape activism, culminating in current debates around consent. In the second part, I read Kate Elizabeth Russell's 2020 novel *My Dark Vanessa* to attend to how a fictional survivor's experience attests to both the necessity of consent and the failure of it.

DOI: 10.4324/9781003358756-4

Modern Representations of Sexual Violence within US Media: A Brief History

Scholars tend to locate the emergence of the modern narrative of sexual and/or gender-based violence in the US within the latter half of the twentieth century.[2] These narratives shifted towards representing rape as rape and to focusing on the experiences of the survivor. Robin E. Field argues that up until the 1960s rape in narrative functioned merely as a "rhetorical device to signify cultural anxieties" or as "a trope for other social concerns."[3] Within these narratives, the experiences of victims of rape were largely ignored in favor of the emphasis on the broader social concerns these narratives helped to illustrate, or, if sexual violence was alluded to, the focal point of the narrative often rested within the point of view of the assailant. However, mid-century, in conversation with second-wave feminist anti-rape activism, narratives representing sexual assault began to refocus their attention away from the perspective of the rapist, hitherto hardly named as such, and onto the experiences of the survivor.[4] In 1991 *Rape and Representation* established the connection between rape and representations of rape, and literature scholars since have gone on primarily to argue for the ethical/didactic function of rape narratives in fiction: "a critical mandate of rape fiction is to educate readers about 'what rape is.'"[5] These texts (Field writes specifically of what she terms "rape fiction") "insist upon understanding rape *as* rape."[6]

Though the evolution of the US rape narrative within the twentieth century has been beneficial insofar as sexual assault is represented as reprehensible, scholars, both inside and outside the discipline of literature, continue to be critical of many of the dominant modern media frameworks for telling stories of rape. Linda Martín Alcoff argues, for example, that the use of survivor stories as a commodity for television audiences' consumption in the 1980s contributed to a "collective disempowerment" around practices of speaking out.[7] The US day-time television industry catered to/contributed to a growing interest in "salacious" stories of rape and incest popular in the 1980s. These shows constructed the speaker of sexual violence as a figure of audience curiosity. "Initially, the shows used the power of the stories to draw out the audience's emotional response as a way to generate interest and a felt connection to both the show and the host."[8] But, eventually, "survivors' stories were sensationalized and exploited by the media, in both fictional and dramatic reenactments and 'journalistic' forums. The presence of real survivors, as opposed to actors, provided a shock value by breaking social taboos, but it could also satisfy the sadistic voyeurism of some viewers."[9] Shock value, it turns out, has a short shelf life. To keep ratings up, day-time television resorted to bringing in experts who contested survivor stories and explained these stories away as the products of misguided or pathological liars. These "experts" frequently portrayed survivors as "damaged, weak, and dependent on expert help."[10] Pathology, not justice, sells, and the focus on the survivor's story within this framework often comes at her expense.

Another framework popular in the latter half of the twentieth century/early twenty-first century is what Tanya Serisier calls the "rape memoir." These narratives are "autobiographical accounts" in which "the experience of rape and its aftermath [is] the defining event of the story, as opposed to auto-biographical works that include discussions of rape as one element in a life narrative."[11] Following the growing interest in rape narratives in the 1980s, Serisier describes the boom of "rape memoirs" in the mid 1990s into the 2000s; she includes within this genre Charlotte Pierce-Barker's *Surviving the Silence* (1998), a collection of survivor's stories including Pierce-Barker's, and infamous cases like Trisha Meili's *I Am the Central Park Jogger* (2004).[12] Leigh Gilmore identifies a subset of the rape memoir as the "neoliberal life narrative."[13] In these narratives, the success of the story is framed around the survivor's ability to overcome the violence done to her and her subsequent trauma; such success is the result of her hard work and "grit," much like other neoliberal life narratives.

In addition to the problematic suggestion that a survivor's success is dependent on her unique and individual ability to "get over it," a disproportionate number of rape memoirs published during this time document the assault of white, het-erosexual, cis-gendered middle-class women by strangers who were typically economically disadvantaged and men of color.[14] These accounts persisted in overabundance despite the fact that sexual assaults are much more statistically likely to be committed by acquaintances than by strangers, and the fact that intra-racial sexual violence and domestic abuse is much more common than inter-racial sexual violence and domestic abuse. More so, while not necessarily the intent of the speaker, the preponderance of this type of narrative is founded on longstanding racist stereotypes about Black men in the United States. Thus, these memoirs aided to skewing public opinion about the frequency of stranger and intra-racial rape to the detriment of groups vulnerable to racism and/or poverty and perpetuated racist stereotypes.

The stereotypes reproduced by the rape memoir also affect the representa-tional limits of the victim. The only "suitable" rape victim is the white, cis-gendered, economically stable, heterosexual woman.[15] Like the sensationalized narratives of day-time television, the neoliberal life narrative is a narrow window: though the focus has shifted onto the survivor herself, this focus abnormalizes, pathologizes, or, as Gilmore argues, "promote[s] individual life experiences as examples of a generic humanity and eschew[s] historical and political analysis or contextualization."[16] For Gilmore, because neoliberal life narratives tell the story of a heroine who overcomes her violation by working hard by specifically "working on herself," they thereby abstract away from an analysis of larger socio-cultural attitudes or political structures in place that blame women who speak out against sexual assault; Gilmore uses Jeannette Walls's *The Glass Castle* (2005) as her primary example. It is up to the survivor to make lemonade out of lemons—that is, to cope with the hand she has been dealt, and those who manage to succeed are valorized. Just as Serisier argues, for Gilmore, these memoirs ultimately present "suitable survivors," whose overabundance in published accounts during this time decreased room and "tolerance for other life narratives" within public discourse.[17]

In contrast, many contemporary narratives of sexual and gender-based violence represent the act of speaking out as itself worthy of attention *because* of the difficulties of doing so. They provide context for why so many survivors choose (or are forced) to stay silent in the first place. Commonly held assumptions make judgments about who "deserves" rape or who is responsible for the rape or who can be "raped" at all, which render survivors who speak out about sexual or gender-based violence uncreditable and make auditors less likely to believe in the factuality of their claims.[18] A subgenre of literary narratives published around the social media campaign, #MeToo (2017), take up these concerns explicitly. Examples include *Vox* (Christina Dalcher), *Putney* (Sofka Zinovieff), *Those Who Knew* (Idra Novey), *The Nowhere Girls* (Amy Reed), *The Water Cure* (Sophie Mackintosh), *Women Talking* (Miriam Toews), *Trust Exercises* (Susan Choi), *My Dark Vanessa* (Kate Elizabeth Russell), *Leda and the Swan* (Anna Caritj), *Love & Virtue* (Diana Reid), and *His Favorites* (Kate Walbert). Similarly, narratives of sexual and/or gender-based violence published prior to #MeToo have also seen a resurgence in popularity; key examples include *Luckiest Girl Alive* (Jessica Knoll), *Speak* (Laurie Halse Anderson), and Margaret Atwood's landmark *The Handmaid's Tale*. These are by no means comprehensive lists. In this context, speaking out has the capacity to change cultural biases against survivors.[19]

Well known within US anti-rape activism, "speaking out" is the act of testifying to a personal experience of sexual or gender-based violence. Proponents of speaking out are committed to "the transformative political potential of experiential storytelling."[20] Within this tradition, speaking out is intended to empower its subjects, bring survivors together, and produce social change. Serisier argues, "feminist anti-rape politics is founded on the belief that producing and disseminating a genre of personal experiential narratives can end sexual violence."[21] "The very act of speaking out—on the printed page and at public meetings—was a courageous first step for many women in naming the unnameable [sic] and identifying rape as an act of violence and hatred against all women," wrote Robin Warshaw in 1988 of 1970s anti-rape activism in the US, one origin point for the practice.[22] These events "demonstrated the epistemological primacy and political power of women's experiential knowledge around sexual violence."[23] Sexual and gender-based violence remove agency. Speaking out transforms a survivor back into a subject. Speaking about violence can become an act of community building and activism.

As the preceding history evinces, narrative, both fiction and non-fiction, literary and non, has had a long history of imbrication with US anti-rape activism; speaking out is, of course, narrative based. Contemporary narratives of sexual and/or gender-based violence can be distinguished by the three major changes to discourse around sexual violence to come out of activism from the latter half of the twentieth century. First, as mentioned, the paradigm for rape has shifted from stranger rape to acquaintance rape.[24] Second, sexual violence is now not seen as rare, but as pervasive.[25] And, third, a "dimensional view"—the view of rape as occurring on a continuum with other forms of sexual victimization—has replaced a "typological view." The typological view at the time used a very narrow definition of rape; for example, in the US, marital rape was not a crime in any state prior to 1970 and was not a crime nationwide until 1993. The dimensional view, by contrast, focused on the intersections of abuse, violence, and victimization, intersections most common within situations of domestic violence.[26] The feminist call to expand the definition of rape was thus "underpinned with a commitment to looking at rape in the context of other coercive sexual experiences in women's lives," in part because the typological approach failed to protect against many situations in which non-consensual sexual intercourse occurs.[27] Researchers began to ask women about "a range of other forced sexual acts and/or coerced or forced forms of sex, besides rape. Implicitly, while rape is an extreme act, it could be seen as existing on a continuum with more subtle forms of coercion, from an unwanted kiss to unwanted sexual intercourse submitted to as a result of continual verbal pressure."[28] Gavey goes on to say that when viewed dimensionally, "over 50 per cent of women reported having had some experience on this continuum of sexual victimization," which underscores that these three features—prevalence, proximity to assailant, and relationality—are interconnected and mutually reinforcing.[29] Popular parlance for the dimensional view includes the newer term rape culture.

The prevalence, proximity, and relationality of sexual and gender-based violence all speak to both the necessity and failure of consent as a concept and a practice. Because of these factors, the expectation of consent should be in the foundation of the experience. But, not only does sexual and gender-based violence persist, prompting sociologists such as Jennifer S. Hirsch and Shamus Khan to study the cultures around sexual violence (Hirsh and Khan study college campuses),[30] but, as certain literary works demonstrate, consent *is* often already within the foundation of the experience.

Fiction presents compelling case studies. Because in literature we can be privy to the thoughts and desires of these characters who do, in certain instances, provide verbal consent, we can see how their words do not align with their internal desires or wishes. For example, Kristen Roupenian's short story "Cat Person" (2017) describes a sexual encounter in which consent is given, yet the protagonist doesn't understand how *not* to give her consent. Carmen Maria Machado's short story "The Husband Stitch" (2017) unspools the obligations a wife feels to consent to her husband's desires against her own and the husband's easy willingness to oblige himself. Kate Walbert's novel *His Favorites* (2018) poignards the adult teacher who preys on minors, those who are not capable of consenting, and the institutions that protect him to protect themselves in part by undermining a survivor's capacity to speak and be heard as credible. In the novel *My Dark Vanessa* (2020), consent as a practice is actually used against the protagonist, Vanessa Wye by her assailant, Jacob Strane.

My Dark Vanessa

In the remainder of this chapter, I read *My Dark Vanessa* to illustrate how consent is co-opted and used against Vanessa. The novel has two parallel storylines: in one, Vanessa is fifteen, in the other Vanessa is thirty-two. In the wake of #MeToo (not named in the novel but heavily implied) thirty-two-year-old Vanessa Wye is confronted by her past, namely the relationship she had as a teenager with her adult literature teacher, Jacob Strane. This relationship begins when Vanessa is fifteen. *My Dark Vanessa* is thus an excruciatingly detailed dramatization of statutory rape. At the outset of the novel, Strane has been accused of abuse by another former student, prompting more students to come forward and the history between Strane and Vanessa to again get dredged to the surface. But Vanessa, instead of allying with Strane's accusers, women who were girls in her exact position, remains one of Strane's staunchest allies: she is consistently unwilling to blame Strane; she won't contribute to a developing journalism story covering allegations of abuse from another student; and she doesn't believe the other women who speak out about abuse at Strane's hands. In part, Vanessa's loyalty can be explained by the fact that (she believes) she has consented to sexual and emotional abuse that spans over fifteen years.

At thirty-two Vanessa refuses to be what she calls a "good victim," and, as the novel unravels the entanglement between Vanessa and Strane that began when Vanessa was fifteen, we learn how and why she feels she can't be. Vanessa is trapped within logics (her own, her assailant's, society's) that prevent her from understanding herself as a victim of longstanding sexual abuse. Vanessa refuses the term victim: "I search endlessly for myself," Vanessa explains, "but never find anything truly accurate. Girls in those stories are always victims, and I am not [...] I am not a victim because I never wanted to be, and if I don't want to be, then I'm not. That's how it works. The difference between sex and rape is a state of mind."[31] This a dangerous and devastating bright line: it highlights the conflict between the imperative for the survivor to be the ultimate arbiter of her experience with the necessity for objective criteria for defining an act of sexual assault.

Vanessa's resentment of victimhood echoes the sentiments of critics such as Katie Roiphe, who has argued that women have been trained, to their detriment, to see themselves as victims.[32] Yet Vanessa's refusal to see herself as a victim of abuse isolates her, first as a child, then as an adult. Moreso, it protects her abuser, who was forty-two to Vanessa's fifteen. Here are the facts of the case: Vanessa was fifteen and he forty-two, Strane sexually assaulted her for years, and this abuse spans over more than half of Vanessa's life. Yet Strane manages to cultivate a specific interpretation around the act of giving and receiving consent that nullifies the stark conclusions everyone else in Vanessa's life (besides Strane) draws from these facts. Consent becomes imbricated with victimhood. Thirty-two-year-old Vanessa protests to her therapist, Ruby,

"No, listen to me. Don't act like I don't know what I'm saying. He never forced me, ok? He made sure I said yes to everything, especially when I was younger. He was careful. He was good. He loved me."

(DV 318–19)

Victims, those who do not consent, Vanessa believes, are unloved. Unspecial. Powerless. Vanessa, on the other hand, has consented. She identifies with Sylvia Plath's "Lady Lazarus," which concludes "Out of the ash/I rise with my red hair/And I eat men like air."

Yes, the man who grooms, assaults, and emotionally preys on Vanessa for years was the one to give her that poem.

Because of *My Dark Vanessa*'s first-person narrator, readers can see how Vanessa's early decision making is marked by her desire to please Strane. Readers are uniquely privy not just to Vanessa's speech, but to her thoughts, desires, and doubts; her confusion over Strane's intentions; self-recrimination; and her inexperience, commensurate with her age, with determining the answers to what she wants and how she understands herself. In the space where Vanessa should be determining these things about herself for herself, Strane first inserts himself. This is how it begins. When he gives her a copy of Sylvia Plath's *Ariel*, he says:

"Is it ok that it reminded me of you?"
    I lick my lips, lift my shoulders. "Sure."
"Because the last thing I want to do is overstep."
    Overstep. I'm not sure what he means by that, either, but the way he gazes down at me stops me from asking any questions. He suddenly seems both embarrassed and hopeful, like if I told him this wasn't ok, he might start to cry.
    So I smile, shake my head. "You're not."
    He exhales. "Good"

(DV 38)

Consent is implicated within this structure of grooming in which Strane presents a problem (his emotional discomfort/pain) and the opportunity to assuage it (for Vanessa to agree with him). The novel rehearses many similar scenes in which Strane acquires her consent, but Vanessa's internal narration belies the "yes" she provides him with pain, confusion, discomfort, irritation, fear of repercussions, lack of interest, et cetera. The pattern has been established: saying yes means pleasing Strain. When he rapes her for the first time, he says "'Do you want me to fuck you?'" and Vanessa thinks, "It's a question, but he isn't really asking" (DV 102).

Around Vanessa's early "yeses," Strane builds a fortress around her, and the patterns he establishes when Vanessa is fifteen persist into an age when she is legally capable of consenting. Her yesses, he claims, prove that she is just as responsible as he is. If anything, they prove she is more complicit, since he has borne the legal burden of their relationship. Strane uses consent to entrap Vanessa and to indemnify himself. He makes her responsible for his crimes. He even goes so far as to get her to agree to her own expulsion: he gives her a fake story to tell the headmaster when rumors about them precipitate an investigation, that Vanessa lied about an affair between the two of them to get attention. Vanessa complies and is expelled. Why would she consent to such treatment?

In posing this question, I want to highlight the importance of focusing on the way the survivor experiences this abuse. Two primary ideas form the bedrock of Vanessa's thinking: a desire to be desired, which, if reciprocated, marks her as special and powerful, and the belief that this desire and power simultaneously makes her deserving of whatever happens to her (both of which Strane cultivates and exploits). And if she is loved and if she deserves the abuse (two contradictory but self-sustaining ideas), then she cannot be a victim, in her eyes. After explaining this to Ruby, her therapist, Vanessa implores, "I just really need it to be a love story. You know? I really need that. [...] Because if it isn't a love story, then what is it?" (*DV* 319). In reporting the veracity and force of Vanessa's feelings so faithfully, the novel presents *both*, a story of sexual assault and a love story—not because one excuses or negates the other, but because both are a part of Vanessa's experience, and only one explains how the other has come to pass and perpetuates itself.

It is important to consider consent in this context, despite the fact that legally Vanessa cannot consent when Strane begins grooming her at the age of fifteen, because it allows us to understand Vanessa. Vanessa's status as a minor, and therefore her inability to consent, is relevant for the ultimate condemnation that occurs (though Strane commits suicide before he can be brought to trial), but consent as it is practiced by Vanessa and Strane is critical for understanding how Vanessa understands what has happened to her, and why she cannot see herself as a victim. Vanessa's resentment of victimhood and her insistence upon her own consent serve as coping mechanisms for Vanessa. She has said yes, so she is equally, if not more, responsible.

As the novel unfolds, we are reminded of a crucial distinction: To be a victim is not to fail to take responsibility for one's actions. To be a victim is to grapple with how one's core agency has been, in that moment, taken away. It is to be faced with the threat of powerlessness, a threat to which Vanessa assigns not injustice, but shame. "'He was so in love with me,'" Vanessa explains to her therapist,

> "'he used to sit in my chair after I left the classroom. He'd put his face down on the table and try to breathe me in' [...] 'Vanessa,' she says gently, 'you didn't ask for that. You were just trying to go to school.' I stare out the window over her shoulder, at the harbour, the swarming gulls, the slate-gray water and sky, but I only see myself, barely sixteen with tears in my eyes, standing in front of a room of people, calling myself a liar, a bad girl deserving of punishment."

> (*DV 265*)

To be a victim you cannot be someone's beloved, Strane has groomed Vanessa to believe. To be desired is to be powerful, and to be powerful and desirable is to be responsible. After all, Vanessa consented.

Conclusion

The imbrication of Strane's actions and Vanessa's thinking about her own desires in this example implicates consent. Literary works like *My Dark Vanessa* are important not because they suggest we should jettison consent as a practice, but because in attending to a concept's weakness we might ultimately make it stronger. Consent is an important boundary line, and yet experience is often so much harder to define than what can be quantified by yes or no, or by the difference between seventeen years of age and eighteen: "I need someone to show me the line," Vanessa thinks, "that's supposed to separate twenty-seven years older from thirteen years, teacher from professor, criminal from socially acceptable. Or maybe I'm supposed to encompass the difference here. Years past my eighteenth birthday, I'm fair game now, a consenting adult" (*DV* 346–47). And while Vanessa's refusal to be a "good victim" has been touted as the novel's most controversial element, I think, in light of the continued necessity and failure of consent as a practice, the novel's most controversial and compelling element is how at its core it provokes us to question, how can you be both abused and loved? How, as a reader, can one both honor a survivor's experience and also hold fast to the bright line of consent? The weight of these things is to be found in narrative accounts. Perhaps to be a victim is the cumulative weight of all these things, not an identity but a feeling, and to be a survivor, the act of carrying of it.

Notes

1 Title IX is the most common name for the US Civil Rights amendment prohibiting discrimination on the basis of sex in any school or education program that receives federal funding. Former President Trump's administration had rolled back many of the expanded protections for survivors laid out by the Obama administration. In June of 2022, the Biden administration announced its plan to reinstate regulations abandoned by the Trump administrations and to expand protections by adding "clarifying text [to the amendment] to include protections against discrimination based on sexual orientation and gender identity to strengthen the rights of LGBTQI+ students." Dustin Jones, "Biden's Title IX reforms would roll back Trump-era rules, expand victim protections," *NPR* (June 23, 2022): https://www.npr.org/2022/06/23/1107045291/title-ix-9-biden-expand-victim-protections-discrimination.

2 Kenneth Plummer argues the contemporary rape narrative came into its own from the 1970s to the 1990s. Plummer, *Telling Sexual Stories: Power, Change, and Social Worlds*. New York: Routledge, 1995, 49.

3 Robin E. Field, *Writing the Survivor: The Rape Novel in Late Twentieth-century American Fiction*. Clemson: Clemson University Press, 2020, 10, 9–10.

4 At the height of the culture wars, some narratives would swerve back to representing the assailant as embattled and unduly persecuted.

5 Field, *Writing the Survivor*, 15. See also, Lynn A. Higgins and Brenda R. Silver, *Rape and Representation*. New York: Columbia University Press, 1991.
6 Field, *Writing the Survivor*, 20.
7 Linda Martín Alcoff, *Rape and Resistance: Understanding the Complexities of Sexual Violation*. Cambridge, UK: Polity Press, 2018, 181.
8 Alcoff, *Rape and Resistance*, 178.
9 Alcoff, *Rape and Resistance*, 180–81.
10 Alcoff, *Rape and Resistance*, 181.
11 Tanya Serisier, *Speaking Out: Feminism, Rape and Narrative Politics*. Basingstoke, Hampshire: Palgrave Macmillan, 2018, 47.
12 Charlotte Pierce-Barker, *Surviving the Silence: Black Women's Stories of Rape*. New York: W. W. Norton, 2000. Trisha Meiji, *I Am the Central Park Jogger: A Story of Hope and Possibility*. New York, Scribner, 2004.
13 Gilmore, *Tainted Witness: Why We Doubt What Women Say About Their Lives*. New York: Columbia University Press, 2017, 93.
14 See Serisier, *Speaking Out*, 47.
15 See, Terrion L. Williamson, "What Does That Make You? Public Narration and the Serial Murders of Black Women," in *Where Freedom Starts: Sex Power Violence #MeToo*. Verso Press, 2018, 73–86. By and large, these limitations persist in the current publishing marketplace: though the trend has shifted towards representing acquaintance sexual assault (a trend reinforced by the explosion of #MeToo on social media in 2017), the marketplace remains dominated by accounts of heterosexual, cisgendered, white middleclass women; a 2020 survey reports that the publishing industry itself is 76% white. See: https://www.publishersweekly.com/pw/by-topic/industry-news/publisher-news/article/82284-new-lee-and-low-survey-shows-no-progress-on-diversity-in-publishing.html. Authors of color report their failure to sell or promote to the same degree their own narratives due to gatekeeping and racial biases of publishers. In some cases, these authors claim their narrative presents content almost identical to those sold by white counterparts. One such case involves Kate Elizabeth Russell's *My Dark Vanessa* (2020), a novel that will be discussed later at length, and Wendy C. Ortiz's memoir *Excavation* (2014). Ortiz has accused Russell of plagiarizing elements of her memoir for Russell's much anticipated and widely promoted novel. In response, Russel has explained publicly that *My Dark Vanessa* was based on experiences she herself had when she was a teenager. The controversy resulted in *My Dark Vanessa* being dropped by promotions as influential as Oprah's book club.
16 Gilmore, *Tainted Witness*, 93.
17 Gilmore, *Tainted Witness*, 94. Gilmore also critiques the rise of the self-help genre, a genre not specific to survivors, within this framework. See Gilbert, *Tainted Witness*, 111–15.
18 See, for example, Merril D. Smith's list of the following commonly held attitudes about rape: "victims deserve, cause, invite, ask for, or want to be raped; victims who get raped could have avoided it and therefore are at fault; and victims are sexually promiscuous, or they are sexually active with the offender, and thus she/he was a willing partner in the sex act." Smith, *The Encyclopedia of Rape*. Westport, CT: Greenwood Press, 2004, 191.
19 While this shift is laudatory, dominant contemporary discourse is by no means radical. Narratives published continue to be predominantly white and to foreground the experiences of cis-hetero women.
20 Serisier, *Speaking Out*, 4.
21 Serisier, *Speaking Out*, 4.
22 Robin Warshaw and Mary P. Koss, *I Never Called It Rape: The Ms. Report On Recognizing, Fighting, and Surviving Date and Acquaintance Rape*. New York: Harper & Row, 1988, 1.
23 Serisier, *Speaking Out*, 6.

24 RAINN reports that eight of out ten acts of sexual violence are committed by perpetrators who are known to the victim, and that 57% of sexual violence is committed by perpetrators who are white: https://www.rainn.org/statistics/perpetrators-sexual-violence.

25 See, Nicola Gavey, *Just Sex?: The Cultural Scaffolding of Rape*. Second ed. New York: Routledge, Taylor & Francis Group, 2019, 59–60.

26 Gavey describes how this shift towards a dimensional view within anti-rape activism was derived out of and in opposition to the narrower, typological legal definition of rape in the 1980s. Gavey, *Just Sex?*, 61. Research precipitating this shift to dimensional thinking about rape is extensive. Gavey also cites Diana E. H. Russell, *Rape in Marriage*. New York: Macmillan, 1982; Gavey, "Sexual victimization among Aukland University students: How much and who does it?" *New Zealand Journal of Pyschology* 20, no. 2 (1991): 63–70; and research by Liz Kelly (1987, 1988a, 1988b), Richard J. Gelles (1977), and David Finkelhor and Kersti Yllö (1983, 1985). Gavey, *Just Sex?*, 60. Liz Kelly, "The continuum of sexual violence," in J. Hanmer and M. Maynard (eds), *Women, Violence, and Social Control*. Basingstroke and London: Macmillan Press. Kelly, "How women define their experiences of violence," in K. Yllö and M. Bograd (eds), *Feminist Perspectives of Wife Abuse*. Newbury Park: Sage, 1988a, 114–32. Kelly, *Surviving Sexual Violence*. Cambridge, UK: Polity Press, 1988b. Richard J. Gelles, "Power, sex, and violence: The case of martial rape," *The Family Coordinator* 26. no. 4 (1977): 339–47. David Finkelhor and Kersti Yllö, "Rape in marriage: A sociological view," in Finkelhor, R. J. Gelles, G. T. Hotaling, and M. A. Straus (eds), *The Dark Side of Families: Current Family Violence Research*. Beverly Hills: Sage, 1983, 119–30. Finkelhor and Yllö, *License to Rape: Sexual Abuse of Wives*. New York: The Free Press, 1985.

27 Gavey, *Just Sex?*, 60.

28 Gavey, *Just Sex?*, 60. The "Sexual Experience Survey" was designed as a part of Koss's research on the prevalence of rape. See, Koss and C. J. Oros, "Sexual experiences survey: a research instrument investigating sexual aggression and victimization," *Journal of Consulting & Clinical Psychology* 50, no. 3 (1982): 455–57.

29 Gavey, *Just Sex?*, 60.

30 See, Jennifer S. Hirsch and Shamus Khan, *Sexual Citizens: A Landmark Study of Sex, Power, and Assault on Campus*. New York: W. W. Norton & Company, 2020.

31 Kate Elizabeth Russell, *My Dark Vanessa*. New York: Harper Collins, 2020, 270 (hereafter cited in-text as *DV*).

32 See Katie Roiphe, *The Morning After: Sex, Fear, and Feminism*. Boston: Back Bay Books, 1994; and Roiphe, "The Other Whisper Network: How Twitter feminism is bad for women," *Harper's Magazine* (March, 2018), https://harpers.org/archive/2018/03/the-other-whisper-network-2/.

3

SM, THE LAW, AND AN OPAQUE SEXUAL CONSENT NARRATIVE

Alexandra Grolimund

Having left prison, my acute anger at the injustice of the trial fuelled my determination to get our case heard by the European Human Rights Commission in an
attempt to have the laws that led to our convictions changed. Our case will be a
historic one in the continuing movement towards greater sexual freedom. The
verdict will be vitally important to those who believe that what consenting adults
do in private is nobody's business but their own. Through the Countdown on
Spanner Campaign, the SM and human-rights organisations have raised awareness of the issues at stake. At the most extreme end of the scale, it remains an
offence in law for anyone to spank his or her partner if the mark that is left lasts
more than a few hours, regardless of whether the spanking was consensual.

Thanks to our case, attitudes towards SM are changing rapidly. Not only has it
become a more acceptable form of behaviour, but one can also see its influence on
mainstream culture, fashion and safer sex practices. As OutRage so aptly put it, it
is high time the judges were evicted from the nation's bedrooms.

Antony Brown, Operation Spanner defendant, in an interview with the
Independent, 12th October 1996

Introduction

Gayle Rubin (1999) in the epochal *Thinking Sex* characterized sadomasochists
as occupying the lowest tiers of hierarchical sexual value. Could it be that this
is still the case? BDSM,[1] and particularly sadomasochism (SM), draws increasing attention in mainstream culture, especially due to the popularization of
films including Lars von Trier's *Nymphomaniac*, Netflix's *365 Days* and the
ubiquitous *50 Shades of Grey* trilogy. BDSM practice in private homes expanded as a subculture, growing internationally through the 20th century. The history of this culture has been scarcely documented as part of research into social
movements expanding sexual liberties internationally (Stein 2021).

DOI: 10.4324/9781003358756-5

Despite its rising visibility, consensual BDSM remains criminalised.[2] The opaque legal area this sexual practice and identity occupies however, proves rife for rumination regarding law's paternalistic regulation of sexuality. This criminal act as part of a legal legacy of problematic judicial and legislative decisions results from a set of consequential moments in history and a temporal trajectory stemming from a seminal case, which will this year celebrate its 30th anniversary: *R v Brown* [1993] UKHL 19, [1994] 1 AC 212.

Brown, which saw a group of men prosecuted and convicted for consensual sadomasochistic sex, is discussed in law modules across the United Kingdom as one of the biggest legal challenges to the limits of consent. The infamous judgement held that notwithstanding consent, the sadomasochistic libido constitutes no effable reason for harm-doing. It was met with backlash from the queer community, whose indignant protests championed bodily autonomy and discrimination.

The problem is one of legal complexity, but also opacity; it lies in the mystification of the practice, and the divergence in understandings of consent between lawmakers and practitioners. The paradox remains: one seemingly cannot consent to sadomasochistic sex in the view of the law – despite consent underpinning the practice. The legal principle's recent resurrection as part of the Domestic Abuse Act 2021 (DAA) as a direct result against the 'rough sex defence' necessitates a timely remembrance of the case's problematic legacy and conflation of sexual gratification (via BDSM) and sexual violence in tandem with consideration of how activist reaction is reincarnated in the present. This chapter will begin with a brief analysis of *Brown* and the problematic legal framework remaining as its legacy. It will then assess public reactions to *Brown* as they pertain to narratives of consent. The discussion will conclude by considering these narratives as applied to contemporary legal developments, namely the DAA.

R v Brown and a Problematic Legal Legacy

This analysis will be relatively brief and provide a backdrop for the ensuing discussion, as most academic study on the case is considered extensively from a legal perspective and best frames the case's complexity from this perspective.[3] With the recent reiteration of its precedent legal framework in mind, it is necessary to explore said framework's core legal principles and facets, its criticisms and contextual underpinnings.

In 1987, the Metropolitan Police's Obscene Publications Branch or Squad (OPS) launched the 'Operation Spanner' investigation into a supposed 'ring' of men involved in sadomasochistic group sex. Police were handed videotapes of men engaged in BDSM activities – the origins of said tapes unknown definitively. Some reports say police carried out over 100 interviews, which led to the Crown Prosecution Service (CPS) charging 16 men with various offences including assault.

Fifteen were convicted and sentenced Thursday, December 20th 1990 at the Old Bailey. No jury was involved; Judge James Rant ruled that consent would not provide a defence to the charges of assault, the men in turn pleading guilty. Their sentences ranged from prison time to minor fines; 8 men were jailed immediately, 11 convicted of assault. Particularly novel was the offence of 'aiding and abetting actual bodily harm upon oneself' – some of the 'victims' having also been 'perpetrators'.

Though Rant accepted all the men had consented, no money had been exchanged for the videos, and that the videos weren't meant for wider circulation, he saw the acts as 'degrading and vicious' (Young 1990). Recognizing the decision's restrictions on private sexual acts, he underscored the court's edifying duties:

> Much has been said about individual liberty and the rights people have to do what they want with their own bodies, but the courts must draw the line between what is acceptable in a civilised society and what is not.
>
> *[ibid.]*

After a failed attempt at the Court of Appeal, the case ascended to the House of Lords, where five of the men's conviction for assault was to be (re)considered – all five faced charges under section 47 and three faced charges under section 20 of the Offences Against the Person Act 1861 (OAPA).[4]

The point of law of general public importance was to be heard by the Law Lords:

> Where A wounds or assaults B occasioning him actual bodily harm in the course of a sado-masochistic encounter, does the prosecution have to prove lack of consent on the part of B before they can establish A's guilt under section 20 or section 47 of the Offences against the Person Act 1861?
>
> *(Giles 1994, p.102)*

In other words: does consent matter, when the result is bodily harm? In a landmark 3:2 decision, the Court ruled against the men, formulating the precedent that still lasts today: one cannot consent to bodily harm or greater for the purposes of 'sexual gratification'.

A Victorian Precedent and Defining 'Bodily Harm'

When contemplating the relevance of the law, specifically OAPA, to the prosecutions of the Spannermen in the House of Lords, Lord Lowry calls *R v Brown* 'an unusual case' (p.254). Given that the case had no direct precedent, the Lords' incredibly narrow decision, in tandem with their reliance on various incongruent case law, suggests their apparent difficulty with the acts and their criminality. The Victorian-era legislation still guiding this area of the law is the first point of concern. It is of note firstly, that the subject matter does not fall under the law of sexual offences, but rather non-fatal, non-sexual offences. The Act itself and its outdatedness as applied to current issues have been heavily criticised.[5]

Beyond the charges themselves falling under an ostensibly outdated statute, the judges' reliance on the 1882 *R v Coney* ([1882] 8 QBD 534) case to frame their decision over a century later also seems a stretch. The judges in *Coney* sought to discourage prize fighting, ruling that consent of both parties to an injurious activity is no defence for assault, if the injury extends to the public. Prize fighting, beyond being 'mischievous' and a 'disorderly exhibition', endangers the lives and health of the participants and is not in the 'public interest'.

Whereas consent is concretely defined as it pertains to sexual offences, it is piecemeal guided by the case law when it concerns offences against the person. The Lords' interpretation in *Brown* is central to the contemporary understanding of consent in this area of the law. In essence, a victim's effective consent[6] may absolve someone of criminal liability, as a defence.[7] But the Lords construed harm as prima facie unlawful; the resulting legal framework requires that for mere assault, the prosecution must prove the victim didn't consent, but for offences amounting to actual bodily harm (ABH) or greater, the prosecution doesn't need to demonstrate non-consent in order for the defendant to be charged.

'Bodily harm', based on the 1934 case of *R v Donovan* ([1934] 2 KB 498) has 'its ordinary meaning' and incorporates any injury that interferes with a person's health or comfort:

> Such hurt or injury need not be permanent, but must, no doubt, be more than merely transient and trifling.

This definition is also problematic because injury that is merely *'transient and trifling'* incorporates even minor injuries, including scratches, bruising and swelling (Child et al. 2021, p.244). The Lords in *Brown*, in construing consent as a defence rather than an element of offence, required the defence therefore to provide evidence of 'lawfulness' of an activity as the result of social utility or otherwise, rather than a prosecutorial demonstration of non-consent to raise an offence. Any injury more than 'transient or trifling' is therefore criminalised. However, they identified certain caveats – activities carried out for 'good reason'.

'Good Reason'

Adding an additional layer to the puzzle, the judges cited the resulting principle of *Attorney-General's Reference (No. 6 of 1980)* – that it is not 'in the public interest' for people to inflict harm on each other for no 'good reason'. The majority opinion sees sadomasochism as no such good reason because of its potential to harm both the immediate victim as well as the general public. More importantly though, the moral justifications in support of their opinions – in picking apart what constitutes a 'good reason' – signify a deeper motivation. The majority premised their argument largely on an equation of sadomasochism with violence. Lord Templeman's judgement sees the sadomasochistic tendency as a violent one, and this linearity permeates his and the other majority judges' explanations. Sadomasochism and violence are repeatedly likened and equated. This is clear in Templeman's weighing of the appellant's privacy against public needs:

> Society is entitled and bound to protect itself against a cult of violence. Pleasure derived from the infliction of pain is an evil thing. Cruelty is uncivilised.
>
> (R v Brown, *p.237*)

Through the Lords' detangling of acceptable versus non-acceptable exemptions of consensual harm, the *Brown* judgement established, or in a sense *summarized* the acceptable activities for which consent can be provided as an acceptable defence to bodily harm. In Lord Templeman's words, when violence is intentionally inflicted, consent matters only if the injury was a foreseeable incident of a *lawful activity* in which the person injured was participating.

It is the meaning of the term *lawful* that allows the case to contribute a fundamental development of an array of categorical exemptions to public prosecution, pertaining to the inevitability of consensual harm. These 'consent-categories' which delineate exempted activities in the public interest and 'good reasons' from consensual harm include surgery, ritual circumcision, tattooing, ear-piercing, parental chastisement, violent sports and games and… 'jostling in a crowd'. Thus, the ruling found sadomasochism had no good reason, and in turn consent to it was not an acceptable defence for bodily harm. Child and Ormerod summarize that the legal complexities arising from such categories, 'have not been designed in accordance with particular legal principles or with regard to any legal or medical notions of acceptable harm' (2019, p.245). The inclusion and exclusion of certain categories remain the result rather of an arbitrary moral balancing act. The resulting legal oddity sees sexual gratification, excluded by the ruling, share the same rationale and confusing predicament as the category of sports, an example of consensual harm with the potential to easily result in more detrimental injury.

'Dubious Consent' and Negating Express Consent for the Purposes of 'Sexual Gratification'

This hyper-specificity or inscrutability of the phrasing 'for the purposes of sexual gratification' is borrowed, along with the transient and trifling threshold, from *Donovan*, which delineates that *Coney's* public interest exceptions do not allow consent to 'flagellation for the purposes of sexual gratification'. Again, as part of non-sexual offences, here, valid consent in the eyes of the law, transforms into 'dubious consent': the men's consent, when for the purposes of sexual gratification, was dubious, despite being confirmed as fully valid – expressed, and effective.[8] The consent of the participants was undisputed by the legal system at every stage of the process in the case's ascension to the House of Lords.

Nevertheless, on moral and social grounds (i.e., 'public health'), it is clear that the judges doubted the consent was truly valid. They emphasized the younger age of the newly recruited participants and risk of proselytization and corruption of the young, the nature of the need for video recordings, the free flow of blood and spread of HIV, the (hypothetical) mixture of sadomasochism with drugs and drink, and the possibility that other practitioners would not be so 'controlled or responsible' as the men were.

It seems ironic that the Courts expressly deemed the sexual acts at hand to be gratifying, yet this did not factor into the consideration of the consent above. It is clearer then, that as a consequence of the contextual factors, the law sees gratification in a heteronormative, or simply normative manner. It does not consider gratification in its positive sense, but rather in the ways it cannot possibly be gratifying. This is made apparent by Lord Templeman:

> There was no evidence to support the assertion that sado-masochist activities are essential to the happiness of the appellants...sado-masochism is not only concerned with sex. Sado-masochism is also concerned with violence. The evidence discloses that the practices of the appellants were unpredictably dangerous and degrading to body and mind and were developed with increasing barbarity and taught to persons whose consents were dubious or worthless.
>
> (R v Brown, p.235)

Summarizing the opaque consent-categories formulated in Brown, Child and Ormerod's write, 'What is included here remains, to some extent, an accident of history, and is not based on degrees or risks of harm' (2019, p.247). In a final disappointing decision, the European Court of Human Rights also decided against the men, ruling that though there was a breach of their right to privacy, it was necessary for the purposes of protecting public health (*Laskey, Jaggard and Brown v United Kingdom* (1997) 24 E.H.R.R. 39). Beyond the legalities of the case, its historical context is easily missed by the literature. It is worth then, returning to the 'accident' that spurred the contemporary predicament, and in particular the activism forgotten by history.

Activism in London: A Campaign for 'SM Rights'

Considering its weight, it is worth viewing Operation Spanner as part of a wider sociolegal legacy, rather than an ephemeral moment. As a case study of lived experiences of the trial, the position of those involved in it might tell us what the future holds in the wake of the legal principle's resurfacing today. As the *Brown* defendants formulated a campaign to fight for their cause at the European Court of Human Rights, so too did fellow SMers. The politically driven 'SM rights' protest was the first of its kind in Britain, sparking an international following and grounding a monumental seat in sexual history.

This is in part due to the case's overlap with policing of sexuality generally. Thatcher's conservative government dealt a substantial blow to the earlier progress made for LGBT politics in Britain. Though the Sexual Offences Act 1967 officially decriminalized homosexual activities between consenting men in private, it upheld the criminalization where more than two persons were involved or simply present, placing queer men in a precarious position. Amongst allegations of judicial law-making and legal paternalism, academic criticisms of the judgment cited blatant homophobia against the backdrop of an HIV/AIDS epidemic (Moran 2003, pp.83–84). In the Court of Appeal, Lord Lane had said of one participant, 'It is some comfort at least to be told, as we were, that (he) is now it seems settled into a normal heterosexual relationship.'[9] The clearest example furthering this theory is the judgment in the 1996 case of *R v Wilson* ([1996] 3 W.L.R. 125, [1997] Q.B. 47) involving consensual sexual activity between a married couple. A husband branded his wife's buttocks with a hot knife at her request.[10] Russell L.J., reading the judgement of the court, distinguished the branding from the 'extreme' nature of those acts in *Brown*, drawing a direct parallel between the branding in question and tattooing:

> Mrs. Wilson not only consented to that which the appellant did, she instigated it. There was no aggressive intent on the part of the appellant…the appellant's desire was to assist her in what she regarded as the acquisition of a desirable piece of personal adornment, perhaps in this day and age no less understandable than the piercing of nostrils or even tongues for the purposes of inserting decorative jewellery.
>
> *(p. 50)*

The judgement's tone presents a distinct departure from the disgust seen in *Brown*, the Lords finding:

> Consensual activity between husband and wife, in the privacy of the matrimonial home, is not, in our judgement, normally a proper matter for criminal investigation, let alone criminal prosecution.
>
> *(ibid.)*

The argument here is though, that the outcry in response to what many saw as blatant homophobia, took on a more expansive tone – British SMers formulated the first cohesive and coordinated 'SM rights'[11] campaign, fighting not only against discrimination but also for the rights of sadomasochists and the centrality of consent to bodily autonomy.

Growing mainstream visibility of SM in the 1970s was part of the general advancing sexual revolution, including in magazines, music and fashion, as well as the popularity of communal areas like sex clubs and leather bars (Stein 2021, p.64). But lesbian sadomasochists had spurred contemporary visibility of sado-masochism as a political issue. Their vociferous efforts originated as part of the

FIGURE 3.1 Demonstrator at SM Pride 1993
Gordon Rainsford Archive, Bishopsgate Institute

feminist debates of the latter half of the 19th century, and more granularly in the pro-sexuality movement formulated throughout the late 1970s and 1980s as a counter to radical feminist campaigns. Sadomasochism and sexuality as a vehicle for women's equality via sexual agency was one of the central themes of the 'sex wars' against anti-sex feminists and the accompanying 1982 Barnard Conference (Love 2011). Gayle Rubin wrote in its aftermath: 'In addition to self-defence, S/M lesbians have called for appreciation for erotic diversity and more open discussion of sexuality' (1999, p.167).

Historian Stephen K. Stein's analysis of BDSM communities in the United States and their organization into politically active groups is among a scarce scholarship of studies of sadomasochist groups (2021, p.189). Stein's work finds the centrality of consent at the heart of early BDSM organizations' mobilization, in particular the Safe, Sane and Consensual (SSC) framework as revolutionary in creating a central uniting principle for the BDSM community (2021, pp. 98–101). The phrase, adopted in 1983, amalgamated various organizations' definitions of BDSM. SSC was both inwardly defining, as an educational guideline for the sadomasochist community, but also outwardly as a demonstration of the respectability of the community to critics; it 'became both the community's definition of BDSM and a litmus test for appropriate behaviour within the community' (Stein 2021, p.120). The extent to which practitioners are versed in this framework is arguable, but consent nonetheless lies at the foundational core of the communities' development.

Britain had yet to create its own formal, public BDSM organization. Compared to their American counterparts, sadomasochists' sexual expression took place in private, at private parties, rather than in public. That is not to say the SM scene was not also foundational to the sexual revolution beginning to flourish in 1970s Britain. While British sadomasochists and fetishists were influenced by American BDSM publications, the Americans were influenced by British fetish fashion and its stylization of BDSM (Stein 2021, p.140). By the 1990s, British venues hosting the fetish-scene blossomed. Despite this growing scene, the SM scene faced a series of challenges as activists tried to distance themselves from their common association with negative stereotypes; they 'sought to disentangle BDSM from rape, murder and fascism, and affirm BDSM as consensual, joyful and fun' (Stein 2021, p.51).

It can be argued then, that the response to Operation Spanner, in the form of SM activism, is Britain's response to its American predecessors; the first for-mulation of coordinated SM activism in the United Kingdom. The campaign for 'SM rights' finds its impetus in the founding of Countdown on Spanner in August 1992. In November of 1992, the inaugural SM Pride parade of more than 700 people marched through London and in 1995, the Spanner Trust was established to provide assistance to the Spanner defendants, lobby for a change in British law to legalize sadomasochism and provide assistance to any person subjected to discrimination on the basis of marginalized sex.

Backlash to the Spanner trials saw the first ever cohort of SM activists cam-paign for their rights in England. Organizations including Liberty, Outrage, the Spanner Trust and Countdown on Spanner Campaign, protested for sexual liberty. Feminists Against Censorship lent their support as well in their cham-pioning of reclamation of power and control via sadomasochistic practices.

The Countdown on Spanner Campaign created the first ever SM Pride march, which saw thousands flock to Central London, parading for SM and queer privacy and sexual liberty. Networks of campaign groups internationally donated to the Spanner Trust, which supported the men in their defence also at the European Court. Peter Tatchell, spokesman for OutRage, said of the ECHR decision: 'The state has no legitimate business invading the bedrooms of con-senting adults and dictating how they should have sex' (Dyer 1997).

In addition to privacy though, the campaign for SM rights focused on the primacy of consent to SM practices and the civil liberties assuring bodily autonomy. Liberty's legal officer defined the deep tie between consent and privacy rights: the state 'had no right to interfere with the private lives of consenting adults' (Cohen 1995).

The campaign stressed the importance of education, one campaigner said: 'Education is very important. Tying people up is complicated. We go down to the smallest detail, like explaining how nerves in the thumb can be cut if you make a mistake with the knots' (Cohen 1995). Scotland Yard officers even attended workshops, expressing their intention not to prosecute consenting adults (Cohen 1995).

Yet the protests also support Langdridge's (2006) argument that the limitations of sexual citizenship – and respectability sought by sadomasochists demanding their rights – are coupled with the dialectical element of transgression. The protesters remained true to the unconventional aspects of their sexuality – the organisers said that wearing of masks during the protest, for example, 'ensures anonymity and also looks very pervy' (Cohen 1995).

Domestic Abuse Act and Re-equation of Sadomasochism with Violence

The 30-year-old case finds a striking contemporary statutory foothold in the DAA, cementing its legacy. There has also been one recent prosecution under its auspices. A body modifier, in *R v (B)M* ([2018] EWCA Crim 560) was found guilty of assault, despite the consent of his consenting customers/ 'victims' of bodily harm for body modifications, including a tongue splitting, ear and nipple removal, and sentenced to several years' prison time. This was the first recent sobering example that there could be prosecutions under the precedent.

The Domestic Abuse Act 2021 though, has reintroduced the sexual element to the equation, so prosecution becomes ever more possible. On the heels of the #MeToo movement, against a backdrop of hypervigilance to sexual violence and sexual consent, arose an attention to a particular group of court cases, focusing on the deaths of several British women as a result of alleged 'rough sex gone wrong'. The deaths of Natalie Connelly, Grace Millane, and Sophie Moss sparked international outrage as the (male) defendants in these cases insisted in court that the women consented to, and explicitly asked for, the rough sex that resulted in their deaths.

The 'rough sex defence' or '50 shades of grey defence' relies on the idea an assault or death was caused by 'sex games gone wrong'. The sex defence in such a case claims an assault or death during the course of sexual activity was an accident, and unintentional. Central to the defence is that consent by a victim or beyond affirmation a more proactive 'she asked for it', absolves a defendant from guilt for having caused death (Buzash 1989; Cowan et al. 2020; Edwards 2020; Bows, Herring 2020). A defendant's claiming of this narrative relies on the idea that a victim consented, not to their death, but to 'a certain level of "rough" sexual activity' that caused eventual harm (Bennett 2021, p.169). It further aims to shift attention away from the defendant, and towards the victim and their character or sexual history (Edwards 2020, pp.301–302). The aim is that, by relying on the defence of consent, the perpetrator may be successful in receiving a less serious charge or lighter sentence (Bennett 2021, p.170).

American jurist George E. Buzash first brought academic attention to the rough sex defence, defining it as a charge to murder that:

asserts that the victim literally 'asked for' the conduct that led to the homicide and that the homicide was the result of sexual practices to which the victim consented, and may have even demanded.

(1989, p.558)[12]

In the contemporary context, the rough sex defence might be seen to have transformed further, into the 'BDSM defence'. The defence, in this case, claims that a victim consented to sex involving BDSM (as 'rough sex') – this BDSM then accidentally leading to unintentional consequences, such as death (Bennett 2021, p.170). It could also bring a victim's interest in BDSM to the juries' attention, making it more plausible that the victim consented to the activity which led to their assault or death. This equation of BDSM with non-consensual sexual violence in a myriad of divergent circumstances under the resurgent umbrella term 'rough sex defence' notably obscures the law's ability to deal with it: in other words, 'these rhetorical moves are misleading because they conflate claims of BDSM in non-fatal cases with claims of BDSM in fatal offense cases' (Bennett 2021, p.177); in addressing proposals to legalize BDSM, this would permit killing in the course of BDSM – something that is practically speaking completely at odds with BDSM culture (Bennett 2021, p.178). Of course, consensual BDSM can result in death, but this is the result of failure to mitigate harm rather than intentional malice. A defendant's reliance on a victim's consent to rough sex might be further supported if their narrative makes reference to a specific fetish interest, and one that is gaining mainstream popularity. The courtroom gesture to BDSM is a proverbial double-edged sword, bonding a legitimate sexual kink with fatal sexual violence, whilst addressing the reality that there is an educational facet to the kink if it is to be safe.

The We Can't Consent to This (WCCTT) campaign, formed at the end of 2018, made its aim to abolish the defence in addressing violence against women and girls resulting from actions claimed to be consensual. The campaign targets the normalized violence against women represented by cases involving the rough sex defence; it suggests this normalization is the result of extreme pornography and its influence on men who assaulted women, and 'romanticized' violence on platforms like Tumblr, TikTok and Instagram as well as *50 Shades of Grey* and *365 Days*, in addition to online guides educating on safe strangulation. MPs Harriet Harman and Mark Garnier, in a show of support across the political aisle, lobbied the Government together with the campaign group pushing for a change in the law. The campaigners' efforts finally came to fruition, as the Domestic Abuse Bill received Royal Assent in April 2021.

Section 71 states:

1. This section applies for the purposes of determining whether a person ('D') who inflicts serious harm on another person ('V') is guilty of a relevant offence.
2. It is not a defence that V consented to the infliction of the serious harm for the purposes of obtaining sexual gratification (but see subsection (4)).[13]

Notably, a Policy Paper praising the statute outlines the DAA's legal effect as extending beyond a context of domestic abuse to incorporate any situation

> where a person consents, or is said to have consented, to the infliction of serious harm (or, by extension, their death) for the purposes of obtaining sexual gratification.
>
> *(Home Office 2022)*

The passage of the statute was hailed as a major success, being that it finally 'abolished' use of the rough sex defence in court (Topping 2022; Devaney 2021; Evans 2021). Home Secretary Priti Patel tweeted the clause marks its 'end' (Priti Patel [@pritipatel] 2020).

The statute, however, drew immediate criticism pointing to the fact that celebration may have come too soon. Many a lawyer has pointed out that, legally speaking, the statute doesn't actually *change* the law (Ormerod, Laird 2021, p.718; BCL Solicitors LLP 2020; n.d.; Reed n.d.). In fact, they explain, there never existed such a defence in the first place. Intent, rather than consent, is the sole factor a jury must consider when considering murder and assault cases. While consent can aid in disproving intent, it is not a defence in and of itself. More importantly, the law simply reifies the existing common law principle; it adds nothing new to the legal toolkit available to defence lawyers. The statute 'appears to do no more than state the clear position at common law' (Ormerod, Laird 2021, p.718), as an explicit iteration of the *Brown* principle. In essence, the new statute simply reaffirms the legal precedent that follows from the 30-year-old case, rather than adding any new content, in that it simply repeats that consent is not a defence to serious harm for sexual gratification. So it seemingly does little in the way of creating new or detracting from old policy surrounding BDSM. Its passage, though, suggests that statutory law might then be a stronger tool than common law and legal precedent, cementing the principle in the bona fide milieu of contemporary legislative action. The incredulity once felt by Spanner activists is overshadowed by demands of campaigners against domestic violence. Though the law does little in the way of changing law *per se*, it is a stark reminder of its limitations on bodily autonomy.

The gendered nature of the campaign against rough sex defence is understandable – the Office for National Statistics reports that in England and Wales the victim was female in 73% of domestic abuse cases, in the year ending March 2021.[14] But it is also problematic in that it supports criminalization of consensual BDSM activities in order to eradicate gender violence, specifically non-consensual abuse of women by men (Bennett 2021). In stressing the need for reform to address non-consensual rough sex, there is again a scepticism of the possibility or reality of consensual rough sex, a dubious prospect. In addressing BDSM, these discussions, though centring on acts where consent is either not clear or expressly non-consensual, take a seemingly negative and gendered view of the practice generally.

Some legal academics see legal reform related to the sex defence as just one opportunity in the feminist campaign against sexual violence, as complementing a wider cultural pushback. Their view is that the invocation of arguments like the rough sex defence by men against women is representative of the broader 'cultural representations of women's insatiable desire for sexual violence redolent in misogynist film, advertising, fiction and journalism' (Edwards 2020, pp.295–296). Edwards, stressing the importance of feminist judgements as furthering the 'moral will on the side of the right', suggests that such representations of BDSM are symptomatic of a patriarchal society, which in turn continues to dominate the courtroom (2020, pp.311 and 296). The DAA section, then, is less about changing a long-standing legislative position, and more about generally 'shutting down…avenues of legal misogyny' and 'the way in which women are constructed both within and outside the law' (Edwards 2020, p.311).

Bows and Herring argue that there is not enough evidence to demonstrate women's interest in and enjoyment of consensual BDSM; to the contrary, they explain – on the basis of two psychological studies – that fetishism and sadism arouses more men than women and that more men than women report engaging in BDSM (Bows, Herring 2020, p.533). They further suggest that anything in the direction of 'roughness' in the course of a sexual encounter is unwanted by women; they cite a BBC Radio survey that found under half of women who experienced acts constituting rough sex, such as choking, spitting and biting, said they were wanted (Bows, Herring 2020, p.533). The women who 'wanted', let us even dare to say 'desired' these acts are eschewed as is their the narrative of sexual pleasure, replaced by one of nonconsensual sexual violence. They quote Edwards' (2017) argument that there is no evidence demonstrating that erotic asphyxiation heightens a women's libido. It is insinuated that women, 'generally', have a negative experience with rough sex regardless of consent, further conflating consensual/wanted with the non-consensual, 'unwanted'. The gendered nature of the arguments against the rough sex defence, whilst trying to underscore the importance of consent, seemingly dispels women's consent from the equation in favour of an 'evidentiary' dislike of SM, i.e., they could not possibly consent to roughness in the course of sex…they could not possibly want it. What if the male population described above comprises mostly queer men? This would complicate the indication here generally, that men have sadistic tendencies towards women. Moreover the isolation of men and their interests should not discount the, albeit smaller, figure of women who do enjoy and engage in BDSM – or other gendered, or gender nonconforming practitioners for that matter.

According to Bennett (2021) though, legal regulation of BDSM across Western common law countries is similar in that their approach to the rough sex defence is prefaced on a 'bogus BDSM argument'; the argument validates criminalization of BDSM on the ground that defendants could otherwise use *false* claims of BDSM to reduce their criminal liability for non-consensual abuse. The argument is flawed in that it assumes that the law cannot distinguish between genuinely consensual BDSM and non-consensual abuse, what Bennett calls the 'assumption of indistinguishability' – this is contestable especially if legal professionals are educated about BDSM culture, reversing their traditional mischaracterization of BDSM as simply dangerous sex (Bennett 2021, pp.170–174). The argument also exceptionalizes BDSM above other regulated injurious activities, in an arbitrary move to extinguish consensual BDSM claims amongst other difficult defence claims because 'they are somehow too hard for the law to deal with' (p.176). Instead, the activities are re-equated with violence, putting practitioners at risk and their consent seen again as dubious, given the nature of the activity in which they are participating.

The Opacity of the Law and Possible Dangers for Practitioners

Given BDSM's ubiquity in popular culture and the increasing popularity of kink and fetish-oriented sex clubs in places like London, there is a timely need to reconsider the implications of these laws and the re-equation of sexual violence and sexual pleasure. Perhaps the reason why consent is considered so dubious here is because of its connectedness to prurient concerns surrounding BDSM. The law, in considering the perceptions, beliefs and lived experiences of practitioners might develop a more nuanced approach to consent, going from 'dubious consent' to a serious consideration of effective consent in the context of BDSM activities.

Academic literature on the BDSM subculture has encompassed various disciplines in the past few decades (Weinberg 2020) beyond its pathologized past, supports the importance of consent to the practice (Langdridge, Barker 2013), supporting the need for legal refinement. The use of safewords is central to the fundamentals of consent education (Bezreh et al. 2012). Power structures at the core of BDSM interactions mean practitioners navigate these via approaches to consent considered outside the normative; thus, neoliberal constructions of consent central to legal interpretations (i.e., yes means yes and no means no) fail to capture their complexity (Fanghanel 2020). Even when the community relies on forms of explicit consent, the negotiation of it during the practice is also ongoing and nuanced, or continued through the practice (Beres, MacDonald 2015). Going beyond neoliberal understandings of consent involves considerations of consent that are critical of it and provide open dialogue, and which can identify potential abuse – this involves a collective social responsibility (Barker 2013). Bauer (2021) has recently pointed to the importance of collective spaces to both foster, but also demystify consent in establishing guidelines as well as enforcing them.

Despite the practice's mainstreaming, the law's position as precedent in both statutory and common law requires scepticism that practitioners are immune from prosecution.[15] Legal case law on the issue of sadomasochism is problematic for practitioners. How are they to understand the *transient and trifling* threshold? Further, it remains unclear as to the law's application to non-married couples and activity involving varying sexual orientations or gender identities. How would the CPS approach prosecution of a couple, or a group of people, depending on these factors, given the blurry legal guidance? Of further consideration is how the referential circumstances would make a difference, i.e., if someone disapproves of their neighbour's kinky sexual lifestyle, could this result in a phone call to police and subsequent arrest?

On an equal note, how might civil society as activism be reincarnated? With the lack of contemporary prosecutions, the SM activist groups in Spanner have quieted. Would a new prosecution spark similar outrage? Take the recent example of Tower Hamlets Council's targeting of Klub Verboten and Cross-breed, queer-inclusive and kink-oriented clubs (Doherty 2022). After the Council threatened to shut them down over nudity, protesters called on kink, leather and BDSM communities to join together, ultimately dismantling the Council's plans (Ahmed 2022). Could raids of such clubs be premised on the new statute, and if so, will the same community band together in protest?

Brown's international recognition in legal scholarship and beyond demonstrates its contemporary significance (Bennett 2021, p.165; Herring 2017). It remains to be seen how future prosecutions will view the law.[16] Thirty years after the historic *Brown* ruling, the categorical criminalization of BDSM has done more than remain...it has been reaffirmed. The recent conflation of fatal and non-fatal references to BDSM – whether in actuality or as a hyperbolic defence narrative – seems less concerned with the specifics of harm caused, but more with BDSM as a lifestyle or identity choice itself. This is especially apparent given the incongruence between the initial application of the principle to a group of men having group sex, and now to protecting women from fatal cases of domestic violence. The arguments in either direction are byproducts of their reference to social utility. It is this historical near-sightedness, the amnesic vantage point of which has led to a replication of existing law without consideration of its many long-standing critiques, that could place inadvertent consequential limitations on sexual liberty.

The role of the law is clear, both confining BDSM to a legalistic arbitrary threshold and also stigmatizing it by placing it on a shelf amongst non-consensual violence once again. This threatens the existence of the practice in the future. Bennett insists that the decriminalization of BDSM is 'the most crucial initial legal step towards sexual citizenship' for practitioners (Bennett 2021, p.162). Rather than its pejorative position in the Domestic Abuse Act, BDSM's regulation might be reconsidered in terms of the incongruous yet overlapping principles surrounding offences against the person and sexual offences in Victorian-era criminal legislation. BDSM as envisaged in the way of sexual offences rather than non-fatal offences against the person, its end goal of 'for the purposes of sexual gratification' in mind, can be more clearly scrutinized along the lines of consent. As consent historically lies at the centre of the practice, what more do practitioners have to add in the way of distinguishing it from sexual violence? How does the reality of BDSM assist the law in distinguishing non-consensual from consensual sexual gratification, beyond the confines of 'yes' and 'no'? The sonorous overtones of media and defence lawyers aside, what might BDSM pracitioners add to the discussion decades on from post-*Brown* activism?

It seems the disgust of non-normative sexuality and stigmatization of BDSM seen in the original *Brown* ruling still guides the recent hasty passage of laws. Will the new law receive a counter-response by the SM community similar to the past? If so, what could it look like? The central question remains, if we are sceptical, dubious of consent when it is established as valid, what credence does this lend to consent, the establishment of which we hold so unequivocal in manners of sexual relationships in the 21st century? Further, by decriminalizing consensual sexual acts causing no serious or permanent injury, what capacity is freed within the criminal justice system to deal with cases (notoriously back-logged) of legitimate sexual violence?

Notes

1 BDSM, an abbreviation for bondage, discipline/domination, sadism/submission, and masochism involves a range of consensual sexual practices falling under the umbrella of kink, or non-normative sexual practices and identities. Sadomasochism involves the giving and receiving of pain and humiliation for pleasure.

2 I refer here to the English and Welsh landscape, but this of course extends through the Commonwealth's reliance on the laws in question. It is also apparent in international law, which I will touch on at the end of this article.

3 See Bamforth 1994; Bix 1997; Edwards 1993; Moran 1995; Khan 2014. That is not to discount the work of Bill Thompson in *Sadomasochism* [1994], a self-admittedly 'non-academic' book (p.13) dedicated entirely to the case which proposes a criminological defence of sadomasochism from a criminological perspective.

4 The offences under scrutiny by the Lords were sections 47 and 20, though as it belongs to the grouping, section 18 should also be considered for emphasis of the others. We can examine these as a spectrum, beginning with the least harmful acts amounting to more than mere assault and battery represented in section 47. Falling under the category of assault, this section outlines the offence of 'any assault occasioning actual bodily harm' (ABH). Section 20 outlines the offence of causing bodily injury, either with or without a weapon: 'unlawfully and maliciously wound or inflict any grievous bodily harm upon any other person, either with or without any weapon or instrument…'. Section 18 outlines the offence of wounding and/or causing GBH with intent to do GBH: 'unlawfully and maliciously by any means whatsoever wound or cause any grievous bodily harm to any person, … with intent, … to do some … grievous bodily harm to any person…'.

5 So much so that the Law Commission presented a report on the matter to Parliament in 2015 (*Reform of Offences against the Person*, No 361). See also (Horder 1994; Leigh 1976; Gardner 1994; Eugenicos 2017; Gibson 2016; Demetriou 2016; Child et al. 2021, pp.281–286)

6 Child and Ormerod (2021) stress that consent as a defence in the realm of non-fatal offences against the person, including to assault and battery, 'is vitally important' to such offences. Where contact is made consensually, or expected/apprehended as consensual, there will be no liability for assault or battery. The two necessary characterizations of this consent are that it is – similar to the 'willing and enthusiastic' terminology used by the judges – expressed and/or implied and effective. Express consent is the most straightforward of the elements, and entails V expressly consenting to the contact with D. Implied consent likewise is also common, and entails

'touching which, although not explicitly consented to, is part of everyday life'; it assumes that, as part of being in everyday society, we expect or more directly, foresee, some sort of contact with other people. In the same vein, consent can only be valid if it is effective; it must require the victim's mental capacity, knowledge (i.e. 'informed consent'), and freedom from fraud/duress on the part of the defendant, in order to be valid.

7 Non-consent could also be considered as an element of offence, rendering it as a defence unnecessary. The *Brown* majority approach, in treating consent as an element of the appellants' defence, deemed the case law as pointing to a preference against this approach. This position, beyond necessitating consent as expressed and effective, which the men's consent was deemed as being, requires of it a third characterization: it is to be related to a context of *lawful* conduct or harm (the meaning of which will be discussed in the following section).

8 Perhaps this is most apparent in that some of the 'victims' were also charged as perpetrators.

9 (p.235) As iterated by Lord Templeman.

10 A doctor became aware of the presence of the marks during a medical exam, reporting this to police.

11 Not to be confused with sexual minority (SM) rights.

12 The defence's utilization in 1989 as part of the 'Preppie Murder' case had become the "updated 1990's version of the "she asked for it" defence" to rape that had for decades saw a victim's conduct replace a defendant's actions as the focus of a trial, Buzash argues. It is notable that while Buzash focuses on the offence of murder, the contemporary debate is broader, also encompassing non-fatal offences. Consent by a victim, in Buzash's view serves to sway a jury since in their eyes a defendant seems 1) less blameworthy, but also 2) less likely that they acted with intent.

13 The Act further creates a new criminal offence of non-fatal strangulation and suffocation (s. 70). Here too, the statute states consent is also not a defence when the victim suffers serious harm and there was intention or recklessness on the part of the defendant.

14 'Domestic Abuse Victim Characteristics, England and Wales – Office for National Statistics'. https://www.ons.gov.uk/peoplepopulationandcommunity/crimeandjustice/articles/domesticabusevictimcharacteristicsenglandandwales/yearendingmarch2021.

15 Beyond the DAA's retention of this problematic legacy, Laskey also persists as its kin in Strasbourg as the precedent in international human rights law. The European Court, in its guidance on the right to privacy, notes the awkward place of sadomasochism amongst rights related to gender identity and sexual orientation; it retains that Article 8 rights to privacy do not prohibit criminalization of SM (Guide on Article 8 of the European Convention on Human Rights). See also *K.A. and A.D. v. Belgium*.

16 In the recent *R v Paterson* [2022] (EWCA Crim 456) case, the judgement of the Court of Appeal relied on Brown as a key authority, but refused to provide a 'full discussion' of its centrality to the case in detail, which considered vitiated consent as related to the 'medical exemption' to serious harm. A full discussion might be expected in the appeal to this case., which could provide an entirely new perspective on Brown. For a preliminary analysis of this case, see (Thomas, Pegg 2022).

References

Ahmed, A., 2022. Queer nightlife groups organise protest to 'Save Kink Spaces' in Tower Hamlets [online blog]. *Mixmag*. Available at: https://mixmag.net/read/save-kink-spaces-protest-tower-hamlets-kink-queer-nightlife-klub-verboten-news.

Bamforth, N., 1994. Sado-masochism and consent. 57*Criminal Law Review*661.

Barker, M., 2013. Consent is a grey area? A comparison of understandings of consent in *Fifty Shades of Grey* and on the BDSM blogosphere. *Sexualities*, 16 (8), pp.896–914. doi:10.1177/1363460713508881.

Bauer, R., 2021. Queering consent: Negotiating critical consent in les-bi-trans-queer BDSM contexts. *Sexualities*, 24 (5–6), pp.767–783. doi:10.1177/1363460720973902.

BCL Solicitors LLP, 2020. 'We can't consent to this': *R v Brown* and the Domestic Abuse Bill [online blog]. BCL Solicitors LLP. Available at: https://www.bcl.com/we-ca nt-consent-to-this-r-v-brown-and-the-domestic-abuse-bill/.

Bennett, T., 2021. A fine line between pleasure and pain: Would decriminalising BDSM permit nonconsensual abuse? *Liverpool Law Review*, 42 (2), pp.161–183. doi:10.1007/s10991-10020-09268-09267.

Beres, M.A., MacDonald, J.E.C., 2015. Talking About sexual consent: Heterosexual women and BDSM. *Australian Feminist Studies*, 30 (86), pp.418–432. doi:10.1080/08164649.2016.1158692.

Bezreh, T., Weinberg, T.S., Edgar, T., 2012. BDSM disclosure and stigma management: Identifying opportunities for sex education. *American Journal of Sexuality Education*, 7 (1), pp.37–61. doi:10.1080/15546128.2012.650984.

Bix, B., 1997. Consent, sado-masochism and the English Common Law. *QLR*, 17 (2), pp.157–176.

Bows, H., Herring, J., 2020. Getting away with murder? A review of the 'rough sex defence'. *The Journal of Criminal Law*, 84 (6), pp.525–538. doi:10.1177/0022018320936777.

Brown, A., 1996. I'm not a sadistic person; I don't do serious harm [online]. *The Independent*. Available at: https://www.independent.co.uk/life-style/i-m-not-a-sadis tic-person-i-don-t-do-serious-harm-1358133.html.

Buzash, G.E., 1989. The 'rough sex' defense. *The Journal of Criminal Law and Criminology (1973-)*, 80 (2), p.557. doi:10.2307/1143805.

Child, J., Ormerod, Q.C., 2019. *Smith, Hogan, and Ormerod's Smith, Hogan, and Ormerod's Essentials of Criminal Law*. Oxford, United Kingdom: Oxford University Press.

Child, J., Ormerod, D.C., Smith, J.C., 2021. *Smith, Hogan, and Ormerod's Essentials of Criminal Law*. Fourth edition. Oxford, United Kingdom: Oxford University Press.

Cohen, N., 1995. 'Perverts' on parade for the right to practise safe sadism [online]. *The Independent*. Available at: https://www.independent.co.uk/news/uk/home-news/p erverts-on-parade-for-the-right-to-practise-safe-sadism-1599215.html.

Cowan, R., Meghan, H., Justyna, G., 2020. Consent to serious harm for sexual gratification: not a defence. Response to the Department of Justice public consultation [online]. Queen's University Belfast Human Rights Centre. Available at: https://www.qub.ac.uk/research-centres/human-rights-centre/outputs/.

Demetriou, S., 2016. Not giving up the fight: A Review of the Law Commission's Scoping Report on Non-fatal Offences Against the Person. *The Journal of Criminal Law*, 80 (3), pp.188–200. doi:10.1177/0022018316646656.

Devaney , S., 2021. What The New Domestic Abuse Act Means For Women [online]. *British Vogue*. Available at: https://www.vogue.co.uk/arts-and-lifestyle/article/dom estic-abuse-bill-changes.

Doherty, S., 2022. Fetish clubs are under attack from Council Using 'archaic' laws [online blog]. *Vice*. Available at: https://www.vice.com/en/article/wxdkgy/klub-verbo ten-crossbreed-tower-hamlets-council.

Domestic Abuse Act2021. An Overview. Criminal Law Blog. Kingsley Napley [online]. Available at: https://www.kingsleynapley.co.uk/insights/blogs/criminal-law-blog/dom estic-abuse-act-2021-an-overview.

Dyer, C., 1997. Jailed sado masochists lose case in rights court. *The Irish Times*.

Edwards, S., 1993. No defence for a sado-masochistic libido. *The New Law Journal*, 143(6592).

Edwards, S., 2017. Assault, strangulation and murder – Challenging the sexual libido consent defence narrative. In: Reed, A. ... Smith, E., eds. *Consent: Domestic and Comparative Perspectives*. Substantive Issues in Criminal Law. Milton Park, Abingdon, Oxon; New York, NY: Routledge.

Edwards, S.S., 2020. Consent and the 'rough sex' defence in rape, murder, manslaughter and gross negligence. *The Journal of Criminal Law*, 84 (4), pp.293–311. doi:10.1177/0022018320943056.

Eugenicos, A.-M., 2017. Should we reform the Offences Against the Person Act 1861? *The Journal of Criminal Law*, 81 (1), pp.26–32. doi:10.1177/0022018316685478.

Evans, R., 2021. Your campaign to end the 'rough sex' defence has become law [online]. *Grazia*. Available at: https://graziadaily.co.uk/life/in-the-news/domestic-abuse-bill-royal-assent-rough-sex-defence/.

Fanghanel, A., 2020. Asking for it: BDSM sexual practice and the trouble of consent. *Sexualities*, 23 (3), pp.269–286. 10.1177/1363460719828933.

Gardner, J., 1994. Rationality and the rule of law in offences against the person. *The Cambridge Law Journal*, 53 (3), pp.502–523. doi:10.1017/S0008197300080934.

Gibson, M.J.R., 2016. Getting their 'act' together? Implementing statutory reform of offences against the person. *Criminal Law Review*, 9, pp.597–617.

Giles, M., 1994. *R v Brown*: Consensual harm and public interest. *Modern Law Review*, 57 (1), pp. 101–111.

Herring, J., 2017. Chapter 16. *R v Brown (1993)* [eBook]. In: *Landmark Cases in Criminal Law*. Hart Publishing, pp. 333–356. Available at: http://www.bloomsburycollections.com/book/landmark-cases-in-criminal-law.

Home Office, 2022. Policy Paper: Consent to serious harm for sexual gratification not a defence. Available at: https://www.gov.uk/government/publications/domestic-abuse-bill-2020-factsheets/consent-to-serious-harm-for-sexual-gratification-not-a-defence.

Horder, J., 1994. Rethinking non-fatal offences against the person. *Oxford Journal of Legal Studies*, 14 (3), pp.335–351.

Khan, U., 2014. *Vicarious Kinks: S/M in the Socio-Legal Imaginary*. University of Toronto Press. doi:10.3138/9781442668096.

Langdridge, D., 2006. Voices from the margins: Sadomasochism and sexual citizenship. *Citizenship Studies*, 10 (4), pp.373–389. doi:10.1080/13621020600857940.

Langdridge, D., Barker, M.-J. eds., 2013. *Safe, Sane, and Consensual: Contemporary Perspectives on Sadomasochism*. New York, NY: Palgrave Macmillan.

Leigh, L.H., 1976. Sado-masochism, consent, and the reform of the criminal law. *The Modern Law Review*, 39 (2), pp.130–146. doi:10.1111/j.1468-2230.1976.tb01449.x.

Love, H., 2011. Diary of a conference on sexuality, 1982. *GLQ: A Journal of Lesbian and Gay Studies*, 17 (1), pp.49–78. doi:10.1215/10642684-10642010-016.

Moran, L.J., 1995. Violence and the law: The case of sado-masochism. *Social & Legal Studies*, 4 (2), pp.225–251. doi:10.1177/096466399500400204.

Moran, L.J., 2003. *Laskey v The United Kingdom*: Learning the limits of privacy. *The Modern Law Review*, 61 (1), pp.77–84. doi:10.1111/1468-2230.00129.

Office for National Statistics2021. Domestic abuse victim characteristics, England and Wales. Office for National Statistics [online]. Available at: https://www.ons.gov.uk/peoplepopulationandcommunity/crimeandjustice/articles/domesticabusevictimcharacteristicsenglandandwales/yearendingmarch2021.

Ormerod, D., Laird, K., 2021. *Smith, Hogan, and Ormerod's Criminal Law* 16th ed. New York: Oxford University Press.

Patel, Priti [@pritipatel], 2020. We have published a clause to end so-called 'rough sex defence' which enables perpetrators to avoid justice by claiming their victims consented to rough sex. Our thanks to @mark4wyreforest, @HarrietHarman, @Wecantconsentto, @GraziaUK and others for their relentless campaigning. *Twitter*. Available at: https://twitter.com/pritipatel/status/1278361627939819523.

Price, H., 2021. Domestic Abuse Bill: For these victims, a new law is long overdue [online]. *BBC News*. Available at: https://www.bbc.com/news/uk-56945169.

Reed, G., New law seeking to ban 'rough sex defence' unlikely to change trial outcomes – The Justice Gap [online blog]. Available at: https://www.thejusticegap.com/the-so-called-rough-sex-defence-is-unlikely-to-change-the-outcome-of-trials/.

Rubin, G., 1999. Thinking sex: Notes for a radical theory of the politics of sexuality. In: Parker, R.G., Aggleton, P., eds. *Culture, Society and Sexuality: A Reader*. Social aspects of AIDS. London: UCL Press, pp. 143–178.

Stein, S.K., 2021. *Sadomasochism and the BDSM Community in the United States: Kinky People Unite*. New York: Routledge.

Thomas, M., Pegg, S., 2022. 'Proper medical purpose': Reviewing consent and the medical exemption to offences against the person: R v Paterson [2022] EWCA Crim 456. *The Journal of Criminal Law*, 86 (4), pp.281–286. doi:10.1177/00220183221115272.

Topping, A., 2022. Refuge chief Ruth Davison: 'We face a growing need, but there is optimism' [online]. *The Guardian*. Available at: https://www.theguardian.com/society/2022/jan/04/refuge-chief-ruth-davison-domestic-abuse-support-growing-need-optimism.

Weinberg, T.S., 2020. The beginning of the sociological study of BDSM: A personal reflection. *Sexualities*, 24(5–6). doi:10.1177/1363460720961288.

Young, David., 1990. 15 men convicted of degrading and vicious practices. *The Times*, December 20.

4

WHAT'S IN A NAME (OR EVEN PRONOUN)?

EJ-Francis Caris-Hamer

Identities are an essential part of the way we live in society. They help us to express who we are, acknowledge the differences and similarities between us, and enable us to access basic human rights with regard to healthcare, education, economic and social inclusion. Names are an important part of our identities as they are often given to us by parents based upon deeply held historical, cultural, and personal preferences of our parents/guardians. In addition, names are often associated with and reflect the sex identity we are assigned at birth. However, what if the name you were given after birth does not reflect the person you are developing into? What if, as you are growing up, your gender identity (often assumed to be aligned with your assigned sex identity), conflicts with your sex assigned at birth and you no longer see yourself as part of the cisgender community?

For those who are part of the non-traditional gender conforming/non-cisgender community who challenge cultural essentialist views (i.e. those who identify as non-binary, gender queer, trans binary/non-cisgendered or non-conforming genders), there is increasing visibility in people actively choosing alternative pronouns such as the singular 'They/Them', 'Ze/Zir' and 'Ey/Em', as well as changing of names, whether this is shortening names, for example from Ashley to Ash, from Sarah-Jane to SJ, choosing names associated with the opposite cis-gender identity, or choosing a name perceived as more gender neutral. For those who are under the age of eighteen, choosing alternative pronouns and names as part of their social identity has proven a difficult transition within the education system and has become, for some, a focus of the frontline debate on gender topics amongst popular media, politicians, parents and staff members working in schools (*The Observer*, 2022). For example, in May 2022 Suella Braverman[1] criticised schools that take an unquestioning approach toward transgender pupils, insisting they do not have to accommodate such a community because those

DOI: 10.4324/9781003358756-6

under eighteen cannot change their name legally without parental consent (Wheale, 2022). Three months later, *The Telegraph* published a report stating that 'Headteachers will continue to decide whether to tell guardians about a child changing their identity' (Clarence-Smith, 2022: 1). This chapter explores the complexities of navigating the debate surrounding pronouns/names and considers who should exercise the right to consent to a student using their preferred pronouns/names in schools. I address questions such as: Does being under the age to legally change your name mean that any social transitioning of personal identity and how it is represented should be decided by people other than the person whose identity it is? Should individuals have agency over their own identity, or should pronouns and names only change within the education system if the school staff and parents/guardians give consent?

Gender identity in an educational context

Those students who are part of the non-traditional gender conforming/non-cisgendered (NCG) community are becoming far more visible at all levels of the education sector. The Census (2021) found that 16–24-year-olds have the highest proportion of a NCG identity (1% identifying as trans and 0.26% identifying as non-binary) compared to the overall population of 0.5% who identify as either trans or non-binary.[2] The Stonewall School Report (2017) found that 24% of respondents said they were trans/non-binary or questioning their gender identity. Being able to choose one's own pronoun/name enables one to make one's personal identity about sex and gender and even sexuality visible, where those identities may otherwise be hidden in everyday life. The use of chosen pronouns can represent a conscious choice on the part of the individual to express themselves and overtly convey how they want to be represented. Schools are a fundamentally vital environment for young people, as it is where they spend a significant amount of their time. All students, including gender-questioning/non-binary/trans, should feel safe and free from discrimination in schools, including, of course, during interactions with teachers and other support staff who are responsible for creating and reinforcing the culture within a school.

Unfortunately, research has shown that schools can often be hostile environments for NCGs because these students are continually faced with cis-gendered, often binary-normative assumptions and practices regarding gender identities, through gendered toilets and changing rooms, which games to play in PE, during lessons, and potentially what name they register under. Consequently, the NCG community suffers from daily discriminations more so than the LGB community (Stonewall School Report, 2017; LGBT Scotland, 2018), which in turn can lead to negative mental health and wellbeing (Formby, 2013; Dellenty, 2019; Glazzard & Stone, 2019; Glazzard, 2019; Bower-Brown et al., 2021) and safeguarding concerns.

Social transitioning

Social transitioning is defined as when someone changes their social identity; it is a term often used when someone chooses to express their gender identity in a way that is different from their assigned sex identity (Olson et al., 2022). Forms of social transitioning for the context of this chapter include change of names and pronouns (adopting 'they/them', 'Ze/Zir', or 'Ey/Em'), which express a gender-neutral stance or when a chosen pronoun is opposite to their assigned sex identity (sometimes known as binary trans). I use the term 'social' to indicate the fact that the change of name/pronoun has not occurred through legal means, i.e. change of name deed. Those who adopt non-conforming gender identities may identify as non-binary, gender questioning, gender queer or trans. Young people with non-binary or trans identities increasingly seek for their chosen identities to be recognised by schools. However, such a request can become complicated in a school context if there are contested legal, moral, and social perceptions around who should give consent for the use of chosen pronouns/names when those who wish to make the change are not legal adults.

Current equality laws and policies regarding non-conforming genders

Suella Braverman has reportedly expressed that schools need not comply with the gender preferences of pupils whose identity does not align with their assigned sex identity. Braverman bases this assertion on the fact that in the UK people cannot legally undertake a change in their gender identity through the Gender Recognition Act until they reach eighteen years (*Independent*, 2022; *The Guardian*, 2022). Braverman states that schools can continue to treat students as the sex they were assigned at birth under the law. 'They don't have to say "OK, we're going to let you change your pronoun or let you wear a skirt or call yourself a girl's name."' (*The Guardian*, 2022).

However, Braverman's perspective is too simplistic and fails to recognise that many youths explore their gender identities and may desire to socially transition in ways that do not require legal changes. In addition, Braverman fails to consider that schools are required, by law, to adhere to the Equality Act, 2010, under which gender reassignment is a protected characteristic (regardless of any medical procedures). Based upon the case law of *Taylor v Jaguar Range Rover*, this can also include non-binary genders (*R v Taylor*, 2022). Thus, if someone continues to 'dead name'[3] an individual, 'mis-gender', or purposely call someone by their non-chosen pronoun, this can constitute harassment and discrimination. Also, schools are subject to the Public Sector Equality Duty (PSED), which requires the education sector to include the views of all groups when considering the culture and daily function within the sector (in this context students, teachers, and parents). The PSED requires educational institutions to eliminate unlawful discrimination, to create a space for equality of opportunity and foster good relations between people (PSED, 2022).

As it stands, there is no official guidance for schools around NCG identities from the government. In May 2022, the then Secretary of State for Education Nadhim Zahawi promised that consultation and guidance would be provided to schools on how to support NCG students. Zahawi further stated that such guidance would be published in September 2022. However, due to government turmoil during 2022 including the appointment of three different Education Secretaries, any form of consultation was delayed until 2023 (Children & Young People Now, 2022). Current existing guidance includes dealing with issues related to parental responsibility and safeguarding. Parental responsibility guidelines state that 'Schools are required by law to engage with pupils' parents' and 'a person with parental responsibility can make decisions about their child's upbringing' (PRG, 2022). One could interpret this as suggesting that parents should have consent regarding whether a child may be called by their preferred name/pronoun. However, the policy also states that 'It will be for schools, on a case-by-case basis, to consider the level of information (if any) that is provided to parents' (PRG, 2022). As such, it could also be interpreted that schools can choose how they engage with parents, e.g., parents may inform the school that their child's gender identity has changed, but equally a school could choose *not to* require consent from the parent if the child informs the school of the change themself.

Under safeguarding guidelines, schools and staff working within schools must consider 'at all times, what is in the best interests of the child' and schools must 'prevent impairment of children's health and development...and take action to enable all children to have the best outcomes' (KCSIE, 2022: 6). A reasonable interpretation of this may be that best interest of the child includes being enabled and empowered in the exploration of their chosen gender identity within a safe space, and that this should be supported by schools.

These laws and guidelines provide multiple interpretations regarding decisions around who should consent to a change in a student's name/pronoun which causes confusion. For example, 'Sex Matters'[4] produced guidance for schools, using laws such as the Equality Act 2010, and claimed that 'The law is clear that children remain boys and girls, male and female, whatever their feelings about gender or the decisions they may take as adults...Imposing *"preferred pronouns"* on teachers or pupils denies their freedom of expression' (Sex Matters, 2022: 5–11). Using the same Equality laws but interpreting an opposing position on gender identity, Mermaids[5] published a 'toolkit' for educational institutions and those who work with children, expressing the need to support the inclusion of NCG identities within schools to promote student wellbeing (Mermaids, 2022). As such, clear guidelines from the government are important. McEntarfer & Lovannone (2022) highlight that without adopting a changing name policy, schools are potentially forcing students to have to 'come out' to every teacher, student, and administrative staff member on an on-going daily basis, which can lead to increased anxiety, feelings of 'othering', and gender dysphoria.

The topic of NCG identities in education is subject to much debate amongst popular media, government officials, and academics, yet simultaneously can prove to be somewhat under researched because NCG is often wrongly conflated with sexuality identity. Much existing research focuses on Lesbian, Gay, and Bisexual (LGB) students with less nuanced discussions around the diversity of gender identities amongst young people (Dugan et al., 2012; Bower-Brown et al., 2021). It is important to recognise that the needs of transgender and non-binary students can differ from LGB students (McEntarfer & Lovannone, 2022). In addition, academic research on this topic often involves studying Higher Education (Braver, 2017; McEntarfer & Lovannone, 2022), which fails to consider that students under eighteen may require some form of consent by an appropriate adult to enact chosen identities, whether that adult be a member of staff in a school or their parent/guardian/carer. Lawrence & Mckendry (2019: 9) indicate that 'education sectors…are sites of empowerment for individuals and society', therefore they should prove to be safe spaces where individuals can develop a better understanding of themselves and others, through agency. This raises the question: When a child wants to socially transition their gender identity by changing their name and/or pronouns, who should be given agency to make the change? Who gets to consent?

Methods

The data for this discussion is based on in-depth interviews with forty teachers, twenty identifying as male and twenty identifying as female. The stipulation was that they had to be working in the 11–19 education sector in England and teaching a secondary school subject. In addition, in September 2020, the new Relationships and Sex Education (RSE) was launched, which meant that for the first time, LGBTQIA identities and relationships were included within the curriculum as topics of discussion.[6]

Teachers interviewed taught in a range of schools including State maintained, Academies, Pupil Referral Units (PRU – those students who cannot be taught in a mainstream school), and Independent. Eight teachers taught in religious schools (Catholic, Jewish, and Church of England). Five taught in a single-sex school. Teachers held a variety of positions: Twenty-four teachers held the title 'Teacher of…(Subject)', fourteen would be considered as Middle Leaders because they were either head of department/subject, head of faculty, lead in SENCo (Special Educational Needs Coordinator) or Head of Year. Two teachers were members of the senior leadership team (SLT), with the title of Assistant Principal. Nine of the teachers were also the lead/representative of LGBT+ club/society and were leading in LGBT+ inclusion within their school.

Interviews were conducted during the Covid-19 pandemic, which meant that throughout this period, there were times when schools were closed for many students and much teaching was conducted remotely. When schools were open, there were strict restrictions regarding any interactions between students and teachers. This meant that some interview questions involved discussions about how the Covid-19 pandemic impacted queer inclusion within schools from the teachers' perspective. Each teacher was interviewed twice. The first set of interviews took place in the Autumn term of 2020 (completed by end of October 2020) and the second set of interviews took place during the summer term and summer holidays of 2021. As a result of Covid-19 research restraints, interviews were conducted online. This enabled a more demographically representative sample as there were fewer costs involved related to travel, and more flexibility for conducting the interviews.

Using Semantic Thematic Analysis, I identified broad shared descriptive ideas and beliefs across the two sets of interviews with teachers (Braun & Clarke, 2022; LeCouteur & Young, 2022). Inductive analysis was adopted in that the themes were driven by the data. I explored teachers' perspectives in relation to queer inclusion and the barriers to queer inclusion, with a specific focus on the discussions, beliefs, and experiences that teachers had around pronouns, NCG identities, and consent, using a queer lens (Braun & Clarke, 2012 & 2023).

Utilising a queer theory lens framework enables the consideration of how the increased *'usualising'*[7] of changing one's pronoun/name evokes forms of disruption, resistance, and potential conflict within schools (between students, teachers, and school leaders, and in some cases the schools' relationship with parents), and subsequently in the education sector more widely (Butler, 1993; Airton, 2018). Such a perspective interrogates taken-for-granted assumptions around binary and non-traditional gender conforming identities (e.g., the assumption that the only pronouns used by staff/students are he/she) which can inhibit agency and diversity amongst students (Butler, 2004; McDonald, 2017). By adopting a queer lens, I am able to make visible the complexities that teachers, students and parents navigate regarding who is impacted by the process and acceptance regarding who holds the power of ultimate consent to the name/pronoun changes of a student. Using a queer lens also enables a disruption of the notion that gender identities are fixed within a binary of male/female, masculine/feminine, regardless of the age of a person.

Context of non-cis gender identities within a binary school culture

Of the forty teachers interviewed, there were many discussions from teachers around students' identities which fell under the umbrella of non-conforming gender (NCG). Teachers noted that there was an increase in the number of students who questioned their cis-gender identity (CGI) and/or wanted to change their pronouns/name. One participant, River, talked about how students were feeling more confident and comfortable discussing gender questioning statuses, and other teachers mentioned there had been a general shift in how schools discuss and acted upon the issue when students wanted to change their pronouns and names on the school register system. Seventy-eight per cent of the teachers interviewed discussed NCG identities and expressed an understanding for the need to consistently support students with the questioning of their CGI, how both teachers and especially students negotiated this with parents and the need to establish clear policies that are supportive towards all stakeholders (schools, teachers, students, and parents).

It is important to note that all teachers interviewed had a positive attitude towards LGBTQIA topics and these identities being both visible and supported within schools e.g., none expressed that only he/she pronouns should be used. Discussions reflected the difference in experiences of the teachers, and thus reflected confidence regarding speaking to and acting upon requests from students, school leaders, and parents. However, teachers also commented that whilst they as individuals were supportive toward the NCG community, the school system itself remained largely a hostile environment for NCG students, where microaggressions were commonplace, because school structures maintained and reinforced the gender binary. Teachers identified the continued binary language in their school policies such as around PE activities and changing rooms, toilet usage, and school uniforms. One participant, Sawyer,[8] discussed how school uniforms (the fact only girls are allowed to wear skirts at his school) helped to reinforce a binary structure of male/female identities and thus contributed to the structural problems around inclusion. As a member of his schools SLT (Senior Leadership Team i.e., assistant headteacher), he has been campaigning to remove school uniforms. However, in general, participants expressed that when teachers have tried to resist the binary structures reinforced by schools, whether that be the Academy Trust or the SLT, they were often subjected to negative sanctions. For example, Briar had this to say:

> I've had a trans student challenge the fact that she felt there wasn't enough visibility or explanation about being trans in the school...I was an NQT[9] then...I tried to create some lessons and I got told off because it was one of those schools where everyone has to teach the same thing at the same time. You're not allowed to do anything of your own

The teachers' perspectives regarding the lack of support and often hostile environments around those with NCG identities has been previously suggested (Bower-Brown et al., 2021). Briar's experience supports the idea that in educational institutions there is often a culture where identities that exist outside the gender binary of male/female are 'othered', especially through language and policy practices (Jorgensen-Rideout, 2017). One teacher interviewed reported that students had been 'troubled because who they are just isn't there, they're not allowed to be who they want to be' (Sawyer). Other teachers also mentioned how students who were part of the NCG community felt alienated because the school refused to call them by their chosen pronouns/names, and these students often underperformed in their studies, especially in instances where the students' parents were also not supportive of their chosen pronouns/names.

One could argue that changing the registration system to enable students to be identified by their chosen name and pronoun is a form of resistance to the structured binary that schools reinforce. Blair mentioned how their school created a supportive atmosphere regarding changing a student's name on the register, illustrating it can be done relatively simply:

> We've had a couple of emails about it as matter of fact, 'this child will now be this'. It was changed overnight…and I thought that was actually really lovely because it wasn't…, there was no song and dance.

However, some teachers also mentioned the contradictions that schools enacted when it came to allowing students to be called by their preferred name. Some teachers mentioned that binaries are western practices. For example, some eastern cultures, such as Turkey, do not recognise 'him/her', and instead use 'they' for everyone. Other teachers mentioned that often they would call students by a shortened but assigned sex-consistent version of the students name, e.g. calling Cassandra, Cassie or Cass with no controversy. Briar expressed their frustration at the discrimination that exists regarding names:

> There are 600 Muhammads that go by their middle name, or a nickname… we've got many Nigerian kids whose everyday name is like one syllable of their name…we have so many examples of why it's bullshit discrimination [to single out NCG name changes].

Briar expresses how NCGs are othered in their school because discussions around parental consent, along with policies on changing names, were not paralleled in relation to other situations related to other identities such as ethnicity where the choice to use an alternative name to their given name was enacted without a discussion about or the need for parental consent. There is no law regarding the changing of pronouns, and SIMS,[10] as a computer programme, could easily accommodate an extra option box that states pronoun – 'They/Them' or 'Ze/Zir'. Thus, one may question why there is a debate about whether parents should give consent to a student choosing to use a different name or pronoun than was assigned to them at birth.

Safeguarding: A term used to justify both why parents *should* have consent and why parents *should not* have consent

A key element of safeguarding is to ensure 'All practitioners should make sure their approach is child centred. This means they should consider, at all times, what is in the best interests of the child' (KCSIE, 2022). Government policy emphasises that educational institutions should 'prevent the impairment of children's mental and physical health or development…and take action to enable all children to have the best outcomes' (KCSIE, 2022). Safeguarding is considered more important than ever for teachers; one participant stated that whilst teachers are educators, they increasingly perform a pastoral role due to the increase in the number of children who no longer live with their biological parent (s). Tan stressed that children 'all have to feel safe, most importantly they have to feel heard, they have to feel included in all conversations'. Tan's comments remind us that adhering to safeguarding policies can play an important role when considering whether parents should be the only stakeholders required to provide consent regarding whether their child may change their pronoun/name in school.

Interviews with participants found that teachers used the word 'safeguarding' to justify either their own, or the schools, decisions/actions relating to whether parents were required to consent to their child socially[11] changing their name and pronoun. All teachers discussed how they felt it was important to work with parents whose children were part of the NCG community and encouraged students to speak to their parents to create transparency. However the teachers also recognised that there could be safeguarding reasons why parents should not be informed about a child/student questioning their gender identity, e.g. if there is a possibility that the child may face abuse at home due to prejudicial attitudes.

Teachers interviewed used 'safeguarding' to justify why parents should provide consent regarding pronouns/name changes, and conversely, they also used 'safeguarding' as a reason why consent should instead lie with the child/student wishing to change their name/pronoun identity. Some teachers stated that it would be a safeguarding issue if schools changed the student's name but failed to tell the parents. Francis discussed a number of incidences where a child wanted to change their name/pronoun and the school adhered to the request only later to find that the parents had not been aware of this, which resulted in difficult situations due to reports going home in the new name (alongside the existing legal name). One participant, Cove, mentioned that their schools' stance is that parents must give consent for pronouns/names to change because the school feels that 'it stops any kid who thinks that's funny...our kids have that sense of humour'. Both Cove, and another participant, Lux, discussed their disagreement with the rules, stating that within the LGBT community group in the school, the students do go by their chosen identity, which has been accepted by the students as a compromise. Here safeguarding was used by teachers to ensure students were considering changes seriously, suggesting children may not be mature enough to make decisions relating to their own identity, yet also to protect staff against awkward conversations with parents. Both these stances highlighted an attempt to negotiate the issue of parental consent, but both, in different ways, failed to centre the welfare of the child as the priority which is a basic expectation of safeguarding. In addition, there remains the assumption that the binary identity assigned to these students from an early age is – and should – remain so, regardless of the potential harm this could cause those who are part of the NCG community. Such potential harm includes increase in negative mental health (anxiety and depression) including suicidal ideation (Su et al., 2016; DuBois et al., 2018), as well as increases in risky behaviours such as alcohol and drug misuse (Truszczynski et al., 2022).

With regard to safeguarding, there were instances where teachers and schools recognised that balance is important, and that it may not always be in the interests of the student to only make changes of names/pronouns on the register if/when parents' consent. For example, Cameron mentioned:

> One trans girl who came back [to school after lockdown] and said that mum stopped using their correct pronouns...mum had initially been OK with it and had been using her pronouns and stuff like that, then had just suddenly stopped doing it.

Riner, another participant, mentioned how some parents had been 'particularly negative' toward their child after their child disclosed their gender questioning identity. Another teacher mentioned how a gender questioning student was kicked out of the home and was forced to sofa surf. These incidences highlighted how some students home lives can be unsupportive with regards to their gender identity.

Teachers interviewed generally attempted to adopt a safeguarding and child centred approach and many discussed talking to students who came to them about this issue. Riner explained that he discussed with students the 'ramifications' of changing name/pronouns and encouraged students to approach things like this with their parents 'and then with their parents backing...so that student now goes by a male name and he/him pronouns'. Two other participants, Dan and Landry, explained to students that the school could change their pronoun and name on the school system informally, whilst also highlighting that until the child changed their name legally (which would require parental consent until the age of eighteen), certificates would include the name assigned to them at birth. Avery, another participant, stated that their school must follow local authority guidance which states parents must be informed about such changes unless there is a safeguarding issue such as the child being faced with abuse from the people they live with.

Most teachers interviewed attempted to provide space and agency for students through supporting them by listening to their struggles/concerns, guiding them by signposting to external support, and encouraging students to be comfortable with their identity. They also recommended that students should communicate with their parents and explained the school could help with such communication with the aim of increasing transparency around conversations occurring between students and teachers, whilst not breaching confidentiality. Another participant, Francis, stated 'We're looking at the policy for name changing to make it easier...and trying to do it in a way that includes the whole family'. Most of the teachers who spoke about parents and consent felt that it was important for parents to be informed but not to exercise overall consent regarding whether a student wants their name changed, as Landry stated, 'the sky doesn't fall in if a student uses a different name or pronoun'. Other teachers point to discrimination related to the fact that other students were allowed to exercise name preference without needing consent from parents in a range of other situations. Thus, a name change seemingly becomes an issue *only* when related to gender-identity. Avery noted that parents were not consulted when students 'came out', and thus questioned why parents should be consulted when students wished to change their name/pronoun.

The complexity of relationships with parents and who has the power to 'consent'

As mentioned in the literature, the education sector is subject to the Public Sector Equality Duty, which requires the sector to foster good relations between people (in this case local authorities, parents, students, and the school) by listening, reflecting, and responding to the schools' communities. Within the context of NCG identities, this can prove difficult when schools are obligated to consider the view of parents who may oppose their child's lived experience, and when parents disagree with each other.

Some teachers mentioned that there had been no discussion on the part of school leaders with regard to whom should have consent regarding a child/student's chosen name/pronoun, and as such they felt school leaders were a little out of their depth when it came to creating policies pertaining to NCG and sexuality identities. Blake and Sawyer are the LGBT+ leads within their respective schools. Both expressed how even they as inclusive leads on this matter, would like more support and guidance from the government. Blake said:

> We need...clear drivers around our legal obligation. We have very conflicting advice around our obligations under the Equality Act in terms of gender identity, and gender identity is actually protected...and so what are our actual, genuine legal obligations here?

Teachers felt that they were having to navigate what they thought was the right thing to do regarding the issue of consent with students. Many of the teachers expressed their support for their students in their provision of some autonomy and felt that the infrastructure of all schools (such as school uniforms and attendance registers) should change to ensure students everywhere are supported regarding their NCG identities.

For those schools who did have a policy, albeit an informal and often verbal one, all teachers stated that from the schools' perspective, parents should play an active role in consenting to whether their child could identify with their chosen name/pronoun in school. Some teachers expressed that their schools provided a very clear message regarding the fact that it is the parent alone who should exercise consent for name changes or the use of chosen pronouns. The common reason for this, according to the teachers interviewed, was that schools feared complaints from parents, and the potential of bad publicity, especially if the school embraced a religious ethos. When asked why the school was taking baby-steps towards inclusion Avery pointed out 'parental pressure and negative publicity...they go on public forums...and we are an RI (Requires Improvement) school'. Another teacher said, 'The deputy head running the meeting was wanting to do something...making sure we are being more inclusive in school, but concerned with the fact we're a Catholic school, what would parents think?' (Dexter). Aubrey expressed that inclusive pronoun language was not taken seriously in their school because the school wants to 'avoid all the backlash from parents'.

It is important to recognise not all religious schools shared the same fear of inclusion, as some teachers working in religious schools expressed how open the school was with acknowledging and embracing the LGBT+ community within the school, as well as having a clear inclusive policy regarding pronoun/name changes. So, for some schools, concern regarding parental response to their approach could lead to *positive* outcomes for NCG identities and ultimately produce an impact for inclusion. For example, Ocean talked about a year eight student who identified as 'they/them', whose parents were very vocal and 'helped to raise some awareness and understanding amongst SLT [senior leadership team]'. However, there is a need to acknowledge this approach *is* reactive. A potential concern with the reactive nature of schools could include the fact that outcomes remain dependent upon individual parental responses, which could be either positive or negative.

Teacher participants also frequently discussed the complex relationship between the schools as institutions, teachers working within the schools, and parents, when handling the fragility of topics that challenge heteronormative social norms. Teachers also stressed how the views of these different entities may differ from one another. For example, Sawyer and Blake mentioned how some parents expressed openly queerphobic views and those parents were supportive of their child expressing such views within the school environment, reinforcing the ideology that cis-binary genders are the norm. This parental support for the gender binary contributed to 'othering', as well as creating difficulties for those teachers who are trying to promote a culture of inclusion, equality, and diversity within the school. Harper gave an example where there was conflict between a mother and her child, and this conflict was illustrated in the conversations the teacher had with the mother. The mother believed her child was experiencing a phase and was certain her child would grow out of it. Harper said:

> It took a week of back and forth between me and mum, for me to say 'actually ignoring this is not going to make it go away...we need to be on the same page...in terms of supporting her, because it is inevitable that there is going to be struggles'...but her parents are refusing to accept that it's even a thing.

Francis gave an example where the parents were in conflict with *each other* over their child's non-cisgender status:

The parents had split up. So, the dad was absolutely fine with it and he lived with that. So, we always refer to 'he', because he is, but when we spoke to mum, mum refused to acknowledge 'he' pronouns and refer back to their dead name and stuff...so eventually we just dealt with dad because mum was struggling with it...so again, it's about having those policies in place for us as teachers.

In both of these examples we see teachers intentionally engaged in discussions with parents with the hope of ensuring that all parties support the child's choices and that all are in agreement. Equally, we can recognise the labour on behalf of the teachers attempting to navigate the issue with the idea that they want to support the student and meet the student's needs by allowing them to freely explore their identity in what teachers hope is a safe space.

Although schools seemed to mostly have a consistent view that parents should exercise consensual input to their child's use of names/pronouns in schools, individual teachers often embraced a different approach and were supportive of the child having more autonomy regarding the decision. For example, Harper teaches in a religious school and stated repeatedly that the school is not progressive in relation to updating policies to be both sexuality and gender inclusive, as well as the school fearing challenge from parents. As such, the school refused to change a particular students' name/pronoun because the parents were not supportive. Harper believed that the child/student should give consent for themselves saying: 'the children need to know that it is not up to the parents' as they believed that the welfare of the child/student should come before parental beliefs. Teachers such as Evan and Briar discussed how, whilst some parents were not supportive and refused for pronouns/names to be changed, during the LGBT+ clubs/societies they led, the chosen pronouns and names were used regardless of the lack of parental consent. In the example provided by Francis, the school also felt that parents certainly had a part to play in consent, but they took the active decision of speaking to the parent who did support their child, thus choosing the path of consent that aligned best with the child's/student's wishes. This illustrates aptly how, although parents' consent was seen as important with regards to NCG identities being expressed in schools, often teachers' views differed from the view propagated by the school. Thus, in many cases it appeared schools and their teaching staff negotiated consent differently between institutions but also between students. Many of the teachers who disagreed with the schools' approach to the issue of who has the power to consent tried to consider different ways around this issue so that they could support what the child wanted and to provide them with some autonomy. However, this effort by teachers was not found to be consistent across schools and was determined by the luck of having a teacher willing to undertake this pastoral labour even when they know that there may be conflicting differences between what the parents wanted and what the child/student wanted.

Discussion

The teachers interviewed highlighted the complexities involved with decisions regarding who ought to consent when a student wishes to change their name/pronoun, along with the negotiations teachers engaged in so that they could ensure the wellbeing of the students they teach. Teachers highlighted how the schools they worked in remained binary-normative through the insistence on continued structures and practices. These included gendered uniforms, gendered toilets, and the default assumption that pronouns on school registers only currently refer to 'him/her' rather than offering a non-binary option, along with the failure to allow all students, regardless of ethnicity or gender, to have a preferred name on their school records alongside their legal name. These practices have been viewed as discriminatory and can create a hostile environment for the NCG community (Stonewall School Report, 2017; LGBT Scotland, 2018), and consequently the information divulged during the interviews challenged the expectation that the education sector is unequivocally a safe space for *all* students, free from discrimination and ensuring the welfare of the students is the priority.

Education is argued to be a "*microcosm of society*" (Caris-Hamer, 2022: 145), functioning as the bridge between family and the wider social world. Given this, it is important that the education sector exposes students to different views to those of their parents. There needs to be some managed separation between some parents' expectations regarding what is accepted within the culture and curriculum of a school, and a genuine reflection and exploration of the wider world in which we now live. This chapter further reflects how relationships between parents and children, similarly to relationships between the school and parents, can prove to be complex.

In an era where it has been argued that education ideology is within its 'third wave'– sometimes called 'parentocracy' – where parents have a choice of schools they can send their child to (Brown, 1990), such conflict between schools' views and parents' ideological beliefs can prove difficult. Such strain was illustrated during interviews when teachers expressed that they felt their schools had failed to discuss topics such as NCG identities in a comprehensive and open manner due to the potential responses (real or perceived) from parents. The fear that parents will no longer send their child to the school which consequently could have a serious impact on school funding and the schools' ability to function effectively to a high standard was seen by teachers as having a significant impact on how schools handled issues related to NCG. Teachers suggested that as a result of threats to funding, senior leaders often adopted a strategic silence on sensitive issues to avoid conflict with some parents, regardless of the fact that negative reactions in no way reflect the reactions of *all* parents. Schools not addressing minority gender topics and practices can fail to engage with all members of the community and this does not reflect the reality of wider society that we all live in. At a time when other institutions, for example the media, seem to be keen to embrace inclusion, this seemingly leaves the education sector significantly behind. The overt invisibility and lack of such discussions and surrounding actions can cause harm to marginalised communities, supress healthy debates about pronouns/name changes and consent within, and how these issues are related to safeguarding of children.

Some of the teachers stated that whatever the policy (even if such policies were informal and verbal) the school had on the issues around gender identity, there was a need for students to be given a safe space to be able to explore their own identities. These teachers found ways for students to navigate this within the school environment, by focusing on what they thought was right for each individual student. Yet even this approach created somewhat of a lottery, because not all schools had teachers that were willing to take on such pastoral work. Clear guidance from the Department for Education would provide a more consistent approach and a clearer position regarding supporting students who question their gender identities rather than school policies being based upon the subjective beliefs of senior leaders. Furthermore, supportive, inclusive guidelines would also provide authoritative policy support for schools to fall back on when/if parents complain.

In reality, despite the best efforts of teachers, only some schools adopted an approach that adheres to safeguarding policies that were centred around the child's wellbeing. Importantly, teachers pointed out that under different, non-LGBTQ+ circumstances, having a preferred name is perfectly acceptable without asking for parental consent. In addition, if a student comes out as LGBTQIA, schools were not obliged to contact parents unless it is a safeguarding concern, e.g., students taking part in 'risky' behaviour. Teachers interviewed felt that whilst it is important for parents to be informed of their child's questioning of gender identity, due to the social nature of a change in name/pronoun (rather than a legal change), children/students should have the agency to choose their own identity. The teachers felt that such decisions are inherently personal to the individual, and that seeking the consent of a guardian who may have emotional biases and/or prejudices around the NCG community could prove harmful to the wellbeing of the student. It must be noted that these views may not reflect the opinions and thoughts of teachers who did not participate in the research. Under the Equality Act 2010, the law protects people from harmful practices such as dead-naming in an array of environments as it can be considered a form of harassment. Because this law is not restricted to age or public institution, it should be adhered to by schools for NCG students to ensure the safety and wellbeing of all.

Finally, I argue that we must remind ourselves that binary genders are a social construct. Within other cultures 'him/he' and 'her/she' are not recognised, and instead 'they/them' or other non-gender specific pronouns are used. As such, if western culture were to adopt a gender fluid, neutral stance as part of the culture within schools, this would negate the need for the debate regarding consent on this issue and could help cease the 'othering' of students who do not fit the binary-normative experience. Ultimately, schools need to be a safe space for students to explore and develop who they want to be.

Notes

1 Suella Braverman has been a conservative MP since 2005 in the UK. At the time (May 2022), she was the Attorney General for the government. She is currently the Home Secretary.
2 NB: This is the first time The Office for National Statistics has asked a gender identity question in The Census (2021). There are no known statistics across the UK for young people under the age of 16 other than data obtained from Stonewall School Report for England and Wales.
3 Referring to a transgender or non-binary individual by a name they used prior to transitioning, such as their birth name.
4 This is a UK-based organisation (non-profit) with a mission to raise awareness that sex matters in public policy and culture.
5 Mermaids is a UK charity that has emerged since 1995 and supports gender diverse, non-binary, transgender young people, and their families, offering advice to professionals who work with young people and their families.
6 The RSE curriculum in England was launched in September 2020. However, due to the Covid-19 pandemic, schools were able to delay the official implementation until the summer term of 2021. Some schools opted for the delay, other schools did not.
7 Term used (first heard from Sue Sanders) instead of 'normalising' that focuses on increasing the visibility of identities within a specific setting, in this case education (Schools Out, 2023)
8 Please note that all pseudonyms are gender neutral names and pronouns have been chosen by the participant teachers themselves.
9 This is a term used in the UK to identify someone as a 'Newly Qualified Teacher'. From 2021, the term has changed to Early Careers Teacher (ECT).
10 SIMS (Student Information Management System) collects student data for institutional and state reporting.
11 I use the term 'socially' because the child/student has not legally changed their name, this is their preferred name similar to a nickname or a shortened version of a name which is added as an 'also known as' to their school records.

References

Airton, L. (2018) The de/politicization of pronouns: Implications of the NO Big DEAL Campaign for gender-expansive educational policy and practice. *Gender and Education.* 30(6): 790–810.

Bower-Brown, S., Zadeh, S. and Jadva, V. (2021) Binary-trans, non-binary and gender questioning adolescents' experiences in UK schools. *Journal of LGBT Youth.*

Braun, V. and Clarke, V. (2012) Thematic analysis. In Cooper, H. Camic, P.M. Long, D. L. Panter, A.T. Rindkopf, D. and Sher, K.J. (Eds). *APA handbook of research methods in psychology. V2. Research Designs: Quantitative, qualitative, neuropsychological, and biological.* Pp.57–71.

Braun, V. and Clarke, V (2022) *Thematic Analysis: A Practical Guide.* London: SAGE Publications.

Braun, V. and Clarke, V. (2023) *Thematic Analysis Revised.* Available: https://uwe-reposi tory.worktribe.com/preview/1043068/thematic_analysis_revised_-_final.pdf Accessed: 16/ 01/2023.

Braver, D. (2017) Complexities of supporting transgender students: Use of self-identified first names and pronouns. *College and University Washington.* 92(3): 2–6, 8–13.

Brown, P. (1990) The 'Third Wave': Education and the ideology of parentocracy. *British Journal of Sociology of Education.* 11(1): 65–86.

Butler, J. (1993) Critically Queer. *GLQ: Journal of Lesbian and Gay Studies*. 1(1):17–32.

Butler, J. (2004) *Undoing Gender*. New York: Routledge.

Caris-Hamer, EJ (2022) Beyond binary boxes: Challenging the status quo. In Wilson, H. and Kara, B. *Diverse Educators: A Manifesto*. London: University of Buckingham Press.

Children & Young People Now (2022) DfE to consult on gender identity guidance for schools in 2023. Available: https://www.cypnow.co.uk/news/article/dfe-to-consult-on-gender-identity-guidance-for-schools-in-2023 Accessed 14/12/2022.

Clarence-Smith, L. (2022) Schools left to write own transgender rules 'behind parents' backs'. *The Telegraph*. 2 August 2022. Available: https://www.telegraph.co.uk/news/2022/08/02/schools-left-write-transgender-rules-behind-parents-backs/ Accessed 11/10/2022.

Dellenty, S. (2019) *Celebrating Difference: A Whole-School Approach to LGBT+ Inclusion*. London: Bloomsbury Education.

Dugan, J.P., Kusel, M. and Simounet, D. (2012) Transgender college students: An exploratory study of perceptions, engagement, and educational outcomes. *Journal of College Student Development*. 53(5): 719–736.

DuBois, S.N., Yoder, W., Guy, A.A., Manser, K. and Ramos, S. (2018) Examining associations between state-level transgender policies and transgender health. *Transgender Health*. 3(1): 220–224.

Formby, E. (2013) Understanding and responding to homophobia and bullying: Contrasting staff and young people's view within community settings in England. *Sexuality and Social Policy*. 10(4): 302–316.

Glazzard, J. and Stone, S. (2019) *Supporting LGBTQ+ Inclusion in Secondary Schools*. Norfolk: Witley Press.

Glazzard, J. (2019) The role of schools in supporting the mental health of young people who identify as LGBTQ. Available: https://www.leedsbeckett.ac.uk/blogs/carnegie-education/2019/01/the-role-of-schools-in-supporting-the-mental-health-of-young-peope-who-identify-as-lgbtq/ Accessed 1/7/2019.

Independent (2022) Suella Braverman: Schools do not need to comply with gender preference of pupils (10 August 2022). Available: https://www.independent.co.uk/news/uk/suella-braverman-schools-policy-exchange-attorney-general-b2142016.html Accessed 10/08/2022.

Jorgensen-Rideout, S. (2017) Beyond theory: Queer theory in practice. *The Post Hole*. 50. Available: https://www.theposthole.org/read/article/379 Accessed 29/09/2022.

KCSIE (2022) *Keeping Children Safe in Education*. Available: https://assets.publishing.service.gov.uk/government/uploads/system/uploads/attachment_data/file/1101454/Keeping_children_safe_in_education_2022.pdf Accessed 30/10/2022.

Lawrence, M. and Mckendry, S. (2019) *Supporting Transgender and Non-Binary Students and Staff in Further and Higher Education: Practical Advice for Colleges and Universities*. London: Jessica Kingsley Publishers.

LeCouteur, A. and Yong, A. (2022) Television commentary on women's and men's Australian Rules football: A thematic analysis. *International Review for the Sociology of Sport*. 57(5): 693–714.

LGBT Scotland (2018) *Life in Scotland for LGBT Young People*. Available: http://www.lgbtyouth.org.uk/media/1354/life-in-scotland-for-lgbt-young-people.pdf Accessed 10/10/2022.

McDonald, J. (2017) Queering methodologies and organizational research: Disrupting, critiquing, and exploring. *Qualitative Research in Methodologies and Organizational Structure*. 12(2): 130–148.

McEntarfer, H.K. and Lovannone, J. (2022) Faculty perceptions of chosen name policies and non-binary pronouns. *Teaching in Higher Education: Critical Perspectives*. 27(5): 632–647.

Mermaids (2022) Trans Inclusion Schools Toolkit. Available: https://mermaidsuk.org.uk/wp-content/uploads/2019/12/BHCC_Trans-Inclusion-Schools-Toolkit-_Version4_Sept21.pdf Accessed 14/12/2022.

Olson, K.R., Durwood, L., Horton, R., Gallagher, N.M. and Devor, A. (2022) Gender identity 5 years after social transition. *Paediatrics*. 150(2):e2021056082.

PRG (2022) Dealing with issues related to parental responsibility. Available: https://www.gov.uk/government/publications/dealing-with-issues-relating-to-parental-responsibility/understanding-and-dealing-with-issues-related-to-parental-responsibility Accessed 25/10/2022.

PSED (2022) Public Sector Equality Duty. Available: https://equalityhumanrights.com/en/advice-and-guidance/public-sector-equality-duty Accessed 28/10/2022.

R v Taylor (2022) *Ms R Taylor v Jaguar Land Rover Ltd*: 1304471/2018. Available: https://www.gov.uk/employment-tribunal-decisions/ms-r-v-jaguar-land-rover-ltd-1304471-2018 Accessed 20/07/2022.

Schools Out (2023) *The Rainbow Flag Award*. Available: https://www.rainbowflagaward.co.uk/the-classroom/the-classroom-inspiration/ Accessed 1/03/2023.

Sex Matters (2022) Sex and gender identity: Keep your pupils safe and comply within the law. Available: https://sex-matters.org/wp-content/uploads/2022/10/Sex-Matters-and-Transgender-Trend-schools-guidance.pdf Accessed 14/12/2022.

Stonewall School Report (2017) *Stonewall School Report*. Available: https://www.stonewall.org.uk/school-report-2017 Accessed 23/08/2022.

Su, D., Irwin, J.A., Fisher, C., Ramos, A., Kelley, M., Menduza, D.A.R., and Coleman, J. D. (2016) Mental health disparities with the LGBT population: A comparison between transgender and non-transgender individuals. *Transgender Health*. 1(1):12–20.

The Census (2021) Office for National Statistics. Available: https://www.ons.gov.uk/peoplepopulationandcommunity/culturalidentity/genderidentity/bulletins/genderidentityenglandandwales/census2021 Accessed 06/02/2023.

The Guardian (2022) Attorney general says schools do not have to accommodate children's gender wishes (27 May 2022). Available: https://www.theguardian.com/society/2022/may/27/attorney-general-says-schools-do-not-have-to-accommodate-childrens-gender-wishes Accessed 27/07/2022.

The Observer (2022) Pronouns, loos and uniforms: How schools become the gender wars frontline (20 August 2022) Available: https://www.theguardian.com/education/2022/aug/20/pronouns-loos-and-uniforms-how-schools-became-the-gender-wars-frontline Accessed 14/12/2022.

Truszczynski, N., Singh, A.A., Hansen, N. (2022) The discrimination experiences and coping responses of non-binary and trans people. *Journal of Homosexuality*. 69(4): 741–755.

Wheale, S. (2022) School leaders criticise Attorney General's advice on trans pupils. *The Guardian*, 30/05/2022. Available: http://www.theguardian.com/education/2022/may/30/school-leaders-criticse-attorney-generals-advice-on-trans-pupils Accessed 30/05/2022.

PART II
Shifting Meanings of Consent

5

"WHAT DO I CALL THIS?"

The Role of Consent in LGBTQA+ Sexual Practices and Victimization Experiences

Brooke de Heer

Sexual consent is a complex concept that is not clearly defined or experienced. It can include elements of verbal negotiation and non-verbal expression which can be interpreted differently by different people. Literature on sexual consent has overwhelmingly focused on heterosexual understandings and practices of consent in sexual interactions, further limiting our knowledge related to sexual communication outside the female/male relationship binary. This hetero-normativity, or a reliance on heterosexual cisgender experiences as normal and dominant to the exclusion of queer or gender non-conforming experiences (Marchia & Sommer, 2019; Warner, 1993), has provided a very narrow exploration of sexual consent. The current chapter seeks to widen the scope of sexual consent to include lesbian, gay, bisexual, transgender, queer, asexual+ (LGBTQA+[1]) experiences, practices, and insights which illuminate the impact of decades of queer oppression and gendered norms and scripts that typically govern sexual negotiation and consent.

Historically, oppression of people that deviated from the gender and sexual orientation binary was commonplace in most patriarchal societies (Worthen, 2020). Specifically in the United States and other Western nations that hold strong undertones of patriarchal values, heterosexual cisgender normativity has dominated mainstream culture, sidelining and devaluing LGBTQA+ experiences and realities. Thus, social power relies upon sexual and gender identity, along with other identity categories such as race and ability, with those that fall outside the margins being politically, socially, and economically disadvantaged (Buist, Lenning, & Ball, 2018; Worthen, 2020). Crenshaw (1989, 1991) coined the term intersectionality to explain multiple oppressive identities and the subsequent disadvantages of that positioning in society. Focused originally on the marginalization of Black women, intersectionality has been expanded to LGBTQA+ individuals to explore the impact of multiple oppressive identities

DOI: 10.4324/9781003358756-8

(e.g. lesbian women of color). Cho (2013) explains that intersectionality is not exclusive to certain minoritized groups and demonstrates its applicability as a framework for understanding overlapping identities that include sexual and gender identities. In relation to LGBTQA+ stigma, race, ethnicity, and LGBTQ identity can intersect to create discriminatory stereotypes. Labels such as gay and transgender have been linked with whiteness among both heterosexual and LGBTQA+ communities as well as white and communities of color (Han, 2007; Hunter, 2010; Whitley, Childs, & Collins, 2011; Worthen, 2020). As such, LGBTQA+ people of color often experience increased instances of homophobia/transphobia or discriminatory treatment.

Traditional gender and sexual scripts – which are internalized, socially constructed norms related to gender roles and sexual interaction that people draw from to guide behavior, responses, and emotions – promote intersectional discriminatory treatment as well as queer oppression generally. Research indicates that mainstream sexual scripts, which purposely exclude LGBTQ+ experiences, exemplify gendered notions of sexual behavior, such as the man initiates sexual contact and the woman responds (Jozkowski & Peterson, 2013). These hetero-normative scripts are pervasive and widespread because, historically, they have been the *only* representation of sexual behavior available. As such, queer people are forced to rely on them as well, creating incongruence in their desires and actions and what is considered acceptable via sexual scripts (de Heer, Brown, & Cheney, 2021). This not only impacts their ability to navigate the intricacies of sexual consent and negotiation but furthers marginalization and othering of LGBTQA+ people. Heterosexual, cis gender discourse and scripts are problematic in that our understanding of sexual consent and interactions is constrained by heteronormative values and dismissive of alternative identities (Beres, 2007).

Sexual Consent

Sexual scripts (Gagnon & Simon, 2005; Simon & Gagnon 1984) are an important element to understanding sexual consent. Sexual consent is uniquely complex and often incorporates varying ideas of what it looks like and how it is given, most of which are based in antiquated constructions of gender norms and sexual scripts. For example, women are supposed to be modest and never actively seek sex and on the contrary, men are expected to always be up for sex. These expectations can cloud or negate expressions of authentic consent, or more importantly, non-consent. This is particularly important for LGBTQA+ people who not only have experienced forced exposure to heteronormative sexual scripts but also have to figure out how those scripts apply to sexual consent in their queer relationships.

In the United States, consent is dictated by state laws related to rape or sexual assault, which often define the absence of consent, typically referring to incapacitation or force during a sexual encounter. In the last 10 years, there has been increased attention to the concept of affirmative consent, which is grounded in the idea that consent is *not* present unless it is affirmative, voluntary, and freely given. Conversations about the utility of affirmative consent have been ongoing at the state law level as well as within college and university policy. While many have commended the movement toward affirmative consent policies, feminist scholars and activists have questioned the utility of the concept, with critiques grounded in notions of patriarchal power and the inability for consent to be "freely given" (Beres, 2007; Pugh & Becker, 2018). This argument is further contextualized within marginalized groups.

The critique of sexual consent posed by intersectional feminists unveils consent as a socially constructed phenomenon controlled by those with power and privilege. In other words, marginalized groups based on race, class, gender, or sexual identity may be limited in their ability to provide true sexual consent within the constraints of a society that functions on inequality (Alcoff, 2018; Baker, 2008; Ehrlich, 2003; Loick, 2020; Mackinnon, 1989). Patriarchy, which places seen and unseen limitations on anyone that deviates from a white, herterosexual, male identity, promotes unequal power distributions across all spheres of life, including the interpersonal sphere where sexual consent lives. Thus, marginalized people may not have the power to freely express their wants and needs related to sexual consent and interaction.

Research over the last 20 years on unwanted but consensual sex, also called coerced consent or forced consent, has investigated heterosexual women's experiences of consenting to sex but having no desire to actually engage in sex (Peterson & Muehlenhard, 2007; Thomas, Stelzl & Lafrance, 2017). From a feminist framework, this research provides empirical validation of the impact of patriarchal power on sexual consent; women are consenting to sex without true intent or interest, often because acquiescence is safer and easier than refusing (Bay-Cheng & Eliseo-Arras, 2008; Hayfield & Clarke, 2012; O'Sullivan & Allgeier, 1998). Research suggests that male-dominated cultural and social norms prescribe women to concede to sex with men to avoid undesirable consequences of declining (Baker, 2008; Gavey, 2005; Thomas, et al., 2017). For example, women often cite that in order to avoid conflict related to declining sex, i.e. relationship tension or violence, they will comply with the request. Unfortunately, research on unwanted but consensual sex has focused on heterosexual women, thus it can only provide insights into the impact of *gendered* secondary status and lack of power related to sexual consent.

While structural constraints related to patriarchal power are typically applied to women, women are not the only marginalized group to experience exploitation and discrimination because of the established masculine hierarchy. As discussed earlier, queer people and communities have historically been ostracized from mainstream acceptance because they challenge patriarchal notions of gender and sexual norms (Buist, Lenning, & Ball, 2018; Worthen, 2020). Given this secondary social status, it is likely that some LGBTQA+ people may experience unwanted but consensual sex in ways similar to heterosexual women. In other words, queer people have been put in comparable or worse positions of powerlessness relative to heterosexual women and therefore may have parallel experiences of forced or coerced sexual consent.

Research, both past and present, demonstrates just this; sexually minoritized people experience coercive and forced sexual consent at disproportionately high rates (Messinger & Koon-Magnin, 2019; Ray, et al., 2021). Renzetti (1992) was among the first to investigate coercion in lesbian couples and found that coercive tactics like threats or manipulation can be used to gain consent between two women. More recently one study found that well over half (58%) of sexually minoritized women reported experiencing coerced sexual violence, which was 16 percentage points higher than heterosexual women (42%; Ray, et al., 2021). Similarly, sexually minoritized men were found to experience coerced sexual violence more often than heterosexual men *and* women – 44% of sexually minoritized men reported experiencing coercion compared to 24% of heterosexual men and 42% of heterosexual women (Ray, et al., 2021). Additionally, Hackman, Bettergarcia, Wedell, & Simmons (2022) found some uncertainty in how LGBTQA+ people identify verbal coercion related to sexual assault. Participants in this study noted that heteronormative assumptions blur the lines between verbal coercion and sexual assault problematizing if and when sexual coercion would be considered sexual assault.

It should be noted that research on sexual coercion in any population rarely interfaces with sexual consent. Each concept is discussed independently and very rarely do studies on sexual coercion also involve discussion of sexual consent, and vice versa. Sexual coercion, both physically and verbally, is often a critical component of unwanted but consensual sex and can likely be attributed to forced consent, yet they are rarely talked about in tandem. The inherent power dynamics, typically dictated by patriarchal values and gender norms, imbedded in coercive interactions that naturally impact consent are often mentioned and explored by scholars, but are never used to frame issues of coercion and consent under the same umbrella. For example, Eaton and Matamala (2014) explain how increased heteronormative beliefs (man is dominant, woman is submissive) lead to more acceptance of and experiences with verbal sexual coercion, without any mention of how this factors into the concept of sexual consent (the word "consent" does not appear in the manuscript). Most would argue that any use of coercion to gain compliance or consent to sex would be classified as non-consensual in that the consent was not freely given and was the product of power hierarchy where one person felt compelled to acquiesce. But power hierarchies and patriarchal underpinnings are absent from considerations of sexual consent in law which may explain why traditionally scholars have separated sexual coercion from consent.

The current work acknowledges the relationship between coercion and consent and seeks to discuss the two in parallel as they relate to and are influenced by inequitable power dynamics present in sexual encounters. This approach follows work by other scholars who have argued that issues associated with power in sexual contexts should be expanded past the man/woman gender binary. While power differentials can always be present, men are not the only people who can hold power in a sexual encounter and women do not always play a passive, powerless role. This is accentuated in same-gender sexual interactions. In line with research that suggests that man/woman dichotomies related to coercive practices are inappropriate because men and women are heterogeneous and have intersecting identities that impact how they engage with others (Donovan & Barnes, 2021; Stark & Hester, 2019), the current work looks to step outside rigid gender binaries to explain experiences of sexual coercion and consent.

Two Studies on LGBTQA+ Sexual Consent and Victimization

In an attempt to investigate queer experiences with sexual consent and victimization, we carried out two studies with individuals who identified as LGBTQA +. Our primary intent across both studies was to explore how LGBTQA+ identities understand sexual consent, experience forced or coerced consent, characterize sexual victimization, and seek help after victimization. The research utilized focus groups and one-on-one interviews, and was guided by feminist and queer theoretical frameworks. LGBTQA+ people were asked to share their thoughts and experiences on consent and victimization. Study 1 used focus groups and open dialog to facilitate discussion among LGBTQA+ people on the topic of sexual consent. Study 2 used one-on-one semi-structured interviews with LGBTQA+ people who had experienced unwanted sexual contact or assault to investigate how individuals characterized and thought about their victimization. Incentives for participation were provided for both studies which was important for both recruitment purposes and more importantly, to ensure that participants received some sort of compensation for sharing their time and personal stories. Below, the projects and respective findings are summarized and implications of the research are discussed.

Study 1

Study 1 (de Heer et al., 2021) included five focus groups consisting of between five to nine self-identified LGBTQA+ participants in each. Many gender and sexual identities were represented in the focus groups including female, male, nonbinary, genderqueer, gender fluid, bisexual, gay, lesbian, queer, pansexual and asexual. Focus groups lasted approximately one hour and all participants were supplied with a resource list if they felt any discomfort after participating in the conversation about sexual consent. Questions were posed to participants centering on where they learned about sexual consent, the varying meanings of sexual consent, the role of sexual consent in sexual encounters, and aspects of sexual consent that are unique to the LGBTQA+ community. There was open dialogue and discussion among the participants about different topics and thoughts or feelings about consent that provided examples of different experiences eliciting rich data for analysis.

Participants expressed a general understanding of sexual consent that seemed to be largely accepted and not approached as taboo within the LGBTQA+ community, yet participants communicated that queer identity and relationships pose some unique challenges relative to sexual consent (de Heer et al., 2021). Those challenges were organized along four primary themes (see Table 5.1). The primary themes identified through this research are particularly interesting in light of other research that discusses consent in heterosexual interactions. For example, the lack of comprehensive sexual education in US schools is not only problematic for queer youth, but has also been argued to uphold harmful stereotypes and disseminate false information that negatively impacts cis-heterosexual youth as well (Kantor, Santelli, Teitler, & Balmer, 2008). Conversely, the other three themes appear to be quite unique to queer people and highlight the layered complexities of consent for gender and sexual minoritized individuals.

These themes all incorporate elements of queer discrimination and marginalization that have worked to suppress LGBTQA+ connectedness and acceptance. In turn, the queer community's ability to openly express and explore their sexuality has been limited, forcing them to function within heteronormative assumptions and values of sex and consent. For example, many participants expressed that sex in the queer community looks different from traditional expectations of sex among heterosexuals, contributing to gaps in understanding and communication about what acts should require explicit consent. One participant noted:

> "It doesn't necessarily just mean, ok, penetration, this is sex. There are a lot of different things that constitute as sex to me that I don't think for some of my heterosexual friends, is necessarily sex to them."

Another participant shared: "all those other categories of sex are now all the places where non-consent can happen". One compelling point identified through this

TABLE 5.1 Study 1 LGBTQA+ Sexual Consent Themes

Theme	Explanation
Heteronormative sex education	Heteronormative sex education is pervasive and perpetuates misconceptions about sexual consent for LGBTQA+ people
Sex in the queer community	Differing ideas of what constitutes sex among the LGBTQA+ community can be an obstacle in determining consent
LGBTQA+ trauma (individually and collectively)	Recognizing trauma, coercion and victimization within the queer community is important when navigating sexual consent
Dual identities (gender and sexual identity)	Discriminatory responses to non-traditional gender and sexual identities impacts attitudes, feelings, and experiences of sexual consent

research is that LGBTQA+ people have been active in shifting the narrative around sexual consent within their community. They clearly identify the ramifications of historical oppression on freedoms related to sex and partnership and work to create an environment where sexual consent is openly and willingly discussed. For example, one participant commented:

> "My experience specifically being in the queer community, one there's more of a shared, a lot more shared experiences with sexual violence and trauma. So there's a general ability to be more tuned in, and want to seek that out, that consent, in different ways."

Many participants expressed an increased sense of responsibility about open communication regarding sexual wants and desires because they recognized that trauma and victimization within the queer community is disproportionately high (see de Heer et al., 2021 for a detailed description of the study and findings).

Study 2

The second study utilized interviews with LGBTQA+ individuals that experienced unwanted sexual contact or sexual assault (de Heer, Lipschutz, & Shevat, 2023) and sought to center queer survivor voices and explore what constitutes and contributes to help-seeking behavior after victimization. Fifteen LGBTQA+ identifying individuals were interviewed, with most interviews lasting approximately an hour. A semi-structured, open-ended interview format was used to allow space for participants to share their story in the way they wanted (Weller, et al., 2018). After the participants had shared as much or as little about their experience as they were comfortable with, participants were asked follow-up questions to reflect on their thoughts about the experience and help-seeking behaviors after victimization, responses to that help-seeking, and subsequent mental health outcomes. Due to the sensitive nature of the information shared in the interviews, all participants were provided with resources for reporting and recovering from sexual assault.

Fifteen participants shared a total of 32 incidents of unwanted sexual contact, with eight of the participants discussing more than one incident. Participants represented a number of different sexual and gender identities including bisexual women, lesbian women, lesbian asexual women, queer women, queer gender nonconforming individuals, queer transgender individuals, and queer men. It should be noted that the LGBTQA+ community is vastly diverse and grouping the varying identities together may not adequately represent the lived experiences of individual members (van Anders, 2015). While our study included participants that identified in a number of different ways, findings are in no way generalizable to the entire queer community.

There was great variability in the types of unwanted sexual contact discussed by the participants. Three incidents out of 32 were classified as stranger rape, 22 incidents were perpetrated by someone the participant was close with, either a family member, friend, or intimate partner, and seven incidents involved a general acquaintance. Fifteen of the 32 incidents occurred when the participants were children (under 18 years of age). Additionally, 22 of the incidents involved heterosexual cisgender men perpetrators, six involved lesbian or queer women perpetrators, two incidents involved heterosexual women perpetrators, and in two incidents the identity of the perpetrator was unknown. Coercive tactics including verbal manipulation or incapacitation were used in the vast majority of instances of unwanted sexual contact.

Three primary themes were identified from the interviews and are summarized below (see Table 5.2). Relative to research on consent among heterosexuals, the three themes discussed below with queer people reflect similar findings across the literature, with the exception that queer identity seems to accentuate and problematize disclosure responses, understanding their sexual victimization, and mental health outcomes. For example, negative disclosure responses to any victim regardless of sexual or gender identity are harmful and subsequent mental health issues are prevalent in many victims of sexual violence (Campbell, et al., 2001) not just LGBTQA+ victims. However, intersectional research that explores the impacts of overlapping oppressed identities suggests that negative outcomes are amplified for queer people because of their vulnerable social positioning (Buist, Lenning, & Ball, 2018; Worthen, 2020).

Overall, findings suggest that disclosure responses, both negative and positive, directly impact help-seeking and that tendencies to normalize and rationalize the experiences as a means to understand it are detrimental to help-seeking behaviors.

TABLE 5.2 Study 2 LGBTQA+ Sexual Victimization Themes

Theme	Secondary Theme	Explanation
Disclosure responses	- Negative disclosure experiences - Positive disclosure experiences	Negative responses impact future *effective* help-seeking attempts and positive disclosure responses were most common with informed mental health professionals
Understanding sexual victimization	- Downplaying, rationalizing, not understanding what happened	Disclosure and help-seeking was inhibited for those that had trouble understanding/defining what happened and those that downplayed or normalized the behavior
Mental health outcomes		Shame and self-blame stemming from the victimization and disclosure responses was related to more severe mental health outcomes (depression, suicide attempts, etc.)

For example, many participants expressed that their own understanding of their experience with unwanted sexual contact was limited, evidenced through voiced comments and questions like:

> "At first, I was kind of in shock cuz I was just like I don't know what happened. What do I call this? I was just so confused, like does this even count as sexual?"

Another participant explained:

> "I guess it was kind of romanticized, the way that I had viewed it back then. So I told a romanticized version of it, so there was nothing inherently wrong with it at face value."

Additionally, problematic mental health outcomes were also readily discussed by participants including anxiety, depression, and suicide ideation that often were proceeded by feelings of shame and self-blame. While not a primary theme related to help-seeking, coercive methods to gain access to sex (sexual acts) was common and added further complexity to whether consent was present or not, which in turn, diluted clarity related to understanding and conceptualizing what occurred. For example, one participant shared:

> "I didn't want to kiss him, I didn't wanna do any of that. But I felt coerced into doing just like one step further... But overall, I had said no, previously. Like when I look back at it, it's like I had said no from the get go, kind of, and he just kept, kept pushing to do more."

These themes again emphasize the disparate impact of heteronormative influences related to responses from others when an LGBTQA+ person discloses unwanted sexual contact and a queer person's ability to understand their experience with sexual violence and coercion within a heteronormative framework.

Limitations

Qualitative research, while greatly impactful at demonstrating lived experiences through participants' own voices, is limited in terms of representation and generalizability. The current studies utilized focus groups and interviews with LGBTQA+ identifying people to capture their feelings, thoughts, perceptions and experiences with sexual consent and victimization, but the data and findings produced from these studies may not be representative of all LGBTQA+ people. We recruited both community and student participants from a relatively queer-friendly area/community which may have impacted their experiences or perceptions related to consent and victimization. Additionally, sharing information about sexual contact is often very personal and participants were advised to only discuss what they were comfortable with; thus these studies may only present a portion of experiences, thoughts, feelings that participants were willing to discuss.

As discussed earlier, the queer community is extremely diverse and recognizing the varying identities within the group is important. The current studies were limited in how many different identities were represented (e.g. gay men, nonbinary people, transgender people) and therefore cannot speak specifically to what specific identities experience or provide recommendations aimed at specific subgroups. Broadly, the current studies can represent individual experiences linked to identity and how LGBTQA+ oppression and discrimination has impacted sexual experiences.

Conclusion and Implications

The two research projects reviewed above provide some needed insight into queer understanding of and experiences with sexual consent and sexual violence. Voices of marginalized groups have been relatively absent from sexual consent literature, leaving a substantial gap in our comprehensive knowledge related to the impact of structural oppression and discrimination on consent processes. Taken together, one of the most important findings to surface from the two studies is the impact of the *lack of* representation, examples, and scripts that reflect LGBTQA+ identities within the context of sexual interactions. Both studies identified that queer participants had misconceptions and questions about navigating sexual contact. This centered on not having a clear understanding of what constitutes sex between LGBTQA+ people, thus adding significant complexity to consent processes and normalizing or rationalizing unwanted sexual contact because of the traditional heteronormative framing of sexual violence.

Findings from these two studies suggest that we expect LGBTQA+ people to find the destination (a consensual, mutually enjoyable sexual experience) without providing them a map of how to get there. Understandings of sexual consent have been socially constructed around cisgender, heterosexual norms, leaving queer people with two options; try to figure out how they fit into the heteronormative narrative or start from scratch and create their own narrative. Outcomes from these two studies suggest that trying to work within the heteronormative narrative is detrimental to queer people in a number of ways: 1) sexual consent understandings being muddled because LGBTQA+ scripts and experiences may not reflect those portrayed in heterosexual interactions and 2) queer people not being able to recognize or define unwanted sexual contact because it falls outside the cis-gender heterosexual depiction of rape or sexual assault. On the other hand, LGBTQA+ people have the space to create a new narrative, where queer representation and identities are prioritized and celebrated. This approach – stepping outside heteronormative expectations – is where the queer community can inform and elevate sexual consent and victimization research and practice. As discussed in de Heer et al. (2021), further understanding of gender and sexually minoritized peoples' consent practices illuminates intricacies of sexual consent and victimization that are *not* entrenched in heterosexual gendered expectations that govern behavior. There is much to be learned from the queer community as they navigate through and embark upon exploring sexual communication outside gender and sexual identity constraints.

Experiences with non-congruent heteronormative assumptions and expectations were expressed in both studies, from the erasure of queer people in sex education to being a target of sexual violence because of their sexually minoritized identity. These experiences induce internalized feelings of self-blame, doubt and normalization of inappropriate behavior related to LGBTQA+ sexual interactions. As discussed in de Heer et al. (2023) researchers and practitioners in the field, including clinicians, advocates, and medical personnel should devise research designs and best practice guidelines that prioritize inclusivity, diversity, affirmation, and safe spaces for LGBTQA+ people. While living in a world that is dominated by cisgender heteronormative mindsets can be challenging for the queer community, outcomes from the two studies highlight that these shared experiences can create a space of strength, support, and increased empathy and communication around sexual consent and victimization which can ultimately serve to protect and empower the sexually minoritized.

Note

1 The term LGBTQA+ is used to describe individuals who identify as homosexual, bisexual, asexual, transgender or any nonconforming sexual orientation and/or identity. Highlighting differences in social identity (similar to work by Schulze & Koon-Magnin, 2017) is critically important to understanding how different identities within the LGBTQA+ community experience consent and sexual violence. The term queer is also utilized as an inclusive representation of this diverse group.

References

Alcoff, L. M. (2018). *Rape and Resistance*. John Wiley & Sons.

Baker, J. (2008, January). The ideology of choice. Overstating progress and hiding injustice in the lives of young women: Findings from a study in North Queensland, Australia. *Women's Studies International Forum*, 31 (1), 53–64.

Bay-Cheng, L. Y. and Eliseo-Arras, R. K. (2008) The making of unwanted sex: Gendered and neoliberal norms in college women's unwanted sexual experiences. *Journal of Sex Research*, 45 (4), 386–397.

Beres, M. A. (2007). 'Spontaneous' sexual consent: An analysis of sexual consent literature. *Feminism & Psychology*, 17 (1), 93–108.

Buist, C. L., Lenning, E., & Ball, M. (2018). Queer criminology. *Routledge Handbook of Critical Criminology* (pp. 96–106). Routledge.

Campbell, R., Ahrens, C. E., Sefl, T., Wasco, S. M., & Barnes, H. E. (2001). Social reactions to rape victims: Healing and hurtful effects on psychological and physical health outcomes. *Violence and victims*, 16 (3), 287–302.

Cho, S. (2013). POST-INTERSECTIONALITY: The curious reception of intersectionality in legal scholarship. *Du Bois Review: Social Science Research on Race*, 10 (2), 385–404.

Crenshaw, K. (1989). Demarginalizing the intersection of race and sex: A black feminist critique of antidiscrimination doctrine, feminist theory and antiracist politics. *University of Chicago Legal Forum*, 139.

Crenshaw, K. (1991). Mapping the margins: Intersectionality, identity politics, and violence against women of color. *Stanford Law Review*, 43 (6), 1241–1299.

de Heer, B., Brown, M., & Cheney, J. (2021). Sexual consent and communication among the sexual minoritized: The role of heteronormative sex education, trauma, and dual identities. *Feminist Criminology*, doi:15570851211034560.

de Heer, B., Lipschutz, S. & Shevat, S. (under review, 2023). "I was just so confused, like does this even count as sexual assault?": Understanding LGBTQA+ sexual victimization, help-seeking, and mental health outcomes. *Journal of Gender Studies*. Forthcoming.

Donovan, C., & Barnes, R. (2021). Re-tangling the concept of coercive control: A view from the margins and a response to Walby and Towers (2018). *Criminology & Criminal Justice*, 21 (2), 242–257.

Eaton, A. A., & Matamala, A. (2014). The relationship between heteronormative beliefs and verbal sexual coercion in college students. *Archives of sexual behavior*, 43 (7), 1443–1457.

Ehrlich, S. (2003). *Representing Rape: Language and Sexual Consent*. Routledge.

Gagnon, J. H., & Simon, W. (2005). *Sexual Conduct: The Social Sources of Human Sexuality*. Chicago: Aldine.

Gavey, N. (2005) *Just Sex? The Cultural Scaffolding of Rape*. New York: Routledge.

Hackman, C. L., Bettergarcia, J. N., Wedell, E., & Simmons, A. (2022). Qualitative exploration of perceptions of sexual assault and associated consequences among LGBTQ + college students. *Psychology of Sexual Orientation and Gender Diversity*, 9 (1), 81.

Han, C. S. (2007). They don't want to cruise your type: Gay men of color and the racial politics of exclusion. *Social Identities*, 13 (1), 51–67.

Hayfield, N. & Clarke, V. (2012) 'I'd be happy with a cup of tea': Women's accounts of sex and affection in long-term heterosexual relationships. *Women's Studies International Forum*, 35 (2): 67–74.

Hunter, M. A. (2010). All the gays are White and all the Blacks are straight: Black gay men, identity, and community. *Sexuality Research and Social Policy*, 7 (2), 81–92.

Jozkowski, K. N., & Peterson, Z. D. (2013). College students and sexual consent: Unique insights. *Journal of Sex Research*, 50 (6), 517–523.

Kantor, L. M., Santelli, J. S., Teitler, J., & Balmer, R. (2008). Abstinence only policies and programs: An overview. *Sexuality Research and Social Policy*, 5, 6–17.

Loick, D. (2020). "… as if it were a thing." A feminist critique of consent. *Constellations*, 27 (3), 412–422.

MacKinnon, C. A. (1989). *Toward a Feminist Theory of the State*. Harvard University Press.

Marchia, J., & Sommer, J. M. (2019). (Re) defining heteronormativity. *Sexualities*, 22 (3), 267–295.

Messinger, A. M., & Koon-Magnin, S. (2019). Sexual violence in LGBTQ communities. *Handbook of Sexual Assault and Sexual Assault Prevention*. Springer, 661–674.

O'Sullivan, L. & Allgeier, E. R. (1998) Feigning sexual desire: Consenting to unwanted sexual activity in heterosexual dating relationships. *The Journal of Sex Research*, 35 (3): 234–243.

Peterson, Z. D., & Muehlenhard, C. L. (2007). Conceptualizing the "wantedness" of women's consensual and nonconsensual sexual experiences: Implications for how women label their experiences with rape. *Journal of Sex Research*, 44 (1), 72–88.

Pugh, B., & Becker, P. (2018). Exploring definitions and prevalence of verbal sexual coercion and its relationship to consent to unwanted sex: Implications for affirmative consent standards on college campuses. *Behavioral sciences*, 8 (8), 69.

Ray, T. N., Lanni, D. J., Parkhill, M. R., Duong, T. V., Pickett, S. M., & Burgess-Proctor, A. K. (2021). Interpersonal violence victimization among youth entering college: A preliminary analysis examining the differences between LGBTQ and non-LGBTQ youth. *Violence and Gender*, 8 (2), 67–73.

Renzetti, C. M. (1992). *Violent Betrayal: Partner Abuse in Lesbian Relationships*. Sage Publications.

Schulze, C., & Koon-Magnin, S. (2017). Gender, sexual orientation, and rape myth acceptance:Preliminary findings from a sample of primarily LGBQ-identified survey respondents. *Violence and Victims*, 32 (1), 159–180.

Simon, W., and Gagnon, J. H. (1984). Sexual scripts. *Society*, 22, 53–60.

Stark, E., & Hester, M. (2019). Coercive control: Update and review. *Violence against Women*, 25 (1), 81–104.

Thomas, E. J., Stelzl, M., & Lafrance, M. N. (2017). Faking to finish: Women's accounts of feigning sexual pleasure to end unwanted sex. *Sexualities*, 20 (3), 281–301.

van Anders, S. M. (2015). Beyond sexual orientation: Integrating gender/sex and diverse-sexualities via sexual configurations theory. *Archives of Sexual Behavior*, 44 (5), 1177–1213.

Warner, M. (1993). *Fear of a Queer Planet: Queer Politics and Social Theory*. Minneapolis: University of Minnesota Press.

Weller, S. C., Vickers, B., Bernard, H. R., Blackburn, A. M., Borgatti, S., Gravlee, C. C., & Johnson, J. C. (2018). Open-ended interview questions and saturation. *PloS One*, 13 (6), e0198606–e0198606. https://doi.org/10.1371/journal.pone.0198606.

Whitley, B. E., Childs, C. E., & Collins, J. B. (2011). Differences in Black and White American college students' attitudes toward lesbians and gay men. *Sex Roles*, 64 (5–6), 299–310.

Worthen, M.G. (2020). *Queers, Bis, and Straight Lies: An Intersectional Examination of LGBTQ Stigma*. Routledge.

6

HOW DRUNK IS *"TOO DRUNK"* TO CONSENT?

A Summary of Research on Alcohol Intoxication and Sexual Consent

Kristen N. Jozkowski and Carli Hoffacker

In this chapter, we review research which examines the effects of alcohol intoxication on sexual consent and consent-related constructs, including the effects of alcohol intoxication on people's feelings of consent, consent communication, consent perceptions, and intent to engage in sexual behavior. We conclude with recommendations for consent promotion-based sexual assault prevention initiatives.

Alcohol use is a significant risk factor for sexual violence, especially among university students (Basile & Smith, 2011; Cantor et al., 2019; Krebs et al., 2016), as alcohol use by perpetrators and victims prior to or during sexual assault is common (e.g., Abbey, 2002; Armstrong et al., 2006). Indeed, sexual behavior without consent achieved via force, coercion, or other means, such as intentional intoxication for the purposes of acquiring sex, constitutes sexual assault (e.g., Cantor et al., 2015). According to the National Sexual Violence Resource Center (n.d.), "Alcohol-involved sexual assault occurs when a victim's intoxication from alcohol impairs their cognitive and physical functions to the extent that they are unable to consent to sexual activity." At the same time, university students report engaging in consensual sex after having consumed alcohol (e.g., Herbenick et al., 2019; Jozkowski & Wiersma, 2015). Approximately one in five university men and one in six university women report that they or their sexual partner were drunk during their most recent *consensual* sexual event and importantly, most of these events were described as wanted and pleasurable to some degree (Herbenick et al., 2019).

How do we reconcile "consensual drunk sex" (Muehlenhard et al., 2016) and alcohol-involved sexual assault? A defining characteristic of sexual assault is nonconsensual sexual behavior that occurs when someone is **too intoxicated to give consent** (Koss et al., 2007; Muehlenhard et al., 2017), begging the question—*how intoxicated is too intoxicated to consent*? This question plagues

DOI: 10.4324/9781003358756-9

sexual assault prevention educators as alcohol-involved sexual behavior—both consensual and nonconsensual—is common. In this review we summarize research examining the ways sexual consent and alcohol are intertwined. We focus on university students given that consensual and non-consensual alcohol-involved sexual behavior is common in this population. First, we provide a brief overview of sexual consent. Second, we discuss the ways alcohol intoxication may influence people's feelings regarding consent (i.e., internal consent). Third, we discuss how university students perceive alcohol-related behaviors as consent cues, and the effects of alcohol intoxication on consent communication and interpretation (i.e., external consent). In these sections, we discuss the effects of alcohol intoxication on constructs related to, but distinct from, consent such as sexual intent, interest, and availability. Then we discuss consent promotion-based sexual assault prevention initiatives, focusing on the inclusion of alcohol. Finally, we conclude with recommendations for prevention initiatives.

Conceptualizations of Sexual Consent

Consent is defined as one's freely given communication of one's feelings of willingness to engage in a particular sexual behavior, with a particular person, within a particular context (Hickman & Muehlenhard, 1999; Jozkowski & Willis, 2020). Consequently, consent comprises (1) internal feelings of willingness (i.e., internal consent) that are (2) externally communicated to another person (i.e., external consent communication). Because sexual consent involves communication to other people, it also comprises (3) interpreting a partner's external communication of their willingness to engage in sexual activity (i.e., external consent interpretation; Jozkowski et al., 2014a, 2014b; Muehlenhard et al., 2016). People more commonly associate external consent with "sexual consent," because we think of the communicative action of indicating agreement or willingness to another person. However, people typically experience feelings that lead them to the decision to consent. Internal consent represents that internal constellation of feelings people experience associated with their willingness to engage in sexual behavior (Jozkowski et al., 2014b; Willis et al., 2021a) and internal consent is often associated with external consent (Willis et al., 2019a).

   Internal consent has been operationalized into five distinct categories: (1) physical response—feelings associated with the body's automatic response to engaging or exciting stimuli; (2) comfort/safety—feelings associated with calm assurance and absence of worry or distress; (3) arousal—feelings associated with having sexual interest to engage in sexual activity; (4) agreement and wantedness—feelings associated with a desire and willingness to engage in sexual activity; and (5) readiness—feelings associated with confidence to engage in sexual behavior (Jozkowski et al., 2014b; Walsh et al., 2019; Willis et al., 2021a). University students report experiencing this range of feelings during consensual sexual encounters (Javidi et al., 2022; Jozkowski, 2013; Jozkowski et al., 2014b; Walsh et al., 2019, 2022). As such, while constructs such as sexual arousal or sexual interest may contribute to feelings of internal consent, on their own, they are not sufficient to constitute consent. Importantly, internal consent is a flexible construct that acknowledges variability and diversity in feelings (Jozkowski et al., 2014b; Willis et al., 2021a). These internal consent feelings have been applied to encounters that people perceive as consensual—but the degree that people experience these feelings varies across as well as during encounters (Willis et al, 2021a). For this reason, feelings such as interest and arousal should not be conflated with consent itself, despite being related.

External consent communication and interpretation have also been operationalized into five distinct categories: (1) explicit verbal cues—straightforward verbal statements communicating agreement to engage in sexual behavior; (2) implicit verbal cues—verbal statements that imply agreement to engage in sexual behavior; (3) explicit nonverbal cues—nonverbal behaviors or actions that are sexually explicit and imply agreement to engage in sexual behavior; (4) implicit nonverbal cues—subtle nonverbal behaviors or actions that imply interest in sexual behavior; and (5) no response signals—not resisting or saying no to sexual behavior and not seeming uncomfortable or distressed (Hickman & Muehlenhard, 1999; Jozkowski et al., 2016).

Sexual Consent and Alcohol

University students express an ability to orient sexual consent within alcohol-involved encounters (i.e., sexual encounters in which one or both/all partners had consumed alcohol; Jozkowski et al., 2017, 2018; MacNeela et al., 2014; Orchowski et al., 2022). For instance, university students (1) report engaging in consensual sexual activity while intoxicated (Herbenick et al., 2019; Jozkowski & Wiersma, 2015), (2) report feeling confident in their ability to consent to sex while intoxicated (Drouin et al., 2019; Jozkowski et al., 2023a), and (3) cite cues related to alcohol as indicators for how they communicate and interpret consent (Jozkowski et al., 2018). At the same time, university students who reported consuming alcohol in the past 30 days were more likely to report nonconsensual sexual experiences or experiences in which their willingness to engage in sexual behavior was questionable during that time than those who had not consumed alcohol (Marcantonio et al., 2021). As such, the relationship between alcohol and sexual consent is multifaceted. In this section, we discuss the ways alcohol intoxication influences sexual consent, specifically highlighting its impact on the three different conceptualizations of consent. Further, we discuss ways alcohol intoxication can lead to misinterpretation regarding external consent.

Internal Consent and Alcohol

According to findings from two studies, alcohol-involved sexual encounters were associated with decreased feelings of safety/comfort and readiness (Jozkowski & Wiersma, 2015) as well as diminished levels of wantedness

(Herbenick et al., 2019). Similarly, co-alcohol and cannabis-involved sexual encounters were associated with diminished levels of internal consent, specifically, feelings related to safety/comfort as well as feelings related to agreement and wantedness (Willis et al., 2021b). Such findings suggest that alcohol use alone *or* in combination with cannabis leads to decreases in one's subjective level of internal consent. However, in another study, alcohol-involved sexual encounters were not associated with wantedness and arousal (Cooper et al., 2016), which are critical aspects of internal consent (Jozkowski et al., 2014b). In summary, alcohol intoxication seems to influence internal consent, although the directionality of those associations is unclear.

External Consent and Alcohol

We discuss two pathways through which alcohol can influence consent communication: (1) alcohol as a cue indicating external sexual consent or a related construct (e.g., sexual interest), and (2) alcohol intoxication as a factor that influences the ways external consent is communicated and interpreted.

Alcohol-related Behaviors and Alcohol Contexts as External Consent Cues

University students perceive behaviors associated with alcohol (e.g., alcohol consumption; purchasing an alcoholic drink) or interactions occurring in alcohol contexts (e.g., flirting in a bar) as indicators of sexual availability, sexual interest, and potentially indicators of external consent (Abbey & Harnish, 1995; Jozkowski et al., 2018; Leigh et al., 1992; Lindgren et al., 2009; Orchowski et al., 2022). On the one hand, this interpretation may sometimes be a faithful proxy for students' sexual availability. Indeed, students indicate sometimes consuming alcohol or attending social functions where alcohol will be provided (e.g., fraternity party) because they are open to or interested in sex (Lindgren et al., 2009). Because sexual interest contributes to internal consent, it is understandable that someone may, in good faith, assume that if a person is interested in having sex, they may be more inclined to consent to sex, which can explain the interpretation of these behaviors as external consent cues. On the other hand, being interested in sex is definitively different from expressing external consent to any given sexual behavior (Jozkowski et al., 2018; Muehlenhard et al., 2016). It is inappropriate (and indeed may increase the likelihood of nonconsensual sex) to unequivocally conflate external consent with sexual interest, availability, or intent.

Importantly, extant research has demonstrated that consent perceptions are distinctly gendered and rely on heteronormative assumptions. Interpretations of alcohol-related cues differ by gender, and alcohol-related cues are applied differently to women's behavior compared with men's.[1] For example, men report interpreting women's engagement in alcohol-related behaviors as definitive indicators of women's willingness to engage in sexual behavior (Jozkowski et al.,

2018; Righi et al., 2019). Such alcohol-related behaviors include women getting intoxicated at a party, on a date, or in a private location with a person they just met, or being severely intoxicated and leaving a party with a person they just met (Wood et al., 2019). In these instances, men perceived women's alcohol behaviors as more reliably indicative of women's sexual willingness than women claimed the same behavior to be for themselves (Wood & Davis, 2017). However, Davis et al. (1999) found that most women reported consuming alcohol and even getting drunk during dates when they had no intention of having sex with their partner. And women do not claim that such alcohol-related behaviors (e.g., consuming alcohol) mean they do or will consent (Jozkowski et al., 2018). Yet, according to qualitative studies examining university students' external sexual consent communication, men report that the act of women consuming alcohol or being intoxicated at a bar or party indicated women's sexual *consent*. In those same studies, women reported engaging in such behavior to suggest sexual *interest*, but that such behavior does not equate to consent (Jozkowski et al., 2018; Orchowski et al., 2022). As such, these interpretations are problematic for two broad reasons: (1) indicating interest is not equivalent to expressed external consent, as interest may exist when consent does not; and (2) the signals men perceive as sexual interest (i.e., women's engagement in alcohol-related behaviors) may be inaccurate to begin with. Men's inability to accurately appraise women's signals may be magnified when men are intoxicated. According to Alcohol Myopia Theory (Steele & Josephs, 1990), after consuming alcohol, men may be myopically focused on these alcohol-related behaviors and situational expectations, which they perceive to indicate women's consent. As a result, they may disregard refusals or indicators that consent is lacking, perhaps explaining why intoxication increases men's propensity toward sexually aggressive behavior (Abbey & Helmers, 2020; Abbey et al., 2014).

These findings are not without complexity. For instance, although women indicated that alcohol-related behaviors were rarely unambiguously indicative of their *own* sexual intentions, they appraised *other women's* actions in the same way men did (Wood & Davis, 2016, 2017). Of note, both women and men applied these interpretations to women's alcohol-related behaviors, but not men's behaviors, reflecting an important sexual double standard (Jozkowski et al., 2017).

Alcohol-related behaviors may be linked to sexual willingness because people, especially women, who have consumed alcohol (or who are believed to have consumed alcohol), are perceived by others as being more sexually aroused, easy to seduce, sexually available, or more likely to engage in sexual behavior than those who had not consumed alcohol (Davis & Loftus, 2004; Lindgren et al., 2009). Supporting this claim, university students were more inclined to perceive sexually aggressive behavior perpetrated by a man on a woman in a vignette as consensual when the two characters had consumed alcohol (Norris & Cubbins, 1992). Alcohol use may also be interpreted as an external consent indicator because university students believe that consuming alcohol can facilitate sexual communication via lowering inhibitions. In this regard, students believe they will feel more assertive communicating about pursuing sex when they are intoxicated (Lindgren et al., 2009). Unfortunately, according to a systematic review alcohol consumption actually decreases women's risk recognition (Melkonian & Ham, 2018).

Additionally, alcohol use is part of some university students' sexual scripts (i.e., socially constructed beliefs or guidelines that people hold and ascribe to regarding how sexual interactions should unfold; Gagnon & Simon, 2005), which comprise consuming alcohol and moving from a public, often alcohol-involved, setting to a private setting such as leaving a bar to transition to a person's home (Beres, 2010; Jozkowski et al., 2018; Jozkowski & Willis, 2020). Because this trajectory is considered normative and expected, men may equate such behavior to women indicating their consent (Jozkowski et al., 2018). This interpretation is problematic because just prior to experiencing sexually aggressive behavior, intoxicated women report engaging in some consensual sexual behavior (Harrington & Leitenberg, 1994) and importantly, women specifically indicated that transitioning from a public, alcohol-involved setting to a private setting may indicate *interest* in sexual behavior, but, again, does not equate to consent to sexual behavior (Jozkowski et al., 2018).

In summary, expression and interpretation of alcohol-related behaviors as external consent cues differ troublingly along gendered lines, such that women who engage in drinking behaviors may experience sexual *interest*, which is sometimes interpreted by men as an expression of *consent* itself. This is problematic because consent is conceptualized as agreement to participate in a specific sexual activity with a given partner at a given time (Jozkowski & Willis, 2020), whereas interest may be experienced and expressed much more generally, without time-specified, behavioral, or other parameters, and can occur in the absence of actual consent. Unfortunately, the conflation of sexual interest, availability, or other related constructs with consent itself or cues of external consent emerges as a major theme in the exploration of alcohol-related sexual communication. This is concerning because to conflate the time-bound and behaviorally specific expression of consent with interest (which can be experienced in a general way across many circumstances) removes the agency of either participant to actually withdraw their consent to a sexual act, logically increasing the risk for nonconsensual activity.

Effects of Alcohol Intoxication on External Consent

Alcohol intoxication also influences the ways people externally communicate and interpret sexual consent. This is because alcohol intoxication impairs cognitive functioning making it difficult for people to both attend to and process complex stimuli (Chermack & Giancola, 1997; Steele & Josephs, 1990), thus diminishing people's ability to appropriately communicate and accurately interpret subtle, implicit cues (Connell, 2015; Griffin et al., 2010). It is important to note this because university students primarily use nonverbal and implicit cues to communicate and interpret external consent (Jozkowski et al., 2014a, 2014b; Muehlenhard et al., 2016; Willis et al., 2019b).

In one study, intoxicated non-partnered university students reported using less explicit external consent communication cues during alcohol-involved sexual encounters compared with encounters that did not involve alcohol (Jozkowski & Wiersma, 2015). In another study, young adults who binge drink relied on no response signals more often (e.g., not saying no; not actively refusing; Hickman & Muehlenhard, 1999; Jozkowski et al., 2016) than active consent cues (i.e., explicit and implicit, verbal and nonverbal consent cues; Willis & Jozkowski, 2019) to communicate and interpret external sexual consent (Marcantonio et al., 2021). More frequent binge drinkers may rely on context rather than active consent cues because alcohol impedes people's ability to process complex stimuli such as active consent cues. According to Alcohol Myopia Theory, it may also be the case that highly intoxicated men were myopically focused on specific context cues that they conceptualized as indicating consent, disregarding other indicators or signals that behavior may not be consensual (Steele & Josephs, 1990).

Again, the ways in which alcohol intoxication influences external consent communication is gendered and relies on heteronormative assumptions. For instance, in laboratory studies, men who were intoxicated were more likely to misperceive or overperceive women's actions as indicating sexual interest compared with their sober counterparts (Farris et al., 2010). Intoxicated men were more inclined to recognize a woman's positive cues of sexual interest and less inclined to consider her negative cues of disinterest (Abbey et al., 2005). Similar findings have been documented in more recent work—specifically that intoxicated men were more inclined to perceive women as more sexually aroused and their behaviors indicative of sexual intent than sober men (e.g., Davis et al., 2012; Farris et al., 2010). In addition, when intoxicated, men were more inclined to perceive "ambiguous social interactions" as women indicating sexual intent than sober men (Santaguida et al., 2022). This is particularly troubling because alcohol intoxication seems to facilitate misperceptions more among men who hold rape-supportive attitudes. Indeed, according to Benbouriche et al. (2018), men who endorse rape-supportive attitudes are more inclined to perceive ambiguous cues (i.e., implicit and nonverbal communication) as sexualized. Similarly, Parkhill et al. (2009) found that perpetrators who were highly intoxicated were more inclined to perceive women as more interested in sex than women report being. Again, this may lead some men to make assumptions about consent, especially if men are intoxicated and potentially myopically focused on engaging in sexual behavior.

Alcohol's Effect on People's Perceived Ability to Consent

Because alcohol-involved sexual assault is defined as a sexual act that happens when at least one party is *too intoxicated to consent* to sex, it is prudent to consider how people make decisions about one another's ability to consent. In one laboratory study, researchers found no meaningful differences in young adults' interpretation of consent and refusal indicators among characters in a vignette based on whether participants were intoxicated or sober; there were also no meaningful gender differences (Jozkowski et al., 2023b). Although this and the other aforementioned laboratory studies lend valuable insight into the effects of alcohol intoxication on perceptions of sexual intent, they lack some ecological validity due to the highly controlled nature of the research environment. As such, it is also important to consider research occurring in naturalistic settings. According to this work, alcohol intoxication does not seem to influence young people's perceived ability to consent to sex. Indeed, findings from two studies conducted in alcohol-involved contexts—one in a bar and another at tailgates[2]—indicate that upwards of 90% of intoxicated young adults indicated they could consent to sex, despite participants consuming on average five alcoholic drinks and variability in their breath alcohol content (BrAC [.00-.32]). In other words, participants with both higher and lower BrAC indicated they could consent (Drouin et al., 2019; Jozkowski et al., 2023a). This lack of variability in perceived ability to consent despite variability in BrAC suggests that alcohol intoxication may not influence the extent that people *believe* they could consent.

Drouin et al. (2019) and Jozkowski et al. (2023a) also examined people's perceptions of their friend's ability to consent to sex while intoxicated. Once again, there was overwhelming endorsement that, despite variability in intoxication levels of friends, participants believed their friend could consent to sex. However, there were some important gender differences. Men were more inclined to perceive their male friend as able to consent, irrespective of intoxication level, than women were to perceive about their female friend. When asked why they thought their friend could consent, common reasons included that participants did not think their friend was "*that intoxicated*" (Jozkowski et al., 2023a). These findings are consistent with other work that suggests that university students report feeling confident in their ability to consent to sex while intoxicated because they believe that alcohol intoxication does not influence their sexual decision-making abilities or that they are "*not that drunk*" (Marcantonio & Jozkowski, 2022). Thus, according to these university students, people can be very intoxicated, but still able to make decisions related to consent. Collectively, these findings highlight the question—*how intoxicated is too intoxicated to consent to sex*?

Consent Promotion-based Sexual Assault Prevention Education

This question—*how intoxicated is too intoxicated to consent to sex?*—seems particularly important for those involved in sexual assault prevention initiatives (SAPI) to consider. Findings from extant research suggest that alcohol and sexual consent are intertwined in important ways. Unfortunately, sexual consent promotion-based SAPI are limited in the ways they address alcohol-involved sexual behavior. For instance, although alcohol is often mentioned in many sexual consent definitions, clear consensus regarding the point at which alcohol intoxication infringes on ability to consent is lacking (Muehlenhard et al., 2016). Even when intoxicated to the point that they experience impaired judgment, young adults report feeling confident in their ability to consent to sex (Drouin et al., 2019; Jozkowski et al., 2023a). However, given frequent confluence between alcohol use and nonconsensual experiences, the presence and consumption of alcohol clearly present an important context to consider when addressing consent-based sexual assault prevention. In this section, we provide an overview of some consent promotion-based SAPI, specifically describing the extent that they discuss alcohol. We then provide recommendations for consent promotion-based SAPI to address regarding alcohol.

Where Is the Discussion of *Alcohol* in Consent Promotion-based SAPI?

Sexual assault prevention initiatives vary in terms of format and topic, with several addressing consent as part of larger initiatives and some exclusively focusing on sexual consent (for reviews see DeGue et al., 2014 and Jozkowski, 2022). Notably, according to the Campus Sexual Violence Elimination (Campus SaVE) Act, institutions of higher education in the United States are required to implement some form of SAPI that includes a bystander component (RAINN, 2022). Sexual consent is sometimes addressed in the context of these bystander initiatives. For example, RealConsent is an interactive, web-based program aimed to increase prosocial intervening behaviors, change attitudes and normative beliefs about sex, rape, and masculine gender roles, and increase knowledge of consent (Salazar et al., 2014). Additionally, programs such as the Enhanced Assess, Acknowledge, Act Sexual Assault Resistance program in Canada focus on verbal and physical self-defense tactics, but also promote healthy communication (Senn et al. 2015, 2017), which may include discussions of consent. And Elemental similarly combines physical and verbal self-protection training with content on recognition of sexual threats, communication in relationships, and importantly consent (Holtzman & Menning 2015). Unfortunately, because consent is often not the focus of such programs, the definitions and information provided as part of these programs is generally limited and such programs typically cannot address the nuances of alcohol intoxication related to consent in detail.

Affirmative consent policies or standards are other mechanisms to address sexual assault among university students (Bennett, 2016; Jozkowski, 2016). In this context, consent is often defined as a voluntary, active form of communicating willingness, agreement, or permission to engage in sexual behavior. Unlike other university-based initiatives, affirmative consent policies or standards typically *do* address or remark on alcohol intoxication. Some definitions clearly state that for there to be affirmative consent, people cannot be incapacitated, but it may be difficult to decipher incapacitation. For example, according to the definition of incapacitation in the context of consent provided on Indiana University's website (2022):

> A person is incapable of consent if they are unable to understand the facts, nature, extent, or implications of the situation due to drugs, alcohol, a mental disability, being asleep or unconscious, or based on their age (pursuant to Indiana law). With respect to alcohol and drugs, intoxication and/or impairment are not presumptively equivalent to incapacitation.

This definition highlights that being incapacitated precludes one's ability to consent, yet it also acknowledges that one can be intoxicated and sex can still be consensual. There is little guidance on how to navigate these states for oneself or for others such as partners or friends whom people may be a bystander for. In that vein, researchers have highlighted barriers to affirmative consent promotion initiatives, particularly focusing on the need to address alcohol-involved sexual behavior (Johnson & Hoover, 2015; Jozkowski, 2016, 2022; Willis & Jozkowski, 2018).

Other SAPI include social marketing campaigns designed to promote consent communication such as *Consent is Sexy, Consent is Good, Joyous, & Sexy*, and *Define Your Line* (Holz et al., 2018; Hovick & Silver, 2018; Thomas et al., 2016). These campaigns attempt to take a sex-positive approach by highlighting the benefits of communicating consent. However, such initiatives fail to address consent specifically in the context of alcohol-involved sexual behavior given that they are somewhat limited in scope.

As another example, Planned Parenthood promotes consent by stating that "Consent is as easy as FRIES" where FRIES stands for "Freely given, Reversible, Informed, Enthusiastic, and Specific." "Freely given" is defined as "Consenting is a choice you make without pressure, manipulation, or **under the influence of drugs or alcohol**" (emphasis added; Planned Parenthood, 2022). Similarly, in some of their educational material, Planned Parenthood states that "obviously if a person is drunk, high, passed out, or asleep, it is not okay to do sexual stuff with them. They can't consent when wasted or unconscious. So doing this is actually rape." Although it is encouraging that alcohol intoxication is mentioned in the context of consent and sexual violence prevention in this initiative, the information is limited. Because we know that people do engage in sexual behavior while intoxicated, stating a parameter that consent cannot be freely given when someone is *"under the influence of alcohol"* is not realistic and may cause people to disregard other information.

The "Consent: It's simple as Tea" Public Service Announcement (PSA) is another example of a consent promotion-based SAPI. This PSA was developed by internet blogger Emmeline May in 2015 and became part of Thames Valley Police department's and Thames Valley Sexual Violence Prevention Group's sexual violence prevention campaign: #ConsentIsEverything in the United Kingdom. The PSA went viral on YouTube worldwide. It uses drinking tea as

an analogy for sexual behavior and discusses sexual consent within this analogy. For example, the video describes if a person were to ask someone if they
wanted to drink tea and that request was declined, it would be wrong to force
tea on the declining party; in this case, forcing tea would not be consensual in
the same way forcing sex on someone after they had refused would not be
consensual, emphasizing that consent is as simple as asking about tea. The PSA,
though informative about certain aspects of consent, again fails to adequately
address alcohol involved sexual behavior. The PSA briefly references alcohol-
involved sex by stating that forcing an unconscious person to drink tea is
wrong. Realistically, there are various stages of intoxication one can experience
prior to passing out. This PSA does little to engage with the nuance of those
situations.

Recommendations for Consent Promotion-based SAPI

Given these limitations, we provide some recommendations for consent
promotion-based SAPI. First, it may be challenging for SAPI to include
detailed information about consent in alcohol-involved contexts because
empirical research is lacking. To that end, we echo scholars who have called
for **more research specifically aimed at understanding how people consent
while intoxicated** (Drouin et al., 2019; Jozkowski & Wiersma, 2015; Jozkowski et al., 2023a). We recommend that such **research include gender- and
sexual-minority groups**.

We also recommend that **consent promotion-based SAPI discuss alcohol in
more nuanced ways.** Consent initiatives ought to shift away from addressing
"drunk sex" as a homogenous category considered to be nonconsensual. Due to
the risks posed by misinterpretation of alcohol behaviors as external consent
cues and the risks posed by alcohol intoxication such as impacting men's
recognition that further advances are unwanted, SAPI may benefit from providing guidance for navigating consent in the context of alcohol specifically.
Educators can advise young people to embrace more explicit forms of consent
communication when one or both partners have been drinking given the ripe
opportunity for misinterpretation of more implicit or nonverbal communication
cues. In this context, it is important to **address problematic gender norms
associated with sexuality that in turn influence consent during alcohol-involved
sexual encounters.** Assumptions that alcohol use and alcohol-related behaviors
are interpreted as consent for women are inaccurate. Instead, it is important to
distinguish between sexual interest, arousal, and consent, underscoring our
recommendation that SAPI be more nuanced when addressing consent.
Although promoting explicit, affirmative consent is a good first step, **we argue
that interventionalists need to craft and tailor outreach to adequately address
the complexities of consent in the context of alcohol use.** Affirmative consent
policies and standards can be helpful, but we encourage them to be part of a
multi-pronged approach.

Conclusion

It is common for university students to engage in consensual sexual behavior after having consumed alcohol. However, compared with other tactics (e.g., force or threat), sexual assault experienced by students most commonly occurs when someone is "too drunk to consent" (Herbenick et al., 2019). Unfortunately, there is no clear metric that can be used to determine whether someone is too intoxicated to consent to sex (Wood et al., 2019). It is important to rigorously examine the effects of alcohol intoxication on consent given the ubiquity of both alcohol-involved sexual assault and "consensual, drunk sex" experienced by university students (Muehlenhard et al., 2016; Rosenberg et al., 2019). In this review, we highlight how alcohol use (1) influences internal consent feelings in meaningful ways, (2) can be interpreted as sexual interest, intent, or availability, which may lead people, particularly men, to make inaccurate assumptions about women's external consent, and (3) can influence people's perceptions of external consent, particularly that men may perceive women as consenting to sexual behavior when, in reality, they are not. Additionally, and importantly, current consent promotion-based SAPI do not adequately address the complexities of alcohol intoxication and sexual consent. To that end, we recommend a more nuanced and comprehensive approach to educating about sexual consent in the context of alcohol-involved sexual encounters.

Notes

1 Samples comprising people who identify within the gender binary make up most of the research reviewed in this chapter. As such, our discussions of gender differences compare women and men. Research examining sexual consent among people who do not identify within the gender binary is significantly lacking and thus warranted.
2 According to Jozkowski et al. (2023), tailgates are "social events typically held in parking lots or fields in association with sporting events or concerts. They often involve consuming alcohol."

References

Abbey, A. (2002). Alcohol-related sexual assault: A common problem among college students. *Journal of Studies on Alcohol*, 14(Suppl. 14), 118–128. https://doi.org/10. 15288/jsas.2002.s14.118.

Abbey, A, & Harnish, R.J. (1995). Perception of sexual intent: The role of gender, alcohol consumption, and rape supportive attitudes. *Sex Roles*, 32 (5), 297–313. https://doi.org/ 10.1007/BF01544599.

Abbey, A., & Helmers, B. R. (2020). Sexual aggression analogues used in alcohol administration research: Critical review of their correspondence to alcohol-involved sexual assaults. *Alcoholism: Clinical and Experimental Research*, 44 (8), 1514–1528. https://doi.org/10.1111/acer.14388.

Abbey, A., Wegner, R., Woerner, J., Pegram, S. E., & Pierce, J. (2014). Review of survey and experimental research that examines the relationship between alcohol consumption and men's sexual aggression perpetration. *Trauma, Violence, & Abuse*, 15 (4), 265–282. https://doi.org/10.1177/1524838014521031.

Abbey, A., Zawacki, T., & Buck, P. O. (2005). The effects of past sexual assault perpetration and alcohol consumption on men's reactions to mixed signals. *Journal of Social and Clinical Psychology*, 25, 129–155. https://doi.org/10.1521/jscp. 24.2.129.62273.

Armstrong, E. A., Hamilton, L., & Sweeney, B. (2006). Sexual assault on campus: A multilevel, integrative approach to party rape. *Social Problems*, 53 (4), 483–499. http s://doi.org/10.1525/sp.2006.53.4.483.

Basile, K. C., & Smith, S. G. (2011). Sexual violence victimization of women: Prevalence, characteristics, and the role of public health and prevention. *American Journal of Lifestyle Medicine*, 5 (5), 407–417. https://doi.org/10.1177/1559827611409512.

Benbouriche, M., Teste, B., Guay, J.-P., & Lavole, M. E. (2018). The role of rape-supportive attitudes, alcohol, and sexual arousal in sexual misperception: An experimental study. *Journal of Sex Research*, 56 (6), 766–777. https://doi.org/10. 1080/00224499.2018.1496221.

Bennett, J. (2016, January 10). Campus sex ... with a syllabus. *New York Times*. (Online Edition). Retrieved from http://www.nytimes.com/2016/01/10/fashion/sexua l-consentassault-collegecampuses.html.

Beres, M. A. (2010). Sexual miscommunication? Untangling assumptions about sexual communication between casual sex partners. *Culture, Health, and Sexuality*, 12, 1–14. https://doi.org/10.1080/13691050903075226.

Cantor, D., Fisher, B., Chibnall, S. H., Townsend, R., Lee, H., Thomas, G., et al. (2015). *Report on the AAU Campus Climate Survey on Sexual Assault and Sexual Misconduct*. Washington, DC: Association of American Universities. http://ias.virginia.edu/sites/ias. virginia.edu/files/University%20of%20Virginia_2015_climate_final_report.pdf.

Cantor, D., Fisher, B., Chibnall, S., Harps, S., Townsend, R., Thomas, G., ... & Madden, K. (2019). *Report on the AAU Campus Climate Survey on Sexual Assault and Misconduct*. Westat, Rockville, Maryland: Association of American Universities. https://www.aau.edu/sites/default/files/AAU-Files/Key-Issues/Campus-Safety/Revised% 20Aggregate%20report%20%20and%20appendices%201-7_(01-16-2020_FINAL).pdf

Chermack, S. T., & Giancola, P. R. (1997). The relation between alcohol and aggression: An integrated biopsychosocial conceptualization. *Clinical Psychology Review*, 17 (6), 621–649. https://doi.org/10.1016/S0272-7358(97)00038-X

Connell, M. (2015). Expert testimony in sexual assault cases: Alcohol intoxication and memory. *International journal of law and psychiatry*, 42, 98–105. https://doi.org/10. 1016/j.ijlp.2015.08.013.

Cooper, M., O'Hara, R., & Martins, J. (2016). Does drinking improve the quality of sexual experience? Sex-specific alcohol expectancies and subjective experience on drinking versus sober sexual occasions. *AIDS and Behavior*, 20 (S1), 40–51. doi:10.1007/s10461-015-1136-5.

Davis, D., & Loftus, E. F. (2004). What's good for the goose cooks the gander: Inconsistencies between the law and psychology of voluntary intoxication and sexual assault. In W. T. O'Donohue & E. Levensky (Eds.), *Handbook of Forensic Psychology* (pp. 997–1032). New York: Elsevier Academic Press.

Davis, D., Follette, W. C., & Merlino, M. L. (1999). Seeds of rape: Female behavior is probative for females, definitive for males. In *Psychological Expertise and Criminal Justice* (pp. 101–140). Washington, DC: American Psychological Association.

Davis, K. C., Schraufnagel, T. J., Jacques-Tiura, A. J., Norris, J., George, W. H., & Kiekel, P. A. (2012). Childhood sexual abuse and acute alcohol effects on men's sexual aggression intentions. *Psychology of Violence*, 2, 179–193. https://doi.org/10.1037/a0027185.

DeGue, S., Valle, L. A., Holt, M. K., Massetti, G. M., Matjasko, J. L., & Tharp, A. T. (2014). A systematic review of primary prevention strategies for sexual violence perpetration. *Aggression and Violent Behavior*, 19, 346–362. https://doi.org/10.1016/j.avb.2014. 05.004.

Drouin, M., Jozkowski, K.N., Davis, J., & Newsham, G. (2019). How does alcohol consumption affect perceptions of self- and friend-intoxication and ability to consent to sexual activity?, *Journal of Sex Research*, 56 (6),740–753, doi:10.1080/00224499.2018.1509290.

Farris, C., Treat, T. A., & Viken, R. J. (2010). Alcohol alters men's perceptual and decisional processing of women's sexual interest. *Journal of Abnormal Psychology*, 119 (2), 427–432. https://doi.org/10.1037/a0019343.

Gagnon, J., & Simon, W. (2005). *Sexual Conduct: The Social Sources of Sexual Conduct* (Second Edition). Piscataway, NJ: Transaction Books.

Griffin, J. A., Umstattd, R., & Usdan, S. L.(2010)Alcohol use and high-risk sexual behavior among collegiate women: A review of research on Alcohol Myopia Theory, *Journal of American College Health*, 58(6), 523–532, doi:10.1080/07448481003621718.

Harrington, N. T., & Leitenberg, H. (1994). Relationship between alcohol consumption and victim behaviors immediately preceding sexual aggression by an acquaintance. *Violence and Victims*, 9 (4), 315–324.

Herbenick, D., Fu, T. C., Dodge, B., & Fortenberry, J. D. (2019). The alcohol contexts of consent, wanted sex, sexual pleasure, and sexual assault: Results from a probability survey of undergraduate students. *Journal of American College Health*, 67 (2), 144– 152. https://doi.org/ 10.1080/07448481.2018.1462827.

Hickman, S. E., & Muehlenhard, C. L. (1999). "By the semi-mystical appearance of a condom": How young women and men communicate sexual consent in heterosexual situations. *Journal of Sex Research*, 36 (3), 258–272. https://doi.org/10.1080/00224499909551996.

Holz, K. B., Fischer, A. R., & Daood, C. J. (2018). The role of men's beliefs in shaping their response to a sexual violence prevention program. *Psychology of Men & Masculinity*, 19 (2), 308–313. https://doi.org/10.1037/men0000091.

Holtzman, M., & Menning, C. (2015). A new model for sexual assault protection: Creation and initial testing of Elemental. *Journal of Applied Social Science*, 9 (2), 139– 155. https://doi.org/10.1177/1936724414536394.

Hovick, S. R., & Silver, N. (2018). "Consent is sexy": A poster campaign using sex-positive images and messages to increase dyadic sexual communication. *Journal of American College Health*. https://doi.org/10.1080/07448481.2018.1515746.

Indiana University (2022). *Stop Sexual Violence: What is Consent?* Retrieved on October 30, 2022 from: https://stopsexualviolence.iu.edu/policies-terms/consent.html.

Javidi, H., Widman, L., Evans-Paulson, R., & Lipsey, N. (2022). Internal consent, affirmative external consent, and sexual satisfaction among young adults. *Journal of Sex Research*, online advance of print. https://doi.org/10.1080/00224499.2022.2048628.

Johnson, A. M., & Hoover, S. M. (2015). The potential of sexual consent interventions on college campuses: A literature review on the barriers to establishing affirmative sexual consent. *Pure Insights*, 4 (5), 1–8. Retrieved from https://digitalcommons. wou.edu/pure/vol4/iss1/5?utm_source=digitalcommons.wou.edu/pure/vol4/iss1/5& utm_medium=PDF&utm_campaign=PDFCoverPages.

Jozkowski, K. N. (2013). The influence of consent on college students' perceptions of the quality of sexual intercourse at last event. *International Journal of Sexual Health*, 25, 260–272. https://doi.org/10.1080/19317611.2013.799626.

Jozkowski, K. N. (2016). Barriers to affirmative consent policies and the need for affirmative sexuality. *University of the Pacific Law Review*, 47 (4), 741–772.

Jozkowski, K. N. (2022). Sexual consent and the prevention of sexual aggression. In Orchowski, L. M., & Berkowitz, A. (Eds.). *Engaging Boys and Men in Sexual Assault Prevention: Theory, Research, and Practice.* Elsevier.

Jozkowski, K. N., & Wiersma, J. D. (2015). Does alcohol consumption influence college students' consent to sex? *International Journal of Sexual Health*, 27 (2), 156–174. doi:10.1080/19317611.2014.951505.

Jozkowski, K. N., & Willis, M. (2020). People perceive transitioning from a social to a private setting as sexual consent. *Psychology & Sexuality*, 11 (4), 359–372. doi:10.1007/s13178-020-00439-9.

Jozkowski, K. N., Canan, S., Rhoads, K. E., & Hunt, M. (2016). Methodological considerations for conducting a content analysis of sexual consent communication in mainstream films. *Sexualization, Media & Society.* doi:10.1177/2374623816679184.

Jozkowski, K. N., Manning, J., & Hunt, M. E. (2018). Consent 'outside the bedroom': Exploring heterosexual college students' perception of consent cues in social settings. *Women's Studies in Communication*, 41 (2), 117–139, doi:10.1080/07491409.2018.1470121.

Jozkowski, K. N., Marcantonio, T. L., & Hunt, M. E. (2017). College students' sexual consent communication and perceptions of sexual double standards: A qualitative investigation. *Perspectives on Sexual and Reproductive Health*, 49 (4), 237–244. doi:10.1363/psrh.12041.

Jozkowski, K. N., Marcantonio, T. L., Willis, M., & Drouin, M. (2023a). Does alcohol consumption influence people's perceptions of their own and a drinking partner's ability to consent to sexual behavior in a non-sexualized drinking context? *Journal of Interpersonal Violence, 38(1-2)*, 128-155. doi:10.1177/08862605221080149.

Jozkowski, K. N., Marcantonio, T. L., Ford, K., Willis, M., Ham, L., Wiersma-Mosley, J. D., & Bridges, A. (2023b). The effects of alcohol intoxication on perceptions of consent and refusal indicators in a fictional alcohol-involved sexual encounter. *Journal of Sex Research.* Online advance of print. doi:10.1080/00224499.2023.2242838.

Jozkowski K. N., Peterson, Z. D., Sanders, S. A., Dennis, B., & Reece, M. (2014a). Gender differences in heterosexual college students' conceptualizations and indicators of sexual consent: Implications for contemporary sexual assault prevention education. *Journal of Sex Research*, 51 (8), 904–916. doi:10.1080/00224499.2013.792326.

Jozkowski K. N., Sanders, S. A., Peterson, Z. D., Dennis, B., & Reece, M. (2014b). Consenting to sexual activity: The development and psychometric assessment of dual measures of consent. *Archives of Sexual Behavior*, 43 (3), 437–450. doi:10.1007/s10508-013-0225-7.

Koss, M. P., Abbey, A., Campbell, R., Cook, S., Norris, J., Testa, M., Ullman, S., West, C., & White, J. (2007). Revising the SES: A collaborative process to improve assessment of sexual aggression and victimization. *Psychology of Women Quarterly*, 31 (4), 357–370. https://doi.org/10.1111/j.1471-6402.2007.00385.x.

Krebs, C., Lindquist, C., Berzofsky, M., Shook-Sa, B., Peterson, K., Planty, M., & Stroop, J. (2016). *Campus Climate Survey Validation Study: Final Technical Report: BJS*, Office of Justice Programs. https://evawintl.org/wp-content/uploads/BJSCampusClimateSurveyValidationStudy.pdf.

Leigh, B. C., Aramburu, B., & Norris, J. (1992). The morning after: Gender differences in attributions about alcohol-related sexual encounters. *Journal of Applied Social Psychology*, 22 (5), 343–357. https://doi.org/10.1111/j.1559-1816.1992.tb01544.x.

Lindgren, K. P., Pantalone, D. W., Lewis, M. A., & George, W. H. (2009). College students' perceptions about alcohol and consensual sexual behavior: Alcohol leads to sex. *Journal of Drug Education*, 39 (1), 1–21. 10.2190/DE.39.1.a.

MacNeela, P., Conway, T., Kavanagh, S., Kennedy, L. A., & McCaffrey, J. (2014). Young people, alcohol, and sex: What's consent got to do with it? Exploring how attitudes to alcohol impact on judgements about consent to sexual activity: A qualitative study of university students. NUI Galway. https://www.drugsandalcohol.ie/21286/1/Whats-Consent-Full.pdf.

Marcantonio, T. L., & Jozkowski, K. N. (2022) Do college students feel confident consenting to sex after consuming alcohol? *Journal of American College Health*. Online advance of print. https://doi.org/10.1080/07448481.2021.1943413.

Marcantonio, T. L., Willis, M., & Jozkowski, K. N. (2021). Effects of typical and binge drinking on sexual consent perceptions and communication. *Journal of Sex & Marital Therapy*, 48 (3), 273–284. doi:10.1080/0092623X.2021.1986445..

Melkonian, A. J., & Ham, L. S. (2018). The effects of alcohol intoxication on young adult women's identification of risk for sexual assault: A systematic review. *Psychology of Addictive Behaviors*, 32 (2), 162–172. https://doi.org/10.1037/adb0000349.

Muehlenhard, C. L., Humphreys, T. P., Jozkowski, K. N. & Peterson, Z. D. (2016). The complexities of sexual consent among college students: A conceptual and empirical review. *Journal of Sex Research*. doi:10.1080/00224499.2016.1146651.

Muehlenhard, C.L., Peterson, Z.D., Humphreys, T. P., Jozkowski, K. N. (2017). Evaluating the One in Five Statistic: Women's risk of sexual assault while in college students. *Journal of Sex Research*, 54 (4–5), 549–576. doi:10.1080/00224499.2017.1295014..

National Sexual Violence Resource Center. (n.d.). *Sexual Assault Response Toolkit Section 5: Sexual Assault Response*. Retrieved October 4, 2022, from https://www.nsvrc.org/sarts/toolkit/5-1.

Norris, J., & Cubbins, L. A. (1992). Dating, drinking, and rape: Effects of victim's and assailant's alcohol consumption on judgments of their behavior and traits. *Psychology of Women Quarterly*, 16, 179–191.

Orchowski, L. M., Oesterle, D. W., Moreno, O., Yusufov, M., Berkowitz, A., Abbey, A., … & Borsari, B. (2022). A qualitative analysis of sexual consent among heavy-drinking college men. *Journal of Interpersonal Violence*, 37 (7–8), NP5566–NP5593.

Parkhill, M. R., Abbey, A., & Jacques-Tiura, A. J. (2009) How do sexual assault characteristics vary as a function of perpetrators' level of intoxication? *Addictive Behavior*, 34, 331–333.

Planned Parenthood (2022). Sexual consent. https://www.plannedparenthood.org/learn/relationships/sexual-consent#:~:text=Consent%20is%20easy%20as%20FRIES,influence%20of%20drugs%20or%20alcohol.

RAINN. (2022). *Campus SAVE Act*. Retrieved on October 30, 2022 from https://www.rainn.org/articles/campus-save-act.

Righi, M. K., Bogen, K. W., Kuo, C., & Orchowski, L. M. (2019). A qualitative analysis of beliefs about sexual consent among high school students. *Journal of Interpersonal Violence*, 1–27. https://doi.org/10.1177/0886260519842855.

Rosenberg, M., Townes, A., Taylor, S., Luetke, M., & Herbenick, D. (2019). Quantifying the magnitude and potential influence of missing data in campus sexual assault surveys: A systematic review of surveys, 2010–2016. *Journal of American College Health*, 67 (1), 42–50. https://doi.org/10.1080/07448481.2018.1462817.

Salazar, L. F., Vivolo-Kantor, A., Hardin, J., & Berkowitz, A. (2014). A web-based sexual violence bystander intervention for male college students: Randomized controlled trial. *Journal of Medical Internet Research*, 16 (9). https://doi.org/10.2196/jmir.3426, e203.

Senn, C. Y., Eliasziw, M., Barata, P. C., Thurston, W. E., Newby-Clark, I. R., Radtke, H. L., & Hobden, K. L. (2015). Efficacy of a sexual assault resistance program for university women. *New England Journal of Medicine*, 372 (24), 2326–2335. doi:10.1056/NEJMsa1411131.

Senn, C. Y., Eliasziw, M., Hobden, K. L., Newby-Clark, I. R., Barata, P. C., Radtke, H. L., & Thurston, W. E. (2017). Secondary and 2-year outcomes of a sexual assault resistance program for university women. *Psychology of Women Quarterly*, 41 (2), 147–162. https://doi.org/10.1177/0361684317690119.

Santaguida, M., Dubé, S., Williams, M., Eidus, C., Vachon, D., Johnson, A. (2022). Alcohol Myopia and high-risk sexual behavior among college students. In Lykins, A. D. (Ed.) *Encyclopedia of Sexuality and Gender*. Cham: Springer. https://doi.org/10.1007/978-3-319-59531-3_108-1.

Steele, C. M., & Josephs, R. A. (1990). Alcohol myopia: Its prized and dangerous effects. *American Psychologist*, 45 (8), 921–933. https://doi.org/10.1037/0003-066X.45.8.921.

Thomas, K. A., Sorenson, S. B., & Joshi, M. (2016). "Consent is good, joyous, sexy": A banner campaign to market consent to college students. *Journal of American College Health*, 64, 639–650.

Walsh, K., Honickman, S., Valdespino-Hayden, Z., & Lowe, S. R. (2019). Dual measures of sexual consent: A confirmatory factor analysis of the Internal Consent Scale and External Consent Scale. *Journal of Sex Research*, 56 (6), 802–810.

Walsh, K., Drotman, S., & Lowe, S. R. (2022). Latent profiles of internal and external consent during a recent sexual encounter. *Archives of Sexual Behavior*, 51 (2), 821–831.

Willis, M., Blunt-Vinti, H. D., & Jozkowski, K. N. (2019a). Assessing and addressing the need for more diverse samples regarding age and race/ethnicity in sexual consent research. *Personality and Individual Differences*, 149, 37–45. doi:10.1016/j.paid.2019.05.029.

Willis, M., Hunt, M. E., Wodika, A., Rhodes, D., Goodman, J., & Jozkowski, K. N. (2019b). Contexts when college students use explicit verbal sexual consent cues. *International Journal of Sexual Health*, 31 (1), 60–70. doi:10.1080/19317611.2019.1565793.

Willis, M., & Jozkowski, K.N. (2018). Barriers to the success of affirmative consent initiatives: An application of the Social Ecological Model. *American Journal of Sexuality Education*, 12 (3), 324–336, doi:10.1080/15546128.2018.1443300.

Willis, M., & Jozkowski, K. N. (2019). Sexual precedent's effect on sexual consent communication. *Archives of Sexual Behavior*, 48 (6), 1723–1734. https://doi.org/10.1007/s10508-018-1348-7.

Willis, M., Jozkowski, K. N., Bridges, A. J., Veilleux, J. C., & Davis, R. E. (2021a). Assessing the within-person variability of internal and external sexual consent. *Journal of Sex Research*, 58 (9), 1173–1183, doi:10.1080/00224499.2021.1913567.

Willis, M., Marcantonio, T. L., & Jozkowski, K. N. (2021b). Internal and external sexual consent during events that involved alcohol, cannabis, or both. *Sexual Health*, 18 (3), 260–268. https://doi.org/10.1071/SH21015.

Wood, E. F, & Davis, D. (2016). Perceived and actual probative and definitive value of sexual behaviors in college students: Which behaviors have most potential for miscommunication? *Society for Personality and Social Psychology* (January).

Wood, E. F., & Davis, D. (2017). Perceived versus actual links between intoxication and sexual availability. *American Psychology Law Society* (March).

Wood, E.F., Rikkonen, K.J., Davis, D. (2019). Definition, communication, and interpretation of sexual consent. In O'Donohue, W., Schewe, P. (eds) *Handbook of Sexual Assault and Sexual Assault Prevention*. Cham: Springer. https://doi.org/10.1007/978-3-030-23645-8_24.

7

TWO WRONGS MAKE IT RIGHT

Perceptions of Intoxicated Consent

Laurie James-Hawkins and Veronica M. Lamarche

Tarana Burke started the #MeToo campaign on social media in 2006 in an effort to bring more attention to sexual violence against women (Groggel et al., 2021; Johnson and Hawbaker, 2018). The #MeToo movement has made the issue of consent more visible across the western world (Groggel et al., 2021). It also spurred an increased focus on research related to consent among young adults, as well as issues of consent and consent training on university campuses (Muehlenhard et al., 2016; Jozkowski and Willis, 2020). While definitions of consent vary, in relation to sexuality a commonly used definition is "one's verbal or nonverbal communication of willingness to engage in sexual activity" (Drouin et al., 2018, p. 741). One outcome of the #MeToo movement has been renewed calls for policies and laws that adopt an affirmative consent standard (Curtis and Burnett, 2017). Affirmative consent is typically defined as "Yes means Yes" suggesting that enthusiastic and positive consent is necessary for consent to be present (Curtis and Burnett, 2017).

Policies regarding affirmative consent (i.e. Yes means Yes[1]) have proliferated on university campuses and in laws in multiple countries in an effort to reduce endemic sexual violence (Jozkowski and Willis, 2020). While these efforts are laudable and necessary, it has been suggested that affirmative consent policies and programs oversimplify the concept of consent (e.g. "Consent is Sexy"[2], "Consent: It's Simple as Tea"[3], "Yes Means Yes"; Muehlenhard et al., 2016; Jozkowski et al., 2018). Young adults in particular have also criticized these efforts as being at odds with their lived experiences in which consent is much more nuanced (Koven, 2021; Groggel et al., 2021; Humphreys, 2004; Curtis and Burnett, 2017), and often not verbally communicated (Jozkowski and Wiersma, 2015), in direct opposition to most campaigns that call for enthusiastic and often verbal consent. Thus, while the need for affirmative consent is evident, we must also focus on what many young adults see as the grey areas of consent so that they have the tools to effectively assess when sexual assault or rape has occurred.

DOI: 10.4324/9781003358756-10

Feminist perspectives on consent suggest that the power differentials present in patriarchal societies mean that women have little agency to consent to sex. Indeed, sex is heavily imbued with specific gender-based expectations (Hunt et al., 2022; Muehlenhard et al., 2016). In line with traditional gender and hetero-normative sexual scripts, men are stereotyped as being insatiable and sexually aggressive, and as the initiators of sexual activity while women are stereotyped as sexual gatekeepers (Hunt et al., 2022; Muehlenhard et al., 2016). As a result, men are seen as active agents who *have* sex, while women are seen as passive agents who *allow* men to have sex with them (Loick, 2020). Belief in these traditional gender roles that frame men as agentic and women as passive has also been associated with men engaging in sex without consent and sexual violence (Cowley, 2014; Hunt et al., 2022).

In addition to the broader context complicating consent for all ages, young adults often have sex while under the influence of alcohol, which is endorsed by cultural norms that encourage alcohol consumption during social interactions (Armstrong and Hamilton, 2013; Wade, 2017). Alcohol consumption is particularly important when it comes to the issue of consent (Bednarchik et al., 2022; Hunt et al., 2022; Jozkowski et al., 2018). However, research on the impact of alcohol on consent among young adults is limited and has focused almost exclusively on young adults who are attending university (Jozkowski and Wiersma, 2015; Jozkowski et al., 2022; Orchowski et al., 2022). Given that sexual assault or rape is often defined by universities, police and court systems as lack of consent (Muehlenhard et al., 2016; Orchowski et al., 2022), and that there is a documented connection between alcohol consumption on the part of the victim and/or perpetrator and sexual violence (Carline et al., 2018; Jozkowski and Wiersma, 2015; Muehlenhard et al., 2016), the scarcity of research on how alcohol impacts perceptions of consent is especially surprising (Jozkowski, 2015).

The limited research on alcohol and consent that does exist has found that most young adults *feel* that they are still capable of consenting to sex after consuming alcohol (Drouin et al., 2018; Jozkowski et al., 2022; Marcantonio and Jozkowski, 2021b). One recent study by Marcantonio and Jozkowski (2021b) found that university students felt that as long as they were not black out drunk, they were able to consent to sex. Some students in this study felt that alcohol consumption was not relevant because it did not hinder their ability to consent. However, others felt that alcohol and consent were incompatible with one another, and that consent cannot be given while under the influence of alcohol. Other recent studies have found similar results (Marcantonio et al., 2022; Jozkowski et al., 2022). At the same time, research has also shown that alcohol-consumption increases the risk of sexual violence (Marcantonio and Jozkowski, 2021b; Marcantonio et al., 2022), illustrating that just because consent *could* be possible in the presence of alcohol, some people continue to take advantage of the vulnerability created by intoxication. Further research is therefore needed to determine how, when alcohol is present, young adults perceive consent and how they incorporate alcohol into these judgments.

Here, we present findings from a study in which we asked young women, aged 18 to 24, to read an ambiguous scenario from the perspective of a young adult woman who describes a casual sexual experience involving excessive alcohol consumption, and then asked the participants to identify if consent was present and if the scenario described a rape. Critically, we then asked them to explain what it was in the scenario that led them to make the decisions they did regarding the presence of consent and/or rape. The reasons our participants gave, illustrate the varied and complex understandings young women have in terms of how they think about consent, rape, and alcohol. Most interestingly, we found that alcohol consumption was used to support judgments that consent was present and that it was absent, as well as to support conclusions that a rape had and had not occurred. These results illustrate some of the grey areas around understanding of consent. Participants in the study used the same reason – alcohol – to support a wide variety of conclusions about the ambiguous scenario presented. We conclude with a discussion of the issues this raises for today's consent training efforts and offer some suggestions for how we might move forward in both studying and teaching about sexual consent as a complex and socially situated concept that goes far beyond our current definitions of consent as "simple".

The Study

To begin to address the question of how young people today think about consent, we ran a study with 793 young heterosexual women, aged 18 to 24 from across the United Kingdom. Data were collected from December 10, 2018 to March 10, 2019 using Prolific Academic, with each participant paid £5.00/HR (pro rata) for their participation. Ethical approval for the study was received from the University of Essex ethics committee. Participants were asked to read an ambiguous scenario about a sexual encounter between a man and a woman and then tell us if consent was present (yes/no) and if a rape had occurred (yes/no). Each participant saw four different scenarios and these two questions were answered for each scenario (see Lamarche and James-Hawkins, 2022). Scenario number two was then shown a second time and participants were asked to explain why the first time they read the scenario they said yes or no as to whether the scenario describes a rape. Our scenario depicted a situation in which a young woman meets a man in a pub while out with friends, she drinks with the man, and she then wakes up in his bed the next morning:

> I decided to go out to the pub with some mates from work. While I was waiting at the bar for another drink, this guy Tom started chatting me up. Before I knew it, we were both so drunk – I'm afraid to look at how much I spent on drink! I must have agreed to go back to his because I woke up in his bed the next morning. It's been a while since I've had sex with someone. At least he was hot I guess.

Our primary interest was in seeing how the participants explained the scenario and the reasons they used to support their rationale and interpretation, not in endorsing any one response as correct. We found that our participants responded in three primary ways to the consent and rape questions: 1) that consent was given and no rape had occurred (discussed below as CY-RN), 2) that consent was not given and a rape occurred (discussed below as CN-RY), and 3) that no consent was given, but no rape occurred (discussed below as CN-RN). Across these groups, the most common rationale used by all participants to explain their rationalization for whether a rape had occurred was that both parties in the scenario were drunk. What was most interesting is that this same reason, drinking, was used by different participants in different ways, and led to different decisions about whether or not a rape had occurred and/or whether consent had been given. These results provide a brief insight into how young adults apply the issue of consent in ambiguous situations, and in doing so reveal the ways in which consent is perceived by young adults as a grey area, with many participants struggling to reach a conclusion. Below, we present the data from women in each of the three groups identified above and explore how they used alcohol as a way to support their differing judgments.

Findings

Consent, Yes – Rape, No (CY-RN)

The first group of people identified in the sample included respondents who believed that consent was present in the scenario, and that the scenario also did not describe a rape. One of the most common rationales used to explain why the presented scenario did *not* depict a rape was that *both* parties were drunk. Participants felt that the concept of consent was not something that was terribly useful in determining whether a rape occurred when both parties were cognitively impaired. One person summarized this by saying, "They were both drunk so how can one person be to blame?" While all of the CY-RN participants indicated on their first reading of the scenario that consent had been given and no rape had occurred, when asked to explain what they used to determine that no rape had occurred, they often decided that consent *had not* been given, but that as *neither party* was in a state to consent the event could not be labelled as a rape. Essentially, participants felt that though they could not, on reflection, say that consent was present when both parties were cognitively impaired, this meant that there was equal and shared responsibility and thus equal and shared blame. One participant explained this well:

> I believe that although no one should have been having sex on this occasion as being too drunk isn't really consensual sex but at the same time if they were both ridiculously drunk and had sex, no one can be blamed.

Lack of blame and lack of responsibility for their actions was clearly attributed to both parties. Equally, the idea of consent, or lack thereof, was not considered to be the sole factor in determining whether a rape had occurred. From this perspective, the perceived mutuality of the state of mind of both participants was more important than the issue of consent. One participant described this, "I don't think this was a rape because both parties got willingly as drunk as each other. It wasn't a rape per se, but the both of them weren't really capable of consenting." Another participant agreed with this assessment: "They were both drunk, neither person could have fully consented, they are both equally responsible." These participants placed the emphasis on shared diminished capacity rather than the idea of absolute or "enthusiastic" consent in reaching their judgment that a rape had not occurred.

Interestingly, several participants assessed the situation from the perspective of the man's well-being, as well as the woman's. These participants challenged traditional sex scripts by suggesting that it was equally important to determine if the man had the capacity to consent, and felt it was possible that the man in the scenario may have been *less* able to consent to sex than the woman: "They were both so drunk. Just because she was drunk doesn't mean it was his fault. He could have been less fit to consent than her." It is clear from these statements that at least some of the young adult participants in the study did not equate the lack of consent with rape when they perceived the man in the scenario to be equally drunk and unable to consent. Thus, rather than looking at the woman as a victim, participants looked for mitigating factors, such as both people being unfit to consent, to explain why they said that no rape had occurred. What is most interesting about this group is that they relied on the idea of *responsibility* rather than consent to assess the situation and appeared to feel that in a situation in which both people could not consent, consent was not the right metric to use to determine whether a rape had occurred. Even more interesting is that this perspective led the participants to initially indicate that consent was present in the scenario. Yet, when asked to explain why they felt a rape had not occurred, they often backtracked on the idea that consent had been given, and instead argued that neither party had consented and explained that in this situation it was necessary to use other cues to decide whether a rape had occurred, rather than relying exclusively on the presence or absence of consent.

In the absence of explicit consent, one of the factors that this group used to determine whether a rape had occurred was any indication of coercion or force, which this group of participants felt was not present in the scenario. One participant put it this way: "They were both drunk, not like either is in a capacity to be coercive/rape the other," while another said: "As both parties were very drunk, I wouldn't say this is rape? Both consensually went home together, there was no coerc[ion] here". Other people focused on whether one person was likely to have been taking advantage of the other, "I decided that it wasn't rape because they were both equally drunk, so it didn't seem like one person was taking advantage of the other", and "Both parties had far too much to drink.

Neither of them should be having sex with new partners, but no one seems to be taking advantage." Thus, because these participants believed that both people being cognitively impaired by alcohol would mutually affect their ability to consent, they turned to rape-script heuristics and looked for evidence that would suggest at least one of the two partners was unwilling (e.g., use of force, coercion). Importantly, this suggests that for some people, a rape requires more than the absence of enthusiastic, or even passive communication of, consent.

Consent, No – Rape, Yes (CN-RY)

The CN-RY group had a much stricter definition of rape and consent, and their direct relationship with one another, compared to the CY-RN. Whereas the CY-RN group believed that the absence/presence of consent insufficiently informed whether or not a rape had occurred, the CN-RY group believed consent was a necessary requirement of sex, and that people cannot consent to sex when intoxicated, ergo drunk sex was equal to rape. Furthermore, justifications showed that these (UK-based) participants subscribed to the legal definition of rape used in England and Wales, which explicitly defines a rape as when a [male] person intentionally penetrates another person with *his penis* (Section 1, Sexual Offences Act 2003). This perspective meant that a scenario depicting a woman who has been drinking and then had sex could be automatically defined as having been raped. The participants in this group did not consider the state of the man. This perspective placed the emphasis on the woman's alcohol consumption to explain why a rape *had* occurred, whereas the CY-RN group used the same explanation – albeit focusing on the intoxication of both the man and the woman – to say that a rape *had not* occurred.

This focus on the woman exclusively was prevalent in the responses in the CN-RY group. For example, one participant said, "Although at the time she may have agreed to have sex, she was drunk and was therefore unable to give consent", and another said, "The woman was in too much of a drunken state to give consent to the man". Some of these participants were also more explicitly willing to place blame on the man in the scenario, regardless of his own intoxication. For example, one participant said, "The reason I believe it describes a rape is if someone is too drunk you cannot legitimately give consent. If she cannot remember getting back to his she must have been too drunk, and Tom should have realised this." More than one participant agreed with the placing of blame on Tom, some going so far as to assume ill intent on his part. One said, "It's absolutely a rape – she was given either a date rape drug, or he let her drink so much she was unable to give consent," while another put it this way, "She was so drunk that she doesn't remember agreeing. Her agreement isn't consent because she was mentally compromised. She also may have been drugged." Another participant also felt that Tom was to blame in the situation, "I do not think consent was given. Consent does not necessarily have to be verbal, but for someone to be so drunk they do not remember – I feel Tom could be viewed as taking advantage." Thus, participants in the CN-RY group were more willing to place the blame on the man in the scenario, despite his alcohol consumption being described as likely to be equivalent to that of the women.

Surprisingly, other participants in the CN-RY group adopted essentially the same reasoning used in the CY-RN group – that both the man and the woman were drunk. However, in contrast to the CY-RN group, for participants in the CN-RY group, both the man and woman being drunk meant that a rape *had* occurred and in some cases that perhaps we should conclude that the man and the woman had *both* raped one another. These participants felt that drunk sex was equal to rape regardless of whether one or both people were drunk. In contrast to the CY-RN group, the CN-RY participants did not appear to be accounting for the possibility of diminished capacity and decision-making on the part of the man, and when they did consider the man's state of mind, they seemed to feel that the only conclusion that could be reached was that the man and woman had raped each other. One participant described this view well, "I believe this does describe a rape, as both participants were drunk and unable to give full informed consent in the situation," while another concurred, saying, "If someone sleeps with someone who is intoxicated, proper consent has not been obtained, meaning it is classed as rape." Thus, while for the CY-RN group consent was seen as not being a particularly useful concept in determining whether a rape had taken place, for the CN-RY group, both parties being drunk and unable to consent was put forward as the reason that a rape *had* occurred. The primary difference between the two groups appeared to be that in the CY-RN group the general feeling was that both parties being drunk meant consent was not a good barometer for assessing whether a rape had occurred, while in the CN-RY group, if a woman engaged in sex while drunk it meant that a rape had occurred even when the man was equally drunk, or in some cases that the man and woman had both engaged in rape as neither could consent. This juxtaposition illustrates both the complexity of consent, and how different people can present essentially the same explanation even when that explanation led them to different and opposite conclusions. While the CY-RN group used the idea that both parties were drunk to more or less set aside the concept of consent and look for mitigating factors which then led them to conclude that no rape had occurred, the CY-RN group used both being drunk as direct support for their conclusion that a rape had occurred.

Consent, No – Rape, No (CN-RN)

The CN-RN group was remarkably similar to the CY-RN group in that they all determined that rape had not occurred. However, the CY-RN group, on first reading the scenario, felt that consent had been given, largely because no force was indicated and that neither party appeared to be taking advantage of the other. In contrast, the CN-RN group decided up front that consent had not been given, but also that even though consent had not been given, no rape had occurred. One participant said, "If they are both equally drunk, then how can one consent and one not? It's not fair to label Tom a rapist if he was equally as drunk." Another agreed saying that in the scenario "It seems as if both people involved were equally drunk, therefore neither of them could properly give consent. However, I don't believe this is rape as neither party forced the other to have sex." Many other participants also pointed to the problems with indicating that only one person was raped when both were described as having reduced decision-making capacity.

One reason participants put forward for their judgment that no rape had occurred was that it was difficult to determine. In other words, the CN-RN group appeared to feel that consent was absent, but they were hesitant to label the scenario a rape, and they expressed this uncertainty when they were asked to explain their no consent but no rape decision. One participant in the CN-RN group put it this way, "It's hard to decide whether this was rape..." The participant then went on to further explain their answer,

> ...as the girl was drunk and most likely unable to give consent. However, she may [have] given consent and known what was going to happen at the time. He was very drunk too so it's hard to know whether he gave consent either, and it doesn't sound like he lured her to have sex on purpose.

This participant felt that consent was in fact fuzzy for both the man and the woman and like participants in both other groups, looked instead for indications that there was some force applied by the man. However, as with this participant, the responses in this group were much more likely to indicate that while they said rape had not occurred, they were uncertain and hesitant in their responses. In fact, a hallmark of responses from the CN-RN group was that, overall, they seemed more uncertain about their responses than those in other two groups. This reticence to ascribe conclusive blame or judgment because of insufficient information about the contextual factors that led to the pair having sex is consistent with social-cognitive models of uncertainty management demonstrating that people care more about fairness in the presence of uncertainty (Van den Bos and Lind, 2002). Even when participants did not explicitly say that they were uncertain, their responses tended to be somewhat longer, and uncertainty was suggested even when not stated. For example, another participant said,

> I think is it not classed as rape as both participants were drunk. The situation does not seem forced, however it cannot be certain if both participants were in the state to consent therefore is not ideal, however I do not think it would be described as rape.

This response indicates uncertainty in their decision without stating it explicitly. While many of the responses they gave were similar to those given in the other groups, the uncertainty they experienced appeared to have led them to the somewhat contradictory response that while no consent had been given, no rape had occurred. Another participant said this,

> This was very tricky as it is hard to make a definitive judgement if both parties were so drunk neither could give consent, but as it was two equally drunk people then it was just two drunk people deciding to have sex.

Similarly, another participant in the NC-NR group discussed in their response what would have needed to have been present for them to consider the event a rape,

> This one is difficult for me. If Tom had not been as drunk then I probably would say yes, this scenario describes a rape. From the information given, I take it that Tom was drunk to a similar level and therefore I believe neither party could be at fault. It could for sure be poor decision making by both parties, but neither party is solely responsible if they are equally drunk, in my opinion.

Like this participant, some other participants also explicitly considered in their responses what would have been needed for them to classify the described event as a rape and explained why they felt the scenario did not reach that threshold,

> It was the fact the statement said "they were both so drunk". It's hard to distinguish if this is rape or not as neither party can remember what happened. If the male had not drunk as much and she was black out drunk I would've said yes it was rape as he was consciously aware that she could not speak for herself. In this case, either party could've raped one another so it's very hard to say if neither have recollection of what occurred.

One participant went so far as to acknowledge that though rape is usually defined as no consent, they did not feel that this definition applied in a situation where both parties were drunk,

> Whilst I believe that there was no consent and that is the definition of rape, they were both unable to consent so neither [was] in a position to say yes or no. They both went for it as much as the other, neither one of them was more to blame.

Overall, the CN-RN group held very similar opinions to the other two groups in terms of what factors were driving their decisions regarding the presence of consent and of rape in the scenario they read. However, despite the overall similarity of reasoning across the three groups, each group came to a different conclusion. While the CN-RY group was the clearest in their judgment that a rape had occurred, all groups suggested that consent, and lack thereof, is not a simple issue. This was especially true for the CY-RN and the CN-RN groups who said that consent is not all that is needed to determine whether rape has occurred, and instead relied heavily on context, often associated with rape myths to make a decision about what the scenario represented.

Discussion

All of the participants were provided with the same scenario, yet they came to very different conclusions regarding whether or not consent had been given, or whether the scenario described a rape. While many consent training programs relying on affirmative consent present the concept of consent as being quite straightforward, the fact that participants read the same scenario and used the same information to arrive at vastly different conclusions illustrates the complexity that exists around the concept of consent in young adults lived reality.

The first group (CY-RN) supported their initial judgment that consent had been given and no rape had occurred by explaining that in the context of an encounter in which both parties were drunk, consent was not a useful concept. These participants instead looked to other cues such as indications of force to make their decisions. The second group (CN-RY) felt that consent had not been given by the woman and so the scenario described a rape. This group of participants used the legal definition of rape as equal to absence of consent on the part of the woman and placed the blame on the man, sometimes stating that they felt force or coercion had been used though this was not present to them in the scenario. The third group (CN-RN) was hesitant to label the scenario a rape, but also felt that consent had not been given. Overall, this group was more uncertain in their responses than were the CY-RN and the CN-RY groups. They struggled with their decision and ultimately said that although no consent was present on the part of the woman, they didn't feel comfortable blaming the man.

Our findings are in line with research that found that young university attending adults sometimes disregard consent when determining whether a sexual assault has occurred (Hunt et al., 2022; Cowley, 2014; Marcantonio and

TABLE 7.1 Summary of reasons why participants felt a rape had or had not occurred

Both Were Drunk		
CY-RN	CN-RY	CN-RN
Both drunk, looked to cues other than consent	Cannot consent when drunk	Both drunk, can't determine consent
Equal blame/ responsibility	Placed blame on man	Not fair to blame man
No force or coercion	Force or coercion likely used	No force or coercion
Man was also drunk	Focused only on woman's intoxication	Man was also drunk

Jozkowski, 2021a). Given the findings of this study, we suggest that the concept of consent is neither simple, nor easily applied, especially since sex usually happens in complex social interactions and in environments which shape people's interpretations of events in different ways. Interestingly, despite legal definitions of rape as lack of consent, many participants did not used the presumed presence or absence of consent to make their decision about whether a rape had occurred, suggesting that many of today's young adult women do not define rape *only* by lack of consent. Therefore, we suggest that consent, or lack thereof, should be regarded as a necessary but not sufficient condition for young women to judge that a rape or sexual assault has occurred. However, given the vastly different conclusions the young women in the study reached with the same information provided, there is clearly more need for consent trainings to address alcohol consumption and sexual activity, as well as how structural gendered power influences people's judgments about sexual consent. By treating consent as black and white, we miss the nuance that can exist in real life, which we believe results in sexual assaults and rapes that do occur potentially being perceived as simply bad sex or as not reaching the threshold of "rape" and therefore not something that should be reported. To decrease rape and sexual assault, and increase reporting of such events when they do occur, we must examine the nuances of consent and be sure that consent training addresses the issues that young women and men face in today's sexual landscape.

In the end, while virtually all the respondents indicated that the presence of alcohol was important to consider, they applied this concept in a wide variety of ways and came to vastly different conclusions about what the presence of alcohol means for sexual encounters. These findings clearly show the complexity of consent as a concept, and the problems inherent in defining rape exclusively in terms of the presence or absence of consent, enthusiastic or otherwise. In line with other authors, we suggest that more nuance and discussion of how sexual encounters take place in the real world is needed (Groggel et al., 2021; Humphreys, 2004; Curtis and Burnett, 2017; Koven, 2021). The ambiguity of consent, especially when alcohol is present, suggests that more needs to be done to clarify and document how young adults operationalize consent. We suggest that determinations of consent and rape may not be as clear cut as the current ideas of "Yes means Yes" and "No means No" suggest. Further, as others have previously noted, gender and gendered dynamics and sexual scripts are critically important to examine considering how the concept of consent is related to determinations of rape in ambiguous situations, especially those when alcohol is present. Until young women feel empowered to behave agentically in sexual situations and can challenge gendered sexual scripts directly in their own relationships, sexual assault and rape will continue to be a major problem, especially in settings such as university campuses where sexual activity while drinking is normative. Consent training aimed at young adults should explicitly address alcohol and the ways in which young adults see alcohol as influencing (or not) their own and others' ability to consent to sex. Highlighting rape myths and the gendered sexual scripts that support those myths is also important so that both the myths and gendered scripts can be challenged and dismantled. Finally, we suggest that universities, police, and governments must endeavour to develop working definitions of consent and rape that more accurately map onto the experiences people have in the real world.

Notes

1 Yes means Yes is a popular affirmative consent campaign that calls for enthusiastic and verbal consent to be given prior to sexual activity. https://www.pbs.org/news hour/education/means-enough-college-campuses
2 Consent is Sexy is a poster campaign aimed at increasing communication between sexual partners; Hovick and Silver, 2019
3 Consent: It's Simple as Tea is a three-minute video cartoon which likens forcing someone to have sex to forcing them to drink tea. https://www.youtube.com/watch? v=pZwvrxVavnQ

References

Armstrong, E. A. & Hamilton, L. T. 2013. *Paying For the Party*. Harvard University Press.
Bednarchik, L. A., Generous, M. A. & Mongeau, P. 2022. Defining Sexual Consent: Perspectives from a College Student Population. *Communication Reports*, 35, 12–24.
Carline, A., Gunby, C. & Taylor, S. 2018. Too Drunk to Consent? Exploring the Contestations and Disruptions in Male-Focused Sexual Violence Prevention Interventions. *Social & Legal Studies*, 27, 299–322.
Cowley, A. D. 2014. "Let's Get Drunk and Have Sex": The Complex Relationship of Alcohol, Gender, and Sexual Victimization. *Journal of Interpersonal Violence*, 29, 1258–1278.
Curtis, J. N. & Burnett, S. 2017. Affirmative Consent: What Do College Student Leaders Think About "Yes Means Yes" As the Standard For Sexual Behavior? *American Journal of Sexuality Education*, 12, 201–214.
Drouin, M., Jozkowski, K. N., Davis, J. & Newsham, G. 2018. How Does Alcohol Consumption Affect Perceptions of One's Own and a Drinking Partner's Ability to Consent to Sexual Activity? *Journal of Sex Research*, 56 (6), 740–753.
Groggel, A., Burdick, M. & Barraza, A. 2021. She Left the Party: College Students' Meanings of Sexual Consent. *Violence Against Women*, 27, 766–789.
Humphreys, T. P. 2004. Understanding Sexual Consent: An Empirical Investigation of the Normative Script For Young Heterosexual Adults. *Making Sense of Sexual Consent*, 209–225.
Hunt, G., Sanders, E., Petersen, M. A. & Bogren, A. 2022. "Blurring the Line": Intoxication, Gender, Consent, and Sexual Encounters Among Young Adults. *Contemporary Drug Problems*, 49, 84–105.
Johnson, C. A. & Hawbaker, K. T. 2018. Metoo: A Timeline of Events. *Chicago Tribune*, 15.
Jozkowski, K. N. 2015. "Yes Means Yes"? Sexual Consent Policy and College Students. *Change: the Magazine of Higher Learning*, 47, 16–23.
Jozkowski, K. N., Manning, J. & Hunt, M. 2018. Sexual Consent in and Out of the Bedroom: Disjunctive Views of Heterosexual College Students. *Women's Studies in Communication*, 41, 117–139.
Jozkowski, K. N., Marcantonio, T., Willis, M. & Drouin, M. 2022. Does Alcohol Consumption Influence People's Perceptions of Their Own and a Drinking Partner's

Ability to Consent to Sexual Behavior in a Non-Sexualized Drinking Context? *Journal of Interpersonal Violence*, doi:08862605221080149.

Jozkowski, K. N. & Wiersma, J. D. 2015. Does Drinking Alcohol Prior to Sexual Activity Influence College Students' Consent? *International Journal of Sexual Health*, 27, 156–174.

Jozkowski, K. N. & Willis, M. 2020. People Perceive Transitioning From A Social to A Private Setting As An Indicator of Sexual Consent. *Psychology & Sexuality*, 11, 359–372.

Koven, J. 2021. *Investigating Women's Sexual Agency and Alcohol Use in the Sexual Consent Process*. Doctoral Dissertation. University of Massachusetts Boston.

Lamarche, V. M. & James-Hawkins, L. 2022. It Happened to a Friend of Mine: the Influence of Perspective-Taking on the Acknowledgment of Sexual Assault Following Ambiguous Sexual Encounters. *Journal of Interpersonal Violence*, 37, Np7343–Np7368.

Loick, D. 2020. "… As If It Were A Thing." A Feminist Critique of Consent. *Constellations*, 27, 412–422.

Marcantonio, T. L. & Jozkowski, K. N. 2021a. College Students' Definition of Non-Consent and Sexual Refusals in the Age of Affirmative Consent Initiatives. *Sex Education*, 1–17.

Marcantonio, T. L. & Jozkowski, K. N. 2021b. Do College Students Feel Confident to Consent to Sex After Consuming Alcohol? *Journal of American College Health*, 1–8.

Marcantonio, T. L., Willis, M. & Jozkowski, K. N. 2022. Effects of Typical and Binge Drinking on Sexual Consent Perceptions and Communication. *Journal of Sex & Marital Therapy*, 48, 273–284.

Muehlenhard, C. L., Humphreys, T. P., Jozkowski, K. N. & Peterson, Z. D. 2016. The Complexities of Sexual Consent Among College Students: A Conceptual and Empirical Review. *Journal of Sex Research*, 53, 457–487.

Orchowski, L. M., Oesterle, D. W., Moreno, O., Yusufov, M., Berkowitz, A., Abbey, A., Barnett, N. P. & Borsari, B. 2022. A Qualitative Analysis of Sexual Consent Among Heavy-Drinking College Men. *Journal of Interpersonal Violence*, 37, Np5566–Np5593.

Van den Bos, K. & Lind, E. A. 2002. Uncertainty Management By Means of Fairness Judgments. In M. P. Zanna (Ed.), *Advances in Experimental Social Psychology*, 34, 1–60.

Wade, L. 2017. *American Hookup: the New Culture of Sex On Campus*. WW Norton & Company.

8

AN APPROACH TO DEVELOPING SHARED UNDERSTANDINGS OF CONSENT WITH YOUNG PEOPLE

Cristyn Davies, Kerry H. Robinson, Melissa Kang and The Wellbeing, Health & Youth (WH&Y) Commission

In simple terms, consent can be understood as permission for something to happen or an agreement to do something. Understandings of consent are informed by legal, medical, ethical, and socio-political discourses that shape attitudes, communication practices, and behaviour. Influenced by local, national, and global contexts, public discourse about consent is generally fore-grounded when high-profile cases involving sexual consent receive media attention. This chapter outlines an approach to collaborating with young people to co-produce principles and strategies to support their consent literacy, especially sexual consent literacy, self-efficacy and involvement in decisions that affect them in different settings and contexts. Developing a shared understanding of consent must begin early in young people's lives to build their awareness, skills, and agency.

Historically, there has been no universally agreed definition of sexual consent, with ongoing debate about what it may mean for different people in various contexts—across time, culture, location, and settings (Muehlenhard et al., 2016). More recent approaches have emphasised affirmative consent, an enthusiastic, mutual agreement communicated by words or actions between young people to participate in sexual activity (Stynes and Kang, 2021). However, young people's communication practices and understandings, embedded in social norms, are often at odds with this gold-standard approach to consent. In the context of sexual decision-making, young people often reproduce dominant gender norms of masculinity and femininity (Templeton et al., 2017). Gendered and sexual social norms are founded within power relations structurally and systematically embedded in sociocultural institutions and practices (e.g., family, religion, and education). There is a fundamental mismatch between the underpinning principles of affirmative consent and the reality of most young people's lives.

DOI: 10.4324/9781003358756-11

Global movements calling out sexual harassment, gender-based violence and inequality communicated through social media have popularised hashtags such as #MeToo, #LetHerSpeak, #TimesUp, #BalanceTonPorc, #NotYourHabibti, #Teknisktfel, #QuellaVoltaChe, and #YoTambien. It is clear from recent social movements and public debate that there is confusion about consent and how young people's understandings of and attitudes about it impact their decisions and practices. In Australia, young people have called for sexual consent to be at the forefront of educational initiatives in school settings and beyond and, consistent with global movements, have described experiences in which sexual consent has been violated. In February 2021, Chanel Contos, an Australian student and sexual consent activist, posted an Instagram story asking her followers if they or someone close to them had been sexually assaulted when they were at school. Following an overwhelming number of responses, Contos launched a petition calling for more holistic and earlier consent education in Australia and the website teachusconsent.com. On this platform, people can share anonymous testimonies of sexual assault (Contos, 2021). The Teach Us Consent movement called for mandated inclusion of consent education in Australian schools. Education ministers around Australia have unanimously agreed to mandate consent education in school settings from 2023.

Contos' successful education campaign built on the powerful advocacy and call for legal reform driven by Saxon Mullins. In 2018, Mullins, now the Director of Advocacy at Rape and Sexual Assault Research and Advocacy (RASARA), appeared on the Australian Broadcasting Corporation's (ABC) investigative current affairs program, Four Corner's episode, 'I am that girl' (RSARA, 2022). She told the story of her 2013 sexual assault and subsequent criminal trials and appeals, which led to the NSW Attorney-General asking the NSW Law Reform Commission to review the section of the NSW Crimes Act that deals with consent relating to sexual assault. Mullin's advocacy catalysed landmark law reform with the NSW Government, which passed an Affirmative Consent Bill through the Upper House on November 23, 2021. The new law stated that consent must be communicated rather than assumed. Mullins and Contos have advocated for the importance of sexual consent legal reform and education, respectively. Grace Tame, 2021 Australian of the year, has led a powerful campaign for systemic change to prevent child sexual abuse and to allow victim-survivors to speak out about their experiences. Brittany Higgins, a former political staff member working at Australia's Parliament House, has also led an effective campaign to prevent gender-based violence within Australian politics, especially within the workplace.

Within these public debates and discussions, the voices and experiences of those young people who are Aboriginal and Torres Strait Islander, culturally and linguistically diverse, gender and sexuality diverse, and those with disabilities or who are socially and economically disadvantaged are not widely represented. Based on our decades of research and collaboration with young people, this chapter proposes an approach to co-developing principles and strategies with young people essential for promoting a shared understanding of sexual consent. This approach foregrounds an intersectional lens to deconstruct dominant discourses that constitute young people's attitudes and underpin their behaviours and practices. Core to this initiative is addressing understandings and practices of consent on young people's terms. Our recent initial consultation with diverse young people about sexual consent highlighted their concerns about understanding different forms of consent, effective verbal and non-verbal language to communicate consent, communicating consent beyond the yes/no binary, understanding consent as a staged learning process, and intersectionality of identity and experiences of negotiating consent, gender, and power.

This chapter provides a background to the key literature relevant to our discussion, providing global and Australian perspectives on consent, sexual violence, and young people. We also discuss sexual communication and the importance of young people's knowledge and skill development. Further, we provide an overview of the literature about sexual consent education and best practice, sexual consent and minority and marginalised groups, and the importance of co-developing sexual consent interventions with young people. An overview of Australian sexual consent laws and consent education follows. The chapter also highlights our theoretical and methodological approach to working with young people. Finally, we outline our proposed collaborative approach to working with young people using a living lab methodology to address sexual consent.

Background

Rates of sexual violence are under-reported globally, and occurrences of sexual activity under pressure, manipulation or intoxication are not accurately captured (Burton, et al., 2021). According to the World Health Organization (WHO), across their lifetime, 1 in 3 women, around 736 million, are subjected to physical or sexual violence by an intimate partner or sexual violence from a non-partner, with these statistics remaining essentially unchanged over the past decade (World Health Organization, 2021). Sexual assault includes unwanted and non-consensual sexual experiences, including those attained by force and when an individual's inability to consent is exploited (Muscari et al., 2022; Fedina et al., 2016). The survivors-victims are frequently adolescents and young adults (Muscari et al., 2022).

There is limited research evaluating programs that include sexual consent education for young people under the age of 15 years. Physical or sexual violence starts early, with 1 in 4 young women aged 15–24 years in a relationship experiencing violence by an intimate partner by the time they reach their mid-twenties (World Health Organization, 2021). Intimate partner violence includes physical, psychological, and/or sexual violence occurring in the context of dating and/or a sexual relationship (Muscari et al., 2022; Breiding et al., 2015). Globally, intimate partner violence is the most prevalent violence against women, affecting around 641 million (World Health Organization, 2021). Further, 6% of women globally report being sexually assaulted by someone other than their husband or partner (World Health Organization, 2021).

Age is a significant factor in adolescents' accounts of sexual readiness, with early adolescence being a critical time when understandings of gender equality become engrained (Templeton et al., 2017; Robinson et al., 2014). Research about heterosexual adolescents' understandings of sexual readiness found that young people may not view initiating sex as problematic, as they generally focus on sexual pleasure rather than potential health concerns. Addressing sexual consent in early adolescence allows young people to critique ideas about gender roles, stereotypes, gender equality and sexual rights and fosters sexual and reproductive health literacy (Templeton et al., 2017; Davies and Burns, 2023).

As highlighted in the introduction, while affirmative consent is considered best practice, research demonstrates gaps in our understanding of how young people communicate in intimate sexual relationships (Widman et al., 2022). Core to young people's sexual communication is developing a shared understanding of consent as an ongoing negotiation rather than a one-off transaction (Stynes and Kang, 2021). How young people obtain sexual consent by reading verbal and non-verbal cues, negotiating safe sexual practices, and managing complex and competing individual and interpersonal needs and goals is yet to be fully understood. Learning about sexual communication that occurs early in relationships can impact future sexual communication, sexual satisfaction, and sexual functioning. Verbal and non-verbal sexual communication about boundaries, pleasure, enjoyment, safety and consent is integral to negotiating sexual interactions as they unfold.

Sexual communication is a multidimensional process including behavioural and cognitive elements (Widman et al., 2022). The transactional communication model proposes that communication is multidirectional, where communicators simultaneously influence each other and jointly create and exchange messages to cultivate shared meaning. This two-way, dialogic model is rarely assessed in adolescent sexual communication literature. The transaction model approach suggests that communication is not simply sending a message but a nuanced and collaborative interaction where young people communicate simultaneously by sending and receiving messages (Widman et al., 2022).

Evaluating the efficacy of sexual consent programs for young people is impeded by a lack of resources, ethical barriers, and valid, consistent, and tailored measures. A systematic review focused on adolescents' views of sexual readiness concluded that a more comprehensive, psychometrically sound measurement of young people's dynamic sexual communication process is required (Widman et al., 2022). In evaluations of consent communication between young people, valid measures that ask about communication with one partner in the context of communication from another partner should be implemented. Historically, there has been reliance on reports of sexual communication from individuals rather than from couples. Most studies have used self-report instruments (e.g., cross-sectional surveys asking about individual experiences of sexual harassment or violence), as they are quicker, easier, and cheaper than observational studies with young people that use scenarios to evaluate their knowledge, understanding and skill set to negotiate sexual consent. Measures that address contextually bound, bi-directional interactions could help researchers better understand the process, informing intervention strategies to address consent communication (Widman et al., 2022).

Another systematic review focused on teaching sexual consent to young people in education settings outlined four main approaches: the risk behaviour approach, a sex-positive approach, a life skills approach, and a socio-culturally adapted approach (taking account of the context in which young people operate, their sexual behaviour and gender roles). In the sexual communication literature on young people, there has been considerable emphasis on sexual risk reduction. Over a third of sexual communication assessments with young people focused exclusively on condom communication, and an additional quarter of assessments focused on safe sex issues, such as sexually transmitted infections (STIs), pregnancy and abstinence (Widman et al., 2022; Goldfarb and Lieberman, 2021). Few studies considered consent, sexuality, pleasure, desire, discussions with partners on sexual or gender identity, media portrayals of sex, peers' sexual activity, or sexual communication using digital technologies.

Best practice suggests that consent education programs adopt a sex-positive and whole-of-school approach, are interactive and inclusive, and enable critical analysis of the impact of sociocultural factors on consensual and non-consensual sexual activity (Burton et al.; 2021; Muscari et al., 2022). Sexual consent education programs documented in the literature in education settings for young people (aged 15–29) are most frequently located in the USA, in university settings, with 1–2-hour sessions, and with varied facilitators and interactive teaching approaches (Burton et al., 2021). Evaluation of consent education in the literature more broadly in school settings is limited for adolescents and virtually non-existent for younger children (Davies and Robinson, 2010; Robinson and Davies, 2008). Consent education in high schools, most frequently included within Comprehensive Sexuality Education (CSE), is generally located in Australia's Health and Physical Education curricula. An effective CSE curriculum requires inclusive sexual health topics, with consent education that scaffolds young people's learning across grades and is embedded in supportive school environments and across subject areas (Goldfarb and Lieberman, 2021). This approach may improve sexual, social, and emotional health and academic outcomes for young people (Skinner et al., 2020; Davies and Burns, 2023).

Most research that includes sexual consent is focused on heterosexual, cisgender and white young people. This is reflected in the lack of comprehensive data on the prevalence and impact of sexual violence on gender, sex and sexuality minorities, people with disabilities, Indigenous women and women from culturally and linguistically diverse backgrounds, despite evidence indicating that these groups are over-represented as survivors and victims of this violence

(Burton et al., 2021; Robinson et al., 2014; Davies et al., 2021; Davies and McInnes, 2012). Research with gay, bisexual and queer (GBQ) men demonstrates that intimate partner violence is prevalent, and there is a need to engage GBQ men in discussions about respectful relationships, sexual ethics, and consent (Salter et al., 2021). This study also highlighted that younger men were more accepting of controlling behaviours in their intimate relationships (Salter et al., 2021). Limited research incorporates an intersectional lens on sexual communication among diverse young people.

Young people are rarely included as research partners and consultants to inform the design and implementation of sexual health promotion strategies related to sexual communication and negotiation of consent (Burton et al., 2021; Ollis et al., 2022). Their contribution to ensuring consent education is relevant and implementable is critical for meeting their needs and promoting long-term health outcomes.

Sexual Consent and Australian Laws

In the context of community understanding of sexual assault law, research shows that consent is a crucial principle in public education (Mason, 2021). However, there is a knowledge gap between the legal meaning of sexual assault and effective community access to that meaning. This is exacerbated by cultural differences, expectations, and language barriers. While there has continued to be considerable focus on young people's understanding of consent, and its relation to gendered violence, some researchers have pointed out the challenges with broader community consent literacy. In the context of sex education and consent, Jen Gilbert has asked: 'Can affirmative consent's misrecognition of the scene of sexual decision-making offer up a new, better vision of sexual relations, for young people especially, one that we should promote even as we fail to live up to that standard ourselves?' (Gilbert, 2018, p. 277). A recent case study undertaken in the Australian jurisdiction of NSW shows that there is a policy failure on the part of the state to educate the public about the law systematically, or changes to the law, regarding sexual assault and the sexual standards inherent in legal regulation (Mason, 2021). Many Australians do not understand consent or the line between consensual sex and coercion (ANROWS, 2018). An Our Watch study highlighted that respondents 12–20 years of age consider girls and women responsible for communicating about consent to participate in sexual activities (Our Watch, 2016). Our Watch is a national leader in the primary prevention of violence against women and their children in Australia. This finding highlights the impact of gender stereotypes and the prevalence of dominant, heterosexual gender power relations.

In Australia, the legal age for consensual sex is 16 years in the Australian Capital Territory (ACT), New South Wales (NSW), Northern Territory (NT), Queensland (QLD), Victoria (Vic.) and Western Australia (WA), and 17 years in South Australia (SA) and Tasmania (Tas.) (Australian Institute of Family

Studies, 2021). Laws regulating sexual consent aim to protect children and young people from sexual exploitation and abuse from adults and older young people. Consent laws determine that children and young people below the age of consent are yet to reach a maturity level that may enable their safe partici-pation in sexual activities (Australian Institute of Family Studies, 2021). For other sexual activities, the criminal legislation relating to different sexual beha-viours and interactions varies across jurisdictions. Most jurisdictions now have a 'similar age' defence for consensual sex for those below the legal age of con-sent (see Table 8.1). Although the legal age of consent throughout Australia is either 16 or 17 years, legislation in the ACT, NSW, NT, SA, Vic, and WA makes it an offence for a person in a supervisory role (e.g. teacher, foster parent, religious official or spiritual leader, a medical practitioner, an employer of the child or a custodial official) to have sexual interactions with a person under their special care who is aged 16 or 17 years (Australian Institute of Family Studies, 2021).

In child sexual assault, a child does not have the decision-making capacity to consent according to the law. In adult sexual assault, consent is absent. In the ACT, NSW, SA, Tas, Vic, and WA, legal defence may be provided when a mutually consensual sexual interaction is between two young people close in age (Australian Institute of Family Studies, 2021). These jurisdictions seek to balance the protection of children and young people from adult sexual exploitation while not criminalising them for having sexual relationships with their peers.

In Australia, it is prohibited to request, access, possess, create, or share sex-ualised images of children and young people under 18 years (Commonwealth) or 16 or 17 years (states and territories) (Australian Institute of Family Studies,

TABLE 8.1 Similar Age' Defence for Consensual Sex

Australian jurisdiction	'Similar age' defence for consensual sex
ACT	Similar age defence for those aged 10 to 15 years, with less than 2-year age difference.
NSW	Similar age defence for those aged 14 or 15 years, where the age difference is not more than 2 years.
NT	No similar age defence.
QLD	No similar age defence.
SA	No similar age defence.
TAS	Similar age defence for those aged 12 to 14 years, with 3 year or less age difference; if age 15 and 5 years or less age difference.
VIC	Similar age defence for those aged 12 to 15 years, where the age difference is not more than 2 years.
WA	A more complicated similar age defence. The person has to believe that the other was 16 years or older, and the age difference cannot be more than three years.

2021; eSafety Commissioner, 2022). Many young people engage in sexting (sending each other nude images of themselves or other young people). They are unaware that they risk criminal charges in doing so in some jurisdictions. However, other jurisdictions have exceptions to these laws allowing for consensual sexting between young people of similar ages (Australian Institute of Family Studies, 2021; eSafety Commissioner, 2022).

After much advocacy, as highlighted in the introduction, some Australian jurisdictions have recently adopted affirmative consent laws. In NSW, the *Crimes Legislation Amendment (Sexual Consent Reforms) Act 2021* implemented reforms taking effect from June 1, 2022. The most relevant reforms to this discussion include:

- clarify consent provisions in the *Crimes Act 1900*, including that consent is a free and voluntary agreement that should not be presumed;
- clarify that consent involves ongoing and mutual communication;
- strengthen laws to confirm that consent can be withdrawn, and that if someone consents to one sexual act, it does not mean they have consented to other sexual acts.

(NSW Government Communities and Justice, 2022)

In Victoria, the *Justice Legislation Amendment (Sexual Offences and Other Matters) Bill 2022* includes changes that will adopt an affirmative consent model and provide better protections for victim-survivors of sexual offences (Premier of Victoria, 2022). The affirmative consent model will be in place from July 2023 unless declared earlier. In May 2022, the ACT Legislative Assembly introduced *The Crimes (Consent) Amendment Bill 2022*, providing a legal definition of consent based on a free and voluntary agreement (ACT Government, 2022). The Bill recognises that consent must not be presumed, that individuals have a right to choose not to participate in sexual activity, and that consensual sexual activity involves ongoing and mutual communication and decision-making.

As pointed out earlier in this chapter, sexual harassment is prevalent, especially among young people, with much of this behaviour culturally entrenched in everyday interactions (Robinson, 2012; Robinson, 2005). Not dissimilar to the relationship between consent and sexual assault, consent is central to an understanding of sexual harassment. Community understandings of sexual harassment are poor, and the relationship between consent and sexual harassment is rendered invisible and irrelevant through the relationship between gender and power (Australian Human Rights Commission, 2020; Robinson, 2013). This phenomenon and its prevalence result from several factors, including the social, cultural, political, and economic inequalities facing girls, women, and gender and sexuality-diverse people inherent in heteronormative and patriarchal societies. Much sexual harassment goes unabated through its normalisation in interactions with girls and young women primarily 'learning to put up with it' (Robinson, 2012; Robinson, 2005). Research with boys and young men in secondary schools in Australia highlights how sexual harassment was integral to performing a dominating, rigidly hetero-normative form of masculinity (Robinson, 2005). Sexual harassment was con-sidered a legitimate and expected means through which boys and men, who identified with this form of masculinity, expressed their gender and sexuality, simultaneously reconfirming their position within their male peer groups (Robin-son, 2005, Robinson, 2012). Girls and female teachers were sexually harassed to assert boys' sexual prowess and to mobilise their masculine power and authority; boys who transgressed gender and sexual norms and/or were known or perceived to be gay or bisexual were also sexually harassed. Consent in these behaviours is not considered relevant as the behaviours are viewed as a 'right' and an expected part of gender expression for some young men. In this context, women and girls are viewed as 'sexually available'. Heterosexism, the beliefs, and behaviours pri-vileging heterosexuality and heterosexual relationships, is foundational to sexual harassment. Both heterosexist harassment and sexual harassment serve to 'punish deviation from traditional patriarchal gender norms', which mandate hetero-sexuality (Australian Human Rights Commission, 2020). Sexual harassment is a powerful tool used against those who transgress social norms of gender and sexu-ality, operating to maintain dominant hierarchical power relations – based on gender, sexuality, and their intersections.

In 1973, Australia ratified the International Labour Organization's Dis-crimination (Employment and Occupation) Convention, and in 1983, the United Nations Convention on the Elimination of All Forms of Discrimination Against Women ('CEDAW'). Anti-discrimination legislation addressing sex discrimina-tion has existed in SA, NSW, and Victoria since the 1970s. In 1984, the Aus-tralian Government introduced the *Sex Discrimination Act 1984* (Cth), which prohibited sexual harassment at work. Under this Act, sexual harassment is:

- any unwelcome sexual advance;
- unwelcome request for sexual favours; or
- other unwelcome conduct of a sexual nature in relation to the person har-assed in circumstances where a reasonable person, having regard to all the circumstances, would have anticipated the possibility that the person har-assed would be offended, humiliated or intimidated.

(Australian Human Rights Commission, 2020)

The Act makes sexual harassment unlawful in certain areas of public life, including employment (Australian Human Rights Commission, 2020).

The Australian Human Rights Commission reports *Respect@work* (2020) and *Everyone's Business* (2018) highlight the vulnerabilities of young people to sexual harassment in the workplace. Young people experience greater precarity as employees as they are often casual workers in retail and service industries, can experience lower levels of pay, generally have lower seniority and authority, have less workplace training, are less likely to be union members, and are less aware of their rights in the workplace. These reports also indicate that employees who are young women, LGBTQ+, culturally and linguistically diverse, and have a disability, are most vulnerable to discrimination and sexual harassment in the workplace.

Consent Education in Australia

While there has been significant advocacy to improve the design and implementation of consent education in school settings, and to mandate this education, more broadly, there are barriers to sexual consent literacy in the community. Three primary pathways to teaching sexual consent have been identified: social marketing campaigns, face-to-face or online programs delivered to young people through educational institutions, and training offered through non-government organisations (Mason, 2021).

Social marketing employs public campaigns to change attitudes and behaviour, such as the 'Stop it at the start campaign', a Commonwealth initiative that aims to advance gender equality and respect for women through effective primary prevention initiatives. This campaign aims to address young people's attitudes to sexual violence through adult influencers: parents, family members, teachers, coaches, employers, and other community role models (Australian Government, 2022). Influencers are encouraged to reflect on their attitudes and converse with young people aged 10–17 years about respectful relationships and gender equality. While this intergenerational approach to improving consent literacy is innovative, a principle at the core of gender equality and preventing sexual harassment and violence, it relies on influencers having a sound understanding of sexual consent and a capacity to communicate this with young people in their lives.

Educational pathways, for example, in universities, primarily employ online programs such as 'Consent Matters' to foster respectful relationships. From 2023, consent education is mandatory in school settings, with changes to the national curriculum requiring age-appropriate consent education from foundation to year 10. Foundation is the first year of compulsory schooling (children aged approximately 4–6 years), while year 10 is the eleventh year of compulsory schooling (young people aged approximately 15–16 years). Health and Physical Education (HPE) is the primary curriculum area for addressing respectful relationships education in the Australian Curriculum for schools. This focus area includes 'negotiating consent, managing relationships online and offline, and dealing with relationships when there is an imbalance of power' (ACARA, 2022; Ollis, 2014). Students learn about establishing and managing respectful relationships and how power imbalances within a relationship can create a dynamic where coercion, intimidation and manipulation can occur, leading to non-consensual or inappropriate behaviour. They also learn to develop positive reproductive and sexual health practices, including sexual consent. Researchers have argued that focusing on a harm prevention approach only foregrounds a deficit model and risks jeopardising commitment to comprehensive CSE education 'that promotes healthy and positive approaches to sexuality' and is, therefore, 'more effective at achieving harm prevention aims' (Marson, 2021, p. 166; Marson, 2022). External providers also offer education programs that schools can employ.

Various non-government organisations address diverse populations' legal, health and counselling needs. Peer education programs have also been developed, such as Consent Labs, an initiative designed by Angelique Wan and Joyce Yu, offering targeted education supporting the development of consent literacy in educational settings (schools and tertiary institutions), parents and guardians (Wan and Yu, 2022).

Theoretical Framework

Consent, especially sexual consent, is perceived by some adults as 'difficult knowledge' to address with children and young people. We understand difficult knowledge within a Foucauldian framework that examines tensions existing within power relations inherent in knowledge (Robinson, 2013; Robinson and Jones-Diaz, 2016; Foucault, 1984). Power relations in discourses of childhood, adolescence, and sexuality constrain children's and young people's access to knowledge. The knowledge that some adults consider inappropriate for children is often associated with highly emotive, challenging, and difficult topic areas to address with children (e.g., death, illness, war, divorce, poverty, violence, sexuality and gender diversity) (Robinson, 2013; Davies and Robinson, 2010). Some adults view these fields of knowledge as developmentally inappropriate for children. This view is underpinned by the dominant discourse that children are too young to comprehend these issues and that addressing them will compromise their perceived innocence. Sexuality, in particular, is considered difficult knowledge for many adults to discuss with children and young people due to socio-cultural taboos and embarrassment. Further, some adults believe addressing these issues with young people is too precarious as adolescence is a period in which they are considered highly impressionable and may encourage engagement in sexual behaviour. However, research demonstrates that educating young people about sexuality and intimate relationships delays sexual debut (Mueller et al., 2008; Davies et al., 2017).

We also view the concept of sexual ethics as foundational to teaching young people consent (Carmody, 2015). Within a Foucauldian context, Moira Carmody's framework of sexual ethics focuses on four main areas: care of the self (taking care of yourself in relationships); care of others; negotiation; and reflection (Carmody, 2015). These concepts are essential in developing an awareness of consent, which is key to sexual ethics, and the process of engaging in consent in relationships. Sexual ethics encourages young people to begin thinking about and communicating ethically about sexual relations, identifying wants and needs, and consenting to sexual interactions. In addressing sexual ethics, young people critically reflect on their desires and wants and how behaviours from a partner make them feel (*care of the self*). Young people also reflect on the impact of their desires and behaviours on their partner (*care of others*). As Carmody points out, negotiating and asking are crucial to building ethical practices (2015). Developing communication and negotiation competencies, including assertiveness skills, are essential to building ethical relationships. Learning to ask permission and talking about the wants and needs of each person in a relationship is essential to understanding consent. Fostering young people's agency to engage in this communication is crucial, especially within the socio-cultural and gendered norms that young people negotiate.

We also employ an ecological framework to understand multiple levels of influence on consent literacy within and across complex systems. The core concept of the ecological model is that behaviour has multiple levels of influence, often including the individual (knowledge, attitudes, skills), intrapersonal (families, friends, social networks), organisational (organisations, social institutions), community (relationships between organisations), public policy (state local laws and regulations), and society (social and cultural norms) (Richard et al., 2011; McLaren and Hawe, 2005). Ecological models can provide comprehensive frameworks for understanding the multiple and interacting determinants of health behaviours.

Methods

To explore these issues further, we propose employing the Living Lab methodology, a user-centred, open innovation ecosystem using iterative feedback processes in real-life settings in research (Swist et al., 2022). The following approach can be adapted to the local context and implemented by others working with young people around sexual consent. The development of this approach is informed by our literature review presented above, alongside our consultation with the Wellbeing, Health & Youth Commission (WH&Y Commission). Both elements inform our proposed series of workshops with young people, which have the following aims:

Aim 1. To identify facilitators and barriers to consent literacy for young people with young people.

Aim 2. To strengthen young people's consent literacy, self-efficacy and involvement in decisions that affect them.

Aim 3. To develop, within a human rights framework, principles relating to consent with young people to support their understanding and decision-making across different settings and contexts.

The WH&Y Commission comprises a cross-institutional group of young people who collaborate with and advise researchers, policymakers and service providers in health research and research translation through ethical engagement. The youth commission is located within the Wellbeing Health & Youth Centre of Research Excellence (WH&Y CRE)—a multi-university research programme funded by the National Health and Medical Research Council (NHMRC) (WH&Y, 2022).

We use Carmody's framework of building sexual ethics in the workshops and employ the Wellbeing, Health &Youth (WH&Y) Engagement Framework (Carmody, 2015; Swist et al., 2019). This latter framework presents a set of values and questions to prompt responses and decision-making that promote ethical engagement practices with young people (Swist et al., 2019). The framework identifies mutual trust and accountability, equity and responsiveness, and diversity and inclusion as the three intersecting pillars enabling youth and adult stakeholder collaboration (Swist et al., 2019; Swist et al., 2022). As part of this approach, we also embed an Integrated Knowledge Translation (iKT) approach, which is a model of research co-production whereby researchers partner with knowledge users throughout the research process and with key stakeholders who can use the research recommendations in practice or policy (Straus et al., 2009; Davies and Sowbhagya, 2022). This ensures that knowledge co-produced by key stakeholders is more likely to inform policy and practice.

Living Lab with Young People

Phase 1: Workshop with young people to generate understandings and values to support youth engagement in consent literacy. In small groups, participants are invited to brainstorm the following issues:

- Gender and power (stereotypes, double standards, contexts such as school, family, work, and sport)
- Intersectionality (the relationship between gender, power, cultural and linguistic diversity, Indigenous perspectives and colonisation, sexuality and gender diversity, abilities and disabilities, age etc.)
- Consent discourses (media, legal, socio-political, medical)
- Communication and consent (consent, assent, verbal, non-verbal, language, communication practices and behaviour)

Output: Participants review and synthesise ideas shared, generate key themes associated with the workshop's key discussion areas, and develop a summary statement to inform the development of principles and strategies.

Phase 2: Workshop with young people to brainstorm their ideas about principles underpinning consent to inform consent literacy. In small groups, participants are invited to brainstorm the following issues:

- A shared understanding of principles
- The role of principles in shaping policy and practice using examples
- The relationship between ethics, principles, and consent literacy

Output: Participants draft key themes around which principles will be developed, informed by both workshops. Together young people and facilitators draft key principles from these themes. Participants also brainstorm strategies for implementing these principles across different settings relevant to young people's lives.

Phase 3: Intergenerational workshop. Key stakeholders from the community working in gender and sexuality-based anti-violence strategies, consent education, and comprehensive relationships and sexuality education are invited to a workshop with the young people who have developed principles underpinning consent to inform consent literacy from their perspectives. The workshop will involve the following:

- Young people present the principles to key stakeholders and explain why these principles are essential to consent literacy and education.
- Key stakeholders mentoring session to provide feedback on the principles developed by the young people.
- Whole group discussion based on the feedback and identification of points to address in reviewing the draft principles.
- Identify potential strategies to activate and implement the principles developed into policy and practice.

Output: Directions for young people to review the principles and identify key areas to target to activate and test the principles in policy and practice.

Phase 4: In this workshop, young people are invited to finalise the principles that are core to consent and develop a strategic plan to activate and test these principles in policy and practice. This workshop involves:

- Reviewing and revision of the principles
- A strategic plan for activating and testing the principles through existing consent education channels (e.g., government campaigns, curricula, educational materials, such as syllabuses, consent labs content, and teaching resources).
- A strategy to monitor progress

Output: From this workshop, a set of fundamental principles will be finalised, a clear strategy for activation and testing will be developed, and a process for monitoring activation and testing will be devised.

Conclusion

This chapter stresses the importance of collaborating with young people to co-produce principles and strategies to support their sexual consent literacy, self-efficacy and involvement in decisions that affect them. We argue that developing young people's consent literacy needs to begin early to build their awareness, skills, and agency. Using participatory, iterative pedagogies such as a Living Lab methodology is foundational to embedding consent literacy within young people's everyday practices and interactions. The literature in this field shows the limited evaluation of consent education programs for young people and poor community understanding more broadly of consent, sexual harassment, and sexual assault. Including young people in the development and implementation of consent literacy programs is uncommon, and there is a dearth of diversity in young people's voices represented in program design, implementation, and evaluation. The development of young people's sexual consent literacy must address the sociocultural discourses underpinning gender and power, foreground the complexities of intersectionality, and be guided by young people's everyday lives, concerns, and practices.

Acknowledgement: Special thanks to Jennifer Nguyen, Betty Nguyen, and John Lewis from the Wellbeing, Health & Youth (WH&Y) Commission.

References

ACARA. 2022. *Curriculum Connections: Respect Matters* [Online]. *Canberra, Australia: Australian Curriculum, Assessment and Reporting Authority. Available: https://www.australiancurriculum.edu.au/resources/curriculum-connections/portfolios/respect-matters/ [Accessed 1st October 2022].*

ACT Government. 2022. *Clearer and Stronger Consent Laws [Online]. Act, Australia: Act Government. Available: https://www.cmtedd.act.gov.au/open_government/inform/act_government_media_releases/rattenbury/2022/clearer-and-stronger-sexual-consent-laws [Accessed 27th October 2022].*

ANROWS. 2018. Are We There Yet? *Australians' Attitudes Towards Violence Against Women and Gender Equality: Summary Findings From the 2017 National Community Attitudes Towards Violence Against Women Survey.* Sydney, Australia: Australia's National Research Organisation For Women's Safety.

Australian Government. 2022. *Violence Against Women. Let's Stop it at the Start. [Online]. Canberra, Australia: Australian Government. Available: www.respect.gov.au [Accessed 1st October 2022].*

Australian Human Rights Commission. 2018. Everyone's Business: Fourth National Survey on Sexual Harassment in Australian Workplaces (2018). Sydney, Australia: Australian Human Rights Commission.

Australian Human Rights Commission. 2020. *Respect@Work: National Inquiry into Sexual Harassment in Australian Workplaces.* Sydney, Australia: Australian Human Rights Commission.

Australian Institute of Family Studies. 2021. *Age of Consent Laws in Australia.* Canberra, Australia: Australian Institute of Family Studies, Australian Government.

Breiding, M., Basile, K., Smith, S., Black, M. & Mahendra, R. 2015. *Intimate Partner Violence Surveillance: Uniform Definitions and Recommended Data Elements. Atlanta, Ga: National Center for Injury Prevention and Control, Centers for Disease Control and Prevention [Online]. Atlanta, Ga: National Center for Injury Prevention and Control, Centers for Disease Control and Prevention. Available: https://www.cdc.gov/violenceprevention/pdf/intimatepartnerviolence.pdf [Accessed 29th October 2022].*

Burton, O., Rawstorne, P., Watchirs-Smith, L., Nathan, S. & Carter, A. 2021. Teaching Sexual Consent to Young People in Education Settings: A Narrative Systematic Review. *Sex Education.*

Carmody, M. 2015. *Sex, Ethics, and Young People,* New York, Palgrave Macmillan.

Contos, C. 2021. *Teach Us Consent [Online]. Australia: Teach.Us.Consent. Available: https://www.teachusconsent.com [Accessed 27 October 2022].*

Davies, C. & Burns, K. 2023. HPV Vaccination Literacy in Sexualities Education. *Sex Education, 23,* 315–323.

Davies, C. & McInnes, D. 2012. Speaking Violence: Homophobia and the Production of Injurious Speech In Schooling Cultures. In: Saltmarsh, S., Robinson, K. & Davies, C. (Eds.) *Rethinking School Violence: Theory, Gender, Context.* New York: Palgrave, Macmillan.

Davies, C. & Robinson, K. H. 2010. Hatching Babies and Stork Deliveries: Risk and Regulation in the Construction of Children's Sexual Knowledge. *Contemporary Issues in Early Childhood, 11,* 249–263.

Davies, C., Robinson, K. H., Metcalf, A., Ivory, K., Mooney-Somers, J., Race, K. & Skinner, S. R. 2021. Australians of Diverse Sexual Orientations and Gender Identities. In: T. Dune, K. Mcleod & R. Williams (Eds.), *Culture, Diversity and Health in Australia: Towards Culturally Safe Health Care.* London: Routledge/Taylor and Francis.

Davies, C., Skinner, S. R., Stoney, T., Marshall, H. S., Collins, J., Jones, J., Hutton, H., Parrella, A., Cooper, S., Mcgeechan, K., Zimet, G. & for the HPV.Edu Study Group 2017. 'Is It Like One of Those Infectious Kind of Things?': The Importance of Educating Young People About HPV and HPV Vaccination at School'. *Sex Education, 17,* 256–275.

Davies, C., Sowbhagya, M. & for the Public Health Association of Australia. 2022. *Comprehensive Relationships and Sexuality Education and Reproductive Health for Children and Young People At School Policy Position Statement [Online]. Canberra, Australia: Public Health Association of Australia. Available: https://Www. Phaa.Net.Au/Documents/Item/5635 [Accessed 27th* October 2022].

eSafety Commissioner. 2022. *Sending Nudes and Sexting [Online]. Act, Australia: Australian Government. [Accessed 27th* October 2022].

Fedina, L., Holmes, J. L. & Backes, B. L. 2016. Campus Sexual Assault: A Systematic Review of Prevalence Research From 2000 To 2015. *Trauma, Violence and Abuse, 19,* 76–93.

Foucault, M. 1984. *The History of Sexuality. Volume 1: An Introduction.* Harmondsworth England, Penguin.

Gilbert, J. 2018. Contesting Consent in Sex Education. *Sex Education, 18,* 268–279.

Goldfarb, E. S. & Lieberman, L. D. 2021. Three Decades of Research: The Case for Comprehensive Sex Education. *Journal of Adolescent Health, 68,* 13–27.

Marson, K. 2021. Consent a Low Bar: The Case for a Human Rights Approach to Relationships and Sexuality Education. *Australian Journal of Human Rights, 27,* 161–169.

Marson, K. 2022. *Legitimate Sexpectations: The Power of Sex Ed.* Victoria, Australia, Scribe.

Mason, G. 2021. Sexual Assault Law and Community Education: A Case Study of New South Wales, Australia. *The Australian Journal of Social Issues, 56,* 409–426.

McLaren, L. & Hawe, P. 2005. Ecological Perspectives in Health Research. *Journal of Epidemiology and Community Health, 59,* 6–14.

Muehlenhard, C. L., Humphreys, T., Kjozkowski, K. N. & Peterson, Z. D. 2016. The Complexities of Sexual Consent among College Students: A Conceptual and Empirical Review. *Journal of Sex Research, 53,* 457–487.

Mueller, T. E., Gavin, L. E. & Kulkarni, A. 2008. The Association Between Sex Education and Youth's Engagement in Sexual Intercourse, Age at First Intercourse, and Birth Control Use at First Sex. *Journal of Adolescent Health, 42,* 89–96.

Muscari, E., Littleton, H. & Cunnane, L. 2022. Emerging Adults' Perceptions of School-Based Sex Education On Consent, Sexual Assault, and Intimate Partner Violence. *Sex Education*.

NSW Government Communities and Justice . 2022. Sexual Consent Laws: Information About Consent Laws Introduced By the Nsw Government *[Online]*. Available: https://dcj.nsw.gov.au/justice/reform-of-sexual-consent-laws.html .

Ollis, D. 2014. The Role of Teachers in Delivering Education About Respectful Relationships: Exploring Teacher and Student Perspectives. *Health Education Research*, 29, 702–713.

Ollis, D., Coll, L., Harrison, L. & Johnson, B. 2022. *Pedagogies of Possibility for Negotiating Sexuality Education With Young People*, London, Bingley: Emerald Publishing Limited.

Our Watch 2016. *The Line Campaign Evaluation: Wave 1 – Report: Summary of Attitudes and Behaviours of Young People in Relation To Consent*. Melbourne, Australia: TNS Social Research.

Premier of Victoria. 2022. *Affirmative Consent Model Now Law in Victoria [Online]. Victoria, Australia: Victorian Government. Available: https://dcj.nsw.gov.au/justice/reform-of-sexual-consent-laws.html [Accessed 27th* October 2022].

Richard, L., Gauvin, L. & Raine, K. 2011. Ecological Models Revisited: Their Uses and Evolution in Health Promotion Over Two Decades. *Annual Review of Public Health 2011*, 32, 307–326.

Robinson, K. H. 2005. Reinforcing Hegemonic Masculinity Through Sexual Harassment: Issues of Identity, Power and Popularity in Secondary Schools. *Gender and Education*, 17, 19–37.

Robinson, K. H. 2012. Sexual Harassment in Schools: Issues of Identity and Power – Negotiating the Complexities, Contexts and Contradictions of this Everyday Practice. In: Saltmarch, S., Robinson, K. H. & Davies, C. (Eds.) *Rethinking School Violence: Theory, Gender, Context*. London: Palgrave Macmillan.

Robinson, K. H. 2013. *Innocence, Knowledge and the Construction of Childhood: The Contradictory Nature of Sexuality and Censorship in Children's Contemporary Lives*. London, UK, Routledge.

Robinson, K. H., Bansel, P., Denson, N., Ovenden, G. & Davies, C. 2014. *Growing Up Queer: Issues Facing Young Australians Who Are Gender Variant and Sexuality Diverse*. Melbourne, Australia: Young and Well Co-Operative Research Centre.

Robinson, K. H. & Davies, C. 2008. Docile Bodies and Heteronormative Moral Subjects: Constructing the Child and Sexual Knowledge in the Schools. *Sexuality and Culture*, 12, 221–239.

Robinson, K. H. & Jones-Diaz, C. 2016. *Diversity and Difference in Childhood: Issues for Theory and Practice*, London, UK, Open University Press/McGraw-Hill Education.

Robinson, K. H., Smith, E. & Davies, C. 2017. Responsibilities, Tensions, and Ways Forward: Parents' Perspectives On Children's Sexuality Education. *Sex Education*, 17, 333–347.

RSARA. 2022. *Rape & Sexual Assault Research & Advocacy* [Online]. Australia: Rape & Sexual Assault Research & Advocacy Ltd. Available: https://rasara.org [Accessed 27th October 2022].

Salter, M., Robinson, K. H., Ullman, J., Denson, N., Ovenden, G., Noonan, K., Bansel, P. & Huppatz, K. 2021. Gay, Bisexual, and Queer Men's Attitudes and Understandings of Intimate Partner Violence and Sexual Assault. *Journal of Interpersonal Violence*, 36, 11630–11657.

Skinner, S. R., Davies, C., Marino, J., Botfield, J. & Lewis, L. 2020. Sexual Health of Adolescent Girls. In: Jane M. Ussher, Joan C. Chrisler & J. Perz (Eds.), *Routledge International Handbook of Women's Sexual and Reproductive Health*. New York: Routledge.

Straus, S. E., Tetroe, J. & Graham, I. 2009. Defining Knowledge Translation. *Canadian Medical Association Journal*, 181, 165–168.

Stynes, Y. & Kang, M. 2021. *Welcome To Consent*. Sydney, Australia: Hardie Grant Children's Publishing.

Swist, T., Collin, P., Nguyen, B., Steinbeck, K. & Dawson, A. 2019b. *Wellbeing Health & Youth Engagement Framework [Online]. Wh&Y Centre of Research Excellence. Available: why.org.au/engagementframework [Accessed 27th* October 2022].

Swist, T., Collin, P., Nguyen, B., Davies, C., Cullen, P., Medlow, S., Skinner, S. R., Third, A. & Steinbeck, K. 2022. Guiding, Sustaining and Growing the Public Involvement of Young People in an Adolescent Health Research Community of Practice. *Health Expectations*, Online First, 1–11.

Templeton, M., Lohan, M., Kelly, C. & Lundy, L. 2017. A Systematic Review and Qualitative Synthesis of Adolescents' Views of Sexual Readiness. *Journal of Advanced Nursing*, 73, 1288–1301.

Wan, A. & Yu, J. 2022. *Consent Labs [Online]. Sydney, Australia: Consent Labs. Available: https://www.consentlabs.org.au [Accessed 1st* October 2022].

WH&Y. 2022. *Wellbeing Health & Youth Centre of Research Excellence [Online]. Australia: Wellbeing Health & Youth Centre of Research Excellence. Available: Wellbeing Health & Youth Centre of Research Excellence [Accessed 1st* October 2022].

Widman, L., Maheux, A. J., Craig, E., Evans-Paulson, R. & Choukas-Bradley, S. 2022. Sexual Communication Between Adolescent Partners: A Scoping Review and Directions for Future Research. *Journal of Sex Research*, 16.

World Health Organization. 2021. Violence Against Women Prevalence Estimates, *2018: Global*, Regional and National Prevalence Estimates for Intimate Partner Violence Against Women and Global and Regional Prevalence Estimates for Non-Partner Sexual Violence Against Women Geneva, Switzerland: World Health Organization.

PART III

Women's Bodies and the Narrative of Consent

9

THE RIGHT TO WITHDRAW CONSENT TO CONTINUING AN UNWANTED PREGNANCY

Aoife Duffy

In 1973, the US Supreme Court in *Roe v. Wade* decided that women's ability to choose whether to continue a pregnancy was protected by privacy rights derived from the US Constitution (balanced against state's interests in regulating later term pregnancies). In *Dobbs v. Jackson Women's Centre* (June 2022), the US Supreme Court overturned this precedent. The dissenting opinions of Justices Breyer, Sotomayer and Kagan in Dobbs observe that the majority decision curtails 'women's rights, and their status as free and equal citizens'. The US Constitution purportedly guarantees equality and liberty for all, but the majority in Dobbs adopted a strict, 'originalist' interpretation of a document over 200 years old, drafted at a time when women were not recognised as equal citizens. This approach is troubling as the Constitution should be viewed as a living instrument capable of responding to historical progress. In reading Roe and subsequent case law, the dissenting judges maintain that this jurisprudence was embedded in 'core constitutional concepts of individual freedom, and the equal rights of citizens to decide on the shape of their own lives'. The current chapter aligns with such views, arguing that the ability to withdraw consent to continuing an unwanted pregnancy is an essential component of autonomy for those capable of gestation. The ability to withdraw consent, in the nomenclature of the dissenting judges in Dobbs, is fundamental to a 'woman's control of her body and the path of her life'. While much of the literature on this topic refers to 'women,' the chapter employs language such as 'those capable of gestation,' or 'pregnant person,' in order to be inclusive; to include women and girls, trans men, non-binary identities, or anyone else who would need to withdraw consent to continuing an unwanted pregnancy during their lifetime.

The right of a pregnant person to withdraw consent to continuing an unwanted pregnancy needs to be universally protected for everyone capable of gestation. Only when this right is protected is social equality possible. Many other rights flow from this ability to give consent or to withdraw consent. It is

DOI: 10.4324/9781003358756-13

not exactly the same as the choice paradigm, which is very familiar in the debate around reproductive rights. The consequences of protecting the right to withdraw consent in these circumstances signify making available the socio-legal, economic, and health provisions that would allow for free withdrawal of consent. While those choices occur in private, the right to withdraw consent is conceived as a public matter of socio-political justice and equality.

First, the chapter tracks through the normative developments of reproductive rights within international human rights law by analysing relevant rights, instruments, and commentary. It summarises the position in international human rights law with regards to reproductive rights and signposts possible directions for greater liberalisation. Then, to explore the right to withdraw consent ideologically, the analysis turns to frameworks on reproductive justice, liberal autonomy and reproductive autonomy, and relational autonomy.

International Human Rights Law

The potential of a right to withdraw consent was present from the outset of thinking on reproductive rights. The right to decide the number and spacing of children was first stated at the Tehran Conference in 1968, and later affirmed in the World Population Plan of Action (adopted in Budapest in 1974). Codified in the Convention on the Elimination of All Forms of Discrimination Against Women (1979), Article 16 obliges state parties to eliminate discrimination against women and ensure 'equality between men and women,' by granting them 'the same rights to decide freely and responsibly on the number and spacing of their children and to have access to the information, education and means to enable them to exercise these rights'. As zero is a number, the only way that this provision can be realised is if the right to withdraw consent to continuing an unwanted pregnancy is protected.

A widely accepted definition of reproductive rights was developed at the International Conference on Population and Development (Cairo, 1994), which entails:

> [R]eproductive rights embrace certain human rights that are already recognized in national laws, international human rights documents and other consensus documents. These rights rest on the recognition of the basic right of all couples and individuals to decide freely and responsibly the number, spacing and timing of their children and to have the information and means to do so, and the right to attain the highest standard of sexual and reproductive health. It also includes their right to make decisions concerning reproduction free of discrimination, coercion and violence, as expressed in human rights documents.

Here the idea of being free to decide on the number of children is at the crux of reproductive rights. In addition, the ability to make decisions regarding reproduction free from coercion appears. If a person capable of carrying a pregnancy is unable to withdraw consent to continuing that pregnancy, decision-making is not 'free of discrimination, coercion and violence'. Similarly, the 1995 Beijing World Conference on Women and its resulting Declaration recognised the right of women to control all aspects of their fertility and that 'equal relationships between women and men in matters of sexual relations and reproduction including full respect for the integrity of the person requires mutual respect, consent and shared responsibility for sexual behaviour and its consequences'. Consent is explicitly framed as an issue of equality and the idea that ensuring equality between men and women requires that the consequences of sexual behaviour should not fall on women alone. The specific consequence under scrutiny here is pregnancy – holding consent to or consent not to continue the pregnancy as a sacrosanct right for the pregnant person.

Access to abortion, as a critical tool for the enjoyment of reproductive rights, has been recognised by various UN human rights bodies under the rubric of the right to life, the right to health, the right to privacy, gender equality, and the right to be free from torture, cruel, inhuman or degrading treatment (Sjöholm, 2017). The Committee on the Elimination of Discrimination Against Women's General Recommendation 19 (1992) on violence against women urged state parties to take measures to prevent coercion with respect to women's fertility and reproduction, and in General Recommendation 21 (1994) the Committee noted reports of 'coercive practices which have serious consequences for women, such as forced pregnancies, abortions or sterilisation'. Around the same time, the Vienna Declaration and Platform for Action specified that forced pregnancies in situations of armed conflict was a violation of international humanitarian law and international human rights law (Altunjan, 2021). In the latter situation it is likely that the threshold to seriousness is understood to be breached because lack of consent to the pregnancy was closely linked to lack of consent at conception in situations of utter powerlessness. From the 1990s, with the establishment of the International Criminal Tribunal for the former Yugoslavia and the International Criminal Tribunal for Rwanda, international criminal law started to address sexual violence that occurred during conflict and mass atrocities. Forms of sexual violence such as rape and enforced pregnancy were codified as crimes against humanity in the Rome Statute of the International Criminal Court (1998). Several years later, Dominic Ongwen, a former commander with the Ugandan Lord's Resistance Army, became the first person convicted by the International Criminal Court of committing 'forced pregnancy,' amongst other crimes (Grey, 2017).[1]

But what of forced pregnancies in non-conflict situations? Or situations where both parties consented to the sexual activity which led to conception, but the person who carries the burden of gestation wishes to withdraw consent to continuing that pregnancy? In 2017, the Committee on the Elimination of

Discrimination Against Women explicitly stated that 'forced continuation of pregnancy' is a form of gender-based violence which may amount to torture, cruel, inhuman or degrading treatment. States that do not protect the ability to withdraw consent hold a form of gender-based violence in reserve, which can have fatal and torturous results. The Committee on the Elimination of Discrimination Against Women has long comprehended the impact of reproductive restrictions on women, because reproductive labour is done by women, and in most societies the burden to raise children also falls on women. This they noted affects women's access to education, to work, and to other activities related to personal development (CEDAW, 1994). One result of the inability to withdraw consent is that disproportionate workloads fall on those forced to continue the pregnancy. This work deepens gender inequality because on the one hand it is unpaid, while on the other it creates obstacles to the benefits of paid employment. Women spend 2.5 more time doing unpaid work than men, and earn approximately 35% of global labour income (UN Women, 2022; World Inequality Report, 2022).

As such, the forced continuation of pregnancy is not prohibited by international human rights law, except in the discrete circumstances of rape, risk to life or the health of the pregnant person, or fatal foetal abnormality. This is because failing to provide for withdrawal of consent in these circumstances is recognised as leading to various socio-economic, and civil and political rights violations. While many commentators point to the aggregate effect of multiple rights being impacted, generally the terrain is conceptualised and litigated through atomised rights: the right to life, the prohibition on torture, cruel, inhumane and degrading treatment, the right to health, the right to privacy, and addressing structural and legal barriers to safe abortion. The next section will consider the latter three lenses through which reproductive rights have been advanced to better understand whether foregrounding these rights has strengthened people's capacity to withdraw consent to continuing a pregnancy.

To assure the ability to withdraw consent requires dismantling structural and legal obstacles, which has been considered at international level. For example, both the UN Human Rights Committee (General Comment 8, 1982) and the UN Committee on Economic, Social, and Cultural Rights (General Comment 22, 2016) urge states not to criminalise women or girls who need to procure abortions and the UN Committee on the Elimination of Discrimination Against Women explicitly urges states to eliminate such laws and to eradicate 'practical barriers to the full realisation of the right to sexual and reproductive health' (see also UN Special Rapporteur on the Right to Health, 2011; Parliamentary Assembly of the Council of Europe calls on states to eliminate barriers to abortion). Such procedural barriers as mandatory waiting periods, third party authorisation, unavailability of good quality medical information and trained professionals, or biased counselling ought to be abolished (Fine et al., 2017). Fine et al. summarise the relevant threads produced by UN commentary as requiring states to ensure 'that legal abortion services are available, accessible (including affordable), acceptable, and of good quality'. While such structural reforms are of course essential to protect the right to withdraw consent, international human rights law has not settled these parameters as a result of granting a universal right to withdraw consent to everyone capable of gestation. Reproductive rights at the international level have advanced through the jurisprudence of hard cases and the prism of discrete (and this chapter argues contingent) rights, to which analysis now turns.

The modern movement for reproductive rights followed the direction set by *Roe v. Wade* whereby the US Supreme Court legalised abortion on the basis of privacy protected by the US Constitution which was deemed to be 'broad enough to encompass the right of a pregnant woman to terminate her pregnancy without state interference' (Palacios Zuloaga, 2021). Patricia Palacios Zuloaga observes that positioning access to abortion under the purview of the right to privacy took hold in a society which valued personal autonomy and state non-interference in private matters; thus, under the rubric of privacy, the right to choose to terminate a pregnancy developed. Likewise, in the European system, the determination of whether or not to reproduce stems from the right to privacy (Sjöholm, 2017). There are several issues with the normative development of reproductive rights under the right to privacy, of which two will be presented. Firstly, to invisibilise reproductive rights as a privacy right rather than an issue of social justice had the unintended consequence of limiting choice, or limiting who could exercise the choice to terminate their pregnancy. Accessing abortion became an exclusive right for those with the resources to make that choice, whereas a social justice approach to abortion rights would have recognised the need for the state to make access to abortion services widely available. The latter, as a matter of social justice, would have signified greater engagement with socio-economic and intersectional analyses of situations where people wished to withdraw consent to continuing pregnancy. This fact was highlighted by radical and critical race feminists who introduced the more comprehensive notion of reproductive justice under which access to abortion could be advanced. In fact, 20 years before the overturning of *Roe v Wade*, Melanie Lee astutely predicted that abortion as a privacy right reduced it to a privilege and this 'laid the foundation for the practical overruling of Roe' (Lee, 2000).

This leads to a second critique of abortion under the right to privacy. Under international human rights law and in many national jurisdictions the right to privacy is not absolute. Shielding the 'choices' of a section of privileged women under the thin right to privacy makes this a gift rather than a right which then is entirely contingent on the political or cultural persuasion of a particular administration at a particular point in time. Unfortunately, the contingency of this 'grant' under the privacy rubric was laid bare by the legal and political engineering of Donald Trump with the US Supreme Court, and the Court's subsequent *Dobbs v. Jackson Women's Centre* (2022) ruling, which removed and restricted reproductive rights for many across the United States. The right to privacy is an inadequate framework for reproductive rights as this is a public, societal and structural issue of equality (Palacios Zuloaga, 2021), and, in the nomenclature of this chapter, it does not universalise the right to withdraw consent to continuing an unwanted pregnancy.

According to Article 12(1) of the International Covenant on Economic, Social and Cultural Rights everyone has the 'right to the highest attainable standard of physical and mental health.' The Committee on Economic Social and Cultural Rights has taken this to include reproductive freedom, 'such as family planning, pre-and post-natal care, and requires the decriminalization of abortion,' according to Sjöholm (2017). The right to health framework suggests that women's health and well-being is intimately connected to the promotion and protection of their reproductive well-being (Weller, 2006). Indeed, the Maputo Protocol (2003) to the African Charter on Human and Peoples' Rights specifies that the right to health of women includes their sexual and reproductive health. In 2011, the UN Special Rapporteur on the Right to Health advocated for the elimination of 'impermissible barriers to the realisation of women's right to health,' as such laws severely restrict women's decision making with respect to their sexual and reproductive health (UN Special Rapporteur on the Right to Health, 2011). However, if reproductive rights are not considered absolute in the way set out in this chapter, administrations enjoy room to argue that these are permissible barriers in their societies.

Another issue for advancing reproductive rights through the right to health is that socio-economic rights lag behind civil and political rights, the former categorised by Karel Vašák as second-generation rights requiring positive state action (Domaradzki et al., 2019). Indeed, from the outset, the conditionality of socio-economic rights was built into the International Covenant on Economic, Social and Cultural Rights – Article 2(1) calls on state parties to take steps towards the progressive realisation of this category of rights according to resources available. Of course, this is a disingenuous argument, for civil and political rights are also contingent on states actively allocating resources, such as in the fulfilment of the right to vote or the right to a fair trial. But it does point to the reality of policy choices, and if those choices are informed by con-servative governments espousing anti-abortion worldviews, the threat to repro-ductive rights is obvious (Palacios Zuloaga, 2021). So reproductive rights under the right to health are also contingent. A more robust and irrefutable framework is needed to dismantle structural violence that prevents the withdrawal of consent to continuing an unwanted pregnancy.

This section will conclude with a summary of the current position to acces-sing abortion in international human rights law. Absolute bans on abortion are considered incompatible with international human rights law (Fine et al., 2017). The Maputo Protocol to the African Charter on Human and Peoples' Rights is the only multilateral human rights treaty which explicitly codifies access to abortion in limited circumstances of 'sexual assault, rape, incest, and where the continued pregnancy endangers the mental and physical health of the mother or the life of the mother or the foetus' (Article XIV, 2, c). Currently the Maputo Protocol has 49 signatories of which 42 are state parties. These exceptions, in which consent to continuing an unwanted pregnancy may be withdrawn, are also reflected in the commentary of treaty monitoring bodies, such as the UN Human Rights Committee, the UN Committee on the Elimination of Discrimination Against Women, and the commentary produced by the UN Special Rapporteur on the Right to Health. In short, at an international level, the view is that abortion may be permitted where the life or health of the pregnant person is threatened (UN Human Rights Committee, UN Committee on the Elimination of Discrimination Against Women), in cases of fatal foetal abnormality (UN Human Rights Committee), and where the pregnancy is the result of rape or incest (UN Human Rights Committee, UN Committee on the Elimination of Discrimination Against Women). Indeed, regarding the rape exception, the UN Committee on the Elimination of Discrimination Against Women was the first treaty monitoring body to explicitly instruct a state party, Peru, to liberalise its abortion laws for pregnancy resulting from rape (*LC v Peru*, 2011).

The difficulty with this position is that it relies on tentative exceptions to the rule of a general ban, rather than completely overhauling that rule to permit withdrawal of consent to continuing pregnancy. Thus, the position is not universalizable to everyone capable of gestation. Of course, this point was not lost on reproductive rights activists and human rights practitioners, who increasingly lean into the notion of reproductive autonomy to bolster and advance access to abortion (Fine et al., 2017). Amnesty International's recently updated policy on abortion (2021) notes that access to abortion is an integral part of sexual and reproductive healthcare, which is key to 'realising individual's reproductive autonomy under full range of human rights'. In 2012, the Committee on the Elimination of Discrimination Against Women advised New Zealand to review its abortion laws and practices to 'ensure women's autonomy to choose'. The UN Special Rapporteur on the Right to Health (2011) noted with concern the impact of proscriptive laws on 'women's dignity and autonomy by severely restricting decision making by women in respect of their sexual and reproductive health'. In 2018, the UN Committee on the Rights of Persons with Disabilities and the UN Committee on the Elimination of Discrimination Against Women issued a joint statement calling for states to repeal laws and policies that impede women's reproductive autonomy and choice. This turn to reproductive autonomy is significant insofar as it is a universalisable norm that could eventually crystallise on such a concept as the right to withdraw consent to continuing an unwanted pregnancy. The rest of the chapter will analyse this notion through the prism of reproductive justice, reproductive autonomy, and relational autonomy. The exceptions to the ban mentioned above also fail to capture the disproportionate impact that unwanted pregnancies have on people who are socio-economically marginalised and already face multiple forms of discrimination in the world.

Reproductive Justice

Over three decades ago, in 1994, the reproductive justice movement was established in the United States by women of colour to bring issues of reproductive freedom within a social justice framework broad enough to contextualise the intersections of gender, race, class, and other forms of oppression (London, 2011). Historically, the mainstream reproductive rights movement had centred the experiences of white middle-class women under the right to choose umbrella without critical reflection of the relative privilege required for the enjoyment of meaningful reproductive autonomy within the pro-choice framework. Feminists, such as Angela Davis, rejected gender essentialism: the idea that a unitary set of women's experiences 'can be isolated and described independent of race, class, sexual orientation, and other realities of experience' (Denbow, 2014). A subset of relatively privileged women could not stand as a cypher for all women. Advanced by the activist SisterSong network composed of 16 groups from four different communities (African American, Native American, Asian American, and Latina), it developed into a truly inclusive movement that aimed to redefine reproductive rights so as to centre 'indigenous women, women of color, trans people, and other people marginalized by existing reproductive choice frameworks' (Johnston & Zacharias, 2017).

Essentially reproductive justice has four objectives: 1) the right to have a child; 2) the right not to have a child; 3) the right to parent a child in a safe and healthy environment; 4) reproductive autonomy and gender freedom for everyone (Roberts, 2015; Ross & Solinger, 2017). Reproductive justice provides critical analysis of how state policies can weaponise women's bodies as a form of reproductive repression. The progressive multiracial organisation, Forward Together, defined reproductive repression as

> the control and exploitation of women, girls, and individuals through our bodies, sexuality, [labor,] and reproduction. The regulation of women and individuals thus becomes a powerful strategic pathway to controlling entire communities. It involves systems of oppression that are based on race, ability, class, gender, sexuality, age, and immigration status.
>
> *(Forward Together, 2005, p. 1)*

The core argument advanced in this chapter is that the right to withdraw consent to continuing an unwanted pregnancy is essential for the enjoyment of autonomy utilises the reproductive justice framework, and aligns with Ross and Solinger who submit that the right to reproduce and not to reproduce is a fundamental right (Ross & Solinger, 2017, p. 9). The shift to reproductive autonomy – the exercise of choices around reproduction – must be contextualised against the social and cultural capital and other resources which can potentially empower and help realise those choices. Transforming reproductive repression to reproductive autonomy and true freedom in reproductive choices requires a sensitivity to context and material resources. This view of reproductive autonomy is capable of being broad enough, while critiquing the fact that traditional autonomy paradigms have excluded some people's access to reproductive options (Johnston and Zacharias, 2017). The next section will sketch out a vision of reproductive autonomy in which the right to withdraw consent to continuing an unwanted pregnancy might be advanced. For this right to be universally applicable and available to everyone capable of gestation, it signifies engaging contextual and intersectional analyses of the ability to withdraw consent.

Reproductive Autonomy

One strand of thinking on reproductive autonomy has developed through the liberal autonomy tradition. Etymologically, the word autonomy originates from the Greek word, αυτονομία, which means 'self-rule' (Hewson, 2001). The liberal autonomy outlook is that people should be able to determine the course of their life plans without interference (Lee, 2000). Essentially people may develop their conception of the good life according to their own beliefs and invoke their plans without constraints from third parties or from the state as long as these plans are not harmful to others (Hevia & Constantin, 2018). Johnston and Zacharias note that autonomous agents are defined with reference to capacities, specifically, the 'ability to deliberate about one's personal goals and the ability to act on the basis of that deliberation' (2017). Self-determination in the absence of force, coercion or interference opens the space for free choice and control over life options (Weller, 2006; Lee, 2000). By this maxim, decisions are free and morally right if individuals can exercise self-governance free from constraint (De Proost & Coene, 2019). Non-interference signifies a restrained state and this is posited as a negative right in liberal autonomy. Of course, the right to withdraw consent to continuing an unwanted pregnancy also engages positive obligations on states to provide for procreative choices for the right to be enjoyed in practice (Lee, 2000). In essence, liberal feminists argue that the decision whether or not to carry a pregnancy to term is crucial for personal autonomy, and that reproductive autonomy is key to unlocking women's liberation (Lee, 2000).

However, there have been numerous critiques of liberal autonomy as a vehicle for women's reproductive autonomy. Penelope Weller (2006) points out that transposing these choices that women make onto a male construct of the autonomous subject divorces those choices from the social, political, and cultural contexts which in reality constrain reproductive autonomy. An even more radical challenge suggests that when patriarchal ideologies are internalised in women this is a force of invisible coercion that precludes the possibility of genuine autonomy (Sjöholm, 2017). Mostly, the critiques point to social contexts, such as structural inequalities and social circumstances, in limiting choices (Weller, 2006). Thus, liberal autonomy and neoliberal discourses fail to take account of 'contextual factors, implicit biases, and power imbalances,' that ultimately present insurmountable constraints on women, particularly poor women, women with disabilities, and women from marginalised minorities (Johnston and Zacharias, 2017).

The next section will clarify current thinking on reproductive autonomy, and marry this to the core argument advanced in this chapter, while the final section leans into the notion of relational autonomy, which is highly sensitised to the social contexts in which choice may be exercised and employs the reproductive justice framework introduced above.

In general terms, reproductive autonomy refers to the individual's ability to make choices with regards to sexuality, pregnancy and childbearing, and the foundation of families (Pereira, 2015). Altujan suggests that reproductive autonomy entails the individual's capacity and ability to make informed decisions about reproduction, including 'all aspects concerning impregnation, pregnancy, and birth. Specifically, reproductive autonomy encompasses the freedom to choose whether, how, and under what circumstances to reproduce' (Altunjan, 2021, p. 77). Decisions about whether or not to have offspring and the circumstances of conception – these choices ought to be realised through the availability of reproductive options (Lee, 2022). Through the liberal autonomy lens, reproductive autonomy signifies 'self rule over their reproductive abilities and decisions' (Lee, 2022). This dovetails the notion of bodily autonomy – that a person has a right to determine what happens to their body (Lee, 2022). As access to abortion increases the pregnant person's choices over what happens to their body, so too does it enhance their reproductive autonomy and their personal autonomy in other spheres. McCleod argues that choices in the reproductive sphere are crucial to people's well-being (McCleod, 2009). Outright abortion bans or discrete exceptions to bans inhibit reproductive autonomy 'by severely restricting decision making by the women in respect of their sexual reproductive health' (Fine et al., 2017), and in terms sustained by this chapter, they prevent the withdrawal of consent to continuing an unwanted pregnancy. The ability to such withdrawal of consent is crucial to reproductive autonomy.

Liberal notions of autonomy tend to decouple individualistic choices from the social context in which those choices occur. Lee points out that traditional liberalism assumes these choices are entirely within a person's control or that they have the resources to exercise such choices (Lee, 2022). Many feminists critique this form of individualistic autonomy unmoored from social relationships, particularly when recognising the uniqueness and complexity of reproductive choices (Laufer-Ukeles, 2011). Thus, the notion of relational autonomy has been advanced as an alternative view of autonomy that 'acknowledges the many social and contextual constraints and pressures that may be placed on choices while simultaneously recognizing that there is value in self-determination' (Laufer-Ukeles, 2011, p. 610). Relational theorists consider individuals as embedded within webs of social relationships. People's capacities and autonomy are influenced – constrained or enabled – by these relationships (Boyd, 2010). Relational theory signals the idea of degrees of autonomy and posits that autonomy is a process rather than a snapshot moment in time, 'selfhood is seen as an ongoing process, rather than something static or fixed' (Sherwin, 1998).

By focusing on and disentangling the relational web in which reproductive choices are embedded, relational theory can take into account constraining factors, such as internal or external constraints. All constraints are highly contextual, but external constraints generally refer to the political, legal, cultural, and economic contexts – and, for example, structured gender power relations in a given society that will constrain or enable reproductive autonomy. The current chapter focuses on external constraints in the realm of law, policy, and health provisions – arguing that these need to be reformed so as to enable the freedom to withdraw consent to continuing an unwanted pregnancy. Nonetheless, it recognises other external constraints and argues that the type of intersectional analyses advanced by reproductive justice needs to be engaged. Additionally, understanding how external factors manifest as internal constraints through the incorporation of certain ideologies that preclude genuine reproductive autonomy is required. The line between external constraints and internal constraints is highly fluid if we consider the way in which patriarchal ideologies, highly structured gender roles, and pro-natalism are internalised through socialisation. These ideologies manifest both as internal and external constraints to the exercise of freedom to withdraw consent to continuing a pregnancy. Different ideologies and technologies could lead to different social structures and consequent divisions of labour. Such commitments as to substantive gender equality, the assumption of equivalent childcare by parents, socio-economic redistribution of resources, degrowth policies in the context of our climate emergency, the elimination of racial hierarchies, and fairness in accessing new reproductive technologies (e.g. artificial wombs) could enhance the socio-political and cultural contexts which frame the right to withdraw consent to continuing a pregnancy.

Conclusion

This chapter argues that the right to withdraw consent to continuing an unwanted pregnancy is essential for the realisation of reproductive autonomy for people capable of gestation. First it tracks through developments in international human rights law, noting that this right is not protected, although outright abortion bans are discouraged. At international level and within regional systems the prohibition on abortion is sustained as the rule with only hard case exceptions to that rule. Perhaps this can be seen as an incrementalistic approach in the name of gradual progress and liberalisation. However, the danger of supporting a rule that only permits extreme exceptions is that these exceptions are contingent 'grants' rather than grounded in a fundamental right. Such exceptions do not protect the right to withdraw consent to continuing an unwanted pregnancy for the pregnant person, and may be taken away according to the political vagaries of the day. This may be the reason why UN commentary, treaty monitoring bodies, UN Special Rapporteurs, and NGOs working in this area are increasingly defining reproductive rights in terms of autonomy and self-determination. While the idea of control over life plans was present in *Roe v. Wade*, it was not as an absolute personal liberty, but as a limited privacy right derived from the US Constitution. The chapter analyses the right to withdraw consent through liberal autonomy and associated feminist critiques of liberalism, settling on the notion of relational autonomy, which by giving context to decision-making can help disentangle limiting factors to reproductive autonomy.

Together with reproductive justice, which can properly assess the socio-economic, cultural, intersectional, and resource implications of being able to consent to continuing a pregnancy or to withdraw consent with dignity, these two paradigms help to identify and dismantle barriers to the right. It is necessary to universalise as a fundamental right the ability to withdraw consent to continuing an unwanted pregnancy because supporting exceptions to a ban means that conservative governments and policymakers can simply remove or reduce these exceptions. Thus, a form of gender-based violence is held in reserve. This is potentially devastating to reproductive autonomy or autonomy more generally for approximately half of the population who may need to exercise the ability to withdraw consent during their lifetime. As a result of *Dobbs v. Jackson*, 13 US states enacted 'trigger' laws designed to ban or severely restrict access to abortion if *Roe v. Wade* fell, and now abortion is illegal in 11 states meaning that one in three American women do not have reproductive autonomy. While internationally the typical trend has been towards liberalisation over the past 25 years, the US is not alone in regressive restrictions as the examples of Nicaragua, El Salvador, and Poland attest. Several UN state parties prohibit abortion entirely, while many others only tolerate limited exceptions to the ban. This signals that continued activism and advocacy is needed to ensure progress towards a universal right to withdraw consent to continuing an unwanted pregnancy for everyone capable of gestation.

Note

1 I would like to thank Carla Ferstman for her insights on this point.

References

Caselaw

Roe v. Wade, 410 U.S. 113 (1973)
Dobbs v. Jackson Women's Health Organization, 19 U.S. 1392 (2022)

UN Commentary

UN Human Rights Committee, General Comment 8 (1982)
Committee on the Elimination of Discrimination Against Women, General Recommendation 19 (1992)

Committee on the Elimination of Discrimination Against Women, General Recommendation 21 (1994)
Committee on Economic, Social, and Cultural Rights (General Comment 22, 2016)
UN Special Rapporteur on the Right to Health (2011) *Report to the General Assembly (criminalisation of sexual and reproductive health)*, A/66/254, 3 August.

Treaties

UN General Assembly, Convention on the Elimination of All Forms of Discrimination Against Women, 18 December 1979, United Nations, Treaty Series, vol. 1249, p.13

References

Altunjan, T. 2021. Historical Perspectives on Reproductive Violence in International Law, in *Reproductive Violence and International Criminal Law*. Springer, 77-136.
Boyd, S. B. 2010. Autonomy for Mothers? Relational Theory and Parenting Apart. *Feminist Legal Studies*, 18, 137–158.
De Proost, M. & Coene, G. 2019. Emancipation on Thin Ice: Women's Autonomy, Reproductive Justice, and Social Egg Freezing. *Tijdschrift Voor Genderstudies*, 22, 357–371.
Denbow, J. M. 2014. Reproductive Autonomy, Counter-Conduct, and the Juridical. *Constellations*, 21, 415–424.
Domaradzki, S., Khvostova, M. & Pupovac, D. 2019. Karel Vasak's Generations of Rights and the Contemporary Human Rights Discourse. *Human Rights Review*, 20, 423–443.
Fine, J. B., Mayall, K. & Sepúlveda, L. 2017. The Role of International Human Rights Norms in the Liberalization of Abortion Laws Globally. *Health and Human Rights Journal*, 19, 69–79.
Forward Together. 2005. A New Vision for Advancing our Movement for Reproductive Rights and Reproductive Justice, 1.
Grey, R. 2017. The ICC's First 'Forced Pregnancy' Case In Historical Perspective. *Journal of International Criminal Justice*, 15.
Hevia, M. & Constantin, A. 2018. Gendered Power Relations and Informed Consent: The I.V.V. Bolivia Case. *Health and Human Rights Journal*, 20, 197–203.
Hewson, B. 2001. Reproductive Autonomy and the Ethics of Abortion. *Journal of Medical Ethics*, 27, 10–14.
Johnston, J. & Zacharias, R. L. 2017. The Future of Reproductive Autonomy. *Hastings Centre Report*. Dec. 47 (Suppl 3), S6–S11.
Laufer-Ukeles, P. 2011. Reproductive Choices and Informed Consent: Fetal Interests, Women's Identity, and Relational Autonomy. *American Journal of Law & Medicine*, 37, 567–623.
Lee, J. 2022. The Limitations of Liberal Reproductive Autonomy. *Medicine, Health Care and Philosophy*, 25.
Lee, M. M. 2000. Defining the Agenda: A New Struggle for African-American Women in the Fight for Reproductive Self-Determination. *Washington and Lee Race and Ethnic Ancestry Law Journal*, 6, 87–102.
London, S. 2011. Reproductive Justice: Developing a Lawyering Model. *Berkeley Journal of African-American Law & Policy*, 13, 71–102.
McCleod, C. 2009. Rich Discussion About Reproductive Autonomy. *Bioethics*, 23, Ii–Iii.

Palacios Zuloaga, P. 2021. Pushing Past the Tipping Point: Can the Inter-American System Accommodate Abortion Rights?. *Human Rights Law Review*, 21, 899–934.

Pereira, R. 2015. Government-Sponsored Population Policies and Indigenous Peoples: Challenges for International Human Rights Law. *Netherlands Quarterly of Human Rights*, 33, 437–482.

Roberts, D. 2015. Reproductive Justice, Not Just Rights. *Dissent*, 62, 79–82.

Ross, L. J. & Solinger, R. 2017. *Reproductive Justice: An Introduction*. University of California Press.

Sherwin, S. 1998. *The Politics of Women's Health: Exploring Agency and Autonomy*. Philadelphia: Temple University Press.

Sjöholm, M. 2017. *Gender-Sensitive Norm Interpretation by Regional Human Rights Law Systems*. Leiden: Brill.

UN Women. 2022 . https://news.un.org/en/story/2022/09/1126901#:~:text=Women%20are%20concentrated%20in%20lower,more%20unpaid%20work%20than%20men.

World Inequality Report. 2022. Executive Summary, 13. https://wir2022.wid.world/www-site/uploads/2022/01/Summary_WorldInequalityReport2022_English.pdf

10

UNLEARNING AGREEMENT

Imagining the Law without Consent[1]

Patricia Palacios Zuloaga

When thinking about how to open conversations with my students about important legal issues, I often find it useful to go back to the beginning, to the place where I first became acquainted with the law. As a result, I find that I often write about law school. I went to a good law school and, in general, I find that my legal education was entirely adequate, in the sense that I graduated knowing all the things that a law graduate was supposed to know at that time. I am many years and many miles removed from my law school, but much of what I learned there still plays a part in how I approach the law today. While the law has changed as I have grown older and moved around the world, the building blocks that make sense of it have largely stayed the same. Concepts like equality, legal certainty, good faith, and *res judicata* come up every day in my work and most of the time what I learned about them thirty years ago is useful to me in untangling the legal issues that occupy my work today.

Having said that, my legal education was not particularly critical. We were taught to learn the law and to understand how the law worked; we were not generally encouraged to question it. All my efforts to challenge my understandings of the law came later and were motivated by my specialisation in women's rights, which requires me to understand how the law is designed and operates to perpetuate the oppression of women. Part of this exercise in challenging what I had learnt involved asking myself about the central role that will plays in law and about how will is operationalised through consent, when will and consent are not synonymous. In trying to understand why consent is so often used as a stand-in for will, I recalled the uneasy feeling that I had as a law student every time we studied consent, which I wasn't able to articulate until I allowed myself to become more critical of the law: that the distance between will and consent is broader the farther you are from power.

DOI: 10.4324/9781003358756-14

When I was asked to contribute a chapter to this publication on consent, I decided to write about the ways in which I learned consent in law school in order to graduate and why I had to unlearn it in order to teach women's rights. In the following pages I will map out my legal education in consent by recalling the courses I took at law school in Chile that helped construct this notion of consent in the service of will. I will then explain why a focus on women's rights forced me to re-evaluate my law school education. I will also suggest that it may well be important to unlearn consent in other areas of law too, despite the supposed risk of chaos that might ensue.

First Year: Introduction to Law

My first lesson in consent came on my first day of law school. I studied in a civil law country[2] that considered it appropriate to define the law *in the law*. Article 1 of my onionskin Civil Code proclaimed that: "The law is a declaration of the sovereign will which, in the manner prescribed by the Constitution, orders, prohibits or permits"[3]. This article introduced me to the legal understanding of will for the first time. Will – in this case sovereign will – meant what the sovereign wanted. We were a constitutional democracy at the time, so the sovereign was all of us. The law then, was a declaration of what all of us wanted.

This is, of course, not true. I will come back to sovereigns later but, in a democracy, laws are made by representatives that are chosen in elections. In the best case, the law reflects the will of the congressperson or member of parliament that I voted for, who is presumed to act on behalf of their constituents. In the worst case, my preferred candidate loses the election, and their opponent is still presumed to act on my behalf. My will regarding the content of the law rarely matters other than in the case of referendums or plebiscites, which ask voters specific questions regarding the proposed content of the law, and which are generally reserved for the most important matters.[4] In the end, will takes shape in the manifestos of political parties and electoral campaign pledges. You vote for the candidate that promises to approach the issues that you care most about in a way that broadly reflects your wishes. You might win, you might lose; the law still binds, whether you like its content or not. None of this is immediately evident in the neatly packaged definition of Article 1 above.

My first lesson about the will of the people was that it is a fiction. The caveat here is that the fiction is necessary. My professor told us that representative democracy was descended from the Athenian Greeks, who would vote on everything in person. He explained that, as society became larger, representatives were necessary to get things done, but the principle was the same. I wrote this down and the class moved on. But it's not the same and for that matter, in exalting the democratic virtues of Athens, my professor did not make much of the fact that women, slaves, and foreign residents were not allowed to vote.

Over the course of my first year, I began to understand that will is tremendously important for the law. It is a bedrock of our understanding of the content and validity of many areas of the law and discovering the shape of that will is what motivates many legal conflicts. Will is sought and described often in different ways and in different parts of the law; sometimes will must be expressed in specific ways, at other times it is presumed. The meaning of will shifts across the law: sometimes it reflects a person's desire, as in how their assets will be distributed after their death; at other times it merely reflects the ability to choose the least bad option. Sometimes, as in the case of Article 1 of the Chilean Civil Code, the presumption of will bears no resemblance to desire and is irrefutable.

First Year: Contract Law

That same year we moved from obligations imposed by the law to obligations we made for ourselves through contracts. We all enter into contracts often, perhaps several times in a day. Every time we agree with someone else about the transfer of property or the provision of a service, we make and fulfil a contract. My professor's example involved us taking the bus to class that day. The bus driver took our money and in exchange allowed us onto the bus and then drove the bus to our university; we both got what we wanted out of the contract. So, contract law is a vehicle for will to be realised and will is an integral part of contracts. Without the expressed will of both parties, there is no contract. I wrote that down too. I didn't like buses though. At the time, the bus system in Santiago was unregulated and bus drivers competed for customers and revenue by using illegal polluting fuels and racing each other to reach passengers at bus stops. They would treat students poorly as we paid a lower fare. The truth is I would rather not have taken the bus, but that was the only way to get to class and I needed to be in class, or I would fail my course.

I was learning that language is important. In contract law we don't talk about "will" or "desire" or "want", we talk about "agreement", and we talk about "consent".[5] In contract law I began to understand that there can be a gulf between what we want and what we agree to. While the textbook version of contracts sees two equal parties satisfy their needs by negotiating the terms of a trade, in real life it's all about the choices that are available to us. In other words: in theory the bus driver and I were equally free to decide if we entered into the contract and to negotiate the terms of that contract. This is another fiction. In reality, the bus driver would not negotiate their fee and I needed to get to class, or the consequences would have been dire, so I was willing to put up with the poor service. I *chose* the poor service; I agreed to it.

Agreement is not the same as will. When contracts are disputed, courts do not look for evidence of what the parties wanted, they look for evidence of what parties agreed to and whether they were free to agree.

The freedom to agree is vitiated by duress where one party causes or takes advantage of an illegitimate pressure on the other that removes their freedom to consent.[6] The question then becomes: what constitutes illegitimate pressure?

Textbooks refer to examples where hypothetical people agree to contracts at gunpoint.[7] But what about limited options?[8] It was too far to walk, and I didn't have a car. I still had a choice: I could have chosen not to take the bus and accepted that by missing class I would fail my degree. Does the existence of this choice to not attend class and therefore fail, make my contract with the bus driver fair? Most legislations have rules that attempt to limit the most egregiously unfair parts of a contract, subjecting them to a test of reasonableness, but these exceptions to contractual freedom don't address the fact that in unequal societies most contracts involve unequal bargaining.[9] I should point out that there are many examples of people entering into contracts in situations far more dire than mine. Think, for example, of the high price of personal protective equipment (PPE) in the early months of the Covid-19 pandemic, which was explained by reference to supply and demand in a healthy capitalist economic system. Not buying PPE at extremely high prices was undeniably a choice for governments and individuals, but was the choice fair? And does it matter to the law? I'll come back to this when I refer to sex.

To be clear though, I have been talking about sex all along. But let's move on.

Second Year: Public International Law

New year, new professor. I learned that state sovereignty was so-called because modern states are the heirs of kings and queens. There was no power above the king – *except God*, my professor was quick to point out – so international law almost always required state consent to create binding obligations. Unlike me, living under the fictional will of Article 1 of the Civil Code, states generally have to agree to international law in order to be bound by it. No-one tells the king what to do.

This idea is codified in Article 38(1) of the Statute of the International Court of Justice which tells the Court that when deciding on disputes between states, it should apply:

1. international conventions containing rules expressly recognised by the contesting states;
2. international custom as evidence of a general practice accepted as law and;
3. the general principles of law recognised by civilised nations.[10]

As a subsidiary source, should the previous three not be enough to clarify the matter, the Court can turn to judicial decisions and the teaching of the most qualified scholars.[11] In practice, the vast majority of law is found in the first two sources: treaties and custom.

Treaties are agreements made between states. They involve states coming together and negotiating an agreement and then expressing their consent to be obligated by that agreement through a formal procedure.[12] For a law student, it looks a lot like a contract; two equal kings with equal amounts of freedom come together to negotiate a deal that satisfies both of their needs. Sovereign equality is a bedrock principle of international law and is enshrined in the Charter of the United Nations.[13] Understanding that modern states are all equal and equally free to negotiate treaties is key to understanding international law. Having said that, I was studying law in a global south developing country, so for me treaty law looked a lot like my bus ride contract: one party with greater needs and less choices accepts a poor offer from a much more powerful counterpart.[14] I didn't ask the professor if this was fair; I didn't reflect on the tight feeling in the pit of my stomach that my increasing concern with fairness was creating. I wrote it down and we moved on.

Custom in international law is also based on state consent. There are two elements that make up international custom: first, a practice, something that states do repeatedly; second, the conviction that the practice is required by law.[15] Lawyers call this belief *opinio juris sive necessitatis*, which is often shortened to *opinio juris*. So, it's not enough to repeat a behaviour, a state must also believe the behaviour is required by law. Proving a repeated practice is relatively easy but proving *opinio juris* is tricky. For one thing, states are collective entities incapable of thought or belief. For another, even if states were human, proving thought processes in court is an incredibly difficult thing, as I would learn the following year in criminal law. States know, however, that while proving belief is difficult, proving a lack of consent to custom is a lot easier if you object to it. Here is where consent features prominently in custom: states that do not want to be bound by emerging customary law are expected to persistently object to it.[16] When required to comply with a rule formed through custom, states that can prove that they persistently objected to the practice can hold that they are exempt from the rule.[17] States that do not want the practice to become law and bind them must make their objection clear to others. Because no-one can force the king to do anything, "[t]he persistent objector doctrine is needed to safeguard non-consenting State's sovereign equality".[18]

Before I move on there are a couple more things to note about how I learnt about consent in international law. First, the third source of international law are the general principles of law recognised by civilised nations. Not just any general principles, but only those acknowledged by *civilised* nations.[19] So, the understandings of the law in nations that are not deemed civilised do not rise to the strength of law. This requirement of civility made me uncomfortable because who gets to decide who is civilised and who is not? Surely only the civilised would be able to tell. The professor, perhaps sensing the discomfort in the room, told us not to worry; Chileans were undoubtedly civilised. We moved on.

Second, some rules are too important to require consent. Peremptory rules of international law, also called *jus cogens*, do not allow states to derogate from them. They are defined as norms "accepted and recognized by the international community of States as a whole as a norm from which no derogation is permitted".[20] This is all well and good until we have to determine which rules have reached the level of peremptory. Here, state consensus, a close cousin of state consent, steps in to help. It is generally understood that the prohibitions of genocide, slavery, racial discrimination and torture are *jus cogens* because all or almost all states consider them to be. So, while states cannot argue a lack of consent to get out of abiding by the rule, the inclusion of the rule in the peremptory group happens via majority consent.[21] This may explain why the prohibition of racial discrimination is *jus cogens* while the prohibition of sex discrimination is not[22].

All of this painted a compelling picture of states' understanding of consent as central to their understanding of their place within the international community. Consent is the basis of international rules because states are sovereign. States are careful to express their consent and the absence of their consent in clear ways, lest they be presumed to consent when they do not actually consent. While all states are theoretically free and equal, only the understanding of civilised states is sophisticated enough to create law.

By this point in my legal education, that tight feeling was getting worse, and I was concerned about what would happen when they started teaching us about sex.

Fourth Year: Criminal Law

In my third year of law school I took a class on the general principles of criminal law, which was followed, in fourth year, by a class on individual crimes. It was in this class that I finally learned how consent was relevant to sex. Or rather, how it wasn't.

When I studied the crime of rape, Article 361 of the Chilean Penal Code established that rape was: "lying with [a] woman in any of the following cases:

1. When force or intimidation is used.
2. When the woman is deprived of reason or her senses, by any cause.
3. When she is under twelve years of age, even when neither of the circumstances expressed in the first two numbers occur".[23]

Two years later, the code was amended to include men as possible victims, and rape became "vaginal, anal or oral carnal access of a person over twelve years of age in any of the following cases:

1. When force or intimidation is used.
2. When the victim is deprived of their senses or when advantage is taken of their inability to resist.
3. When the derangement or mental illness of the victim is abused".[24]

A few years after I graduated the age of consent was raised to fourteen[25] and the victim's inability to resist was reframed as an inability to object.[26]

Even today, after several efforts to patch up its faults, the law doesn't talk about consent explicitly. It does, however, list situations that vitiate consent:

force, intimidation, senselessness, derangement, mental illness. I knew about these impediments to consent from contract law; the contract signed with a gun to my head easily morphed into sex with a gun to my head. The contract would be invalid, and the sex would be rape.

In contrast, UK law states that "[a] person (A) commits rape if:

a   he intentionally penetrates the vagina, anus or mouth of another person (B) with his penis,
b   B does not consent to the penetration, and
c   A does not reasonably believe that B consents.[27]

The differences are stark; in Chile today, anyone can commit rape whereas in the UK only a person with a penis can be a rapist. In Chile the age of consent is fourteen but interestingly, consent itself does not figure in the definition of rape. Chilean law seems to fixate on duress, or force, whereas consent is central to UK law.

You could reasonably understand that consent is present in the Chilean definition, because the possible scenarios that turn sex into rape are all situations where consent is vitiated but it's not that simple. The law seems to require that the victim resist unwanted sex. Under force or intimidation, the victim cannot resist, or their resistance is overpowered; if they are deprived of their senses or otherwise incapacitated, they are unable to resist; if they are deranged or their mental illness is abused, they don't resist whereas they would have (should have) resisted if they were not. The evidentiary questions therefore became: was the victim able to resist sex and did the victim resist sex? If the resistance or an inability to resist was not proven, rape turned back into sex. Even when the term "resist" was amended to "object" in 2010, the victim was still required to *do something* to stop the sex/rape. But what happens when a woman who is mentally healthy does not want to have sex and does not resist/object to sex? If no force or intimidation is used, the answer is that sex would happen, not rape.

Under Chilean criminal law, sex is constructed much like a contract or the creation of international law. Equal parties come together and negotiate sex. All parties have the same amount of power so what is important is agreement. If agreement to sex does not exist, the party that does not want to have sex is expected to object (formerly resist). As a law student, all of this made sense because it all fit together with what I had already learned about will in contract law and public international law. At the same time however, I understood that much like most contracts are not celebrated between equals and most international law is not created among equals, most sex does not happen between equals either. And the understanding of sex isn't the same among people who are not equal.

The UK definition of rape does not refer to force and instead relies on the absence of consent. This consent is understood in much the same way as agreement in contract law; the law does not require that people desire sex, merely that they consent to it. Crucially though, the role of consent does not end there; under UK law, the perpetrator must not reasonably believe that the victim consents (this psychological element is called *mens rea* in criminal law). As sex most often takes place without witnesses, when allegations of rape are made and contested, criminal courts must determine beyond a reasonable doubt (a) if sex took place, (b) if the alleged victim consented and (c) if the alleged perpetrator reasonably believed that the alleged victim consented. None of these requirements are easy to prove, and the process through which courts attempt to discover consent is very often so traumatic that victims do not report rapes and many of those that do, withdraw from the process.[28] Furthermore, prosecutors' inability to prove the absence of consent beyond a reasonable doubt, and pressures to improve conviction rates, often lead them to drop prosecutions.[29]

The Chilean definition of rape that I learned about in law school (an amended version of which remains law today), in opting to forgo the requirement to prove consent, is easier to prosecute as a conviction requires evidence of force or intimidation or the victim's inability to resist/object. But the supposed trade-off for covering far fewer cases of rape than those covered by a consent-based definition (that those far fewer cases are easier to prove) does not necessarily result in higher conviction rates. In a consent-based system the cases of rape where consent is absent through force, intimidation and incapacity are also easier to prove and would also presumably be prosecuted with greater ease than those where consent is simply not present.

Much like my education in contract law did not help me to understand fairness in the exchange of goods and services and my education in international law did not help me to understand fairness in international relations, my education in criminal law did not help me to understand fairness in sex. I understood violence and I understood my role as a potential victim, but law school did not help me to understand the gulf that existed between rape – which was the only sex the law was interested in – and desired sex – which was the only sex that was socially acceptable. The *Other Sex*, which did not fit neatly into either category gave me pause. For example, during the time that I was studying law, my hairdresser was sleeping with a married man who paid the rent on her hair salon. It wasn't love, she said, but rather that they had an agreement. The agreement worked for her, she told me with a shrug; they both got what they wanted out of it. I thought: that's more than I can say about my bus ride contract.

Women and the Law: The Process of Unlearning

I studied law for five years and I studied for the bar for another full year. Almost all of the law that I studied was created by powerful men and almost all of my law professors were powerful men. They made and taught the law that made sense to them, according to their own experiences.[30] The fact that I was not encouraged to question the content of the law meant that, for all of my discomfort with what I learned, my understanding of the law was the understanding that lawmakers and my professors had, an understanding that was built on fictions of equality and agreement.[31] These lawmakers and professors were not generally treated unfairly by the law (or by bus drivers or by sexual partners), so any concerns about fairness were brushed away by an underlying concern with practicality. It would not be practical to allow everyone to vote on every issue like they did in Athens. It would not be practical if every contract had to be properly negotiated. It would not be practical to ask if poorer states were getting the best possible conditions in treaties signed with rich states or if it was fair to make them abide by custom created by and for powerful states. It would not be practical to examine the conditions under which people had sex or to ask whether sex is fair or not.

I dutifully learned the law and did not ask questions, until I began to study women's rights. There was no course on women's rights at my law school when I studied there, but there was a brilliant human rights lawyer on staff who tutored a small group of women law students on human rights law, outside of hours. It was in these sessions where I turned the discomfort that I had felt for years into an understanding of the law that acknowledged the power that was coded into it. I began to read feminist theory, I came to understand that judges and lawmakers were not the infallible monoliths that I had understood them to be but rather people, influenced by their own experiences. I was encouraged, for the first time, to challenge them and the law that they made. I was allowed, for the first time, to imagine a different law, a better one. One that didn't feel so unfair.

That discomfort with the law blossomed into a career. I became a law teacher myself and today I teach on a variety of law courses, including a course on women's rights. I am twenty-five years removed from my law school classroom but here is what I understand about the Chilean crime of rape that I studied: sex happens unless you resist it. This construction of rape as a crime dependent on the resistance of the victim is understandable if you understand that the people that wrote the law on rape were overwhelmingly men. Those men that I elected (or did not elect) to carry out my sovereign will, understood that if someone wants you to do something that you don't want to do, you should resist. They would resist. It's natural to resist. Much like international custom, if a person doesn't resist – and resist in a clear and effective way – it's ok to presume that they wanted the unwanted thing to happen, or at least that they didn't mind enough to bear the consequences of resistance.

Except, this requirement of resistance does not appear in the same way with regards to other crimes. There is no requirement to resist theft[32] or assault[33] or homicide.[34] That is because elite male lawmakers didn't think it reasonable to ever want to be the victim of theft, assault or homicide. Sex, on the other hand, is understood to be a good thing, unless it is rape.

The lawmakers that codify consent-based definitions of rape are mostly concerned with agreement in a contractual sense. Much like in contract law, desire is not relevant, only agreement is relevant. In the absence of duress, it doesn't matter why women like my hairdresser consented, what matters is that she consented.

Given that most sex happens in private and that all cases of rape that come to court involve opposing versions of the circumstances of that sex, judges and juries search for evidence of consent wherever they can find it. So, consent is inferred by what women were wearing, where they were, whether they had ever consented to sex before, whether they drank alcohol, whether they were in a relationship with the alleged rapist. In some legislations, wives are thought to give perpetual consent to their husbands[35] and sex workers have been presumed to consent to any sex.[36] In those legislations both are, legally speaking, unrapable. In some legislations, marriage between the victim and the perpetrator erases the charge of rape.[37]

For some scholars, this ability to consent, even in adverse circumstances is essential to understanding women as fully equal members of society.[38] There are many reasons women have sex; some of those reasons have little or nothing to do with sexual desire. Agreeing to sex in this sense, is a choice available to women to achieve the ends that they wish to achieve, even when the options available to them are limited.

For other scholars, the reality of sex for many women makes the reliance on consent in a traditionally contractual sense to build the crime of rape inappropriate. For those scholars, what matters is the use of coercion to compel sex.[39] The shape of that coercion varies across many different instances of sex from physical force, threats and intimidation on the part of the perpetrator to economic pressure, or societal pressure to engage in sex. Some theorists have gone as far as to hold that because sexism is ubiquitous in society, women are almost never in an equal enough position to meaningfully consent to sex. In this view, sex must be freely agreed between equals and as women suffer structural oppression, they can almost never truly consent.[40]

For years, some feminists attempted to reconceptualise rape from being a crime based on the absence of consent to a crime based on the presence of coercion. This approach had the advantage of doing away with the focus on the behaviour of the victim as a proxy for their willingness to engage in sex and switching instead to a focus on the perpetrator and whether they knew, or should have known, that the circumstances in which the sex took place were coercive.

When I teach this idea of coercion as the important factor in rape, I refer to the case of *Akayesu*, ruled on by the International Criminal Tribunal for Rwanda in 1998.[41] Akayesu, the mayor of the town of Taba, was charged, among other things, with rape and sexual violence in the context of the Rwandan genocide. His defence to the charges was that no rapes had taken place.[42] The Court did well to present the facts of the case in such a way as to make it very clear that the rapes took place in an environment of extreme violence that was clear to everyone involved. Some victims had taken refuge in municipal buildings so that Akayesu could protect them from the genocide.[43] All over the area, there were dead bodies of murdered Tutsis.[44] This was the context in which the rapes took place. In its ruling, rather than attempt to determine whether consent was given and whether that consent was vitiated by duress, the court saw fit to redefine rape as: "a physical invasion of a sexual nature, committed on a person under circumstances which are coercive".[45] Similarly, it redefined sexual violence as "any act of a sexual nature which is committed on a person under circumstances which are coercive".[46]

In essence, what the Court was saying in *Akayesu* is that, in coercive circumstances, the law should not be interested in the presence or absence of consent. Or: even if the victim consented, the sex was still illegal. This was a ground-breaking ruling that took an idea from feminist theory and made it law. However, the Rwandan ruling was not followed widely and, most relevantly, it was not followed by the International Criminal Tribunal for the Ex-Yugoslavia, which – three years after *Akayesu* – also dealt with gendered crimes within the context of a genocide. In the *Foča* case where women were forced into rape camps, the ICTY Trial Chamber found that there was rape, but that rape was a crime based around the absence of consent to sex. It was, however, careful to specify that "[c]onsent for this purpose must be consent given voluntarily, as a result of the victim's free will, assessed in the context of the surrounding circumstances"[47] which suggests that the circumstances in which the consent is given are at least relevant.

On appeal, the ICTY Appeals Chamber clarified that the focus on consent was important to further an understanding that rape is a crime against sexual autonomy, and that it does not require force. It held that

> [a] narrow focus on force or threat of force could permit perpetrators to evade liability for sexual activity to which the other party had not consented by taking advantage of coercive circumstances without relying on physical force.[48]

It followed with:

> [...] the circumstances giving rise to the instant appeal and that prevail in most cases charged as either war crimes or crimes against humanity will be almost universally coercive. That is to say, true consent will not be possible.[49]

So, coercion figures in both understandings of rape, either as the standalone requirement or as a way to vitiate consent. The difference between both approaches can be boiled down to whether judges and lawmakers believe that it is possible to consent to sex in extremely coercive circumstances. The *Akayesu* Court held that in the context of genocidal violence, no consent is possible. The *Foča* Court on the other hand, held that consent – while very rare – is still technically possible and relevant to determining whether sex is rape, even when the sex happens in a rape camp.

The ICTR and the ICTY were precursors to the International Criminal Court which, according to its Elements of Crimes, understands rape as a bodily invasion committed by force, or by threat of force or coercion, such as that caused by fear of violence, duress, detention, psychological oppression or abuse of power, against such person or another person, or by taking advantage of a coercive environment, or the invasion was committed against a person incapable of giving genuine consent.[50]

This mixture of coercion and consent is typical of newer understandings of sexual violence where drafters are eager to avoid the dichotomy and include as many cases as possible.[51] Consent removes the requirement of force and coercion vitiates "genuine" consent.

In class, my students generally warm to the idea of coercion as a more appropriate marker for rape. Pedagogically, *Akayesu* is a clear example of the futility of looking for consent in a context of overwhelming coercion – sex with a gun to your head – so the alternate framing makes sense to them, it seems fairer. As class progresses, however, I see them struggle with the question of whether we can use coercion domestically in the same way for the rapes that they are more familiar with, those that happen outside of genocide and that populate their experiences. Coercion is a spectrum, so the biggest question that they ask themselves is what degree of coercion is necessary to make bad sex rape.

As the women's rights course progresses and we move from violence against women to sexual and reproductive rights, consent rears its head once more, this time in the fact that in many states around the world women cannot consent to abortions and do not consent to sterilisations. So, while consent as an expression of [sovereign] will is a necessary element of sex, it is irrelevant to pregnancy. Women are not sovereigns of their own pregnant bodies.

Looking back, in the same criminal law class where I learned to resist rape, I also learned that if my pregnancy were to threaten my life, I could do nothing to save myself without risking prison.[52] At the same time, around the world, doctors were sterilising women from oppressed groups without their consent as a form of population control.[53] Some years later, a friend of mine who lived with bipolar disorder sought a sterilisation as she very much wanted to avoid pregnancy and could not be confident that she would always be able to use contraception effectively. Her request was denied. Doctors told her that she was too young, that she might change her mind, they did not trust her ability to make such a grave decision for herself. In some legislations around the world, it is common for doctors to require the consent of husbands to sterilise their wives.[54] Recall the unrapable nature of wives; here too wives lack the sovereignty to defy their husbands' wishes.

Coercion seems relevant here too. If women do not control the conditions of the sex that they engage in, removing their ability to change the stakes and therefore forcing them to bear the consequences of that sex is unfair. Furthermore, pregnancy involves hardship for those who do not want to be pregnant. Physical hardship as well as psychological, economic, and social hardships are borne by women and other pregnant people who are denied reproductive healthcare such as abortion and sterilisation. Forcing them to continue pregnancies that harm them is coercive. It's not fair.

Law School Revisited

Even now, some twenty years after I graduated from law school, I find that I still care about fairness; I wonder if that is because of my legal education or in spite of it. On the one hand, concepts such as equality, certainty and justice were pillars of how I was told the law was constructed. On the other, the ability of concepts like will, agreement and consent to achieve those ideals was so often fictional. We kept being told that consent was important when the reality was that it wasn't, or at least what passed as consent for the law wasn't what it should have been; it wasn't what we wanted.

The nuance here is that perhaps consent isn't totally irrelevant for the law, maybe it just wasn't relevant for people like me. I lived in a developing nation, I paid a student bus fare, I had to resist unwanted sex, I had to give birth. What was important seemed to be the consent of the rich nations we traded with, the bus driver, the men who wanted to have sex with me, the lawmakers who wanted me to give birth. In law we were all equal to agree to what we wanted. In life it was the will of the powerful that gave shape to agreement; the rest of us agreed to the least bad option if we were able to agree at all.

Feminist theory afforded us an alternative to rape law that made sense to many people who experience rape. It said that relying on agreement when circumstances are coercive is not fair. It also said that those who create or take advantage of coercive circumstances should not be able to rely on the agreement of their victims to make their sex legal. While we can debate about where on the spectrum of coercion we place the limit that differentiates sex from rape, the idea that coercion is important – either standalone or as a vitiator of consent – seems truer and fairer than a sole focus on contractual consent or a lack of resistance.

To be clear, we are no longer talking about sex.

It took me years to come to this understanding and I am now working my way backwards through my legal education trying to pinpoint all the places where replacing consent with coercion feels fairer.

In practice, agreement, as it is understood in law, often preserves and reinforces pre-existing power dynamics. It is thus central to patriarchy, capitalism and neo-colonialism, among other power structures. If we care about coercion in sex, why not care about it with regards to every other place where we agree under circumstances that are unfair, where we pick the least bad option to avoid a worse fate? Had I ever been brave enough to ask that question in law school I imagine that my professors would have answered that requiring meaningful fairness in contracts, international law or indeed in any other area of law would be impractical. It would threaten legal certainty and make transactions unbearably slow and complicated. If we had to ensure that every contract was fair, the entire system of contracts would grind to a halt, and we could never get anything done. In fact, agreement is so central to so many areas of the law that if we were to question it or replace it – they would say – the result would be chaos.

I think this might be true, life would be more complicated if we replaced a focus on consent with a focus on coercion. It's good to remember though, that I was also told that it would be impractical to examine the circumstances in which every instance of sex is carried out and yet the inclusion of coercion in the examination of rape cases – either standalone or as a vitiator of consent – hasn't been the downfall of sex. Where coercion is relevant, the law requires those with power to consider the circumstances and think about what is fair. This would mean that sometimes those with power would not get what they want. I wonder if this is what we mean when we say that life would be more complicated: that it would force those used to exercising power over others to not abuse that power.

Notes

1 I would like to thank Geoff Gilbert, Emily Jones, and Laurie James-Hawkins for their helpful comments in the drafting of this chapter. All errors herein remain my own.

2 Civil law systems derive from Roman law and are characterised by a preponderance of written legislation, organised into Codes. G Slapper and D Kelly, *The English Legal System* (18th edn, Routledge, 2017) 4.

3 Chilean Civil Code of 1855 art. 1. My translation.

4 Unless you vote in Switzerland. Needless to say, if my position is defeated in a referendum, I am still bound by the law that comes as a result of it.

5 Ewan McKendrick, *Contract Law: Text, Cases and Materials* (10th edn, OUP 2022) 4.

6 Ibid. chapter 18.

7 Ibid. 609; Stephen Smith, "Contracting Under Pressure: A Theory of Duress" (1997) 56(2) *Cambridge Law Journal*, 343.

8 Máiréad Enright, "Contract Law" in Rosemary Auchmuty (ed.), *Great Debates in Gender and Law* (Palgrave 2018) 1–8.

9 E.g., in the UK, the Unfair Contract Terms Act of 1977; in Chile, Title XX of the Civil Code of 1855 covers nullity and termination of contracts.

10 United Nations, *Statute of the International Court of Justice*, 18 April 1946, art. 38.1.a-c.

11 Ibid. art. 38.1.d.

12 United Nations, *Vienna Convention on the Law of Treaties*, 23 May 1969, United Nations, Treaty Series, vol. 1155, art. 2(a).

13 United Nations, *Charter of the United Nations*, 24 October 1945, 1 UNTS XVI, art. 2.1.

14 See Matthew Craven, "What Happened to Unequal Treaties? The Continuities of Informal Empire", (2005) 74 *Nordic Journal of International Law* 335. Also, Emily Jones states: "in proclaiming sovereign equality and state consent, international lawyers apply false, idealised concepts of equality to an unequal reality. The nature of state consent can clearly be questioned, with many treaties being signed under some form of implicit duress, often reflecting global inequalities. Therefore, while states may be formally equal, all sovereign, and all consenting parties in the making of international law, it is evident that this is a legal fiction". Emily Jones, *Feminist Theory and International Law: Posthuman Perspectives* (Routledge 2023) 32. Ann

Orford points out that the sovereign equality regime enshrined in the UN Charter can also be understood as a tool to resist imperialism, although that resistance becomes complicated when considering the UN and its Security Council as imperialistic themselves. Ann Orford, "The Gift of Formalism", (2004) 15 *EJIL* 179, 188.

15 Hugh Thirlway, "The Sources of International Law" in Malcolm Evans (ed.) *International Law* (4ᵗʰ edn, OUP 2014) 98. Antonio Cassese, *International Law* (2ⁿᵈ edn, OUP 2005) 157.

16 *Anglo-Norwegian Fisheries, United Kingdom v. Norway*, I.C.J. Reports 1951, 116, 131.

17 James Crawford, *Brownlie's Principles of Public International Law* (8ᵗʰ edn, OUP 2012) 28. See also, in general, James Green, *The Persistent Objector Rule in International Law* (OUP, 2016).

18 Martti Koskenniemi, *From Apology to Utopia: The Structure of International Legal Argument* (Cambridge University Press, 2006) 443.

19 United Nations, *Statute of the International Court of Justice*, 18 April 1946, art. 38.1.c.

20 United Nations, *Vienna Convention on the Law of Treaties*, 23 May 1969, United Nations, Treaty Series, vol. 1155, art. 53.

21 Koskenniemi (n. 18) 324.

22 Hilary Charlesworth and Christine Chinkin, "The Gender of Jus Cogens" (1993) 15 *Human Rights Quarterly*, 63.

23 Chilean Penal Code of 1874, art. 361. My translation.

24 Ibid art. 361, as modified by Law 19.617 of 1999. My translation.

25 Law 19.927 of 2004, art. 1.5.

26 Law 20.480 of 2010, art. 1.2.

27 UK Sexual Offences Act 2003, Section 1.

28 United Nations, Human Rights Council, Report of the Special Rapporteur on Violence against Women, its Causes and Consequences: Dubravka Šimonović, "Rape as a Grave, Systematic and Widespread Human Rights Violation, a Crime and a Manifestation of Gender-based Violence against Women and Girls, and its Prevention", A/HRC/47/26 (2021) para. 98. Jacqueline Wheatcroft, Graham Wagstaff and Annmarie Moran, "Revictimizing the Victim? How Rape Victims Experience the UK Legal System" (2009) 4 *Victims & Offenders* 265.

29 House of Commons, Home Affairs Committee, Investigation and Prosecution of Rape, Eighth Report of Session 2021–22, 29 March 2022; Kathleen Daly and Brigitte Bouhours, "Rape and Attrition in the Legal Process: A Comparative Analysis of Five Countries", (2010) 39 *Crime and Justice* 565; BBC News, "Why do so Few Rape Cases go to Court?", 27 May 2022; BBC News, "Hidden Rape Conviction Target Revealed", 13 November 2019.

30 Martha Minow, *Making All the Difference: Inclusion, Exclusion, and American Law* (Cornell University Press, 1990) 50–74.

31 Re. the male perspective in law see: Catharine MacKinnon, *Towards a Feminist Theory of the State* (Harvard University Press 1989) 161–163, 169, 237; Hilary Charlesworth, Christine Chinkin and Shelley Wright, "Feminist Approaches to International Law", (1991) 85 *American Journal of International Law* 613.

32 Chilean Penal Code (n 23) states in art. 432 that: "[w]hoever, without the will of the owner and with the intention of profiting, appropriates an asset belonging to someone else using violence or intimidation on the body or force on property commits robbery. If violence, intimidation, or force is not present, he commits theft". My translation.

33 Chilean Penal Code (n 23) states in art. 395 that: "[w]hoever injures, beats or physically abuses another, will be punished as responsible for serious injuries". My translation.

34 Chilean Penal Code (n 23) states art. 391 that "[w]hoever kills another…" My translation.

35 United Nations, Report of the Special Rapporteur on Violence against Women (n 28) paras 69–72.

36 Barbara Sullivan, "Rape, Prostitution and Consent", (2007) 40 *The Australian and New Zealand Journal of Criminology* 127.
37 United Nations, Report of the Special Rapporteur on Violence against Women (n. 28) para. 89.
38 For an overview of the discussion surrounding consent and coercion in rape law see Vanessa E. Munro, "From Consent to Coercion: Evaluating International and Domestic Frameworks for the Criminalization of Rape", in Clare McGlynn and Vanessa E. Munro, *Rethinking Rape Law: International and Comparative Perspectives* (Routledge, 2010) 17.
39 See ibid.; MacKinnon, 171–183.
40 R. Morgan, (1980) "Theory and Practice: Pornography and Rape" in L. Lederer (ed.) *Take Back the Night: Women on Pornography* (New York: William Morrow & Co.) 134–135.
41 *The Prosecutor v. Jean-Paul Akayesu (Trial Judgement)*, ICTR-96-4-T, International Criminal Tribunal for Rwanda (ICTR), 2 September 1998.
42 *Akayesu*, paras 446–448.
43 *Akayesu*, indictment para. 12A.
44 *Akayesu*, paras 115–116, 158,
45 *Akayesu*, para. 688.
46 Ibid.
47 *Prosecutor v. Dragoljub Kunarac, Radomir Kovac and Zoran Vukovic (Trial Judgment)*, IT-96-23-T & IT-96-23/1-T, International Criminal Tribunal for the former Yugoslavia (ICTY), 22 February 2001, para. 460.
48 *Prosecutor v. Dragoljub Kunarac, Radomir Kovac and Zoran Vukovic (Appeal Judgment)*, IT-96–23 & IT-96-23/1-A, International Criminal Tribunal for the former Yugoslavia (ICTY), 12 June 2002, para. 129.
49 *Kunarac et al.* (appeal) para. 130.
50 International Criminal Court (ICC), *Elements of Crimes*, 2011, art. 7(1)(g)-1.
51 E.g., United Nations, Human Rights Council, *A Framework for Legislation on Rape*. Report of the Special Rapporteur on Violence against Women, its Causes and Consequences, 15 June 2021, A/HRC/47/26/Add.1, para. 17; Council of Europe, The Council of Europe Convention on Preventing and Combating Violence against Women and Domestic Violence, November 2014, art. 36.2. Both definitions follow the ICTY *Kunarac* Chamber's understanding of consent evaluated in context.
52 Chilean Penal Code (n. 23) art. 344. The total ban on abortion that was in force when I studied law was amended in 2017 to allow for legal abortion in three cases: 1. Where the life of the pregnant person is at risk; 2. Where the foetus will not survive and; 3. Where the pregnancy is the result of rape or incest. Law 21.030 of 2017.
53 E.g., *Maria Mamerita Mestanza v. Peru*, Case 12.191, Inter-Am. Comm. H.R, 22 October 2003; *V.C. v. Slovakia*, Application no. 18968/07, Council of Europe: European Court of Human Rights, 16 June 2009; I.V. v. Bolivia, Preliminary Objections, Merits, Reparations and Costs, Inter-Am. Ct H.R., 30 December 2016.
54 Rebecca Cook, "Spousal Veto Over Family Planning Services" (1987) 77 *American Journal of Public Health* 271; EngenderHealth, *Contraceptive Sterilization: Global Issues and Trends* (2002 EngenderHealth) 91.

11

BIRTHING CONSENT

Supporting Shared Decision Making and Informed Consent in Labour and Childbirth

Laura Pascoe

My first birth did not go as planned. Yes, we had "healthy mom, healthy baby," and for that I was grateful, but I had wanted to give birth vaginally and ended up with a c-section after more than 24 hours of labour. I experienced grief and played out a series of "what-if" questions as I made sense of my experience. And yet I also felt incredibly empowered by my birthing experience. How could this be? Throughout my labour and birth I was surrounded by an incredible birth team who ensured I was an active and informed participant in all decisions. I consented to everything that happened to me, and I always knew I had the choice to tell my providers to pause, wait, or stop what they were doing. Over the course of the bitterly cold January night and day in which I laboured, I felt respected, cared for, and heard, which made a world of difference. I had also learned a fair bit about birth in my years as a birth doula before my own birth. This no doubt helped me understand that while birth may not go to plan, one's consent should be expected for all procedures and there should always conditions be created to support a positive and empowered experience.

I understood, by the time I consented to having a cesarean, how we had gotten there and felt confident that my birth team and I had done everything we could to achieve my goals. Even in those initial weeks postpartum, my birth team—comprised of my midwife, doula, my partner, my father, and my two cats, who were excellent comfort in the hours of labouring at home—continued to hold space for me. I processed grief and gratitude alongside recovering from major surgery and getting to know my tiny new human, and they validated my emotions and experience alongside me (my cats mostly tried to share lap space with said tiny new human, but the purring was comforting).

Research confirms that a birthing person's[1] well-being and sense of control over and involvement in decisions during labour and birth are vital to creating the conditions for a positive birth experience (Villarmea and Kelly, 2020).

DOI: 10.4324/9781003358756-15

Having one's right to provide or withhold informed consent on an ongoing basis is key to this. And indeed, feeling respected, cared for, and heard during labour and childbirth increases the likelihood one will have a positive birth experience, improves health outcomes for birth giver and baby, and contributes to successful parent-baby bonding (Deherder et al., 2022; Moore, 2016; Vedam et al., 2017). In contrast, feeling dismissed and excluded from decisions made in birth, or experiencing coercion and nonconsent during one's birth experience increases the likelihood of experiencing trauma in birth, which can also lead to poor health outcomes for birthing person and baby (Deherder et al., 2022). Informed consent, as discussed throughout this book, is not about a singular moment or form to fill out but an ongoing process and conversation between relevant parties. In the context of birth, it is helpful to use the concept of *shared decision making*. Shared decision making expands on the concept of informed consent by focusing on a collaborative process in which "you and your caregiver discuss the medical risks and benefits of treatment and any possible alternatives" (Simkin et al., 2018: 8) and there is an emphasis on "honoring informed preferences" (Elwyn et al., 2012: 1362).

This chapter explores why consent and shared decision making in labour and childbirth are so important, the potential impacts when consent is not sought or given, and factors that support shared decision making. I offer concrete strategies for birth givers, health providers, partners, and doulas to facilitate shared decision making and ensure ongoing and informed consent for all birth givers. In particular, this chapter provides key guidance and insight into how health providers and doulas can facilitate informed consent to ensure that no matter what the birth experience, birth givers feel respected, cared for, and heard. To get at some of the structural barriers that make shared decision making elusive for many birth givers and often result in a denial of consent, I also discuss the ways that gender and race (really, misogyny and racism) play out in the context of labour and birth. This chapter draws on personal experiences as both a birth doula and birth giver, as well as relevant academic literature on childbirth and midwifery.

Wait – What Is a Doula?

In the context of birth, a doula is trained to provide informational, emotional, physical, and practical support to a birth giver. Birth doula support typically includes prenatal visits to help the birth giver prepare for labour and birth, continuous support throughout labour and birth, and follow up visits postpartum. Doulas are not medically trained and do not carry out clinical tasks such as vaginal exams or monitoring of the baby. Evidence on doula support shows the benefit they provide, including improving birth outcomes, reducing use of unnecessary pain management and interventions, and increasing the likelihood of having a positive birth experience (Dekker, 2019; Pascoe, 2023). Although doulas can be integral to positive and empowered birth experiences and health outcomes and we have evidence to back this, they remain under-utilized and largely invisible in media and larger cultural representations of birth (Horstman et al., 2017).

Why Are Consent and Shared Decision Making in Childbirth so Important?

Shared decision making should be part of all health care decision making, and it is essential to ensuring informed consent. Informed consent is enshrined in various human rights declaration and international guidelines, and shared decision making is outlined in national guidelines such as the National Institute for Health and Care Excellence in the U.K. (National Institute for Health and Care Excellence (NICE), 2022). The term and case for "shared decision making", rooted in law and ethics, has been around since at least the 1990s (Elwyn, 2021) and is well supported by evidence, having been tested in more than 80 randomized controlled trials in healthcare and showing that shared decision making leads to "knowledge gain by patients, more confidence in decisions, [and] more active patient involvement" (Elwyn et al., 2012: 1362).

There are unique needs and realities of shared decision making and ensuring ongoing consent in the context of birth (Villarmea and Kelly, 2020). For one, use of medical interventions in birth continues to rise in many parts of the world, with the risk of a "cascade of interventions" often not sufficiently conveyed to birth givers (Hodnett et al., 2013). Certainly, some pregnancies and births are high risk and/or require intervention, and birth givers have fought for the right to use pain medication as much as they've advocated for the right to give birth without medication or unnecessary intervention. But, as opposed to a chronic illness or disease that *requires* intervention and treatment, birth is a natural and physiological process that does not inherently require outside intervention. And yet labour and birth can, at times, feel as though it is *happening to you*, which raises the bar for why a deeply embodied experience of consent throughout labour and birth is an extraordinarily critical and transformative aspect of birthing. Childbirth is a very personal event that leaves a lasting impression on those who experience it, and it is of profound importance to create the conditions for a positive birthing experience.

Shared decision making is at the core of such conditions, as is informed consent. In their article focused on shared decision making in the context of childbirth, Villarmea and Kelly emphasize that shared decision making "is sometimes incorrectly interpreted as that the decision has to be shared. It is important to remember that what is shared is the process of decision-making, not the decision itself" (2020: 515). Shared decision making includes recognizing when patients do not want to be involved in or responsible for decisions, but that this should not take away their autonomy or ability to have their preferences heard and respected, particularly in the context of childbirth (Villarmea and Kelly, 2020). In the following case example, I offer insight into how a lack of shared decision making and informed consent can impact a birth giver's experience.

> Emeline[2] had had a rough labour. Her contractions had quickly morphed into a seemingly never-ending cascade of contractions, and she was barely able to catch her breath between them, even in early labour. She revised her original birth plan and requested an epidural, grateful to get some rest and gather her energy for the pushing stage. As baby's head got closer to crowning, the monitors showed baby's heartrate was taking longer to recover between contractions. Although baby's heartrate was not yet indicating an emergency, I watched as the obstetrician pick up a pair of surgical scissors and, over the course of three contractions, cut an episiotomy.[3]

I specify this was not an emergency and the episiotomy was not a quick or singular cut to make the point that there were numerous opportunities for the obstetrician to engage in shared decision making that could have ensured Emeline's consent. At the very least, the obstetrician should have explained to Emeline *what he was doing to her body*, and yet at no point he did. Sadly, this is not uncommon (Malvasi et al., 2021). For example, in a US-based qualitative study on informed consent in birth, researchers found that at least one in five birth givers felt that informed consent was absent or inadequate when complications arose and the majority of respondents felt there should be better policies and processes to ensure informed consent during labour and birth (Ely et al., 2022). In Emeline's case, I was a newer doula at the time and too much in shock to ask the obstetrician to explain what was happening and ensure he sought my client's consent (I am now much better prepared). While I wish I had handled this moment better, it was exacerbated by the fact that the obstetrician *never* disclosed the episiotomy to my client. He only told her, hours after her birth, that she had a third degree tear[4] and had required stitches. When I explained to her and her partner the full details upon their request, although Emeline generously offered her obstetrician the benefit of the doubt, she also expressed frustration that her consent was not sought. She was disheartened that her health provider did not deem it a priority to engage in a shared decision making process that would have allowed her the opportunity to give or withhold her consent or, if the episiotomy was absolutely necessary, provide her information about why this was so and an opportunity to ask questions after the fact. She would reiterate these sentiments in follow up postpartum visits when I asked how she was feeling about her birth experience.

Factors that Facilitate Shared Decision Making and Informed Consent

As Emeline's story illustrates, labour and childbirth are not only defined by the events that occur, but the ways in which those events are interacted with and conveyed by present parties. Like so many things, the process of successful shared decision making that ensures the right to give or withhold consent is not as simple as a job aid or step by step process—although these are excellent ways to provide the scaffolding and shared expectations for shared decision making. Rather, it is about relationships. The power dynamics within these relationships can be particularly tricky given the vulnerability of the birth giver and the stakes of such a transformative experience.

Shared decision making expert Glen Elwyn and his colleagues explain that the following three conditions must be in place for the successful implementation of shared decision making that ensures informed consent: the availability of evidence-based information, guidance on weighing the pros and cons of available choices and alternatives, and "a supportive clinical culture that facilitates patient engagement" (2012: 1). Research has also made clear that the interactions between birther and provider have a huge influence on the birther's experience (Ahmed, 2020; Larkin et al., 2017; MirzaeeRabor et al., 2016; Moore, 2016; Reed et al., 2017). Furthermore, a health provider's opinion is often the biggest influencing factor in a birther's decision making (Moore, 2016), which is of particular importance given that the consent-seeking process often involves a provider emphasizing risk factors with little discussion of alternatives or an exploration of the birth givers preferences and priorities (Nicholls et al., 2021). This means the details of how information and options are communicated from provider to birth giver is of critical importance to shared decision making and the birth givers' ability to give (or withhold) informed consent. Elwyn notes that shared decision making must involve "cognitive, emotional, and relational" (2021: 1591) work to mitigate the uneven power dynamics present in the patient-provider relationship. Other research specifies that "small talk, humor, being familiar with each other, using different senses and taking different positions, e.g., standing, sitting, varying distances" are key to creating a trusting bond (Korstjens et al., 2019: 1). Research with midwives and patients of midwives emphasizes the importance of compassion, personal connection, and empathy (Aktas and Pasinlioğlu, 2021; Hallam et al., 2016) alongside an unbiased presentation of risk and benefits as part of ensuring ongoing informed consent. In a study aiming to identify key criteria and professional competencies for ensuring shared decision making in perinatal care with a particular emphasis on seeking input from midwives, the study found that

> Experts agreed that the regular visits during pregnancy offer opportunities to build a relationship, anticipate situations and revisit complex decisions. Professionals need to prepare women antenatally for unexpected, urgent decisions in birth and revisit these decisions postnatally. Open and respectful communication between women and care professionals is essential; information needs to be accurate, evidence-based and understandable to women.
>
> *(Nieuwenhuijze et al., 2014: 1)*

Villarmea and Kelly (2020) specify that outlining options and leaving the rest of decision-making to the birth giver is not shared decision making, and that ensuring informed consent involves prompting the birthing person to participate based on their preferences and in a way that conveys respect for their agency and right to consent. This includes questions such as "How much information would you like?" "Do you have questions" and "Would you like more time?" (2020: 518). In their article on the contributions doulas make to creating the conditions for informed consent, Ford argues that doulas should be considered "'consent workers' who do complex emotional labor to facilitate the consenting voice of their client" (2021: 111) and serve as a critical "bridge" between providers and birth givers.

The scope and impact of trauma—and the need for trauma-informed care—as it relates to birth is another critical component of shared decision making and protecting birth givers' right to consent. Unfortunately, trauma is not well discussed in the literature on shared decision making, although arguably a lack of trauma-informed care limits the reaches of true shared decision making. Many come into pregnancy, labour, and birth with trauma that may impact their experience, such as past experiences of sexual and/or physical violence or those who do not want to be pregnant/giving birth. This is particularly true in places like the U.S. where access to abortion is limited and some are forced to carry unwanted pregnancies to term. Furthermore, traumatic birth experiences are far too common (20–50%), those with mental health challenges being most at risk for birth trauma, followed by those who face obstetric emergencies and neonatal complications (Simpson and Catling, 2016). Trauma-informed care, or the provision of health care that integrates the potential impacts of trauma, should be integrally woven into perinatal care and the ways in which shared decision making is carried out, and yet it often is not. This also includes trauma-informed doula care which is particularly valuable in contexts where trauma-informed care is not incorporated into hospital guidelines. A trusting and transparent relationship between birth giver and their support and health team is a core part of trauma-informed care (and shared decision making) (Mosley and Lanning, 2020).

There is also substantial influential power of how evidence is framed and presented. Research across cognitive and behavioural science has shown that it is often not *what* is said but *how* (Dolan et al., 2011); this absolutely applies to the birth setting. For example, when providers present evidence in ways that underscores fears or pull the "dead baby card"[5] (Villarmea and Kelly, 2020) it can create a decision-making context that is more coercive than shared and emphasize the provider's power and control over the situation. The birth giver is in a much-strengthened position if they have already sought evidence-based information through childbirth education and/or doula support. They will have a more comprehensive understanding of how the evidence is being presented and what questions to ask to get the information they need to give or withhold their consent and make the right decision for themselves.

Before I outline concrete strategies for facilitating shared decision making and ensuring informed consent, I turn to some of the systemic and cultural-level factors, namely misogyny and racism, that often impede the consent giving process and make shared decision making in perinatal care more complicated for many.

Misogyny and Racism in Perinatal Care

The way birth givers are treated and perceived must take into consideration the ways in which women are treated and viewed more generally. Historically, birth was a woman's space, with birth givers supported by female family members and attended to by a trained midwife, which continues to be a female-dominated occupation. When birth became an area of interest for male physicians and later obstetricians, birth givers were increasingly distanced from the more intimate and intuitive experiences of birth and encouraged to give birth in hospitals. One of the consequences of the medicalization of childbirth was that it embedded into the birth experience a patriarchal and hierarchical relationship between patient and provider. Furthermore, rationality has been traditionally (and incorrectly) associated with being a man, and so birth became yet another place where women were assumed incapable of making their own decisions. In some contexts, this meant women were thought to "deserve" the pain of labour and therefore left to suffer; in others (particularly for wealthier white women) women were believed too fragile for labour and were subdued and placated, including through barbaric means such as Twilight Sleep (McCulloch Dip, 2016). Villarmea and Kelly explain:

> Once women were portrayed as less than rational, it became a small step for a woman in labour to be viewed as somehow hyper-feminine/uterus-ruled, and thus lowest of the low in the rationality scale. As such, she is too easily taken (in practice, not by the law) as unable to engage in SDM [shared decision making] processes that lead to consent.
>
> *(Villarmea and Kelly, 2020: 518)*

The legacy of this misogyny in perinatal care and birth means that, sadly, many women experience childbirth as yet another event along the continuum of gendered and sexualized violence (Villarmea and Kelly, 2020). Rates of obstetric violence are troublingly high globally, ranging anywhere from a third to three-quarters of all women experiencing some form of obstetric violence in childbirth (Bohren et al., 2019; Martínez-Galiano et al., 2021; Mihret, 2019; United Nations General Assembly, 2019). This is unacceptable and must change. This is also all the more reason why understanding perspectives and expertise from midwives and doulas on how to facilitate shared decision making and ensure each birth giver retains the right to give or withhold consent is so important. While individual midwives and doulas may differ, these professions have always been and continue to be women-led and, in addition to taking a more physio-logic approach to birth, their training and orientation towards providing care emphasizes shared decision making, informed consent, and the importance of the birthing person's autonomy.

For pregnant people from Black, Indigenous, and other communities of colour, shared decision making and informed consent is further complicated by systemic racism and discrimination, and experiences of coercion, non-consent, and trauma are much more common among these populations (Logan et al., 2022). For example in Canada, Indigenous birth givers in rural and remote areas are still forced to travel from their communities between 36 and 38 weeks to urban centres until they give birth (Lawford et al., 2018). Not only does Canada's One Health policy further divest from Indigenous midwives and rural maternity care centres, but it makes some of the key ingredients for shared decision making and informed consent—trusting relationship with one's health provider and open lines of communication (Feeley et al., 2020; Nieuwenhuijze et al., 2014; Wilson and Sirois, 2010)—more challenging before labour has even begun (Lawford et al., 2018). Research on racial biases present in assessing and treating pain has shown that people of colour are often not taken as seriously and even dismissed when presenting with pain (Hoffman et al., 2016), which further compro-mises their right to give or withhold consent. Professional tennis player Serena Williams' brush with death in the days following her daughters' birth is one such example (Lockart, 2018), but there are many others including those that ended in tragically preventable deaths (Christian, 2020).

As Canadian Black midwife Chandra Martini reminds us, shared decision making is additionally complicated for racialized populations who may be expected to give consent based on evidence that is not applicable for their population (Martini, 2023). Martini gives an example of her sister, Ashley, declining to keep her newborn admitted for her first few days because of her small birth weight. This was because Ashley and her husband already knew that universal baby weight charts were controversial and understood that customized baby weight charts that took into account the fact that Black babies are often born smaller would be more accurate (Glauser, 2018). But, as Martini explains, "when they brought this up with their nurses, Ashley says, their concerns were dismissed; 'it was like we were stupid'" (Martini, 2023).

While there is still much more work needed to address the disproportionately poor health outcomes for racialized birthing people and their babies, there are many amazing people and organizations who are working to improve the con-ditions of birthing and maternal health outcomes for racialized pregnant people. These include those investing in and encouraging more people of colour to train as midwives and doulas as well as efforts to create more tailored and commu-nity-centred approaches to perinatal care and birthing for these populations (Epoo et al., 2021).

Concrete Strategies to Facilitate Shared Decision Making and Empower Birth Givers

While not an exhaustive list, the following provides key strategies that birth givers and their support teams can employ before, during, and after birth to facilitate the shared decision making process that ensures informed consent (and retains the birth givers' right to withhold consent) that helps create an empowered, positive birth experience.

The Prenatal Period

As the birth giver, childbirth/prenatal education classes are a key way to get prepared and orient to one's preferences and priority areas to become informed. Having a doula is another excellent way to access evidence-based information, ensure continuity of support from pregnancy through postpartum, have someone to remind you of your preferences and support you as you navigate the various decisions one faces during labour and birth, and actively protect and uplift your voice throughout the process. For example, as a doula I help my clients identify, based on their preferences, what interventions they plan to consent to verses those they want to decline. We then work through real-life scenarios ahead of labour and birth to help them concretely think through how they might handle a situation, remember which questions to ask and, if a partner is involved, how that partner could advocate for the birthing person while also ensuring the birthing person has final say on what happens to their bodies. A doula can also help develop a birth plan (also sometimes called a "birth preference plan" in recognition of the unpredictability of labour and birth) which can be used as an advocacy tool (López-Gimeno et al., 2022).

Conversations with one's health provider, the content of which can be greatly informed by childbirth education and prenatal appointments with one's doula, can also spark questions to ask, illuminate areas where you and your provider are (or are not) on the same page about your preferences, and help prepare you for how to ensure your provider seeks your informed consent in an active and ongoing manner when you are in labour. These efforts to prepare oneself prior to labour are critical, as

> it is arguably too late for nursing staff in the hospital to fully educate women about an intervention such as induction of labor to support informed, shared decision making and provide alternative options for something that have already been decided.
>
> *(Moore, 2016: 222)*

In such cases, or where the attending health provider is not known to the birthing person, a doula can provide an invaluable "bridge" between provider and birth giver that facilitates shared decision making and informed consent.

Health providers can create the space for pregnant patients to ask questions and discuss preferences and fears during prenatal appointments. However, many health providers have limited time for each patient due to institutional constraints, and/or are part of a group of providers and are not guaranteed to be the attending provider for the patient's birth. It can be incredibly powerful for such health providers to encourage their patients to attend childbirth education classes and hire a doula. Health providers can also ask their patients if they have a birth plan and go through it with them prior to their birth.

During Labour and Birth

Once the birth giver is in labour (or being induced), shared decision making can be facilitated by bringing a few copies of one's birth plan and offering them to the health team. Remembering that you have a right to make decisions about your body and ask questions to gain clarity is important. A doula can remind you and your providers of your birth preferences and help create the conditions for your ongoing and informed consent throughout your labour and birth experience.

For health providers, shared decision making and informed consent can be facilitated by asking for and honouring a patient's birth plan. I have seen health providers receive a birth plan and say "I'm so glad you have this! Let me share this with the team now and we'll let you know if we have any questions"; I have also seen providers look at the birth plan like it's an unwanted house guest and place it under other documents. While some health providers perceive birth plans as unrealistic or uninformed ideas of what birth will look like, they are nevertheless a window into what a birthing person's preferences are, what they feel prepared to consent to, and can help create a platform for a shared decision making process.

Institutional supports and a culture of patient-centred trauma-informed care will also go a long way in facilitating shared decision making and informed consent. This includes explicit training and job aids in how to seek consent and foster shared decision making, and encouraging and role modelling actively engaging in shared decision making and patient-centred care. For trauma-informed care, health providers need to receive training that increases their understanding of trauma and how it impacts the body, ability to recognize signs and symptoms of a trauma response, understand how to engage with compassion and sensitivity to a patient's trauma response, and avoid retraumatization (Kuzma et al., 2020; Mosley and Lanning, 2020). For example, this should include a more flexible and adaptable set of guidelines around cervical exams through labour (e.g., not expected at regular intervals), and training providers on how to ensure ongoing consent throughout such a procedure.

The Postpartum Period

The "fourth trimester", or the first few months postpartum, continues to be a critical time of vulnerability and processing for a birth giver. Support teams (e.

g., partners, doulas, health providers) should ensure the birth giver has space to process their birth experience and revisit decisions made in a way that encourages them to examine their feelings and experience beyond "healthy mom, healthy baby." This is because many birth givers feel guilty about feeling grief over their birth experience in contexts where "at least mom and baby are healthy" is emphasized. Support should be focused on validating the full range of emotions the birth giver has about their birth.

Future Research and Conclusion

Shared decision making and informed consent are critical to ensuring birth givers feel cared for, respected, heard, and empowered in their birth experience. This in turn translates into better outcomes for birthing person, their baby, and the success of parent-baby bonding. While the realities of shared decision making in the context of labour and birth are influenced by a number of factors, this chapter providers an overview of what shared decision making is, factors that inhibit and support shared decision making and informed consent, and concrete strategies for birth givers, health providers, partners, and doulas to support birth givers in having an empowering experience grounded in an active and ongoing consent-giving process. In a post-Roe era where labour and birth will be increasingly thrust upon those who do not wish it, it is all the more essential that birth giver's rights to make decisions about their own body and provide (or withhold) consent is embedded in all birth health care settings, including through trauma-informed care. Research on the role of doulas in shared decision making and facilitating informed consent is lacking, and an area of future research that would add great value is to understand the role doulas play in supporting shared decision making and ensuring their client's informed consent throughout their labour and birth experience, including how to ensure doula training programs prepare doulas for this task.

Notes

1 I use the terms "pregnant person," "birthing person," "birther," and "birth giver" in this chapter to be inclusive of all women and people of other genders who give birth (e.g., transmen, gender queer and gender non-binary folks). In doing so my intent is not to take away from the ways that for many, birth is a powerful way to identify with the strength and beauty of womanhood. Rather, my goal is to create the conditions for all those who birth, regardless of their gender identity, to feel cared for, respected, and heard. Where research that I cite refers to "women" and "mothers" I use these terms to maintain an accurate depiction of the data.
2 Stories shared from my perspective as a doula are merged experiences from different clients, and I use pseudonyms to protect their right to privacy.
3 An episiotomy is a surgical incision made to your perineum, or the area between the vagina and anus. While episiotomies used to be routine, evidence now makes clear episiotomies can cause more damage than natural tears and should only be used in certain circumstances (Hartmann et al., 2005).

4 Perineal tearing, whether occurring naturally or via an episiotomy, is divided into four categories, or "degrees," with first degree tears the most minor and fourth degree tears the most severe (Ramar and Grimes, 2022).

5 Pulling the "dead baby card" refers to situations when a provider overemphasizes the risk of a baby's death, despite knowing the absolute risk is small. Providers do this, whether intentionally or unintentionally, to short circuit the consent-giving process and gain control over childbirth decision-making.

References

Ahmed HM (2020) Role of verbal and non-verbal communication of health care providers in general satisfaction with birth care: a cross-sectional study in government health settings of Erbil City, Iraq. *Reproductive Health* 17 (35). doi:10.1186/s12978-020-0894-3.

Aktas S and Pasinlioğlu T (2021) The effect of empathy training given to midwives on the empathic communication skills of midwives and the birth satisfaction of mothers giving birth with the help of these midwives: A quasi-experimental study. *Journal of Evaluation in Clinical Practice* 27 (4): 858–867. doi:10.1111/jep.13523.

Bohren MA, Mehrtash H, Fawole B, et al. (2019) How women are treated during facility-based childbirth in four countries: A cross-sectional study with labour observations and community-based surveys. *Lancet (London, England)* 394 (10210): 1750–1763. doi:10.1016/S0140-6736(19)31992-0.

Christian TA (2020) New York woman dies during childbirth days after tweeting concerns about hospital care. *Essence*. Available at: https://www.essence.com/news/amber-isaac-dies-childbirth-bronx-hospital-tweet/.

Deherder E, Delbaere I, Macedo A, et al. (2022) Women's view on shared decision making and autonomy in childbirth: Cohort study of Belgian women. *BMC Pregnancy and Childbirth* 22 (551). doi:10.1186/s12884-022-04890-x.

Dekker R (2019) Evidence on: Doulas. *Evidence Based Birth*. Available at: https://evidencebasedbirth.com/the-evidence-for-doulas/.

Dolan P, Hallsworth M, Halpern D, et al. (2011) Influencing behaviour: The mindspace way. *Journal of Economic Psychology* 33 (1): 264–277. doi:10.1016/j.joep.2011.10.009.

Elwyn G (2021) Shared decision making: What is the work? *Patient Education and Counseling* 104 (7): 1591–1595. doi:10.1016/j.pec.2020.11.032.

Elwyn G, Frosch D, Thomson R, et al. (2012) Shared decision making: A model for clinical practice. *Journal of General Internal Medicine* 27 (10): 1361–1367. doi:10.1007/s11606-012-2077-6.

Ely S, Langer S and Dietz HP (2022) Informed consent and birth preparedness/complication readiness: A qualitative study at two tertiary maternity units. *Australian and New Zealand Journal of Obstetrics and Gynaecology* 62 (1): 47–54. doi:10.1111/ajo.13417.

Epoo B, Moorehouse K, Tayara M, et al. (2021) 'To bring back birth is to bring back life': The Nunavik story. In: *Birthing Models on the Human Rights Frontier: Speaking Truth to Power*. Abingdon, Oxon, UK: Routledge, pp. 75–109.

Feeley C, Thomson G and Downe S (2020) Understanding how midwives employed by the National Health Service facilitate women's alternative birthing choices: Findings from a feminist pragmatist study. *PLOS ONE* 15 (11). Public Library of Science: e0242508. doi:10.1371/journal.pone.0242508.

Ford A (2021) Attuned consent: Birth Doulas, care, and the politics of consent. *Frontiers: A Journal of Women Studies* 42 (2): 24.

Glauser W (2018) Ethnicity-based fetal growth charts could reduce inductions and elective cesarean sections. *CMAJ* 190 (45): E1343–E1344. doi:10.1503/cmaj.109-5670.

Hallam JL, Howard CD, Locke A, et al. (2016) Communicating choice: An exploration of mothers' experiences of birth. *Journal of Reproductive and Infant Psychology* 34 (2): 175–184. doi:10.1080/02646838.2015.1119260.

Hartmann K, Viswanathan M, Palmieri R, et al. (2005) Outcomes of routine episiotomy: A systematic review. *JAMA* 293 (17): 2141–2148. doi:10.1001/jama.293.17.2141.

Hodnett ED, Gates S, Hofmeyr GJ, et al. (2013) Continuous support for women during childbirth. *Cochrane Database of Systematic Reviews* (7). doi:10.1002/14651858. CD003766.pub5.

Hoffman KM, Trawalter S, Axt JR, et al. (2016) Racial bias in pain assessment and treatment recommendations, and false beliefs about biological differences between blacks and whites. *Proceedings of the National Academy of Sciences of the United States of America* 113 (16): 4296–4301. doi:10.1073/pnas.1516047113.

Horstman HK, Anderson J and Kuehl RA (2017) Communicatively making sense of Doulas within the U.S. master birth narrative: Doulas as liminal characters. *Health Communication* 32 (12): 1510–1519. doi:10.1080/10410236.2016.1234537.

Korstjens I, Mesman J, Helmond I van, et al. (2019) Visualizing the art of maternity care practice: a video-reflexivity study on communication and collaboration of professionals and parents. *International Journal of Integrated Care* 19 (4): 646. doi:10.5334/ijic.s3646.

Kuzma EK, Pardee M and Morgan A (2020) Implementing patient-centered trauma-informed care for the perinatal nurse. *The Journal of Perinatal & Neonatal Nursing* 34 (4): E23–E31. doi:10.1097/JPN.0000000000000520.

Larkin P, Begley CM and Devane D (2017) Women's preferences for childbirth experiences in the Republic of Ireland: A mixed methods study. *BMC Pregnancy and Childbirth* 17 (1): 1–10. doi:10.1186/s12884-016-1196-1.

Lawford KM, Giles AR and Bourgeault IL (2018) Canada's evacuation policy for pregnant First Nations women: Resignation, resilience, and resistance. *Women and Birth* 31 (6): 479–488. doi:10.1016/j.wombi.2018.01.009.

Lockart PR (2018) What Serena Williams's scary childbirth story says about medical treatment of black women. *Vox*, 11 January. Available at: https://www.vox.com/identities/2018/1/11/16879984/serena-williams-childbirth-scare-black-women.

Logan RG, McLemore MR, Julian Z, et al. (2022) Coercion and non-consent during birth and newborn care in the United States. *Birth: Issues in Perinatal Care* 49 (5). doi:10.1111/birt.12641.

López-Gimeno E, Seguranyes G, Vicente-Hernández M, et al. (2022) Effectiveness of birth plan counselling based on shared decision making: A cluster randomized controlled trial (APLANT). *PLOS ONE* 17 (9): e0274240. doi:10.1371/journal.pone.0274240.

Malvasi A, Trojano G, Tinelli A, et al. (2021) Episiotomy: An informed consent proposal. *The Journal of Maternal-Fetal & Neonatal Medicine* 34 (6): 948–951. doi:10.1080/14767058.2019.1622677.

Martínez-Galiano JM, Martinez-Vazquez S, Rodríguez-Almagro J, et al. (2021) The magnitude of the problem of obstetric violence and its associated factors: A cross-sectional study. *Women and Birth: Journal of the Australian College of Midwives* 34 (5): e526–e536. doi:10.1016/j.wombi.2020.10.002.

Martini C (2023) Racial disparities in birth outcomes in Canada. In: *An Anthology of Canadian Birth Stories: Inspiring Stories and Essential Guidance for Parents, Parents-to-Be, and Health Providers*. Praeclarus Press.

McCulloch Dip S (2016) Twilight sleep: The brutal way some women gave birth in the 1900s. *BellyBelly*. Available at: https://www.bellybelly.com.au/birth/twilight-sleep/ (accessed 23 October 2022).

Mihret MS (2019) Obstetric violence and its associated factors among postnatal women in a Specialized Comprehensive Hospital, Amhara Region, Northwest Ethiopia. *BMC Research Notes* 12 (1): 600. doi:10.1186/s13104-019-4614-4.

MirzaeeRabor F, Mirzaee F, MirzaiiNajmabadi K, et al. (2016) Respect for woman's decision-making in spontaneous birth: A thematic synthesis study. *Iranian Journal of Nursing and Midwifery Research* 21 (5): 449–457. doi:10.4103/1735-9066.193389.

Moore JE (2016) Women's voices in maternity care: The triad of shared decision making, informed consent, and evidence-based practices. *The Journal of Perinatal & Neonatal Nursing* 30 (3): 218–223. doi:10.1097/JPN.0000000000000182.

Mosley EA and Lanning RK (2020) Evidence and guidelines for trauma-informed doula care. *Midwifery*83: 102643. doi:10.1016/j.midw.2020.102643.

National Institute for Health and Care Excellence (NICE) (2022) Shared decision making. Available at: https://www.nice.org.uk/about/what-we-do/our-programmes/nice-guidance/nice-guidelines/shared-decision-making.

Nicholls JA, David AL, Iskaros J, et al. (2021) Consent in pregnancy–An observational study of ante-natal care in the context of Montgomery: all about risk? *BMC Pregnancy and Childbirth* 21 (1): 1–9. doi:10.1186/s12884-021-03574-2.

Nieuwenhuijze MJ, Korstjens I, de Jonge A, et al. (2014) On speaking terms: A Delphi study on shared decision-making in maternity care. *BMC Pregnancy and Childbirth* 14 (1): 223. doi:10.1186/1471-2393-14-223.

Pascoe L (2023) Evidence on doulas. In: Pascoe L and Leduc J (eds) *An Anthology of Canadian Birth Stories: Inspiring Stories and Essential Guidance for Parents, Parents-to-Be, and Health Providers*. Praeclarus Press.

Ramar CN and Grimes WR (2022) Perineal lacerations. In: *StatPearls*. Treasure Island (FL): StatPearls Publishing. Available at: http://www.ncbi.nlm.nih.gov/books/NBK559068/ (accessed 22 October 2022).

Reed R, Sharman R and Inglis C (2017) Women's descriptions of childbirth trauma relating to care provider actions and interactions. *BMC Pregnancy and Childbirth* 17 (1): 21. doi:10.1186/s12884-016-1197-0.

Simkin P, Whalley J, Keppler A, et al. (2018) *Pregnancy, Childbirth, and the Newborn: The Complete Guide*. 5th ed. Da Capo Lifelong Books. Available at: https://www.amazon.com/Pregnancy-Childbirth-Newborn-Complete-Guide/dp/0738284971 (accessed 13 October 2022).

Simpson M and Catling C (2016) Understanding psychological traumatic birth experiences: A literature review. *Women and Birth* 29 (3): 203–207. doi:10.1016/j.wombi.2015.10.009.

United Nations General Assembly (2019) A human rights-based approach to mistreatment and violence against women in reproductive health services with a focus on childbirth and obstetric violence: Note by the Secretary-General. United Nations. Available at: https://digitallibrary.un.org/record/3823698?ln=en.

Vedam S, Stoll K, Martin K, et al. (2017) The Mother's Autonomy in Decision Making (MADM) scale: Patient-led development and psychometric testing of a new instrument to evaluate experience of maternity care. *PLOS ONE* 12 (2): e0171804. doi:10.1371/journal.pone.0171804.

Villarmea S and Kelly B (2020) Barriers to establishing shared decision-making in childbirth: Unveiling epistemic stereotypes about women in labour. *Journal of Evaluation in Clinical Practice* 26 (2): 515–519. doi:10.1111/jep.13375.

Wilson KL and Sirois FM (2010) Birth attendant choice and satisfaction with antenatal care: the role of birth philosophy, relational style, and health self-efficacy. *Journal of Reproductive and Infant Psychology* 28 (1): 69–83. doi:10.1080/02646830903190946.

12

CONSENT AND WORK

A Postfeminist Analysis of Women Leaders' Acceptance of Long Working Hours

Patricia Lewis

Always being available to work and the necessity of long working hours are central components of contemporary organizational life, particularly for those who have leadership ambitions. Being willing to sacrifice your own time and to privilege work over other life activities is interpreted as emblematic of the ideal worker within present-day professional work settings (Acker, 1990; Blair-Loy, 2001). Indeed, 'pulling all-nighters' is treated as a rite of passage, particularly in global financial services firms such as investment banks. While the necessity of long working hours has been questioned when it has resulted in tragic events such as the early death of Moritz Erhardt, who died after working three nights in a row during a summer internship in London with Bank of America (Day, 2013), this has not stopped the practice. Time spent at work is taken as a key indicator of commitment, drive, ambition and future potential (Ruiz Castro, 2012). This remains the case even as research demonstrates that the long-hours culture characteristic of modern work is detrimental and distressing to both women and men with the former being pushed to choose between family and work and the latter experiencing a persistent disconnection from their family (Padavic et al., 2020).

Conventionally understood in terms of individual choice and free will, 'never-saying-no-to-work' is assumed to be voluntary behaviour. Here, working beyond the requirements of an employment contract is treated as driven by freely given individual consent, a means to 'stand out from the crowd' if you can work longer and harder than anyone else. In other words, it is perceived as a decision taken by an autonomous, empowered individual who can say 'no' if they wish. In this chapter I seek to challenge the idea that choice and freely given consent underpin personal accessibility for the purposes of work and that individuals are free to choose otherwise. In questioning this autonomous freedom to consent, I focus on 'the social forces that shape and influence the communication of consent and the activities that are consented to' (Beres, 2007: 99)

DOI: 10.4324/9781003358756-16

as a means to contextualize and problematize individuals' willing submission to long working hours. Specifically, I mobilize postfeminism as an analytic device to explore the way in which contemporary social forces in the form of postfeminist discourses of individualism, choice, gender difference and balance impact on consenting to work long hours. Through a postfeminist analysis of interviews with women leaders in the City of London, I make visible how consent to long hours is navigated and how acquiescence to work availability 'are influenced by gendered discourses and norms, which generate implicit pressures that disrupt (women's) negotiations of consent' (Burkett and Hamilton, 2012: 817). Accordingly, the chapter explores the way women consent to dedicate long hours to their organization, putting it first before other life activities. While women in leadership positions are assumed to be agentic and autonomous organizational actors, this does not mean they are free from pressure to 'never-say-no'. I consider how the securing of consent occurs within a contradictorily gendered context that calls women to respond to the demands of work while also addressing the traditional responsibilities of home.

The chapter is structured as follows: I begin by depicting the cultural phenomenon of postfeminism and how it is used as an analytical framework. Next, I outline the methodology adopted for the study. Following this I present the empirical data and the interpretation of the findings. The chapter finishes with a conclusion to the study.

Postfeminism and Consent

Originating within the disciplinary field of cultural and media studies and developed through the foundational work of Angela McRobbie (2004) and Rosalind Gill (2007), postfeminism has become an important analytic device through which to investigate how depictions of gender have changed and the effect this has on women's positioning in relation to work and family. The development and take-up of postfeminism as an analytical framework is set within a context of a variety of interpretations of this cultural phenomenon ranging from epistemological and historical shifts within feminism, to a backlash conceptualization that criticizes feminism for making women 'unhappy', to an emphasis placed on the 'success' of feminism in achieving gender 'equality' (Gill, 2007; Projansky, 2001). Nevertheless, while it is acknowledged that there is no definitive interpretation of postfeminism, there is one conceptualization that has gained widespread acceptance in research that seeks to investigate the persistence of gender inequality amid the reconfiguration of gender norms. Here, postfeminism is approached as an object of critique, understood as a mode of governance, identifiable by its selective acceptance of liberal feminist values of agency, choice and empowerment alongside the neoliberal principles of individualism, self-transformation and entrepreneurialism, while also restabilizing traditional gender norms (Lewis et al., 2022). As such, the postfeminist subject is an empowered, agentic woman with economic capacity who at the same time enacts conventional feminine roles, engaging in the traditional rituals of femininity associated with beauty, fashion, the domestic realm, and motherhood. Accordingly, women are called to become the liberated, self-governing, self-reliant, autonomous subject of neoliberalism, aligning with the agentic, choosing, self-transforming but reassuringly feminine subject of postfeminism, (Gill and Scharff, 2011; McRobbie, 2009). Within postfeminist culture, this subject position emerges out of a collection of discourses that connect to each other in a patterned way. This includes discourses of individualism and choice, continuous working on the self, 'natural' distinctions between masculinity and femininity, the valorization of femininity as a psychological and bodily property and retreating to home as a matter of choice not obligation (Gill, 2016; Lewis, 2014; Negra, 2009).

The take-up and incorporation of liberal feminist values of agency, choice and empowerment within postfeminism, impacts on the way consent is understood and given within work contexts. Consensuality is central to feminist interpretations of liberalism with consent understood as 'emblematic of as well as constitutive of autonomy; consent itself is a sort of intrinsic as well as instrumental good' (West, 2017: 816). Thus, within a work context saturated with the norms of a postfeminist gender regime, consenting to work long hours is perceived to empower and increase the autonomy of the individual by providing her with opportunities to gain valuable work experience which can support leadership ambitions. For such consent to be interpreted as valid, it must be voluntary and based on clear information. From this position, if a person chooses and consents to long hours working and there is no 'coercive imposition' (West, 2017: 817), then an improvement in their well-being is perceived to occur through the enhancement of their career prospects. Nevertheless, as West (2017) points out we need to question the sufficiency of consent when judging if the outcome of what we consent to is a good or bad thing for us. Choice by itself does not 'ensure goodness, even if the lack of it is quite bad indeed' (West, 2017: 817). What the taken-for-granted, individualized approach to consent ignores is the *contextualization* of voluntary participation and that in practice consent is not just an individualized practice but is also a relationally constituted process influenced by circulating gender norms.

Methodology

This chapter stems from an interview study of men and women leaders working in the City of London. Using postfeminism as an analytic device, the research sought to make visible the way in which postfeminist gender norms informed men and women's leadership and the constitution of their leadership identities. The research conceptualized leadership as a negotiation between masculine and feminine norms, and aimed to demonstrate how men and women leaders 'do' masculinity and femininity when leading. Interviewees were sourced through a mixture of personal and professional contacts that facilitated the construction of a purposeful, snowball sample. Through this sampling process, forty-eight interviews with senior and mid-level leaders from insurance underwriters, insurance brokers and insurance sector bodies were conducted. Senior leadership positions included CEO of an organization or holding responsibility for a function such as finance or operations at board level. Those in mid-level leadership roles led a particular business area within the insurance field, which often included responsibility for a team of people (Lewis, 2021).

For the purposes of this chapter, the focus is on the interviews with 13 women holding senior leadership roles and 13 women in mid-level leadership positions. The interviews explored a range of topics including how they became leaders, their motivation to lead, the personal transformation they experienced and/or sought as leaders, the challenges they have faced and their description of how they lead. Across the respondents there was a general awareness that men and women in leadership positions were participating in the study but the questions asked around leadership were not expressed in gender terms. Instead, the questions posed related to leadership in general as a means to explore their motivations and experiences as a leader. The purpose of this approach was to provide an open space for interviewees to speak about leadership but within this context, issues of gender did arise over the course of the interview.

The analysis of the interview data was informed by a Foucauldian discursive approach. As such, the interview data is treated as being located within post-feminist constitutive discourses associated with the interpretation of postfeminism developed by Gill (2007). These include postfeminist discourses of individualism, choice, gender difference and balance. In line with the conceptualization of leadership as a negotiation between masculine and feminine norms, I treat discourses of individualism and choice as connected to masculinized attainment in the sphere of work, with discourses around gender difference and balance being associated with femininity (Lewis and Benschop, 2022). These discourses make it possible for certain things to be said and delimit the sayable, empowering the respondents to speak of themselves as particular types of subjects (Bacchi and Bonham, 2016). In relation to consenting to work long hours, what is sayable is that this is the action of a committed, ambitious person and in saying this, the respondents constituted themselves as a 'future leader' of the organization. Additionally, what is important to note here is that when consenting to work long hours, women are constituting their subjectivity through discourses of masculinity but this *must* be done interdependently with femininity (Lewis, 2021). Accordingly, and as, we will see below, consenting to work long hours is complicated by postfeminist gender norms which give rise to a normative requirement that women can't do masculinity – work long hours – without also doing femininity – care for family. In presenting the findings, I include segments from individual interviews that are illustrative of the overall argument and resonate across the wider data set (Pullen and Simpson, 2009). Pseudonyms are used and specific roles are not specified to protect the confidentiality of respondents but whether a respondent is a senior or mid-level leader is indicated.

Findings

Consenting to Work

One key consequence of the emergence of postfeminism is its opening up of the subject position of 'individual' to women, a positioning that they were historically excluded from (Cronin, 2000). At the same time, within postfeminism there is a systematic silence about the impact of structures connected to gender (and other forms of difference) that can exert power over women's experience of work. Instead, emphasis is placed on individual autonomy and responsibility-for-self with 'choice, agency and empowerment (presented) as the watchwords of contemporary feminine experience' (Gill and Donaghue, 2013: 247). This postfeminist individualist emphasis is reflected in respondents' consideration of their path to leadership. All the respondents placed an emphasis on their choices as they took up the discursive stance of the individual with free will to consent to engage in work practices such as long hours working. Indeed, when considering how they were identified as having 'potential' and 'value' in the context of their organizations, being available and willing to work extra hours enabled them to communicate that they have 'worth' and can 'fit in' with this normative organizational requirement. At the same time, it was perceived to be an important way to 'stand out' from their peers. Accordingly, drawing on postfeminist discourses of individualism and choice, respondents' willingness to consent to work when required, was the way by which they were constituted as having value for the organization:

> So, I was a secretary and a really, not very good secretary, but and we didn't have computers right, so this is a long time ago and so part of your job as a secretary is typing and I wasn't a super-good typist but I would come in at like three in the morning so that all my typing was all done before my day started. So, they loved the fact that I was like a 'try-hard'. And so, I think that's my thing, I try really hard…And so all I did was anything anybody asked me to and when I'm telling young people today, I think there's a whole kind of culture around things you will do and things you won't do and that somehow taking a certain task is beneath you or whatever. Especially as you move up along and I do think that the, that you should never do that, I think you should do anything anybody asks you to do. I mean if my Group Chief Executive asked me to go pick up his dry-cleaning, I would do it. Do you know what I mean? That is my mentality.
>
> *(Belinda, Senior Woman Leader)*

In expressing this view, Belinda communicates a strong masculinized attachment to work through her willingness to put in extra hours to get the job done. While she understands her readiness to work tirelessly as her 'thing' – how she is as an individual – she also understands that working long hours is what you do if you want to be identified as valuable within an organization. She demonstrates this understanding when she says she did 'anything anybody asked me' and this willingness to never-say-no is the advice she gives to young people. Embedded in Belinda's account is the liberal assumption in relation to consent, that working long hours is the way value is created for both her and the organization. She benefits because she can make her commitment visible and the organization benefits because the work gets done. Her postfeminist, individualized approach to consenting to work long hours is also evident in her denial of any negative consequences, connected to her gender, of never-saying-no. We can see this when she states that she would go as far as collecting dry-cleaning for her CEO, rejecting the idea that such a request can be interpreted as having gendered connotations with the potential for an adverse impact on her. Rather, she sees her willingness to take on any task as positive and empowering, a view supported by other respondents:

> I think I've been, you know, have I been lucky, I mean you know, the adage, you know, if you work hard, the harder I work the luckier I get. I am a, I'm a grafter and I came with no sort of expectations or, you know, sense of entitlement and I just seem to have kind of had opportunities which I guess you make for yourself by element of right place right time but I guess you make them as well by being kind of good and knuckling down and getting on with it.
>
> *(Phoebe, Senior Woman Leader)*

Again, drawing on postfeminist discourses around individualism and choice, Phoebe emphasises how she is as an individual – 'a grafter' – and that her willingness to work long hours has opened up opportunities for her. Being willing and available to work – 'knuckling down and getting on with it' – is the source of her success. Here, the emphasis is placed on what she has gained from putting work first and she makes a direct connection between working hard and creating opportunity. Phoebe emphasises how she has forged her own path and that being available for work has been central to this. There is no felt sense of coercion, of 'having to work', rather she understands and presents herself as a hard worker, with freedom to realize her potential. Similarly, Stella reflecting on her younger self, places an emphasis on the enjoyment she felt in being heavily involved in work. In particular, she highlights how the chance to bring out her competitive spirit by 'beating people', gave her a felt sense of exhilaration as follows:

> (Working long hours) yes, energising. I enjoyed it, I felt part of something. I knew I was doing well, I was doing better than other people, I had a sense of beating people, you know, which I enjoyed, quite competitive then, this is my 20s, early 30s remember.
>
> *(Stella, Senior Woman Leader)*

From the above, we can see that Belinda, Phoebe and Stella are interpellated by discourses of individualism, choice and empowerment. This manifests in the emphasis they place on their own agency, their own willingness to work long hours and the benefits and opportunities they secured by doing this. They connect their success to their consensual orientation to working long hours and the way this aligns with how they understand themselves as individuals. There is no sense here that they experience any undue pressure to engage in these temporal work practices but that they work like this because this is 'who they are' and because they secure career benefits from working excessively. Accordingly, drawing on the postfeminist discourses of individualism and choice, what is 'sayable' about consenting to work long hours is that this is an individual choice, usually taken up and enacted by agentic, empowered people, who create opportunity for themselves and their organization by never-saying-no to any type of work. They see themselves as gaining social and organizational status by constituting themselves as committed and dedicated to their job (Kuhn, 2006). There is an acceptance that managing long working hours is the responsibility of the individual who is 'read' as ambitious, driven and having value for the organization by always being available to work. Consenting to arduous temporal commitments is presented as deriving from their description of themselves as 'a try-hard', 'a grafter', and 'being competitive', acting to mask the complexities of giving consent (Burkett and Hamilton, 2012). However, as we will see below, within a postfeminist gender regime, discourses of individualism and choice do not stand alone but are entangled with other discourses of gender difference and balance bringing a coercive social force to the giving of consent (Beres, 2007).

Consent and Gender Difference

While consenting to work long hours was largely understood in terms of the choosing, autonomous individual, within the interviews the suggestion that the broader (gender) context can have an impact on choices made and decisions taken was also evident. As Valerie asserts, 'we're female CEOs operating in a world where you don't really fit in' and this gives rise to efforts being made by women to 'fit in' within a context that is numerically and culturally masculine. As Jane states:

> And in a mixed environment, most women will find a way of fitting in with men, rather than vice versa. So, you know you are in a social group you go, it's easier for me to fit in with my husband's friends than it is for my husband to fit in with my friends because we just, you just naturally do that, don't you?
> *(Jane, Mid-Level Leader)*

Drawing on a discourse of gender difference, Valerie and Jane recognize that the gendered context they work in has an impact on their experience of work, including how they communicate consent and the activities they agree to engage in (Beres, 2007). As such, there is a movement away from assuming that giving consent in relation to work is an individualized activity that is only informed by the type of people they are. What is recognized is that how they engage in work activities, which includes consenting to work long hours, does not happen in a vacuum. This signals that in contrast to the individualized mode of consent previously discussed, the social force of the postfeminist discourse of gender difference that circulates within the insurance market, means that the giving of consent may be better understood as a relationally constituted process which takes place within a gendered context.

Recognition of the way in which gender difference impacts on consent to work long hours strongly emerges around family issues. According to Stella 'there's still in certain environments a thought that women should be, you know, why aren't women looking after the children?' As such, taking care of family is treated as a 'woman's issue' with the decisions taken and choices made by women when trying to balance home and work seen as different to men and far more challenging, particularly for those who are planning a family:

> I think I'd put a lot of pressure on myself. And my role is a producing role, it is a very heavily client facing role and we do go out a lot on entertainment, there's a lot of drinking involved so when you think about it, it's not just a year of maternity leave, it's the nine months before...and those are things that men don't really have to think about....I find that quite scary to be honest and how am I going to prove my value if I can't go out and produce my business and be client facing and do what I've always done but I think that's something that I need to kind of battle with and see what else I can do to make sure that my value is still staying there and I don't lose touch with my clients...I think that's a lot of the reason why women leave broking houses at age 30-something to go into underwriting...they can leave at five because well Lloyds is closed...if they need to do notes on the accounts that they write they can do that at home. So, I do think that's why a lot of women go into underwriting but I love broking and I love my job and I don't want to feel that I have to go into underwriting just to be able to stay in the industry and have a family.
>
> *(Nina, Mid-Level Leader)*

Here Nina is reflecting on the decisions she will face when it comes to having a family. Initially, drawing on postfeminist discourses of individualism and choice, she presents her situation in relation to having children as dependent on her individually. She is worried that she will lose her 'value' as being available to entertain clients in the evenings will be more difficult for her both in the run-up to getting pregnant, being pregnant and caring for the baby once born. She articulates her situation in terms of the 'struggle' and 'battle' she will face in maintaining her connection to clients. Nevertheless, halfway through her reflections, she draws on a discourse of gender difference as she considers how men do not have to face the same kinds of issues that she does in relation to family. She recognizes that she is working within a context where women can experience 'gendered forms of coercion' (Burkett and Hamilton, 2012: 824) which 'push' them to change from broking to underwriting as the working hours of the latter are more conducive to balance family and career. Underpinning Nina's reflections is a sense of pressure – she does not want to have to change her job because she 'loves broking' but knows this is a possibility if she is not able to work long hours when she becomes a mother. Nina's ruminations clearly illustrate the complexities that attach to consenting to always be available for work. As a childless woman, she is able to meet this demand and can interpret her actions as based on her own freely made choices. Yet, as her personal situation changes, the gendered pressures underpinning her choices become visible as the ability to interpret her situation solely in terms of her own agency is put under strain.

The coercive social force of gender on the giving of consent also emerges in Belinda's account of how she responded to a request to attend a two-week leadership course following a very busy period of work:

> They had this leadership course (and) my boss, said, you know, 'congratulations, you're going on this leadership course' and I was like, 'Er, no I ain't, I'm not going on that. I have five children, my busy season ends on the 1st of July, you're asking me to go on a course for two weeks on the 8th of July, absolutely no way. I will have been killing myself for four months, absolutely not.' So, he was like 'okay'. And then we used to have a general manager here....and she called me in and basically said, if you don't do this you are sending a message. And I was really taken aback and I've no, because normally I'd say, 'fine take the message', you know. But for whatever reason, I said 'oh I don't want to send a bad message' so I went.

In reflecting on this experience, Belinda draws on discourses of balance and gender difference. In relation to the former, she is constituted by masculine and feminine norms – the former in terms of working long hours during a very busy period and the latter through her need to spend time with her children. In not consenting to go on a leadership course she connects this decision with the completion of a busy period at work when her availability to her family would have been restricted and seeks to 'balance' this by having time with her children so she can focus on their needs. This seems like a clear-cut choice until she is advised to rethink her decision and the message she is sending. While there is no explicit statement of what her refusal to attend the leadership course communicates, Belinda appears to have an implicit understanding of the message her actions convey and immediately states 'oh I don't want to send a bad message'. It is notable that the advice to rethink her decision came from another senior woman. Belinda's original refusal derived from a desire to spend time with her family and the 'bad message' implicitly links to this. As a woman leader and a mother, gender norms deriving from a discourse of gender difference influenced Belinda's initial response and swayed her revised decision to attend the course. While Belinda states that she changed her mind 'for whatever reason', there is a 'tacit knowing' (Burkett and Hamilton, 2012: 821) that not attending means she risks being interpreted as a less committed *woman* leader because she put her family first. Accordingly, consenting to working long hours is influenced by what 'you just know' in terms of how actions will be interpreted. Within a gendered context, a woman leader who is a mother could experience career 'harm' by refusing to attend a senior leadership course. This sense of potential 'harm' is heightened because of the warning she received, demonstrating that her consent to attend was not freely given.

Conclusion

Working long hours and always being available for work is conventionally understood in terms of the actions of ambitious, driven people who demonstrate their commitment to their job through their willingness to privilege work over other life activities. This interpretation was evident in the study data but by itself is not enough to understand the challenges that attach to long working hours and the reasons why people accept this practice. Drawing on postfeminism as an analytic device, the study highlights the way in which the respondents draw on discourses of individualism, agency and empowerment to interpret their willingness to consent as connected to their individual ambition and determination to get the job done. However, the 'story' of long hours working did not end there. What also became clear is the compulsory nature of never-saying-no to work due to the entanglement of individualist discourses with discourses of gender difference and balance, which the interviewees also drew on. The compulsory nature of working long hours, which is 'fed' by postfeminist discourses can act to conceal how consent to work is not just a 'free choice'. What is clear is that consent to work is subject to social forces and is not just down to the ambition and characteristics of an individual. Contextualizing the acceptance of this temporal demand is important if we are to gain understanding of the contradictions experienced. Women leaders see themselves as empowered, autonomous actors free to make their own choices but at the same time are subject to traditional compulsory expectations around family. Challenging each other in relation to how family is managed and the call to put work first even when their preference is not to, is intelligible when we contextualize this contradiction within the bounds of a postfeminist gender regime (Burkett and Hamilton, 2012).

Finally, what emerges in this study is the distress that can attach to consenting to work long hours, an issue also identified by Padavic et al. (2020). We saw Nina's distress in her assessment of her personal situation as she thinks about how she will manage the job she loves and a family. We also saw it in the way

Belinda was 'pushed' to attend a leadership course for fear of sending a 'bad message'. Both women drew on a 'grammar of individualism' derived from the postfeminist context they work within when assessing their situations, and this may allow them to feel as if they can have some control over the challenges they face. Women's desire to have a career within a context which claims that 'equality' has been achieved, can often mean that they remain silent about the challenges and compulsions attached to managing work and family. As Stella, a senior women leader put it in relation to managing work now that she has children: 'It has been horrific, really difficult, extremely hard…even now in the women's organizations there's not really very much open conversation about how tough it is'. Such silence means that a type of 'consensual harm' (West, 2017) is experienced but left unsaid. Focusing on the social forces that attach to consent – here postfeminist discourses – pushes us to consider the culture within which these choices are made and to make visible the harms that attach to never-saying-no to work.

References

Acker, J. (1990) Hierarchies, job, bodies: A theory of gendered organizations. *Gender & Society*, 4 (1): 139–158.

Bacchi, C. and Bonham, J. (2016) Poststructural interview analysis: Politicizing personhood. In Baachi, C. and Goodwin, S. *Poststructural Policy Analysis*. New York: Palgrave Pivot, pp. 113–121.

Beres, M.A. (2007) 'Spontaneous' sexual consent: An analysis of sexual consent literature. *Feminism & Psychology*, 17 (1): 93–108.

Blair-Loy, M. (2001) Cultural constructions of family schema: The case of women finance executives. *Gender & Society*, 15 (5): 687–709.

Burkett, M. and Hamilton, K. (2012) Postfeminist sexual agency: Young women's negotiations of sexual consent. *Sexualities*, 15 (7): 815–833.

Cronin, A.M. (2000) Consumerism and 'compulsory individuality'. In Ahmed, S., Kilby, J., Lury, C., McNeil, M. and Skeggs, B. (eds.) *Transformations: Thinking Through Feminism*. London: Routledge, pp. 273–287.

Day, E. (2013) Moritz Erhardt: The tragic death of a City intern. *The Guardian*, 5 October.

Gill, R. (2007) Postfeminist media culture: Elements of a sensibility. *European Journal of Cultural Studies*, 10 (2): 147–166.

Gill, R. (2016) Post-postfeminism? New feminist visibilities in postfeminist times. *Feminist Media Studies*, 16 (4): 610–630.

Gill, R. and Donaghue, N. (2013) As if postfeminism had come true: The turn to agency in cultural studies of 'sexualisation'. In Madhok, S., Phillips, A. and Wilson, K. (eds) *Gender, Agency and Coercion*. Basingstoke: Palgrave Macmillan, pp. 240–258.

Gill, R. and Scharff, C. (eds) (2011) *New Femininities: Postfeminism, Neoliberalism and Subjectivity*. Basingstoke: Palgrave Macmillan.

Kuhn, T. (2006) A 'demented work ethic' and a 'lifestyle firm': Discourse, identity and workplace time commitments. *Organization Studies*, 27 (9): 1339–1358.

Lewis, P. (2014) Postfeminism, femininities and organization studies: Exploring a new agenda. *Organization Studies*, 35 (12): 1845–1866.

Lewis, P. (2021) Gendered encounters in a postfeminist context: Researcher identity work in interviews with men and women leaders in the City of London. In Stead, V., Elliott, C. and Mavin, S. (eds.) *Handbook of Research Methods on Gender and Management*. Cheltenham, UK: Edward Elgar Publishing, pp. 115–129.

Lewis, P. and Benschop. Y. (2022) Gendered hybridity in leadership identities: A postfeminist analysis. *Gender in Management: An International Journal*. doi:10.1108/GM-07-2022-0238.

Lewis, P., Rumens, N. and Simpson, R. (2022) Postfeminism, hybrid mumpreneur identities and the reproduction of masculine entrepreneurship. *International Small Business Journal*, 40 (1): 68–89.

McRobbie, A. (2004) Postfeminism and popular culture: Bridget Jones and the new gender regime. *Feminist Media Studies*, 4 (3): 255–264.

McRobbie, A. (2009) *The Aftermath of Feminism*. London: Sage.

Negra, D (2009) *What a Girl Wants? Fantasizing the Reclamation of Self in Postfeminism*. London: Routledge.

Padavic, I., Ely, R.J. and Reid, E.M. (2020) Explaining the persistence of gender inequality: The work–family narrative as a social defence against the 24/7 work culture. *Administrative Science Quarterly*, 65 (1): 61–111.

Projansky, S. (2001) *Watching Rape: Film and Television in Postfeminist Culture*. New York: New York University Press.

Pullen, A. and Simpson, R. (2009) Managing differences in feminized work: Men, otherness and social practice. *Human Relations*, 62 (4): 561–587.

Ruiz Castro, M. (2012) Time demands and gender roles: The case of a big four firm in Mexico. *Gender, Work & Organization*, 19 (5): 532–554.

West, R. (2017) Consensual sexual dysphoria: A challenge for campus life. *Journal of Legal Education*, 66 (4): 804–821.

PART IV

Consent in a Digital World

13

CONSENT ISN'T JUST A GIRL'S THING

Gender, Consent and Image Based Sexual Abuse

Claire Meehan

Consent, both sexual and non-sexual, is a vital part of life. Literature on people's views towards sexual consent, non-consent and sexual violence continues to develop, going beyond simplistic ideas that consent is the difference between good and bad sex, and lawful and unlawful sex (Setty 2018). Neoliberal approaches place responsibility for privacy and consent upon individuals, yet the ability for an individual to socially negotiate privacy is challenged due to the presence of an interconnected network (Barker 2013). Therefore, consent operates at the interpersonal, social and cultural levels (Livingstone and Mason 2015). With that being said, the meaning and nature of consent is the cause of some confusion in academia, policy and practice (Carmody 2008). The ability to give consent relies upon a 'good understanding of sexual possibilities, awareness of our own desires and any social and relational pressures upon us, and the confidence to communicate these and to accept, refuse or negotiate others' suggestions' (Attwood et al. 2013, 13). Thus, consent does not happen without context; rather, it is a result of power relations that shape social meanings and sexual relationships (Meehan 2021a).

Traditional sexual scripts align their understandings of sexual behaviour close to 'the male sexual drive discourse' (Hollway 1984), whereby men are expected to be sexually skilled, initiate sex, and strive for multiple sexual partners (Farvid and Braun 2018). This gatekeeper role places responsibility for consent, or indeed non-consent, on women; men ask for consent and women respond (Thorburn et al. 2021; Hunt et al. 2022). In conventional sexual scripts, consent is thought to be expressed in subtle, indirect ways rather than through a direct verbal 'yes' (Edgar and Fitzpatrick, 1993). This has implications for all parties in how they communicate and interpret consent, specifically as non-verbal expressions of consent are likely to be more common than direct verbal articulations (Jozkowski et al. 2014). Unlike non-sexual acts, which can be declined without a clear verbal 'no', a frequent notion is that non-consensual

DOI: 10.4324/9781003358756-18

sex is the result of miscommunication (Coy et al. 2013). To this end, Gavey (2005) demonstrates the forces within society that provide a scaffold where women experience coercive or non-consensual sex. While there are differences between online and offline consent, the continuous blurring of online and offline boundaries challenges the neatness of the notion that private information publicly shared in a virtual setting does not impact a victim's offline life. I begin this chapter by exploring sexting and consent before considering image based sexual abuse and responses in New Zealand. Following an overview of the methods employed in this study, I discuss young people's understandings of consent, and their experiences with breaches of consent and how these have been responded to. The young participants report, including those who had intimate images shared non-consensually, numerous experiences of harm and distress. Yet, discussion and education on consent continue to be gendered, risk-based and abstinence-focused in both ideology and application. Responses to breaches in consent reinforce the status quo, including victim blaming, often victims are punished alongside those who have forwarded the images. Far-reaching change is needed to improve responses and interventions to image based sexual abuse. I conclude that only by understanding and conceptualizing consent within a rights-based framework can we begin to appropriately address image based sexual abuse.

Sexting and Consent

While definitions of sexting vary, Ringrose et al. (2012) broadly define it to include taking and sharing sexually explicit texts and images within peer-networked activity. A set of understandings around consent and privacy underpin sexting practices (Hasinoff and Shepherd 2014). Various reasons for sexting have been reported by young people, for instance flirting, exploring their sexuality and their sexual identities or as a joke or a bonding ritual (van Ouytsal et al. 2017). Research shows that only a small minority of teens make and/or distribute sexting images, but scholars have not reached agreement on whether this results in pleasure, pressure, distress or harm (De Ridder 2019; Döring 2014; Salter et al. 2013; Setty 2018). Young women have reported feeling pressured to consent to producing sexual images, and young men report having to negotiate competitive masculinity in homosocial settings, which includes pressure to 'trade' images (Ringrose et al. 2022). In these cases, young women's bodies are commodified as a social currency of sorts. Creating and sending sexual images requires young women to carefully manage their desire for desirability (Meehan 2021b) and the risk of being labelled a slut (Ringrose et al. 2012).

It has been consistently demonstrated that an obvious gendered double standard persists (Mascheroni et al. 2015, Meehan 2022). Public interest in young women's sexuality has long been attributed to the sexualisation of young women, including renegotiation of the boundary between public and private (McNair 2002), which is intrinsically linked with consent. Reflective of broader sexual scripts, while young women are viewed as being more sexualised (Hasinoff and Shepherd 2014), they are tasked with remaining private, pure and morally responsible for protecting their bodies from male sexuality (Willem et al. 2019). By privileging male sexuality, young women's bodies and their sexual experiences are somehow the property of young men (Ringrose et al. 2012).

Image Based Sexual Abuse

Image-based sexual abuse is the 'non-consensual creation and/or distribution of private sexual images' (McGlynn et al. 2017, 534; Henry et al. 2020). While most intimate images are not forwarded without consent, those that are have the potential to go viral (McGlynn et al. 2017). As well as exploiting a person's sexual identity and violating their sexual autonomy, victims often experience online abuse in addition to experiencing image-based sexual abuse (McGlynn et al. 2017). This includes sexual threats, offensive comments about the victim's appearance, body, sexuality, and sexual agency (McGlynn et al. 2017). Additional harms to the victim can include trauma, depression, bullying, low self-esteem, self-harm and even suicide (Angelides 2013).

If an intimate image or text is shared without the sender's consent, repercussions are almost always more harmful for the woman (Hasinoff and Shepherd 2014). By placing responsibility of risk and harassment on the woman, the implication is that the non-consensual distribution of intimate images is a result of women's supposedly bad choices, which diverts attention away from the people responsible for privacy violations (Hasinoff 2014). Victim blaming narratives are entrenched and breaking of trust by young men is naturalised and accepted (Setty 2019). Women are assumed to be aware and responsible for their choices and their social identities, and told they 'deserve' the negative consequences that may arise (Mascheroni et al. 2015). The 'slut' stigma reduces women's social status and cultural capital (Willem et al. 2019), popular misogyny becomes commonplace (Banet-Weiser 2018), and the cultural practices that reproduce and justify the perpetration of sexual aggression and violence (Rentschler 2014, 67) by men towards women, becomes the norm.

Responding to Image Based Sexual Abuse in New Zealand

In 2019, a study found 250,000 New Zealanders experienced image based sexual abuse. In that same year, Netsafe – the approved internet watchdog for New Zealand – also received 3500 reports of abuse with 85–90 percent of them being from women. Victims of this abuse are often blamed and shamed for the behaviour perpetrated against them (McGlynn et al. 2017). The current legislative provision for image-based sexual abuse in New Zealand is the Harmful Digital Communications Act (HDCA) 2015. The Act, which covers numerous online offences, has a maximum penalty which includes fines of up to $50,000 for an individual, or two years imprisonment. The original emphasis of the Act was on the perpetrator's intent to cause harm to the victim, and the victim's experience of distress. Both are exceedingly difficult to define, let alone measure. This is evident in the court outcomes published by the Ministry of Justice and reported in the press. Only 106 people were charged under the HDCA in 2020, and only 70 percent of those charged were convicted (Bradley 2021). To put this in context, 2019 study found 250,000 people (5 per cent of the population) had experienced image based sexual abuse (Pacheco et al. 2019) and each year Netsafe receives more than 3500 reports of abuse, with around 550 being image based sexual abuse (Bradley 2021). An amendment in 2022, The Harmful Digital Communications (Unauthorised Posting of Intimate Visual Recording) Amendment, changed the focus of the Act to prioritise consent. In this instance, 'consent is given voluntarily and in full knowledge of how the intimate visual recording will be used'. By focusing on consent, or lack of, the amendment will remove some of the limitations of the current Act. This Act is a compelling tool to recognise the harms of image based sexual abuse and it signifies a robust public statement that such conduct will not be tolerated. Nevertheless, law alone is unlikely to provide a panacea in tackling image based sexual abuse and the culture which underpins it.

While this legislation has provided some form of redress for adult women, young women continue to rely on ad hoc resolution, which differs depending on jurisdiction or the school they attend. Instead, sexting and image based sexual abuse are attended to through school-based sexuality education and policies. Sexuality education in New Zealand is a required component of The New Zealand Curriculum and Te Marautanga o Aotearoa (the curriculum statement for Māori medium schools). The Ministry of Education sets out that schools need to provide 'a broad education through a balanced curriculum covering essential learning areas' (MOE 2015). A 2018 report released by the Education Review Office demonstrated that many schools are struggling to teach sexuality education. While the Ministry of Education in New Zealand confirmed that physical/biological/puberty aspects were 'well covered' in compulsory health and PE curricula, fewer than half of secondary schools were covering porn and sexual violence.

In this chapter, I present findings from qualitative small group interviews with young people and one-to-one interviews with teachers exploring their perceptions and practices around sexting and image based sexual abuse. The research focused on how both young people and adults understood consent, sexual images and their perceptions of responsibility, abuse and blame. I argue that to address harmful sharing practices, peer and school responses must move away from the current gendered construction of consent towards a more ethical framework based on inclusion and rights of young people. The following sections commence with an overview of the qualitative data collection before exploring young people's understandings of consent, including the informal norms and values they have created. Following this, I explore participant's experiences of breaches of consent, responses from schools and the implications of this for young people. Finally, I argue that we need to 'de-gender' consent as the first step in the move towards a rights-based framework in which girls are no longer responsibilised as sexual gatekeepers.

Methods

Small friendship group interviews were conducted with 106 self-selecting young people, aged 12–16, in three participating schools in New Zealand. Young people were recruited from one rural co-ed and two urban single sex (one male, one female) schools. In the sample schools, the study was advertised to students, and they self-selected if they were interested in participating.

Small friendship group interviews of established friends in the same year group allowed many of the benefits of a focus group, but overcame some of the limitations, such as the participants not knowing or liking each other. It was hoped that a comfortable small group setting with established friends would be more conducive to providing deeper insights and respecting confidentiality. I provided refreshments and the groups began with a scenario to open discussion then focused on loose topic areas. The participants and I were the only people present at the group interviews which were held in a classroom at each school.

Data were recorded and transcribed by a professional transcriber and I verified the transcripts. Drawing on Braun and Clarke's (2006) thematic analysis framework, data were coded and analysed using a latent approach, which allowed me to move away from the explicit and obvious content of the data, to identify initial organising codes. Common themes were then identified, reviewed, further defined and situated within the scholarly literature.[1] or the purposes of this chapter, perceptions and practices around sexting and image-based sexual abuse, I coded the data for: 1) understanding consent; 2) experiencing breaches of consent; 3) responding to breaches of consent; and 4) towards a rights-based framework of consent. Excerpts below are taken from young people, who are referred to by pseudonyms throughout the chapter.

Understanding Consent

The term 'consent' was rarely used by the young people in this study; 'asking if it's okay' or 'do you agree to' was more common. Consent was often considered to be abstract and passive, more aligned with permission seeking and granting. The participants considered consent to be more important when asking for an image although the young women did talk about how receiving an image without consent, for example unsolicited dick pics, made then feel uncomfortable. In keeping with sexual scripts outlined above, consent was most often communicated non-verbally and implicitly. Requests for 'nudes' usually happened after a period of flirting, and on occasion the requestor would send (usually) his image in the hope of receiving on in return. Consent often happened within this context, which oftentimes made it difficult to 'just say no'.

AMY: It's usually kind of like signalling to that girl that he's keen and he's open to sex.

CLAIRE: What about consent, where does that come in?

AMY: I feel like some guys out there are good with it; are good with the consent and all. Like, if she doesn't want to do it, some guys will be like, 'Okay, I'm not going to pressure you into doing it.' And, then there's the other guys that would be like, 'Oh come on, it will be fine, just do it', and the girl doesn't really have a say.

ANNA: Like, there will be stuff before, he might send something and say it's not a big deal. He's my boyfriend. I should want to do this kind of stuff with him. Things like he does things like says really nice things so compliments you or your things. It's like you owe him something. I mean you're not in the moment to think about the things that could happen. It's not that you don't have respect for yourself; it's that sometimes you don't think about that moment. You only think about that time you guys are talking.

AMY: It could even be like not nude nudes but pictures of you in your bra and undies

While sexting is a relatively recent practice, the young people who participated in this research were creating their own norms and practices around the sharing of nudes. A set of informal norms and expectations around consent were evident in each of the schools visited. Discussions of young women's pleasure was often absent from many of these discussions. Nudes were believed to be for the pleasure of boys, either to masturbate, or for status as part of the gendered homosocial economy (Ringrose et al. 2022).

SARA: If girls go around and send lots of nudes to boys; that's seen as a slut and a really negative thing. Whereas, if you're a guy you'll be seen as a legend, and it's quite the opposite. I think that's probably not cool.

CLAIRE: Why do you think that is?

SARA: Double standards: boys have this image in their head that they have to be so manly.

SIMONA: They want to be better than their mates.

SAM: They compete against one another but girls; we're like… insecure.

Both boys and girls emphasised the potential for the images to be shared non-consensually and they articulated the need for girls to 'be careful' and to be 'sexy but not slutty'.

PETER: A girl sending nudes to everybody would be considered kind of like slutty.

PAULA: Yeah, girls need to be careful. People put labels on them. They start to get a reputation for things that they do instead of who they actually are and stuff like that.

Experiencing Breaches of Consent

Young women were more likely to have experienced a breach of consent. In the group below, we can see how the gendered difference is articulated. While there were reports of it happening to boys, the consensus was that boys would get 'some stick' but then it would be forgotten about. Girls, by contrast, would be subjected to judging, demeaning humour and sexual harassment.

BARRY: Yeah, one of my close friends, his nudes got leaked and they went everywhere; or like all around [town] for I think it was like two months tops, and then everybody has forgotten by now.

BRENDA: But then I think for a guy to send it rather than a girl; it's almost like the environment they're in as well. Their guy friends wouldn't care whereas when a girl's one got leaked to her friends it's like the judging thing again.

BARBRA: Her class would probably just laugh at her and crack up.

BRENDA: If the girl's nudes are leaked to the guy's friends they all see her as an easy target for sex.

When talking about nude images being shared non-consensually, they were often labelled as a 'leak' rather than abuse. In doing so, the response becomes disembodied – the non-consensually sharing of the image is separate to the body, yet the resulting harms are experienced in an embodied way. In a similar vein to their adult counterparts (Henry et al. 2022), those who had been victims of image based sexual abuse described the manifestations of this distress as personal 'I felt attacked, like everyone was attacking me' (Cleo), emotional 'I couldn't believe it, I was really upset' (Ruby), visceral 'it was like mental rape' (Paula), and physical 'I felt so sick that I was sick when it happened' (Mary).

In addition to the gravity of the harm experienced, this was compounded by accusations that 'she was asking for it' as well as young women being victim blamed and slut shamed, regardless of whether or not they felt pressured into creating and sharing the nude in the first place. Yet, in some of the discussions with young women, several identified the gendered imbalance and how the discourse around non-consensually shared nudes seeks to reinforce existing inequalities.

It's probably to do with the fact that throughout history in general, and even now it still exists – it's always been, the men are higher than women; it's how it's been throughout history; and only recently, last few years, is that attempting to be rectified. But it still exists. So, the guys won't... It might do some damage, but it won't last forever. But for the girls, their found as maybe easier targets, and they're like, 'Oh, we can bring them down further.' Something along those lines.

(Ruby)

The intersecting nature of embodied harms, contrasted with neutralizing language which disembodies the action, within the context of a victim blaming discourse, demonstrates the complexity of young women's experiences with image based sexual abuse.

Responding to Image Based Sexual Abuse

Breaches of consent that entailed image based sexual abuse were responded to in formal and informal ways. Schools responded formally through education and discipline policies. Education programmes usually took on a risk-based, abstinence focused stance. In the mixed sex school, classes on consent were targeted more towards female students.

PAULA: Yeah, it's like up to us to say no
PETRA: The boys ask us and we have to decide and that's not right
PAULA: Yeah, consent isn't just a girl's thing

In the all-girls school, consent was covered in some detail and onus was placed on the young women to 'say no'. This approach often neglected to consider the nuance of the context in which consent was being broached. This led to some female participants asking whether boys were taught consent at all.

EMMA: And do guys get taught about consent because we always get taught about consent but do they get taught about consent as well at all boys schools?

Through teaching consent in this way, girls were responsibilised to enforce a gatekeeping role which enabled them to be blamed and shamed if their images were shared non-consensually. Ultimately, they were made responsible for their decisions, even bad decisions (Fine and McClelland 2006). When consent was breached, often both the victim and the perpetrator were punished equally, which frequently entailed suspension from school. For some young women, when both victims and perpetrators were suspended, this led to others who had not necessarily seen the victim's image finding out about it through word of mouth which made the 'shame harder to hide because then everyone knew what had happened' (Paula).

Informally, terminology used by teachers at schools to discuss image based sexual abuse skirted around 'permission' and 'leaks' of intimate images, rather than harassment or violence. The embodied responses of image based sexual abuse, such as dropping a phone, were reduced to 'being shocked' by language that neutralised the visceral reactions to this abuse. Much of the terminology used reinforced hierarchies of male domination and female subordination, providing evidence of the nature of gender imbalances in schools. This was demonstrated in how young students spoke about these interactions, not in a way that made strong links to sexual harassment and gendered abuse (Ringrose et al. 2022). The effect of the informal language used was compounded by perceptions of responsibility and quickness to blame young women for creating intimate images in the first place. This feeds into the formal gendered responses to consent, and breaches of consent, which ratifies the cycle of language, perceptions of responsibility, and speed at which young women were blamed. The implications of formal and informal responses by schools were twofold – gendered harms were further entrenched, where established norms were rigid and hard to challenge; and barriers to help-seeking were erected for young women who had been victims of image based sexual abuse.

Towards a Rights-based Framework of Consent

The informal and formal ways in which consent is gendered in schools, through sexuality education and responding to breaches of consent, continues to uphold the patriarchal status quo. By overlooking the rights and experiences of young women, while continuing to privilege young men's sexuality, a context of entitlement ensures that young women continue to be tasked as sexual gatekeepers (Dobson and Ringrose 2016; Ringrose et al. 2012). The gendered nature of school-based sexuality education and responses means that young women are not recognised as sexual subjects. Both education and responses reinforce the notion that the onus of consent is upon the woman, sexting is risky and harm is inevitable, young women's bodily expressions are shameful and likely to attract shame and blame. The best way to manage this risk and to avoid harm is to not consent to sext – to say no (Hasinoff 2015; Dobson and Ringrose 2016). Through being implored to say no, there are few opportunities for them to engage in legitimate sexual and bodily expression of their own accord (Tolman et al. 2015).

What is needed are opportunities for young people to critically engage with the socio-cultural processes in which they sext, as well as their roles and responsibilities as peers (Hasinoff 2015). By making strides to de-gender sexuality education and responses to breaches of consent, instances and harms associated with image based sexual abuse may be lessened.

There are two key ways schools could initiate this shift. First, an articulation of young people's rights (Dobson and Ringrose 2016) are necessary to disestablish existing gendered norms around sexting and consent as well as the normalisation of harms resulting from image based sexual abuse. These rights should be informed by the socio-cultural context in which young people sext. Albury (2017) posits the importance of these rights as a means to challenge the entrenched assumptions that facilitate the blaming and shaming of victims. The focus should be on young people's rights to explore their sexualities, the right to make informed choices over their bodies and expressions and the right to support if needed. If this was the case, it would be less acceptable to share intimate images non-consensually. In the event of harm, the emphasis should then be on the actions of the perpetrator, not the perceived wrongs of the victim.

Second, schools need to move beyond consent education as protection for young women, who are considered passive pre-victims. Dobson and Ringrose (2016) in their exploration of 'sext education' pedagogies, suggest that for digital sexual ethics to be upheld, it is imperative that schools encourage young people to critically unpack harmful practices. This includes image based sexual abuse and the tendencies towards blaming and shaming young female victims. Moving towards positive sexual rights (Dobson 2018) requires a shift away from a binary of victim versus empowerment. Instead, it is essential that schools delve into the structures of inequality which ensure that some young people are positioned as more obviously the recipients of ethical and consensual treatment, while others are structurally more vulnerable to unethical treatment, abuse and limited opportunities for meaningful consent (Dobson 2018, 2). Sexual citizenship, a concept coined by Evans (1993), has been used by Albury (2016) to focus on the youth culture in which images are taken and shared. Albury argues for a move away from assumptions that sexting is always about risk, objectification and exploitation, to the varied ways that young people practice sexual and bodily self-expression. In this way, Albury (2017) asks how sexuality education pedagogy might include digital sexual rights to focus on ethical decision making, whereby young people are encouraged to challenge gendered norms and harms. In these ways, consent becomes the responsibility of everyone, not just young women as sexual gatekeepers. Sexting, and the culture in which it takes place, is a ripe site for critical co-learning about sex, sexual expressions, relationships, rights, responsibilities and ethics (Albury et al. 2013) and meaningful change to the current provision of sex education. There must be space for a conversation on sexting rights, as well as responsibilities (Albury 2017), even if this does cause initial discomfort as it goes against the status quo.

Conclusion

The HDCA, while established in part to respond to image based sexual abuse, provides no resolution for young victims. Instead, they rely on the school they attend addressing issues of consent. School-based consent education and responses to breaches of consent are informed by gendered double standards. Both education and responses disadvantage young women at all stages of the process, resulting in gendered harms and victim-blaming. This was evident both formally, through school education and discipline policies, and informally, through language and quickness to blame. This approach reinforces entrenched gender norms by de-legitimising young women's right to sexual and bodily expressions and pleasure and reinforcing their role as pre-victims. In doing so, it fails to hold those who perpetrate image-based sexual abuse to account, nor does it address the social, emotional and physical fall-out for the victim including shame and blame. Far-reaching change is needed to improve responses and interventions to image based sexual abuse. There is a pressing need to de-gender consent as the first step in the move towards a framework of sexual rights in which girls are no longer responsibilised as sexual gatekeepers. Only by understanding and conceptualizing consent within a rights-based framework can we begin to appropriately address image based sexual abuse.

Note

1 Ethical approval was obtained from the University of Auckland Human Participants Ethics Committee on 4th May 2016 reference: 017039

References

Albury, K. 2016. Sexting, schools and surveillance: Mediated sexuality in the classroom. In *The Routledge Research Companion to Geographies of Sex and Sexualities* (pp. 383–392). Routledge.

Albury, K. 2017. Just because it's public doesn't mean it's any of your business: Adults' and children's sexual rights in digitally mediated spaces. *New Media Society*, 19, 713–725.

Albury, K., Crawford, K., Byron, P., & Mathews, B.P. 2013. *Young People and Sexting in Australia: Ethics, Representation and the Law*. Sydney: ARC Centre for Creative Industries and Innovation/Journalism and Media Research Centre, UNSW.

Angelides, S. 2013. 'Technology, hormones, and stupidity': The affective politics of teenage sexting. *Sexualities* 16 (5–6), 665–689.

Attwood, F., Bale, C., & Barker, M. 2013. *The Sexualisation Report*https://thesexualizationreport.files.wordpress.com/2013/12/thesexualizationreport.pdf

Banet-Weiser, S. 2018. *Empowered: Popular Feminism and Popular Misogyny*. Duke University Press.

Barker, M. 2013. Consent is a grey area? A comparison of understandings of consent in *50 Shades of Grey* and on the BDSM blogosphere. *Sexualities* 16 (8), 896–914.

Bradley, A. 2021Image-based sexual abuse: Victims with ongoing mental health issues struggle for help from ACC and justice system. *New Zealand Herald* (19th May 2021). Available at: https://www.nzherald.co.nz/nz/image-based-sexual-abuse-victims-with-ongoing-mental-health-issues-struggle-for-help-from-acc-and-justice-system/B2CRMQ47UEATATMY2CYH6SMLE4/.

Braun, V., & Clarke, V. 2006Using thematic analysis in psychology. *Qualitative Research in Psychology* 3 (2), 77–101.

Carmody, M. 2008. *Sex and Ethics: Young People and Ethical Sex* (Vol. 1) Palgrave Macmillan Australia.

Coy, M., Kelly, L., Elvines, F., Garner, M., & Kanyeredzi, A. 2013*Sex without Consent, I Suppose That Is Rape': How Young People in England Understand Sexual Consent*. Office of the Children's Commissioner.

De Ridder, S. 2019. Sexting as sexual stigma: The paradox of sexual self-representation in digital youth cultures. *European Journal of Cultural Studies* 22(5–6), 563–578.

Dobson, A.S. 2018. Sexting, intimate and sexual media practices, and social justice. In Dobson, A.S., Carah, N., Robards, B. (eds), *Digital Intimate Publics and Social Media*. Cham, Switzerland: Palgrave Macmillan, pp. 93–110.

Dobson, A. S., & Ringrose, J. 2016. Sext education: Pedagogies of sex, gender and shame in the schoolyards of Tagged and Exposed. *Sex Education* 16 (1), 8–21.

Döring, N. 2014. Consensual sexting among adolescents: Risk prevention through abstinence education or safer sexting? *Cyberpsychology: Journal of Psychosocial Research on Cyberspace*, 8 (1)

Edgar, T., & Fitzpatrick, M.A. 1993. Expectations for sexual interaction: A cognitive test of the sequencing of sexual communication behaviours. *Health Communication* 5 (4), 239–261.

Education Review Office2018. *Promoting Wellbeing Through Sexuality Education.* Wellington.

Evans, D. 1993. *Sexual Citizenship: The Material Construction of Sexualities.* London: Routledge.

Farvid, P., & Braun, V. 2018. 'You worry,'cause you want to give a reasonable account of yourself": Gender, identity management, and the discursive positioning of 'risk' in men's and women's talk about heterosexual casual sex. *Archives of Sexual Behaviour* 47 (5), 1405–1421.

Fine, M, & McClelland, S. 2006. The politics of teen women's sexuality: Public policy and the adolescent female body. *Emory Law Journal*, 993.

Gavey, N. 2005. *Violence Against Women: Beyond Gender Neutrality.* In Contribution to Special Topic Session, co-presented with Alison Towns at The Women's Convention, Wellington (pp. 3–6)

Hasinoff, A.A. 2014. Blaming sexualization for sexting. *Girlhood Studies* 7 (1), 102–120.

Hasinoff, A.A. 2015. *Sexting Panic: Rethinking Criminalization, Privacy, and Consent.* University of Illinois Press.

Hasinoff, A.A., & Shepherd, T. 2014. Sexting in context: Privacy norms and expectations. *International Journal of Communication* 8, 24.

Henry, N., McGlynn, C., Flynn, A., Johnson, K., Powell, A., & Scott, A.J. 2020. *Image-Based Sexual Abuse: A Study on the Causes and Consequences of Non-consensual Nude or Sexual Imagery.* Routledge.

Henry, N., Gavey, N., McGlynn, C., & Rackley, R. 2022. 'Devastating, like it broke me': Responding to image-based sexual abuse in Aotearoa New Zealand. *Criminology & Criminal Justice*, 1–19.

Hollway, W. 1984. Women's power in heterosexual sex. *Women's Studies International Forum* 7 (1), 63–68.

Hunt, G., Sanders, E., Petersen, M.A., Bogren, A. 2022. 'Blurring the Line': Intoxication, gender, consent, and sexual encounters among young adults. *Contemporary Drug Problems* 49 (1): 84–105.

Jozkowski, K., Peterson, Z., Sanders, S., Dennis, B., & Reece, M., 2014. Gender differences in heterosexual college students' conceptualizations and indicators of sexual consent: Implications for contemporary sexual assault prevention education. *The Journal of Sex Research* 51 (8), 904–916.

Livingstone, S., & Mason, J. 2015. Sexual rights and sexual risks among youth online. London School of Economics and Political Science, commissioned by the European NGO Alliance for Child Safety Online (ENACSO).

Mascheroni, G., Vincent, J., & Jimenez, E. 2015. 'Girls are addicted to likes so they post semi-naked selfies': Peer mediation, normativity and the construction of identity online. *Cyberpsychology: Journal of Psychosocial Research on Cyberspace* 9 (1), 5.

McGlynn, C., Rackley, E., & Houghton, R. 2017. Beyond 'revenge porn': The continuum of image-based sexual abuse. *Feminist Legal Studies* 25 (3): 25–46.

McNair, B. 2002. *Striptease Culture: Sex, Media and the Democratisation of Desire.* Routledge.

Meehan, C. 2021a. Young people's perceptions of young women's engagement in sexting. *Culture, Health & Sexuality*, 1–13.

Meehan, C. 2021b. 'It's like mental rape I guess': Young New Zealanders' responses to image-based sexual abuse. In *The Palgrave Handbook of Gendered Violence and Technology* (pp. 281–295). Palgrave Macmillan, Cham.

Meehan, C. 2022. 'If someone's freaky, everyone loves it. It's all about the drama': Young women's responses and reactions to image based sexual abuse of other young women. *Journal of Gender Studies* 31(2), 231–242.

MOE (Ministry of Education). 2015. *Sexuality Education: Guidelines for Principals, Boards of Trustees and Teachers*. Wellington: Ministry of Education.

Netsafe. 2019. Image-based sexual abuse: A snapshot of New Zealand adults' experiences. https://netsafe.org.nz/wp-content/uploads/2019/01/IBSA-report-2019_Final.pdf.

Pacheco, E., Melhuish, N., & Fiske, J. 2019. Image-based sexual abuse: A snapshot of New Zealand adults' experiences. *SSRN Electronic Journal*. doi:10.2139/ssrn.3315984.

Rentschler, C. 2014. Rape culture and the feminist politics of social media. *Girlhood Studies* 7 (1), 65–82.

Ringrose, J., Gill, R., Livingstone, S., & Harvey, L. 2012. *A Qualitative Study of Children, Young People and 'Sexting'*. A report prepared for the NSPCC.

Ringrose, J., Regehr, K., Whitehead, S. 2022. 'Wanna trade?': Cisheteronormative homosocial masculinity and the normalization of abuse in youth digital sexual image exchange. *Journal of Gender Studies* 31 (2): 243–261.

Salter, M., Crofts, T., and Lee, M. 2013. Beyond criminalisation and responsibilisation: Sexting, gender and young people. *Current Issues in Criminal Justice* 24 (3), 301–316.

Setty, E. 2018. Meanings of bodily and sexual expression in youth sexting culture: Young women's negotiation of gendered risks and harms. *Sex Roles*, 1–21.

Setty, E. 2019. A rights-based approach to youth sexting: Challenging risk, shame, and the denial of rights to bodily and sexual expression within youth digital sexual culture. *International Journal of Bullying Prevention* 1 (4), 298–311.

Thorburn, B., Gavey, N., Single, G., Wech, A., Calder-Dawe, O., & Benton-Greig, P. 2021. To send or not to send nudes: New Zealand girls critically discuss the contradictory gendered pressures of teenage sexting. *Women's Studies International Forum* 85 (3), 102448.

Tolman, D. L., Anderson, S. M., & Belmonte, K. 2015. Mobilizing metaphor: Considering complexities, contradictions and contexts in adolescent girls' and young women's sexual agency. *Sex Roles* 73 (7): 298–310.

Van Ouytsel, J., Van Gool, E., Walrave, M., Ponnet, K., & Peeters, E. 2017. Sexting: Adolescents' perceptions of the applications used for, motives for, and consequences of sexting. *Journal of Youth Studies*, 20 (4): 446–470.

Willem, C., Araüna, N., & Tortajada, I. 2019. Chonis and pijas: Slut-shaming and double standards in online performances among Spanish teens. *Sexualities* 22(4), 532–548.

14

NEGOTIATING CONSENT IN ONLINE KINKY SPACES

Liam Wignall and Mark McCormack

The dominant image of kink in the heterosexual imagination is a *50 Shades of Grey* style form of sexual activity within a monogamous relationship, with high street shops like *Ann Summers* and online stores like *Love Honey* enabling light exploration of kinky acts for those less familiar with kink. This does not reflect the reality of the practices, cultures and identities associated with kink, and how it is present both in the mainstream and multiple subcultures (Simula et al., 2023). To recognize this diversity, and move away from simplistic definitions, kink is best understood as a spectrum of sexual or erotic activities outside normative versions of sex undertaken for sensory, emotional, or intellectual pleasure (see Wignall, 2022). It tends to include a combination of the exchange of power, or perception of this, the infliction/receiving of pain, the wearing of gear, or the fetishization of body parts or objects. Kink can be practiced individually or in groups and can be organised into communities and subcultures. It is *consensual*, with a shared understanding that the activities are kinky. This definition of kink, alongside multiple alternatives (e.g., Moser & Kleinplatz, 2007; Newmahr, 2011;Weinberg et al., 1984; Williams & Sprott, 2022), places significant emphasis on the consent of all people involved in the activities. As such, this chapter explores how people who engage in kink negotiate consent, particularly when meeting others through socio-sexual networking sites (SSNS).

In much of the 20th century, kink tended to be practised in dedicated subcultural venues, often called "dungeons" or similar terms (see Rubin, 1991). These venues were vital in providing a private space to meet others interested in kink in a context where such sexual practices were illegal (or subject to police harassment), where meeting people with similar interests was difficult otherwise, and where the gear associated with kink was expensive. Kink venues still maintain an important status within kink communities (Steinmetz & Maginn, 2014), yet changing queer landscapes and the flourishing of technology has

DOI: 10.4324/9781003358756-19

provided alternative pathways for individuals to engage in kink (Simula, 2019; Wignall, 2022). Contrary to older narratives of needing to be invited into a community or having to *earn one's leathers* (Rubin, 1991), individuals can permeate the boundaries of kink subcultures more easily by engaging with kink-oriented SSNS, creating online profiles to explore these online kink spaces and interact with others (Graham et al., 2016; Wignall, 2017). Indeed, individuals can use the internet to research and learn about kink at their own pace, find others to engage in kink with, and explore kink communities (Hughes & Hammack, 2022). This has occurred alongside a normalization of leisured sexual practices, even if kink sits on the periphery of this (McCormack et al., 2021; McCormack et al., 2022).

It is in this new context of the internet where the dynamics of kink have changed, including on how consent is negotiated. While Wignall (2022; 2019) explores the impact of the internet in detail elsewhere, here we focus on how consent is negotiated and discussed in these new digital contexts, where the "old guard" and more collective practising of kink are not present to provide guidance or enforce rules related to norms and values of kink. Drawing on interviews with 30 gay and bisexual kinky men, we show that there was a lack of knowledge of "safe, sane, and consensual" (SSC; a common framework to distinguish consensual kink from abuse) and related terms; instead, participants highlighted the importance of online safety when engaging with kink SSNS and the importance of ongoing communication for exploring interests and boundaries. Implications of these findings for academics, activists and practitioners are discussed.

Consent in Contemporary Kink Cultures

In mainstream culture, kink practices have often been socially stigmatized, medically pathologized and criminalized (Khan, 2014). Referred to by several terms (including sadism, masochism, S&M, BDSM), kink was framed in these ways because it was seen to be a form of harm perpetrated by people who were psychologically unwell and needed protecting from themselves by the state, whether that be via medics, psychiatrists or the police (Dunkley & Brotto, 2018). As legal regulation and cultural condemnation lessened, practices changed and kink went from being near-totally hidden from mainstream culture to being discussed and present within it (see Wignall, 2022).

During this period, kinksters sought to challenge the stereotypes that persisted around kink (Shindel & Moser, 2011). The language of "*safe, sane and consensual*" (SSC) was adopted by kink practitioners both to counter these dominant preconceptions and as a heuristic about the norms and expectations of consensual kink (Williams et al., 2014). SSC was quickly adopted as a mantra for kink practitioners, activists, and the academic community (Langdridge & Barker, 2013) as a simple and accessible way of countering the pathological framing of kink in broader culture.

Yet as kink cultures developed, SSC came under criticism. It has been critiqued for seeming to distinguish between acceptable and unacceptable forms of kink practice without nuance, perpetuate kink stigma for a subset of practices, and re-enforce normative binaries of sane/insane (Downing, 2007). As such, other terminology has been proposed, including "RACK" (Risk-Aware Consensual Kink) and, more recently, the "4Cs" framework of "Consent, Communication, Caring and Caution" (Williams et al. 2014). The central tenets of consent and caution (safety/risk-awareness) are still present in the 4Cs but highlight the importance of communication within BDSM (Kaak, 2016), and the necessity of caring about kink partners. While the 4Cs is still relatively new, it provides an open space to negotiate the complexities involved in kink.

Beyond this terminology, it is important to focus on *how* risk and consent are negotiated by kink practitioners (Dunkley & Brotto, 2019). Some research has highlighted how this is done for kink organisations and clubs (e.g., Sagarin et al., 2019; Weiss, 2011), but less is known about how individuals who engage in kink outside of these traditional venues understand consent (Coppens et al., 2020; Zambelli, 2017). These individuals may be less invested in kink and exploring it through social media or they may be deeply committed to it but reject venues and collective engagement. Without the structures of these venues, and new discourses and dynamics of consent in popular culture, the ways of negotiating consent may be markedly different for this group of kinky men.

A Note on Methods

Data come from a larger study exploring the experiences of kinky gay and bisexual cisgender men (n=30). Participants' ages ranged from 21 to 62 (M = 27.63). All participants were UK residents at the point of data collection: 27 participants were Caucasian, 2 were Asian, and 1 was Black. Twenty-seven participants identified as gay; 3 participants identified as bisexual. Participants identified with various kinky roles, including Leatherman, pup, and rigger. Twenty-five participants identified with a switch role, with 5 participants identifying with more dominant roles and 7 identifying with more submissive roles within the switch context; the remaining 5 identified as solely submissive.

Participants identified as kinky but differed in levels of immersion into kink communities. As such, participants were classified during analysis as either a community participant or non-community participant. A holistic approach was undertaken to identify these two groups of participants, drawing on participants' understandings of kink, their SSNS profiles, and self-identification. Community participants framed kink as a socio-sexual activity, invested in their online profiles (multiple profile pictures; friends linked to their profiles; profiles containing demographic information; interaction with online forums), described how they had multiple kinky friends and attended kink events, and identified as part of a kink community. Non-community participants described kink as primarily a sexual activity, did not provide as much detail in their online profiles, did not describe connections to kink communities, and actively distanced themselves from a community label. Participants were evenly split across the two groups.

Participants differed with their levels of real-world kink experience, ranging from two years' experience to 20 years of experience (M = 5.9 years).

Interviews lasted approximately 60 minutes on average. They were transcribed and analysed inductively using thematic analysis (Jaspal, 2020), with initial codes grouped into focused codes before being arranged into themes and subthemes. These themes were also discussed with five participants who agreed with them. Ethical approval was granted from the University of Sunderland.

Results

Safety and Consent beyond SSC

Despite the popularity of SSC and similar frameworks in academic research on kink, 25 of the 30 participants had never heard the phrase SSC before, or alternatives including RACK or the 4Cs. Epitomising responses to questions about the terms, David said, "No idea what those terms are", Ben said, "I've no idea of the history of kink", while Thomas said, "I've not heard of them."

The five participants who had heard of at least one of the terms could only offer vague descriptions and did not use them in their own kink engagements. For example, Andy said, "I'm aware of the concepts of SSC and RACK, but I've never heard much about them… I know kink has a long and varied history, but I don't really know anything about it." While not knowing what it was, Sam said, "I've heard of safe, sane and consensual, but don't really know what it is. You can sort of work it out though." Ryan knew about the terms in context of the interview discussion, saying, "I've heard of SSC, as opposed to BDSM being abuse? I don't know RACK though."

It was more than the term SSC falling out of usage, however, as some participants had negative associations with it. For example, Oscar said, "I usually find people who use SSC are the people to avoid. I've heard people use the language, but it's not something I use myself. It reminds me of D&D [drug and disease free] on profiles." Given how D&D has been critiqued as stigmatizing drug use and STIs, this suggests that Oscar views SSC as a similar term that is dated in contemporary kink discourse. Similarly, Andy added, "I just think people who have SSC on their profiles play in a very specific way, and it turns me off." While a lack of knowledge on terminology is understandable for non-community participants, it is noteworthy for community participants, given how SSC is somewhat labelled as the cornerstone of kink (Langdridge & Barker, 2013). This speaks to a potential disconnect between dominant framings of kink and how some practitioners negotiate their play outside of community venues.

With these scripts absent, we now focus on how participants understood risk in terms of their kink practice. Three themes were identified from transcripts: *informal conversations; the importance of sustained communication*; and *unstructured approaches*.

Informal Conversations to Assess Safety and Honesty

Rather than being concerned about elements of safety specific to kink as characterized in SSC language traditionally found in kink subcultures, participants were far more concerned about contemporary risks associated with hooking up online generally, such as "catfishing" and whether their potential partner was "real" (Lauckner et al., 2019). For example, when asked about navigating safety with kink hook ups, George said, "You need to chat to people online for a bit. I normally ask for multiple pictures or very difficult pictures to forge, like their name on their foot. I've always been careful about who I talk to." Drawing on previous experiences, Stephen said, "I ask people to take a picture with the date on it. The first person I messaged online was a catfish. I drove to meet him, and they were a fake, so I learned quickly to check people out."

Rather than adopting a script of SSC or other terminology, participants instead sought to get to know their potential partner online by having extended conversations with them. Lloyd said, "I don't play with anyone until I've spoken to them for a while, to make sure they're not crazy, going to abuse me, rob me or harm me in anyway." Similarly, Harry said, "I speak to people for ages online first. You can work out if they're real, and a bit about their personality... it makes me feel safer." The discussion of harm and abuse by Lloyd, and explicitly mentioning safety by Harry, shows that similar concerns of SSC are present in their experiences and thoughts, but they navigate this through informal conversations rather than specific terminology.

Two participants spoke about asking for other forms of social media as a way of building trust. Sam said, "I might add them on Facebook at some point because that adds another level of realness. If they have a profile with friends and pictures, you will think they're more real." Fred described feeling more relaxed seeing others' social media, saying, "I don't normally let people stay over the first time I've met them. Unless I've had lots of conversations with them, or you have them on Facebook or something and you can see their jobs and friends." One reason why few participants spoke of doing this may be about concerns of sharing their own personal details given the broader stigma around kink in society even as attitudes have liberalized (see Wignall, 2022).

Finally, some participants described precautions taken when meeting for kink hook ups – again, these focused on the risks associated with meeting people online more generally rather than meeting for kinky sex. For example, Neville said, "If I am going somewhere new, I would scribble a note of my location and call the police if I don't get back in time." Similarly, Andy said, "I meet people in public, so if you say no, you're not jumping straight into their car. I don't have *rules*, but I'd like to feel safe, not too dark or lonely, somewhere I could tell the police about." Ben described how on kink SSNS, he felt more comfortable meeting up with people who had mutual friends listed, saying, "I trust the people I'm friends with on [kink SSNS], so if they're also friends with somebody then I feel safer meeting them." Ben's explanation highlights the importance of reputation and community with subcultures (Wignall, 2022). These strategies are not kink specific but for meeting strangers more generally. They also show an explicit understanding of the potential risks involved in meeting strangers balanced with their desire to engage in kink, perhaps more akin to the 4Cs (proceeding with caution rather than "safe").

Consent and the Importance of Communication

In this section, we focus on the role of discussing consent for participants. Good communication was deemed the most important factor when arranging kink sessions through kink SSNS, such as Recon.com and ClubCollared.com. Communication beforehand helped identify mutual kink interests, establish trust, and negotiate consent, including through "limits" (kink activities they will not participate in) and "safe words" (a word used so that the kink play stops immediately). This occurred in a more conversational way and developed organically from participants thinking about the potential risks involved. Depending on the age of participant and how recently they were talking about a previous example, this "chat" was primarily asynchronous text messaging, either on a computer or mobile phone. Recent innovations like voice notes (available on some SSNS and via apps like WhatsApp) were not used by participants, but this speaks to the time of data collection and may change as norms around social media change as well.

Most participants described sustained communication with potential kink hook-ups on SSNS. For example, Thomas said, "I normally have a lot of chat beforehand. I wouldn't put myself in a vulnerable position at first." Similarly, Harry said, "I make sure I talk to people a lot beforehand – what our kinks are, different levels of experience, and some limits." While participants did not want "endless chat" which could be seen as "wank material" rather than an in-person meeting, they recognised the importance of clear communication. However, for some participants, there was a balance between just enough communication and too much, with Kyle saying he did not "want to plan the scenes, because then they would feel too contrived." Here, communication should be used to arrange kinky sex, but not plan *exactly* what would happen. For as Oscar highlighted, kink should be "spontaneous."

This type of communication – discussing interests and things they will not do beforehand – is the primary method by which participants navigated consent. Notably, no participant explicitly used the word "consent" when describing the context or the purpose of these conversations. Instead, participants spoke about making themselves feel "comfortable" about meeting up and a way of agreeing which activities they would engage in. Terms like "limits" were used to describe what they did not consent to, but without using that word.

Kink practices exist on a spectrum with some activities being safer than others, with more risky ones sometimes known as "edge play" or "heavy play". Participants who engaged in practices that were riskier spoke about having more sustained conversations. For example, Caleb said, "There's a high degree of trust involved in any sort of sexual relationship, especially one that involves gear that can go quite badly wrong – I want to know someone at least a bit before I do something like that." Fred also emphasised the importance of establishing trust beforehand, especially if he intended to engage in more "heavy play" (e.g., edge play), so he can discuss "safe words, limits [and] ask how far they can be pushed." He added, "Kink meets can be safer than hook ups – the conversations are longer, and you tend to know more about a person because you chat longer." These extended discussions as a way of developing trust can be understood as indirect discussions of consent, as there is likely an implicit understanding that people would mention what they are interested in doing alongside hard limits. This highlights how the SSC label has fallen out of fashion, because the conversational tone is an implicit way of developing trust and implied consent.

However, while most participants described how they implemented some sort of rules, a minority described how they avoided in-depth communication beforehand or discussions of limits. Sometimes indicating their main kink interests on the SSNS, they would generally meet up and "see what happens" during a kink session. For example, Seamus said, "I just go with the flow really... see what happens." Similarly, when asked about building trust before a scene, David said, "It's common sense I suppose. You can get a gauge on it." The ability to "gauge" a person, was also mentioned by Thomas, who said, "I feel like I'm a fairly good judge of character." Neville described a similar approach to Thomas, but acknowledged the danger of judging people, saying, "If they seem fairly normal, which is a bad measure, it will make me feel more comfortable. I'm not stupid – I know the risks and I tend to ignore them, which is bad." Even with this *laissez-faire* approach, participants still had some rules, with Dean saying:

> I sort of wing it really. I wouldn't let somebody tie me up... You'd also have to be insane to let somebody tie you up in your own house – but that's common sense. I don't do drunk sex and I definitely don't do drunk kink. I avoid drugs as well. I don't hook up with people from a night out... Most of my knowledge has come from meets though – finding out in the moment how to do it.

These participants tended to engage in kinks which could be deemed as less risky, such as power exchange without physical restrictions, or more fetishistic type behaviors, suggesting that participants had already considered the risks and deemed them low enough to not explicitly discuss them. However, research into sexual consent more generally highlights how verbal and behavioral cues can often be misinterpreted (Jozkowski & Peterson, 2013).

Conclusion

This chapter explored how kinky gay and bisexual men negotiate consent and the risks associated with kink activities when planning kink hook ups through SSNS. While academics and activists stress the importance of SSC and RACK, particularly in kink venues, most participants reported not having heard of these terms before, showing a potential disconnect between popular kink discourses on safety and consent, and how kink is conducted, particularly when exploring how risk and consent are explored in home venues compared to public kink venues. This speaks to differences in conceptualizing and communicating safety, consent, and trust, with a greater emphasis on spontaneity and indirect discussion which serves to distance further from organised kink community sessions where SSC and RACK are emphasised.

Participants avoided using the term *consent* in their online discussions when planning kink hook ups. Instead, participants described activities they were interested in and limits, or things they will not do. These conversations were less formal than previous research into how kinky individuals negotiated planned activities and consent (e.g., Rubin, 1991; Sagarin et al., 2019), but still a way of establishing trust. While participants did not use SSC or RACK, their engagement in kink more closely reflected the 4Cs framework (Williams et al., 2014). Participants emphasised the importance of *communication* in kink; negotiated *consent* through describing their interests and limits; and were *cautious* in who they engaged in kink with. Further research could apply the 4Cs framework to kink settings, particularly expanding on the role of *caring*.

This chapter also identified another layer of risk navigated by participants when planning kink activities through SSNS – the risks associated with chatting and meeting others online. Participants placed great importance in verifying the genuineness of their potential kink partner. Indeed, participants created tasks to verify someone's identity and took safety precautions when meeting others. Future research should acknowledge the importance of the internet for kinky individuals and how the use of SSNS creates new challenges and risks. Specifically, research could explore how communication of interests and limits on SSNS prior to engaging in kink is executed in person, focusing on the concept of ongoing consent (see Beres, 2007).

The results of this study may be partly down to the sample of gay and bisexual men, and the experiences of straight kink practitioners may be different. This can be explained somewhat through comparing two popular kink SSNS aimed at the two populations: *FetLife*, a kink SSNS which predominantly caters for straight kink communities and emphasises the importance of interactions through forums and organising *munches* (regular non-sexual events for members to meet offline and socialise); while *Recon,* a kink SSNS for gay and bisexual men, tends to focus more on the individual interactions between its members. For gay and bisexual men, kink may predominantly be about the sex and the activities (Wignall & McCormack, 2017), while for straight kink practitioners, kink could be framed as a ritual which encompasses the pre-activity discussions as part of the kink session (see Sagarin et al., 2015). The important intersections of gender and power are not present in the same way in our sample, and this issue requires further interrogation and understanding in future research.

The lack of explicit discussions of consent are not as alarming as they might initially seem given that most participants navigated the underlying issues through conversation. Even so, the individualistic nature of SSNS apps compared to community venues to engage in kink point to a gap in education around these issues. While some SSNS, like Recon.com, have a range of activities to try and foster these discussions (e.g., a podcast, blog and live events), the structured way of teaching about consent is absent. Furthermore, it is important that kink community leaders and academics also understand the evolving terminology around kink in online spaces and recognize that terms like SSC may not have the valence they used to. Future research should consider how to foster discussions around safety and consent in online environments.

References

Beres, M. (2007). "Spontaneous" sexual consent: An analysis of sexual consent literature. *Feminism & Psychology*, 17(1), 93–108. https://doi.org/10.1177/0959353507072914.

Coppens, V., Ten Brink, S., Huys, W., Fransen, E., & Morrens, M. (2020). A Survey on BDSM-related activities: BDSM experience correlates with age of first exposure, interest profile, and role identity. *The Journal of Sex Research*, 57(1), 129–136. https://doi.org/10.1080/00224499.2018.1558437.

Downing, L. (2007). Beyond safety: Erotic asphyxiation and the limits of SM discourse. In D. Langdridge & M. Barker (Eds.), *Safe, Sane and Consensual: Contemporary Perspectives on Sadomasochism* (pp. 119–132). London: Palgrave.

Dunkley, C. R., & Brotto, L. A. (2019). The role of consent in the context of BDSM. *Sexual Abuse*, 32(6), 657–678. https://doi.org/10.1177/1079063219842847

Dunkley, C. R., & Brotto, L. A. (2018). Clinical considerations in treating BDSM practitioners: A review. *Journal of Sex & Marital Therapy*, 44(7), 701–712. https://doi.org/10.1080/0092623X.2018.1451792.

Graham, B. C., Butler, S. E., McGraw, R., Cannes, S. M., & Smith, J. (2016). Member perspectives on the role of BDSM communities. *The Journal of Sex Research*, 53(8), 895–909. https://doi.org/10.1080/00224499.2015.1067758.

Hughes, S., & Hammack, P. (2022). Narratives of the origins of kinky sexual desire help by users of a kink-oriented social networking website. *Journal of Sex Research*, 59(3), 360–371. https://doi.org/10.1080/00224499.2020.1840495.

Jaspal, R. (2020). Content analysis, thematic analysis, and discourse analysis. In G. Breakwell, D. Wright, and J. Barnett. (Eds.). *Research Methods in Psychology* (pp. 285–312). Sage.

Jozkowski, K. & Peterson, Z. (2013). College students and sexual consent: Unique insights. *Journal of Sex Research*, 50(6), 517–523. https://doi.org/10.1080/00224499. 2012.700739.

Kaak, A. (2016). Conversational phases in BDSM pre-scene negotiations. *Journal of Positive Sexuality*, 2(3), 47–52. https://doi.org/10.51681/1.232.

Khan, U. (2014). *Vicarious Kinks: S/M in the Socio-legal Imaginary*. University of Toronto Press.

Langdridge, D. & Barker, M. (Eds.). (2013). *Safe, Sane and Consensual: Contemporary Perspectives on Sadomasochism*. Palgrave Macmillan.

Lauckner, C., Truszczynski, N., Lambert, D., Kottamasu, V., Meherally, S., Schipani-McLaughlin, A. M., ... & Hansen, N. (2019). "Catfishing," cyberbullying, and coercion: An exploration of the risks associated with dating app use among rural sexual minority males. *Journal of Gay & Lesbian Mental Health*, 23(3), 289–306. https://doi.org/10.1080/19359705.2019.1587729.

McCormack, M., Measham, F. & Wignall, L. (2021). The normalization of leisure sex and recreational drugs: Exploring associations between polydrug use and sexual practices by English festival-goers. *Contemporary Drug Problems*, 48(2), 185–200. https://doi.org/10.1177/00914509211009901.

McCormack, M., Measham, F., Measham, M., & Wignall, L. (2022). Kink in an English field: The drinking, drug use and sexual practices of English festival-goers who engage in kink. *Sexuality & Culture*, 26, 1750–1765. https://doi.org/10.1007/s12119-022-09968-4.

Moser, C., & Kleinplatz, P. J. (2007). Themes of SM expression. In D. Langdridge & M. Barker (Eds.), *Safe, Sane and Consensual: Contemporary Perspectives on Sadomasochism* (pp. 35–54). London: Palgrave.

Newmahr, S. (2011) *Playing on the Edge: Sadomasochism, Risk and Intimacy*. Bloomington, IN: Indiana University Press.

Rubin, G. (1991). The catacombs: A temple of the butthole. In M. Thompson (ed.) *Leatherfolk: Radical Sex, People, Politics and Practice*. Boston, MA: Alyson.

Sagarin, B. J., Lee, E. M., & Klement, K. R. (2015). Sadomasochism without sex? Exploring the parallels between BDSM and extreme rtuals. *Journal of Positive Sexuality*, 1(3), 32–36. https://doi.org/10.51681/1.132.

Sagarin, B. J., Lee, E. M., Erickson, J. M., Casey, K. G., & Pawirosetiko, J. S. (2019). Collective sex environments without the sex? Insights from the BDSM community. *Archives of Sexual Behavior*, 48(1), 63–67. https://doi.org/10.1007/s10508-018-1252-1.

Shindel, A. W., & Moser, C. A. (2011). Why are the paraphilias mental disorders? *The Journal of Sexual Medicine*, 8(3), 927–929. https://doi.org/10.1111/j.1743-6109.2010. 02087.x.

Simula, B. (2019). Pleasure, power, and pain: A review of the literature on the experiences of BDSM participants. *Sociology Compass*, 13(3), e12668. https://doi.org/10.1111/soc4.12668.

Simula, B., Bauer, R., & Wignall, L. (2023). *The Power of BDSM: Play, Communities, and Consent in the 21st Century*. Oxford University Press.

Steinmetz, C. & Maginn, P. J. (2014) The landscape of BDSM venues. In P. J. Maginn and C. Steinmetz (Eds.), *(Sub)urban Sexscapes: Geographies and Regulation of the Sex Industry* (pp. 117–137). Abingdon: Routledge.

Sprott, R. A., & Williams, D. J. (2019). Is BDSM a sexual orientation or serious leisure? *Current Sexual Health Reports*, 11(2), 75–79. https://doi.org/10.1007/s11930-019-00195-x.

Weinberg, T. S., Williams, C. J., & Moser, C. (1984). The social constitutes of sadomasochism. *Social Problems*, 31(4), 379–389. https://doi.org/10.2307/800385.

Weiss, M. (2011). *Techniques of Pleasure: BDSM and the Circuits of Sexuality*. Duke University Press.

Wignall, L. (2023). The role of the internet in research on BDSM. In B. Simula, R. Bauer, & L. Wignall (Eds.). *The Power of BDSM: Play, Communities, and Consent in the 21st Century*. Oxford University Press.

Wignall, L. (2022). *Kinky in the Digital Age: Gay Male Subcultures and Social Identities*. Oxford University Press.

Wignall, L. (2019). Pornography use by kinky gay men: A qualitative approach. *Journal of Positive Sexuality*, 5(1), 7–13. https://doi.org/10.51681/1.512.

Wignall, L. (2017). The sexual use of a social networking site: The case of Pup Twitter. *Sociological Research Online*, 22(3), 21–37. https://doi.org/10.1177/1360780417724066.

Wignall, L., & McCormack, M. (2017). An exploratory study of a new kink activity: "Pup Play." *Archives of Sexual Behavior*, 46(3), 801–811. https://doi.org/10.1007/s10508-015-0636-8.

Williams, D. J., & Sprott, R. A. (2022). Current biopsychosocial science on understanding BDSM/kink. *Current Opinion in Psychology*, 48, 101473. https://doi.org/10.1016/j.copsyc.2022.101473.

Williams, D. J., Thomas, J. N., Prior, E. E., & Christensen, M. C. (2014). From "SSC" and "RACK" to the "4Cs": Introducing a new framework for negotiating BDSM participation. *Electronic Journal of Human Sexuality*, 17(5), 1–10.

Zambelli, L. (2017). Subcultures, narratives and identification: An empirical study of BDSM (bondage, domination and submission, discipline, sadism and masochism) practices in Italy. *Sexuality & Culture*, 21(2), 471–492. https://doi.org/10.1007/s12119-016-9400-z.

15

MOLKA

Consent, Resistance, and the Spy-Cam Epidemic in South Korea

Sarah Molisso

Image-based sexual abuse serves as a reminder of the constant and ever-changing nature of sexual abuse faced primarily by women, perpetrated mostly by men. In recent studies across the UK, Australia, and New Zealand more than one in six of all respondents admitted to engaging in at least one form of image-based sexual abuse: non-consensual taking, sharing, or threat of sharing of a nude or sexual image (Henry et al., 2020). McGlynn et al. (2019) refer to image-based sexual abuse as encompassing three facets:

> taking or creating nude or sexual images or videos without consent, including making 'fake' nude or pornographic images and/or sharing nude or sexual images or videos without consent and/or threatening to take, share or create nude or sexual images or videos without consent.
>
> *(McGlynn et al., 2019, p. 2)*

Responses to the issue in the UK, 'have been ad hoc, piecemeal and inconsistent. In practice, victim-survivors are being consistently failed: by the law, by the police and criminal justice system, by traditional and social media, website operators, and by their employers, universities and schools' (Rackley et al., 2021, p. 293).

This failure is not unique to the UK, Australia, or New Zealand. In South Korea (henceforth Korea), the widespread issue of *molka*, a portmanteau of the words 'mollae' (secretly) and 'kamera' (camera), has shown how cataclysmic this problem is. *Molka* is more akin to the term 'upskirting' in the UK: spy cameras placed in public areas (toilets, changing rooms, motels, offices, clothing, etc.) with the resulting images uploaded to pornography sites. This lack of consent, loss of autonomy, and violation of the private individual has led to victims committing suicide due to the resulting trauma (Taylor, 2019). As with

DOI: 10.4324/9781003358756-20

UK studies, *molka* can leave victim-survivors experiencing 'the abuse as "life-ruining," "hell on earth," a "nightmare…"' (Rackley et al., 2021, p. 298), as evident in the number of recent news articles and documentaries that have been made on *molka* [see Taylor (2019); McCurry (2021); McCurry and Kim (2018); Tabanera (2021); Open Shutters (2022); Stacey Dooley Investigates (2020); and Cyber Hell: Exposing an Internet Horror (2022)].

In Korea, public resistance to the *molka* endemic has been enmeshed with feminist practices, both online and offline. I do not think it is a stretch to say that *all women* are wary of spy-cams: checking cubicles before urinating, filling up small holes with toilet paper, tissue, or chewing gum from previous spy-cam occupancies (Figure 15.1). It is such a standard part of life that there are anti-*molka* posters in toilet cubicles (Figure 15.2), and even stationary shops sell '*molka* detectors', a piece of red plastic which enables the user to detect spy-cams when put on the end of their smartphone's camera (sold by *Artbox*). This chapter demonstrates how consent has emerged as a key feminist issue in Korea and contributes to an understanding of how gendered autonomy is thought about in an international context. Through an examination of different realms of resistance, I argue that subverting misogyny online and offline is an act of regaining the loss of autonomy and consent.

FIGURE 15.1 *Molka* holes in a toilet cubicle
(photo – author's own)

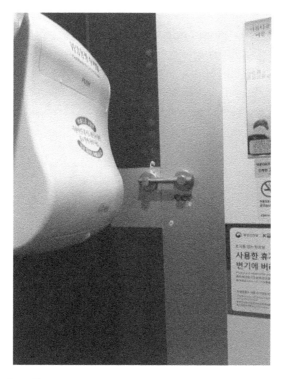

FIGURE 15.2 Anti-*molka* posters
(photo – author's own)

Part 1: *Molka*

> The word *molka* was a neologism in the 1990s referring to a popular
> hidden-camera prank show on TV at that time, but it has since been used
> euphemistically to denote criminal acts that violate the privacy and dignity
> of women and deter them from participating fully in everyday life. This
> tongue-in-cheek shorthand has trivialised the harmful consequences of the
> crimes, including suicides and psychological distress of victims. The word
> has been used so routinely that efforts to replace it with 'illegal filming'
> have been in vain. English terms such as 'upskirting', 'downblousing', and
> 'creepshots' can perform a similar disservice.
>
> *(Y Lee, 2022)*

It might be hard to understand the sheer scale of image-based sexual abuse in
Korea. Within the past ten years, the number of *molka* cases and arrests have
increased, yet the actual rate of crime is thought to be a lot higher. In 2017, of
the 6,465 cases reported, 5,437 arrests were made, yet fewer than 2% of these
(119 perpetrators) were jailed for *molka* crimes (BBC, 2019b; Human Rights
Watch, 2021). From 2012 to 2017, 98% of those arrested for *molka* crimes were

FIGURE 15.3

FIGURE 15.4

men, but 84% of the recorded victims in the same period were women (McCurry and Kim, 2018). Former president Moon Jae In had said that *molka* is a part of daily life (ibid.), and this has appeared to be true.

The scale and range of cases involving image-based sexual abuse has gained various coverage, including: the secret filming and distribution of women by a high-profile K-Pop star, Jung Joon-young [see the *Burning Sun* scandal]; the filming and livestreaming of videos of at least 1,600 motel guests from across the country; the *Nth Room* scandal which saw at least 74 women and 16 children being coerced into making and uploading explicit videos of themselves on the app, *Telegram*; and the international *Welcome to Video* case, whereby the overwhelming majority of those arrested who used the child pornography site were Korean (BBC, 2019a). In 2020, Korea's National Assembly made it easier to prosecute digital sex crimes. Now,

> those who possess, buy, store or watch illegally filmed sexual content can be sentenced to a maximum of three years in prison or 30 million won ($24,660). Before the new legislation was enacted, it was not illegal to possess such content.
>
> *(Al Jazeera, 2020)*

Korea's deeply patriarchal and misogynistic society has allowed these crimes to be engaged with, has fostered a society in which these crimes are *wanted*, and has ultimately accepted these crimes as a norm.

The issues of *molka* feed into the wider narratives of (1) misogyny and violence against women, (2) gender inequality, and (3) feminicide (see Lagarde, 2010). Misogyny and violence are clearly present worldwide, in different iterations. To frame it in a 'Korean context,' I will touch on three widely discussed themes: *Ilbe*, the September 2015 *Maxim* cover controversy, and the 2016 novel *Kim Jiyoung, Born 1982*. *Ilbe*, an alt-right internet community, was created in 2010. Koo (2019) has argued that *Ilbe* operates on a 'politics of hatred' (Koo, 2019, p. 835), that is, mainly men against women. Members of *Ilbe* participate in a type of homosociality: the bonds between these men help maintain the hegemonic structure in Korea, that of patriarchal misogyny and gender inequality. Bird (1996) has argued that homoscociality promotes hegemonic masculinity and is maintained in three ways: emotional detachment, competitiveness, and the sexual objectification of women. Emotional detachment is formed within the family unit as men identify as 'other' to mothers, competitiveness exists within relationships with other men, and the sexual objectification of women idealises male as *better than* female.

The sexual objectification of women is probably the most prolific and obvious part of homosociality and was clearly seen in the *Maxim* cover from September 2015. This recalled issue showed the actor, Kim Byeong-ok, posing in front of a car where there is a woman in the boot with her ankles bound together. The pictures within the magazine show a woman's body in the boot, and Kim dragging along a rubbish sack which the audience is meant to believe is Kim disposing of the body (Hodgson, 2015; Bahk, 2015). These images, along with the headline 'The Real Bad Guy' show the celebration of rape culture and violence against women. However, not all misogyny is as overt as this. The book, *Kim Jiyoung, Born 1982*, was published in 2016 and documents the everyday sexism and misogyny faced by the titular character *Kim Jiyoung*. Some hailed it as a feminist novel, which led to an anti-feminist backlash that had previously only been seen on websites like *Ilbe* (Lee and Lee, 2019; Lee, 2018; Woo and Kim, 2019).

Gender inequality remains high in Korea. In 2021, it ranked 102 out of 156 countries in the 2021 Global Gender Gap Report (World Economic Forum, 2021) largely in part to its low scores in 'political empowerment' and 'economic participation and opportunity'. Related to this violence and inequality is the issue of feminicide, and the state's inactive role in protecting women. In 2016, a 23-year-old woman was murdered in a public toilet near Gangnam station by a man who said that he had 'been "belittled" by women many times in the past' (Lee, 2016). The police ruled that this was not a hate crime. In September 2022, a 28-year-old woman was murdered by her stalker at her place of work, Sindang Station, in Seoul. These crimes are shocking, yet regarding intimate partner violence by men against women in Korea, 'between 2012 and 2015, 313 murder cases of women by their "romantic partners" took place' (Cheng, 2021): the Gangnam murder was a random attack yet was anything but random in the context of patterned violence against women.

The lack of the state's commitment to women's safety is reflected in the practice of the law. Article 14 (1) of the 'Act on the Punishment of Special Cases of Sexual Crimes Imprisonment' was amended in May 2020 to increase the prison sentence for offenders from 5 years to up to 7 years or a penalty from up to ⊠10 million to up to ⊠50 million, which is roughly from around £6,250 to around £31,250 (based on a conversion rate of 1GBP = 1600KRW). In reality, there is little done to perpetrators, and those prosecuted receive nominal sentences. In 2021, the Supreme Court upheld a 42-year prison sentence for Cho Ju-bin, in relation to the *Nth Room* case (J Lee, 2022; D Lee, 2022b), and the creator of the *Nth Room* chat room, Moon Hyung-wook, was sentenced to 34 years.

These lengthy sentences were attached to high profile cases with a large public engagement; a petition signed by nearly 2.7 million people caused Cho Ju-bin to be the first sex offender to have his identity revealed while in police custody (D Lee, 2022b). In contrast, Son Jong-woo of the *Welcome to Video* case received an 18-month prison sentence (Y Lee, 2022; D Lee, 2022a). The case for Korean feminicide is further seen in current president Yoon Suk-yeol's beliefs, which refute 'the idea that gender discrimination is systemic in South Korea, [blame] the country's low birth rate on feminism and [pledge] to abolish the Ministry of Gender Equality and Family – accusing its officials of treating men like "potential sex criminals"' (D Lee, 2022a). If the state is not helping victim-survivors of *molka*, how can they regain autonomy and consent?

Part 2: Regaining Autonomy and Consent

The issues of *molka* and other cybersex trafficking crimes (such as the afore-mentioned *Nth Room* and *Welcome to Video* cases), as well as the ever-present violence against women, represents a profound violation of consent. How then, can victim-survivors of these crimes regain any kind of autonomy? When the state and protective powers are so consistently failing those subjected to *molka* crimes, and when these crimes are repeated so often, how can any kind of consent be recovered? Article 14, Section 1, states that

> A person who takes photographs or videos of another person's body, which may cause any sexual stimulus or shame against the will of the person who was shot, by using a camera or other mechanism which has functions similar thereto, shall be punished by imprisonment with labor for not more than seven years or by a fine not exceeding 50 million won.
>
> *(Seoul Law Group, 2022)*

In the somewhat infamous 'Leggings Case', a defendant was acquitted in 2019 after secretly filming a woman on a bus – she was wearing leggings. The generally accepted parts of the body that 'cause any sexual stimulus or shame' are the breasts, genitals, and buttocks, but the Korean Supreme Court declared this ruling faulty in 2021 as 'whether a person experiences sexual shame or not is not dependent on which body part is filmed, but more contingent on the fact that his or her body was filmed in secret' (Lee and Chung, 2021). This was the first instance in which the idea of sexual freedom expanded from 'a "right to not engage in sexual activity without consent" to a "right to not be sexually objectified against one's will"' (Yonhap, 2021).

In May 2018, a woman was arrested for a *molka* crime. She uploaded a picture of her colleague, a nude male model, taken illegally without his consent. Not only was she arrested only days later, but she

> appeared on the perp walk as though she was a major criminal… Generally, first-time offenders guilty of illegal photo taking and uploading online were released with a warning and their conduct was not publicised by the media in Korea, so this case was exceptional.
>
> *(Jeong, 2020, p. 14)*

What angered bystanders the most was the double standards in the quick and swift response to finding and arresting a female perpetrator, when thousands of male perpetrators continue their crimes uninterrupted. In this instance, it appears that the consent of male victims of *molka* is regarded more highly than that of female or other marginalised victims of *molka*, as seen in the police's speedy reaction and public display of a female perpetrator who had violated the autonomy and consent of a male victim.

The reaction to this hypocrisy was instantaneous. The largest women's rally against male violence was staged, organised through the online café, *Uncomfortable Courage/Courage to be Uncomfortable* (J. Kim, 2021b; Park, 2020), also known as the Hyehwa Station demonstrations. The first rally attracted around 12,000 women, after which it was held on an almost monthly basis. By December, after six rallies, 350,000 accumulated participants in total had taken part in these women-only protests (Park, 2020). The infamous slogan chanted during this protest, 'My Life is Not Your Porn', coincided with other feminist acts of solidarity from the protests' participants. The government responded to these protests with legislative amendments (as discussed earlier) to both toughen penalties and to expand the range of punishable acts (Human Rights Watch, 2021).

Other acts of resistance against hegemonic masculinities and homosociality have preceded and followed this incident. The relentless disregard for women's consent has transcended *molka* crimes and is visible as serious violence against women. Following the 2016 Gangnam Station murder, a Twitter account (@0517am1) was created and called for chrysanthemums and post-it notes to be left at Gangnam Station Exit 10 (closest to the site of the murder) in order for attendees and those paying tributes to explain the violence faced by women (J. Kim, 2021a). In what J. Kim has referred to as 'sticky note activism', the use of post-it notes as a tool to disseminate feminist ideas originated from the online radical feminist group *Megalia*. This sticky note activism has also been seen in response to the Sindang Station murder.

Other *Megalia* activities included the numerous campaigns to eradicate *molka* crimes (Jeong, 2020), as well as the endorsement of the politician Jin Sun-mee (who was appointed Minister of Gender Equality and Family under Moon Jae-in's government in September 2018). Jin led a campaign to shut down *Soranet*, an illegal pornography sharing site founded in 1999 'which was notorious for arranging gang rapes and sharing revenge porn as well as photos and videos taken by spy-cams by the spontaneous participation of users' (Jeong, 2020, p. 95). Following the calls for *Megalians* to donate, the campaign received ₩10 million in donations in 24 hours (Singh, 2016). The site was shut down in 2016, yet only one of the four founders has been prosecuted. Song was arrested in 2018 and sentenced to four-years in jail, fined ₩1.4 billion (£875,000), and was ordered to attend 80 hours of sexual violence prevention education (BBC, 2019c).

However, the images continue to circulate online (Park, 2021), despite the revised Telecommunications Business Act, also known as the 'Nth Room Prevention Law', that went into effect in December 2021, 'making large internet platforms legally responsible for removing illegal content from their servers' (H. S. Kim, 2021). This was met with some opposition, arguing that as it only mandated platforms registered in Korea, and to stop illegal content from being shared on public chat rooms, the law would not have been able to prevent the Nth Room case from happening (Ko, 2021). Piecemeal responses from the state have done little to combat the rise in digital sex crimes; in September 2022, police shared some details of the 'second Nth Room case', in which

> the seven victims who had been discovered so far were even younger than the underage girls in Cho's case [the original Nth Room case]. And the tactics L [the alias used for the suspect] used to lure them in were even more cruel, despite reforms in internet protocols and an increased awareness of child abuse prevention.
>
> *(D Lee, 2022b)*

Molka and other image-based sexual abuse crimes continue in earnest.

Conclusion

The endemic nature of *molka* requires an important and necessary foregrounding in relation to consent. Thompson and Wood (2018) have argued that 'creepshot sites' (sites displaying non-consensually taken or distributed images) provide a forum for 'homosocial online environments that legitimate misogyny through their programming power—and, specifically, their ability to aggregate men holding misogynistic attitudes' (Thompson and Wood, 2018, p. 569), thus expanding on the definition of networked misogyny [see Banet-Weiser and Miltner, 2016]. This online homosociality has stripped away the consent and autonomy on its victims, 'their autonomy, agency, and subjectivity are denied, ignored, or considered subordinate to the desire of the perpetrator to capture non-consensual images' (Thompson and Wood, 2018, p. 568), and victim-survivors of these crimes have limited recourse in claiming back the consent that was taken from them.

While *Megalia* has helped in the war against image-based sexual abuse, its schism and formation of the more extreme radical feminist website, *Womad* 'explicitly pursued an essentialist and separatist politics for women, advocating female superiority and a biological notion of women that excluded trans women' (J. Kim, 2021b, p. 87). This transphobia transcended the online into the offline: the organisers of the Hyehwa Station demonstrations 'limited its membership to "biological females," again, supposedly for the sake of women's safety at the protests… and… request[ed] that participants report any "transgender-looking individuals"' (J. Kim, 2021b, p. 88). An intersectional feminist approach to tackling *molka* is needed – while 80% of cases target women, 'gay, bisexual or transgender men are disproportionately targeted' (Human Rights Watch, 2021), and these marginalised groups have been actively excluded from these large-scale protests which aim to claim back autonomy and consent.

The prison sentences received by the high-profile cases of digital sexual abuse have ranged from shorter to longer prison sentences, neither of which have satisfied bystanders. Olufemi (2020) has argued that 'the problem with sexual violence is that no amount of retribution can stem the consequences of an invasion of bodily autonomy' (Olufemi, 2020, p. 111). While the law was amended in 2020 to increase prison sentences and fines, we know that these spy-cam crimes have led to a number of suicides. How does a 7-year sentence or a 50 million won negate this non-consensual, life ruining act?

> Survivors of digital sex crimes grapple with trauma so deep that it at times leads to suicide... Many others consider suicide. This trauma is often worsened by retraumatizing encounters with police and justice officials, and by the expectation that survivors should gather evidence for their case and monitor the internet for new appearances of images of themselves, which leaves them immersed in the abuse.
>
> *(Human Rights Watch, 2021)*

These suicidal thoughts are not just caused by the incident/incidences of image-based sexual abuse, but are further exacerbated by the criminal justice system, as experienced in victim-survivors within the UK, Australia, and New Zealand (Rackley et al., 2021). What is needed is a societal overhaul of how genders and sexualities are imagined and dealt with. Moving away from a binary, from an *us* and *them* (whether that be members of *Ilbe* or *Womad*), and towards an egalitarian notion of personhood. Practically, this can begin in childhood in the adequate teaching of sex education, which in Korea is often heavily criticised for its lack of inclusivity, misogynistic leanings, and victim blaming among other issues (Goh, 2020; Ryall, 2020). Expansive education and a break away from the conservative Christian hold on Korean governments could be a step towards this kind of future: a more egalitarian future in which consent is societally understood, rather than one in which women are blamed by society, ignored by the state, and further traumatised by institutions.

References

Al Jazeera (2020) 'Leader of S Korea 'sextortion' ring jailed for 40 years', 26 November. Available at: https://www.aljazeera.com/news/2020/11/26/ringleader-of-s-korea-sextortion-ring-jailed-for-40-years (Accessed: 07 October 2022).

Bahk, E. (2015) 'Maxim Korea blasted for lurid cover', *The Korea Times*, 03 September. Available at: https://www.koreatimes.co.kr/www/nation/2015/09/113_186113.html (Accessed: 14 November 2022).

Banet-Weiser, S. and Miltner, K. M. (2016) '#MasculinitySoFragile: Culture, structure and networked misogyny', *Feminist Media Studies*, 16(1), pp. 171–174. Available at: https://doi.org/10.1080/14680777.2016.1120490.

BBC (2019a) 'Dakeuweb' Adongeumnanmul gukjegongjo susa... geomgeodoen 300 yeo-myeong jung 223 myeong-i hangugin' ('Dark Web' Child Pornography International Investigation... Of the 300 arrested, 223 were South Koreans), 17 October. Available at: https://www.bbc.com/korean/news-50078096 (Accessed: 24 October 2022).

BBC (2019b) 'Korea spycam porn: 1,600 fall victim and four men arrested', 20 March. Available at: https://www.bbc.co.uk/news/world-asia-47637734 (Accessed: 07 October 2022).

BBC (2019c) 'South Korea porn: Co-founder of the Soranet site jailed', 09 January. Available at: https://www.bbc.co.uk/news/world-asia-46810775 (Accessed: 15 November 2022).

Bird, S. R. (1996) 'Welcome to the Men's Club: Homosociality and the maintenance of hegemonic masculinity', *Gender and Society*, 10 (2), pp. 120–132. Available at: https://doi.org/10.1177/089124396010002002.

Cheng, S. (2021) 'The male malady of globalization: Phallocentric nationalism in South Korea', *Current Anthropology*, 62(S23), pp. 79–91. Available at: https://doi.org/10.1086/711664.

Cyber Hell: Exposing an Internet Horror (2022) Directed by Choi Jin-sung, Netflix. Available at: https://www.netflix.com/gb/title/81354041 (Accessed: 14 November 2022).

Goh, D. (2020) 'Misogynistic sex education in South Korea is making students have distorted view on sex', *Medium*, 13 July. Available at: https://iufcsol0122.medium.com/sexist-sex-education-is-a-culprit-of-sex-crimes-in-south-korea-8ef18b3c28fc (Accessed: 07 October 2022).

Henry, N., McGlynn, C., Flynn, A., Johnson, K., Powell, A. and Scott, A. J. (2020) *Image-based Sexual Abuse: A Study on the Causes and Consequences of Non-consensual Nude or Sexual Imagery*. London: Routledge.

Hodgson, C. (2015) 'Maxim Korea features a man posing next to a woman tied up in a car boot', *Cosmopolitan UK*, 02 September. Available at: https://www.cosmopolitan.com/uk/reports/news/a38300/maxim-korea-woman-tied-trunk/ (Accessed: 15 November 2022).

Human Rights Watch (2021) '"My life is not your porn": Digital sex crimes in South Korea,'16 June. Available at: https://www.hrw.org/report/2021/06/16/my-life-not-your-porn/digital-sex-crimes-south-korea (Accessed: 07 October 2022).

Jeong, E. (2020) *Troll Feminism: The Rise of Popular Feminism in South Korea*. PhD thesis. University of York. Available at: https://etheses.whiterose.ac.uk/28959/ (Accessed: 07 October 2022).

Kim, H. S. (2021) 'Critics voice their views as Nth Room Prevention Law goes into effect following near unanimous support last year', *The Dissolve*, 16 December. Available at: https://thedissolve.kr/what-they-said-on-the-nth-room-prevention-law/ (Accessed 15 November 2022).

Kim, J. (2021a) 'Sticky activism: The gangnam station murder case and new feminist practices against misogyny and femicide', *JCMS: Journal of Cinema and Media Studies*, 60 (4), pp. 37–60. Available at: https://doi.org/10.1353/cj.2021.0044.

Kim, J. (2021b) 'The resurgence and popularization of feminism in South Korea: Key issues and challenges for contemporary feminist activism', *Korea Journal*, 61 (4), pp. 75–101. Available at: https://doi.org/10.25024/kj.2021.61.4.75.

Ko, J. (2021) '[Newsmaker] Nth room prevention law draws fire for censorship, invasion of privacy', *The Korea Herald*, 13 December. Available at: https://www.koreaherald.com/view.php?ud=20211213000626 (Accessed 14 November 2022).

Koo, J. (2019) 'South Korean cyberfeminism and trolling: The limitation of online feminist community Womad as counterpublic', *Feminist Media Studies*, 20 (6), pp. 831–846. Available at: https://doi.org/10.1080/14680777.2019.1622585.

Lagarde de los Ríos, M. (2010) 'Preface. Feminist keys for understanding feminicide: Theoretical, political, and legal construction', translated by C. Roberts, in R. Fregoso and C. Bejarano (eds) *Terrorizing Women: Feminicide in the Americas*. Durham, NC: Duke University Press, pp. xi–xxv.

Lee, C. (2016) '[FROM THE SCENE] Korean women respond to Gangnam murder case', *The Korea Herald*, 19 May. Available at: http://www.koreaherald.com/view.php?ud=20160519000691 (Accessed: 07 October 2022).

Lee, C. (2018) '[Feature] Feminist novel becomes centre of controversy in South Korea', *The Korea Herald*, 27 March. Available at: http://www.koreaherald.com/view.php?ud=20180327000799 (Accessed: 24 October 2022).

Lee, D. (2022a) 'South Korea's women fear an "Nth Room" repeat now Yoon Suk-yeol's in charge', *South China Morning Post*, 21 May. Available at: https://www.scmp.com/week-asia/people/article/3178566/south-koreas-women-fear-nth-room-repeat-now-yoon-suk-yeols-charge (Accessed: 14 November 2022).

Lee, D. (2022b) 'South Korea hunts down leader of new "Nth Room" as sex crimes soar despite digital reforms', *South China Morning Post*, 25 September. Available at: https://www.scmp.com/week-asia/article/3193545/south-korea-hunts-down-leader-new-nth-room-sex-crimes-soar-despite (Accessed: 14 November 2022).

Lee, J. (2022) '"Baksa Room" leader indicted again for sexual assault charge against minor', *The Korea Herald*, 19 October. Available at: https://www.koreaherald.com/view.php?ud=20221019000649 (Accessed 14 November 2022).

Lee, S. and Chung, E. (2021) 'Supreme Court rules on leggings, shame, covert filming', *Korea JoongAng Daily*, 6 January. Available at https://koreajoongangdaily.joins.com/2021/01/06/national/socialAffairs/secret-filming-peeping-tom-korea/20210106164700578.html (Accessed: 14 November 2022).

Lee, Y. (2022) 'Digital sex crimes: Three lessons from South Korea', *SOAS (School of Oriental and African Studies) Blog*, 1 September. Available at: https://study.soas.ac.uk/digital-sex-crimes-three-lessons-south-korea/ (Accessed: 14 November 2022).

Lee, Y. and Lee, J. (2019) 'Yeonghwa-neun gonggam·chiyu malhaneunde…'Kim Jiyeong' akpeul-e ttodareun sangcheo' (The movie talks about empathy and healing…Another wound from 'Kim Jiyoung' malicious comments), *Maeil Gyeongje*, 28 October. Available at: https://www.mk.co.kr/news/society/9041066 (Accessed: 24 October).

McCurry, J. (2021). 'Online sex crimes crisis in South Korea affecting all women, report finds', *The Guardian*, 16 June. Available at: https://www.theguardian.com/world/2021/jun/16/online-sex-crimes-crisis-in-south-korea-affecting-all-women-report-finds (Accessed 20 November 2022).

McCurry, J. and Kim, N. (2018) '"A part of daily life": South Korea confronts its voyeurism epidemic', *The Guardian*, 03 July. Available at: https://www.theguardian.com/world/2018/jul/03/a-part-of-daily-life-south-korea-confronts-its-voyeurism-epidemic-sexual-harassment?CMP=gu_com (Accessed: 07 October 2022).

McGlynn, C., Rackley, E., Johnson, K., Henry, N., Flynn, A., Powell, A., Gavey, N. and Scott, A. (2019) *Shattering Lives and Myths: A Report on Image-Based Sexual Abuse*, Durham University; University of Kent; RMIT University; Monash University; University of Auckland; Goldsmiths, University of London, pp. 1–24. Available at: https://www.endviolenceagainstwomen.org.uk/wp-content/uploads/ShatteringLivesandMythsFINALJuly2019.pdf (Accessed: 07 October 2022).

Olufemi, L. (2020) *Feminism, Interrupted: Disrupting Power (Outspoken)*, London: Pluto Press.

Open Shutters (2022) Directed by Youjin Do, TIME and Field of Vision. Available at: https://www.youtube.com/watch?v=yQr7Pnag0Yw (Accessed: 14 November 2022).

Park, G. (2021) '"You remove it but it keeps coming back": New laws leave adult digital sex crime victims little recourse', *Hankyoreh*, 12 December. Available at: https://english.hani.co.kr/arti/english_edition/e_national/1022931.html (Accessed: 15 November 2022).

Park, H. (2020) 'Throwing off the corset: A contemporary history of the beauty resistance movement in South Korea', *Dignity: A Journal of Analysis of Exploitation and Violence*, 5 (3), pp. 1–17. Available at: https://doi.org/10.23860/dignity.2020.05.03.01.

Rackley, E., McGlynn, C., Johnson, K., Henry, N., Gavey, N., Flynn, A. and Powell, A. (2021) 'Seeking justice and redress for victimsurvivors of imagebased sexual abuse', *Feminist Legal Studies*, 29, pp. 293–322. Available at: https://doi.org/10.1007/s10691-021-09460-8.

Ryall, J. (2020) 'South Korea withdraws sex education school books after conservative outcry', *Telegraph*, 18 September. Available at: https://www.telegraph.co.uk/news/2020/09/18/south-korea-withdraws-sex-education-school-books-conservative/ (Accessed: 07 October 2022).

Seoul Law Group (2022) Crimes using cameras in Korea | Sex Crime Laws, 12 July. Available at: https://seoullawgroup.com/sex-crime-camera-korea/ (Accessed: 14 November 2022).

Singh, E. (2016) 'Megalia: South Korean feminism marshals the power of the internet', *Korea Exposé*, 26 July. Available at: https://www.koreaexpose.com/megalia-south-korean-feminism-marshals-the-power-of-the-internet/ (Accessed: 07 October 2022).

Stacey Dooley Investigates (2020) 'Spycam Sex Criminals', BBC. Available at: https://www.bbc.co.uk/iplayer/episode/p0872g59/stacey-dooley-investigates-spycam-sex-criminals (Accessed: 14 November 2022).

Tabanera, L. G. (2021). 'What is "Molka" And why is it a serious problem in South Korea?', *Cosmopolitan Philippines*, 14 January. Available at: https://www.cosmo.ph/news/molka-south-korea-hidden-spy-camera-problem-a2520-20210114-lfrm (Accessed: 20 November 2022).

Taylor, J. (2019) 'South Korea: woman reportedly kills herself after being secretly filmed by doctor', *The Guardian*, 02 October. Available at: https://www.theguardian.com/world/2019/oct/02/south-korea-woman-kills-herself-after-being-secretly-filmed-by-doctor-reports (Accessed: 24 October 2022).

Thompson, C. and Wood, M. A. (2018) 'A media archaeology of the creepshot', *Feminist Media Studies*, 18(4), pp. 560–574. Available at: https://doi.org/10.1080/14680777.2018.1447429.

Woo, H. and Kim, J. (2019) '"82 nyeonsaeng Kim Jiyeong" daetgeul bunseok… "yeoseonghyeomo" nolli gujo-reul boda' (Analysis of comments on 'Kim Ji-young, born in 1982… Look at the logical structure of 'misogyny'), *KBS News*, 30 December. Available at: https://news.kbs.co.kr/news/view.do?ncd=4352852 (Accessed: 24 October 2022).

World Economic Forum (2021) *Global Gender Gap Report 2021*, pp. 1–405. Available at: https://www3.weforum.org/docs/WEF_GGGR_2021.pdf (Accessed: 07 October 2022).

Yonhap (2021) 'Man fined in retrial over illicit filming of woman in leggings', *The Korea Herald*, 3 November 2021. Available at: http://www.koreaherald.com/view.php?ud=20211103000696 (Accessed: 14 November 2022).

16

GENDER, POWER AND AGENCY IN ONLINE SEX WORK

An Expanded Framework of (Constrained) Consent in the Context of "Camming"

Panteá Farvid, Rebekah Nathan, Juliana Riccardi and Abigail Whitmer

Social, political, legal and interpersonal understandings of what constitutes *sexual consent* (and consent in general) have become much more nuanced in the contemporary context. Much of this deepened understanding and engagement owes a great debt to ongoing feminist research and theorizing at the fulcrum of gender, power, sexuality and subjectivity. In this chapter, we examine how consent might be understood in the context of a specific form of technologically mediated sex work that is typically referred to as "camming" or online cam modeling. To do this, we first outline how consent has been understood by feminists in the realm of (largely) heterosexuality, how this may be expanded to include broader domains of negotiation within intimacy (i.e., within the relationship, but beyond the interpersonal/immediate sexual contact), followed by the examination of consent and sex work from diverse feminist theoretical orientations. After this, we give a brief overview of what "camming" is and how it unfolds, drawing on empirical research that engages with the contours of the practice (and its reported benefits and drawbacks for cam models). Lastly, we tease out how consent might be conceptualized in this domain, by offering an *expanded framework of consent*, but one that is "constrained" by the context(s) within which camming occurs (drawing on lived experiences of cam models), no matter how much agency is exercised. We engage with the contextual (sociopolitical and structural), vocational (the nuances of the sex work industry), mediated (online), interpersonal (relationship with others), and intrapersonal (relationship with the self) components of camming. We argue that the notion of consent, or the capacity to negotiate consent in the context of camming (and most assuredly beyond), requires a multidimensional and expanded framework, beyond the individual or dyad, which takes into consideration social, political, and economic structures as well as the identity configurations of sex workers/clients.

DOI: 10.4324/9781003358756-21

Interrogating (Sexual) Consent

When the notion of "consent" is evoked, in academia and in daily life, it is typically in the context of sex, sexual negotiation, or sexual assault. The notion of sexual consent, and consent in general, is at the same time seemingly obvious, but also elusive and hard to define. Yet, a firm grasp on what consent is and means is critical when it comes to ethical conduct and a just society. Clarity is important when it comes to the realm of sexual negotiations, but also in a broader sense when it comes to a plethora of daily relationships, labor, research, privacy and other rights. Furthermore, what constitutes consent, or the capacity for an individual to offer full unfettered consent, needs to contend with the relational, sociocultural and economic context in which such a negotiation occurs. And, in the realm of sexuality, the broader structures that shape sexual relations or the politics of a given time or sexual encounter, also becomes important. Lastly, our understanding of consent is not only relevant to in-person events, but the rapidly evolving and complex online domain, and technologically mediated intimacies.

The discourse and literature on (sexual) consent spans the legal, sociological and psychological. Legally, consent can simply mean agreeing, "voluntary", to something that is proposed by another, or to voluntarily agree to an act that another seeks of you (ranging from any contracts to sexual acts). The sociological aspect comes in, when one is to unravel broader questions of what counts as meaningful consent, under what conditions and broader contextual backdrop. Lastly, the psychological component, while linked to both legal and social, can help us unravel how people come to misconstrue the meaning or presence of consent, or willingly go along with unwanted sex, or minimize the experience and impacts of non-consensual sexual contact. It was not long ago that the literature on consent was rther underdeveloped. For example, when Beres (2007) sought literature on the definition of "sexual consent" in 2007, academic database yielded between 30–42 results. Yet, searching for the term "rape" yielded between 2705–8145 results – indicating an alarming lack of engagement with the concept of consent, when lack of consent is arguably at the core of sexual assault. In 2022, a database search for "sexual consent" garners around 2,200 results, showing a much greater engagement with the concept. This is no doubt a response to the call for a deeper examination of the concept, as well the impact of the global #MeToo Movement on the wider, public and more nuanced discussions related to power and sex.

In a deeper analysis of academic definitions of sexual consent, Beres (2007) argued that the most common use of the phrase conceptualizes it as "spontaneous consent". Here, scholars using the term sexual consent do so without explicitly defining consent, and instead rely on the "common sense" meanings of concepts without critically dissecting or outlining them (Beres, 2007). Another way in which consent is "spontaneously" assumed is the presumed gendered nature of the consent – that heterosexual women will be consenting to heterosexual men who are presumed to be ubiquitously willing and eager to have sex (Beres, 2007). Recent work has expanded the categories of how sexual consent is conceptualized across academic literature – arguing for three major trends (Muehlenhard et al., 2016). The first of these refers to *consent as a mental act* – the notion that consent involves an internal state of willingness to engage in sexual acts with other people; whether or not this is communicated with another. In this context, for example, sexual coercion occurs when someone does not what want to engage in sex, and is aware of this feeling, but goes along with sex/sexual contact. Going along with unwanted sex may be due to perceived pressure, actual social or verbal pressure, or due to fear of another person's "rejection reaction" (e.g., violence), or other negative ramifications that may result from saying "no", particularly if there is a power imbalance between two actors (e.g., employer/employee) (see Farvid & Saing, 2022; Gavey, 2019; Pond & Farvid, 2017).

The second theme revolves around the *explicit communication or expression of consent* and involves the direct and clear expression through verbal communication and/or very explicit behavior, which evidently shows the willingness of participation in the sexual act. The third theme then is *inferred or implied consent*, which refers to the interpretation of "signals," usually non-verbal, which imply a willingness to engage in sexual acts (Muehlenhard et al., 2016). This last form of consent is suggested to be the most ambiguous, and yet is the most common type of consent that takes place in sexual exchanges. The reasons for this type of consent being most common may be many, but two main conditions should be noted. The first is that sex, particularly heterosex, continues to be relentlessly non-communicative (due to the continued lack of skills being taught in this area, and ongoing social taboos around open conversation about sexual matters, see Herbenick et al., 2019). Secondly, sexual communication, or the communication of direct consent, is often depicted as "not sexy" (Farvid & Braun, 2018). Popular discourses of sexuality promote spontaneity and passion alongside sexual desire (e.g., Farvid & Braun, 2006), leaving little room of the boringly "adult" and mundane concept of open dialogue when it comes to negotiating sex/sexual acts, particularly in the "heat of the moment".

Sexual consent is not only difficult to define, with its parameters multiple and opaque, but becomes a difficult arena for guaranteeing that two people are on the exact same page. At its most basic, sexual consent may be defined as an agreement by all parties to engage in specific sexual acts (Graf & Johnson, 2021). Yet, how one judges such an agreement becomes difficult to ascertain, particularly when non-verbal behavior or implied consent is involved. Even in instances where there is verbal consent, the power dynamics of a given sexual encounter might mean that such consent is coerced, induced or is part of sexual compliance (Farvid & Saing, 2022). In addition, consent is an ongoing negotiation within a sexual encounter; simply because parties initially agree to engage in sexual acts does not mean that they are stripped of the freedom to retract, or re-negotiate the terms of the sexual exchange. Further complicating the issue is that ongoing "check-ins" and renegotiations of consent are unlikely, due to the dominant discourses of what constitutes sex, sexuality and linear sexual encounters (see Farvid & Braun 2018; Aubrey et al., 2022).

Moving beyond the interpersonal context, the politics of sexuality also become important when considering consent. This is particularly the case when considering the politics of heterosexuality and the norms that govern gender and sex within this context (Farvid, 2015, forthcoming; Gavey, 2019). Within patriarchal society, where there is ongoing gender inequity, heterosexuality is a domain plagued with power imbalances between the men and women who might find themselves in intimate relationships, or in a sexual encounter. Many second-wave radical feminists, for example, argued that women are unable to fully consent to heterosexual sex, due to deeply entrenched power imbalances between men and women, the exploitative nature of sex in this context, and the gendered constructions of male and female sexuality (e.g., Barry, 1996; Dworkin, 1981). West (2008) went further to highlight the "harms of consensual heterosex" and the (gendered) societal pressures which shape "choices" of consent. Examples include the pressure for people to have intercourse with their spouse, because it is assumed as a required part of marriage, or for a man to feel pressured to consent to sex, because it is assumed that men should always desire and be ready for sex (see also Hollway, 1989). Furthermore, contemporary critical feminists have demonstrated the manner in which normative heterosexuality (and constructions of gendered male and female sexuality) continue to provide the scaffolding for sexual coercion, harassment, assault and rape (Gavey, 1992, 2019). The context within which one operates or negotiates sex, is thus fundamentally important when it comes to understanding how constrained one might be in terms of agency or freedom, when it comes to consent. Similarly, such debates about power, sex and consent also exist when it comes to understanding the commercial sex industry.

Consent in Sex Work

Sex work is typically defined as the direct exchange of financial compensation for various forms of sexual acts and services. This can involve erotic massage, pole dancing, pornographic acting, camming, sugar dating, and in-person sex. The in-person sex industry is one that remains profoundly gendered – with most buyers heterosexual men, and most sellers, ciswomen (Farvid, 2017). In this section, we focus on how consent has been understood in the context of in-person sex work (from dancing/stripping to intercourse). An important qualifier to offer at the outset is that sex work is a form of compensated labor – but, in many contexts it is illegal, partially legal and/or not regulated or held to the same labor policies of other (legal) work. Yet, like many other jobs, there are routine requirements of the work that ostensibly complicate how we conceptualize consent. First and foremost, sex work is a (often criminalized) "job", and secondly, it happens to involve bodies, intimate encounters and sex. The scope of what might constitute consent can thus begin rather broadly. For example, at the outset, we might consider what consent to enter the industry looks like (under what conditions do people choose such work), consent to what type of sex work (how do sex workers decide what type of sex work they will do and is there overlap and why), and finally, consent to sexual acts or the parameters of the sex work they engage in. We address these various issues below.

Academic and feminist debates about what constituted "consent" in sex work have mostly been grounded in theory and policy. As such, they have often ignored much of the lived experience of sex workers, how they understand consent and negotiate it after a monetary transaction has occurred (Gerassi, 2015). In general, the literature tends to focus on issues of morality, legality and whether sex work can ever be truly consensual in a heteropatriarchal and capitalist society (Bacik, 2020; Farley, 2004; Reinelt, 2016; Van der Meulen, 2012). There are typically structural as well as interpersonal notions of consent implicated here. There are two opposing camps typically engaged in public and academic debates about the politics and positionality of sex work. Abolitionists are typically coming from a conservative political/religious or radical feminist perspective. These groups have different motivations for seeking to eradicate (or criminalize) sex work but support the same outcome (ending sex work). Radical (and some) Marxist feminists believe sex workers are incapable of truly consenting to sex work because it exists within, and is perpetuated by, a capitalist-hetero-patriarchal society, which enforces the structural oppression of women. Conservative groups, on the other hand, oppose sex-work on the grounds of morality and what they see as the proper place of sex (within heterosexual marriage) (Bacik, 2020). Conversely, there are sex-positive (feminist and/or liberal) movements which support women's right to conduct sex work, as another form of legitimate labor. They advocate for taking seriously the agency of sex workers, and decriminalizing sex work on the grounds that it allows for a safer environment for the workers (Gerassi, 2015). Critical feminists are a smaller faction that often find themselves critiquing the inequalities within sex work (and the broader contexts within which sex work occurs), whilst advocation for sex worker rights (for a full discussion, see Farvid, 2017).

One area where consent might be compromised is the conditions under which many enter the industry. A popular media portrayal of sex work is of the white, educated, middle-class woman who finds personal and financial empowerment by entering the industry. Yet, this privileged positionality and narrative is an outlier, rather than the norm. Large scale surveys indicate that, even in a decriminalized context (like New Zealand), most enter sex work due to financial hardship (Abel, Fitzgerald, & Brunton, 2009) and as an alternative to minimum-wage work that tends to be dirty, degrading or hard on the body. The sex industry is not an easy industry to work in, due to its illegality in many places, the stigma the work carries, and the other risks it can pose (e.g., unpredictable clients, enforcing sexual health measures, escaping criminalization). Hence, the choice to enter the industry itself is often one that is shaped by the larger inequities and the stratification of social and economic privilege along class, gender and race (e.g., the feminization and racialization of poverty). The gendered nature of sex work itself speaks to expectation that heterosexual men must have access to women's bodies for sex and the value of sex as a desired commodity (see Weatherall & Priestley, 2001).

Entry aside, when it comes to discussing services with clients, many have argued that the commercial requirements of the sex industry actually bring to the fore the notion of, and need for, direct negotiations about what will happen in each sexual exchange (i.e., direct negotiation of sexual consent) (Van der Meulen et al., 2013). That is, verbal negotiation and agreement about what a specific session or encounter will involve in terms of compensation and sexual acts. This is a form of direct sexual communication that is rarely seen in non-sex work sexual interactions. Traditional modes of heterosexuality, for example the traditional marriage contract, come imbued with predetermined ideas about what the role of husbands and wives are in such relationships. For example, that a woman provides domestic and sexual upkeep, while the man provides financial support (Farvid, 2017). While discourses of love, romance or duty obfuscate these power relations, in-person sex work brings these firmly into focus (Robinson, 1997).

Exit from sex work can also be tricky. Many women tend to drift in and out of sex work – sometimes using it as a financial fallback option (Curtis et al., 2019). However, completely leaving the industry can be difficult due to stigma and wage discrepancy between other available jobs and the earning potential of sex work (Curtis et al., 2019). The stigma associated with sex work creates massive difficulties for sex workers, across their working conditions, personal lives, and psychical and psychological health (see Benoit et al., 2018). Workers rather than clients bear the brunt of the stigma associated with the sex industry, and are often positioned as the social or moral "problem" rather than the clients who drive demand for, and seek out, paid sex (Farvid & Glass, 2014). Such profound stigma means that many sex workers do not disclose their sex work history to potential employers, are less likely to disclose or discuss their work in their personal relationships, and must engage in extra psychological and cognitive labor when doing so. This secrecy increases isolation, which limits sex worker support systems, meaning that reduced safety-nets (either financial, emotional, or both) decrease the freedom of the choices women make in regard to sex work (Curtis et al., 2019).

When it comes to the parameters of an encounter, it is often argued that these are set by individual sex workers, albeit shaped by shifting demands of the industry (e.g., competition with other sex workers, and the requests of clients). Furthermore, the negotiation of consent "in the moment", even after verbal agreements, can be complicated if clients do not respect the boundaries that are already set in place. While sex workers often speak about their work in business terms (discussing their conversations about the terms and conditions of the interaction before money is exchanged), others describe struggling to say no to an interaction even if it felt "off" (or they were not fully comfortable with it) (e.g., Tremblay, 2021). Many state that if a client wants to instigate something that was not agreed upon at the start of a meeting, they will pause and renegotiate the price.

Discussions of consent typically go beyond the one-on-one exchange and include reflections on the context and structure of sex work. For example, sex workers note that it is easier to set boundaries, and say no to various practices, when they work for themselves (whereas there is pressure to go along with what the client wants, when working for a third party, agency or brothel). Agencies, brothels and clubs can also be exploitative – taking unfairly large percentages of earnings, or barring someone from work as punishment for not doing what clients want. There are also financial vulnerabilities, due to a lack of an enforced minimum wage, inconsistent pricing, slow days (and feeling compelled to accept lower prices due to financial hardship). Clients sometimes use these factors as a means by which to directly exploit the standard terms of the work. While sex work may involve financial, physical and psychological vulnerabilities (similar to some legal but precarious work), it can also be a legitimate source of income, that offers greater control and autonomy over daily life.

The discrepancy in freedoms, women's agency, and the choices they make, is also tethered to structural inequities and the sociopolitical positioning of their identities (Showden, 2011). Indeed, many sex workers belong to marginalized communities, such as being people of color, transgender, undocumented and/or unhoused (Vanwesenbeeck, 2001). If a woman falls into any already minoritized category, sex work can both offer greater freedoms (financial gain/independence) as well as pose risks and opportunities for exploitation. The stigma associated with sex work has almost always included class and race (Wedum, 2014; Brooks, 2021). Black sex workers, for example, are more likely to be arrested, and more likely to be thought of as choosing to be in sex-work; while white women are more likely to be framed as victims of the industry (Phillips, 2015; Brooks, 2021). In the US context, this sentiment dates back to times of slavery, where black women were hyper-sexualized, and seen to be "unrapeable" property (Smith, 2003; Brooks 2021). Further, sex workers are often publicly framed as "sexually, morally and socially inappropriate and … [un] worthy of human dignity" (Tomura, 2009, p. 52). This risk of physical danger increases the need for hiring paid security (if a woman is a sole operator), working with a known minder or "pimp" (who often take a large cut of earnings), or choosing to work in a brothel/agency (which also take about at least half of what a sex worker earns) – creating a complex relationship between ensuring safety and earning money (Marcus et al., 2014).

The notion of consent is no doubt complex when it comes to sex work. It is subject to the demands of a given day, one's financial needs, the norms of the industry, client and employer/agency demands, and market competition. At times, the worker's own sense of boundaries can thus be secondary to other competing demands or needs. Furthermore, the legality of the work adds another layer of complexity. In contexts where sex work is illegal, sex workers can be subject to raced, classed and spatial surveillance or arrest. The boundaries of what constitutes consent in sex work is further complicated when it becomes technologically mediated – or moves online.

Consent in Online Sex Work

The Internet has long allowed communication across the globe, fostering relationships between those who have never met "in the flesh" (Farvid, 2016). While earlier technology was slow and clunky, high-speed Internet, now used in conjunction with webcams, allow people to stay in touch or communicate much more seamlessly online. Sex work is currently technologically mediated in many ways, from sex workers advertising online, staying in contact with clients on social media, and/or developing a client-base or followers via various platforms (Campbell et al., 2019). "Camming", is a form of technologically mediated sex work typically defined as an online session where webcam models, cam girls, or cam models livestream a variety of performances and activities, often sexual in nature, in exchange for money to viewers (Henry & Farvid, 2017). In line with the examinations above, we focus on online sex work that involves ciswomen as cam models, and (assumed) cismen as consumers.

The sector of digital sex work dates back to the inception of the Internet (Jones, 2020), and has gained greater momentum in recent years. The camming industry often overlaps with social media and other forms of sex work such as online pornography and subscription-based content making (such as OnlyFans). This overlap and the blurred lines of media have been further exacerbated by the pandemic, as well as recent growth in these industries, overall. Many that cam often have a coalescence of areas that they work in, such as multiple websites/platforms and in multiple fields of sex work, as well as employing more mainstream social media to grow their client-base. In what follows, we tease out the "nexus of labor" that is typically involved in camming for cam models, as well as examining the subjective experiences of camming, as based on three in-depth works of the practice (Henry, 2018, p. 38; Jones, 2020; Sanders et al., 2018), in order to unpack what consent means in this context. We argue for an *expanded framework of consent* that can more accurately capture the ways in which choices women make in this context are "constrained" by the broader context within which the work takes place, but still denotes the exercise of agency on their part.

The process of camming involves cam models setting up an online profile with various hosting sites that act as a mediator between models and clients. The sites typically have a tipping or token system that viewers purchase and can pay the models with. Most streams are often advertised on social media beforehand, have a title, tip goal, and description, (models can also use tags with different identifiers similar to tags used in online pornography). Content of the stream can vary but typically involve a cam model performing various acts (ranging from mundane daily practices to invasive sex acts) and interacting with their viewers. Many streams also have predetermined acts available where cam models can post an act that they will perform once they reach a certain goal for tokens (or the site's currency) as well as a tip menu displaying available acts that can be purchased for individual tips (Jones, 2020). These goals and menus are a way of pre-determining and stating available content and its price, as prearranged by the models.

Like in-person sex work, camming deals directly with many aspects of consent. In negotiating terms, as mentioned, many models will post available acts, pre-determining and explicitly stating what is available, "the topic and countdown are individualized and set by the model according to what acts they will and will not perform" (Jones, 2020, p. 43). However, these pre-determined agreements can be complicated by on-the-spot demands – which can range from the routine (masturbating or "cum shows"), to the "silly" but dehumanizing (being asked to bark like a dog), to strange kinks (being asked to wear multiple menstrual pads) (Henry, 2018). In an account where boundaries were crossed, one cam model relayed to Jones (2020), her experiences of a customer tipping large and requesting her to perform racialized femininity (with white-supremacy adjacent sentiment), stating:

> And I was just like, no. Like, I could never say that; I wouldn't want to be associated with that….It makes you feel conflicted because they're giving you money and…either I have to kick this guy out, even though he just gave me $50, but I can't let him stay here because he's saying some, like, really messed-up things. So I think they're doing it on purpose; like, they want you to have to feel like you should go along with it because they're paying you for it, and, so, I think that they are trying to manipulate you a little bit by giving you a lot of money and thinking they can do that because they're giving you money for it.
>
> *(p. 171)*

Others describe getting fed-up with the type of content they were repeatedly asked to perform, and the sexual politics or ramifications of performing (mainstreamed) hetero-pornified sexual sessions:

> [You] really annihilate your genitals and bend yourself into a pretzel and hurt yourself and choke yourself…[it reinforces] bad male sexual behavior [when you're] faking orgasms, when you're doing stuff that is genuinely not pleasurable…I just feel like stopping what I'm doing and saying "do you guys know, have you ever touched a woman before? Do you have any understanding of how the female process of sexual arousal and climax works, because this is not it."
>
> *(Henry, 2018, p. 45)*

For many cam models, while camming was initially seen as an easier and safer way to make money in the sex industry, it quickly became clear that the work was actually much more laborious than initially expected. The labor involved in camming spans the digital, physical, and emotional, as well as including "safety work" (Henry, 2018). Digital labor is typically linked to the administrative and marketing activities associated with the online modality. Activities in camming include maintaining high-speed internet, curating appealing and organized online profiles on social media and cam sites, producing bespoke pornography, advertising camming sessions, maintaining contact with clients (especially regular clients) before and after sessions. Physical labor involves any work done to the body in the process of getting ready for a session (e.g., make-up, hair, costuming), or during streaming (e.g., masturbating, sucking/inserting sex toys, spanking and stripping) (Henry, 2018).

A prevalent aspect of camming is the level of contact and intimacy that can be fostered between models and clients before, during and after cam sessions. Similar to in-person sex work "models are selling intimacy, not just sex in public performances...conversation is an integral part of camming and a primary way that cam models sell embodied authenticity" (Jones, 2020, p. 44). Due to this importance placed on "authenticity" many models have highlighted their desire to portray themselves in a way that is congruent with their daily persona, while most note that a large part of camming is the performance of various characters or taking on a sexual persona that is most marketable to the largest group of potential viewers (Henry, 2018). The "emotion work" involved in camming, as with in-person sex work, requires surface to deep acting and "ego work" with clients (O'Brien, 1994). This aspect of the work includes developing and maintaining close/ongoing connections with clients, acting aroused and engaging in sexual banter to elevate men's sense of sexual desirability (Henry, 2018). Akin to subjective experiences of in-person sex work (e. g., Abel, 2011), cam models also describe sometimes "dissociating" during camming sessions, as a way to keep their true feelings or responses hidden from clients, when performing authenticity was not desired (Henry, 2018).

In terms of surface or deep acting, Henry (2018) identified four subject positions that cam models described. These were adopting a *cam girl persona* (doing what the market demanded – a character that was hypersexual, always up for anything, sexually submissive, and responsive to the penetrative acts clients asked them to do online), the *woman next door* (an easy-going, more authentic and relatable persona, less fixed on the demands of clients), the *anxious subject* (being hyper vigilant about the potential negative ramifications of doing cam work), and *the puppet master*. The puppet master was a complex subject position, where women savvily negotiated the gendered camming market, while being award of the gendered norms and power imbalances that were at stake. They saw themselves as a strategic performer who knowingly acted in a manner that they knew clients would like, even though they thought the desires and requests of men were silly, idiotic, unrealistic, or sexist. The

244 Panteá Farvid, Rebekah Nathan, Juliana Riccard, Abigail Whitmer

process of camming also revealed other forms of self-reflection, self-knowledge, and psychic angst. There was frustration around the work, as "completely… killing my sex drive" or creating a vast disconnect between their own sexual desires/preferences, and what they performed (Henry, 2018, p. 55). One woman noted that camming created greater self-awareness around how her unpaid sex life was quite performative, where she sought to be more authentic in that context (see also Fahs, 2011).

Outside of the monetary earnings, camming involves both positive (e.g., feeling more confident sexually, feeling more attractive, getting to know oneself more as a sexual subject) and negative experiences (e.g., anxiety about the process and the risks associated with the work, feeling exploited, feeling inadequate physically). While the physical labor is seen as easier and less psychologically laborious, the digital and emotional labor is vital for garnering and maintaining (repeat) clients – a demand of the work that the cam models could not ignore, if they wanted to make decent money. As one participant noted in Henry's (2018) work:

> The performing itself is easy…but it's the, I guess liaising? With clients or possible clients…I still felt like I had to, y'know, do all those normal, social niceties and be really polite and, ended up kind of engaging in all this, emotional, like, labour? For men? And, it was that part that got really exhausting rather than the actual performative part.

Lastly, safety work (which typically refers to the work women do to maintain their own physical safety on a daily basis, see Vera-Grey, 2016) – was another layer of labor that the women engaged in to keep themselves safe; both psychologically and physically. This work ranges from keeping one's identity secret from clients, hiding the work from friends and family, managing the stigma associated with the work, and dealing with "capping" and removing online capped content (when photos or videos are saved by users and shared without consent). It is also not uncommon for cam models to be defrauded out of money by clients, or end up with higher site fees than expected, or to get kicked off certain platforms without explanation. The lack of legal protection and workers' rights afforded to those in the camming industry (alongside other sex workers) creates a context ripe for the exploitation of cam models (Stegeman, 2021). As such, the gains of working in the industry are offset by a range of complex burdens that need to be considered and astutely negotiated by cam models.

Conclusion

Like in-person sex work, camming is wrought with complex issues when it comes to the worker's rights, agency and capacity to offer or negotiate full consent. As Jones (2020) has argued, camming "is not a utopian paradise. It is an exploitative capitalist marketplace that also reproduces White supremacy, patriarchy, heterosexism, cissexism, and ableism" (p. 61). Camming, like in-person sex work, carries various aspects of benefits and drawbacks, many of these complicated by the digital modality of the work, as well as the demands of the market to offer competitive online sexual services. While cam models negotiate a complex terrain with great skill, typically developing "an ethos of resiliency" (Jones, 2020, p. 131), their experiences indicate a landscape of a constrained, evolving and fluid notion of "consent" – one that is mediated by the social, political, legal, and vocational context. Hence, we argue that when it comes to camming (and beyond), consent needs to be understood as "constrained" by the (unequal) broader landscape within which such work takes place. Although free or unfettered consent may not be fully possible in this context, the agency cam models display in their ongoing negotiations of the terrain indicate a level of engagement with sexual and labor matters that might be more elusive in daily and mundane negotiations of work and sex.

References

Abel, G. M. (2011). Different Stage, Different Performance: The Protective Strategy of Role Play on Emotional Health in Sex Work. *Social Science & Medicine*, 72(7), 1177–1184.

Abel, G. M., Fitzgerald, L. J., & Brunton, C. (2009). The Impact of Decriminalisation on the Number of Sex Workers in New Zealand. *Journal of Social Policy*, 38(3), 515–531.

Aubrey, J. S., Terán, L., Dajches, L., Gahler, H., & Yan, K. (2022). Is Sexual Consent Sexy?: Investigating the Effects of a Televised Depiction of Verbal Sexual Consent on College Students' Sexual Consent Attitudes and Behavioral Intentions. *Health Communication*, 1–10.

Bacik, I. (2020). "If Consent Is Bought, It Is Not Freely Chosen": Compromised Consent in Prostituted Sex in Ireland. *Dignity: A Journal on Sexual Exploitation and Violence*, 5(3).

Barry, K. (1996). *The Prostitution of Sexuality*. New York: NYU Press.

Benoit, C., Jansson, S. M., Smith, M., & Flagg, J. (2018). Prostitution Stigma and Its Effect on the Working Conditions, Personal Lives, and Health of Sex Workers. *Journal of Sex Research*, 55(4–5), 457–471.

Beres, M. A. (2007). "Spontaneous" Sexual Consent: An Analysis of Sexual Consent Literature. *Feminism & Psychology*, 17(1), 93–108.

Brooks, S. (2021). Innocent White Victims and Fallen Black Girls: Race, Sex Work, and the Limits of Anti-sex Trafficking Laws. *Signs: Journal of Women in Culture and Society*, 46(2), 513–521.

Campbell, R., Sanders, T., Scoular, J., Pitcher, J. and Cunningham, S. (2019), Risking Safety and Rights: Online Sex Work, Crimes and "Blended Safety Repertoires". *British Journal of Sociology*, 70, 1539–1560.

Curtis, M. G., D'Aniello, C., Twist, M. L., Brents, B. G., & Eddy, B. (2019). "We Are Naked Waitresses Who Deliver Sex": A Phenomenological Study of Circumstantial Sex Workers' Lives. *Sexual and Relationship Therapy*, 36(4), 438–464.

Dworkin, A. (1981). *Pornography: Men Possessing Women*. London, UK: Women's Press.

Fahs, B. (2011). *Performing Sex: The Making and Unmaking of Women's Erotic Lives*. New York: SUNY Press.

Farley, M. (2004). "Bad for the Body, Bad for the Heart": Prostitution Harms Women Even if Legalized or Decriminalized. *Violence Against Women*, 10, 1087–1125.

Farvid, P. (2015). Heterosexuality. In C. Richards & M. J. Barker (Eds.), *The Palgrave Book of the Psychology of Sexuality and Gender* (pp. 92–108). Palgrave Macmillan.

Farvid, P. (2016). Cyber Intimacies. In N. Naples, R. C. Hoogland, & M. Wickramasingh (Eds.), *The Wiley-Blackwell Encyclopedia of Gender and Sexuality Studies* (pp. 288–292). Wiley-Blackwell.

Farvid, P. (2017). The Politics of Sex Work in Aotearoa/New Zealand and the Pacific: Tensions, Debates and Future Directions. *Women's Studies Journal*, 31(2), 27–34.

Farvid, P. (forthcoming). *Psychology and Heterosexuality: Theory, Research and Practice*. New York: Palgrave Macmillan.

Farvid, P., & Braun, V. (2006). "Most of Us Guys Are Raring To Go Anytime, Anyplace, Anywhere": Male and Female Sexuality in Cleo and Cosmo. *Sex Roles*, 55(5–6), 295–310.

Farvid, P., & Braun, V. (2018). A Critical Encyclopedia of Heterosex. In K. Hall & R. Barrett (Eds.), *The Oxford Handbook of Language and Sexuality*. Oxford University Press (online version).

Farvid, P., & Saing, R. (2022, May). "If I Don't Allow Him to Have Sex With Me, Our Relationship Will Be Broken": Rape, Sexual Coercion, and Sexual Compliance Within Marriage in Rural Cambodia. *Violence Against Women*, 28(6–7), 1587–1609.

Farvid, P., & Glass, L. (2014). "It Isn't Prostitution as you Normally Think of It. It's Survival Sex": Media Representations of Adult and Child Prostitution in New Zealand. *Women's Studies Journal*, 28(1), 46–67.

Gavey, N. (2019). *Just Sex?: The Cultural Scaffolding of Rape* (2nd edn). London: Routledge.

Gavey, N. (1992). Technologies and Effects of Heterosexual Coercion. *Feminism & Psychology*, 2(3), 325–351.

Gerassi L. (2015). A Heated Debate: Theoretical Perspectives of Sexual Exploitation and Sex Work. *Journal of Sociology and Social Welfare*, 42(4), 79–100.

Graf, A. S., & Johnson, V. (2021). Describing the "Gray" Area of Consent: A Comparison of Sexual Consent Understanding Across the Adult Lifespan. *The Journal of Sex Research*, 58(4), 448–461.

Henry, M. V (2018). "You Can Look but You Can't Touch": Women's Experiences of Webcam Sex Work in Aotearoa/New Zealand, Unpublished Master's thesis, Auckland University of Technology, Auckland, NZ.

Henry, M. V., & Farvid, P. (2017). "Always Hot, Always Live": Computer-mediated Sex Work in the Era of "Camming". *Women's Studies Journal*, 31(2), 113–128.

Herbenick, D., Eastman-Mueller, H., Fu, T.-C., Dodge, B., Ponander, K., & Sanders, S. A. (2019). Women's Sexual Satisfaction, Communication, and Reasons for (No Longer) Faking Orgasm: Findings from a U.S. Probability Sample. *Archives of Sexual Behavior*, 48(8), 2461–2472.

Hollway, W. (1989). *Subjectivity and Method in Psychology: Gender, Meaning and Science*. London: Sage.

Jones, A. (2020). *Camming: Money, Power, and Pleasure in the Sex Work Industry*. New York: NYU Press.

Marcus, A., Horning, A., Curtis, R., Sanson, J., & Thompson, E. (2014). Conflict and Agency among Sex Workers and Pimps: A Closer Look at Domestic Minor Sex Trafficking. *The ANNALS of the American Academy of Political and Social Science*, 653(1), 225–246.

Muehlenhard, C. L., Humphreys, T. P., Jozkowski, K. N., & Peterson, Z. D. (2016). The Complexities of Sexual Consent Among College Students: A Conceptual and Empirical Review. *The Journal of Sex Research*, 53(4–5), 457–487.

O'Brien, M. (1994). The Managed Heart Revisited: Health and Social Control. *The Sociological Review*, 42(3), 393–413.

Phillips, J. R. (2015). Black Girls and the (Im)possibilities of a Victim Trope: The Intersectional Failures of Legal and Advocacy Interventions in the Commercial Sexual Exploitation of Minors in the United States. *UCLA Law Review*, 62, 1642–1675.

Pond, T., & Farvid, P. (2017). 'I Do Like Girls, I Promise': Young Bisexual Women's Experiences of Using Tinder. *Psychology of Sexualities Review*, 8(2), 6–24.

Robinson, V. (1997). My Baby Just Cares for Me: Feminism, Heterosexuality and Non-monogamy. *Journal of Gender Studies*, 6(2), 143–157.

Reinelt, J. (2016). Coerced Performances? Trafficking, Sex Work, and Consent. *Lateral*, 5 (2).

Sanders, T., Scoular, J., Campbell, R., Pitcher, J. and Cunningham, S. (2018). *Internet sex Work: Beyond the Gaze*. London: Palgrave.

Showden, C. R. (2011). *Choices Women Make: Agency in Domestic Violence, Assisted Reproduction, and Sex Work*. University of Minnesota Press.

Smith, A. (2003). Not an Indian Tradition: The Sexual Colonization of Native Peoples. *Hypatia*, 18(2), 70–85.

Stegeman, H. M. (2021). Regulating and Representing Camming: Strict Limits on Acceptable Content on Webcam Sex Platforms. *New Media & Society*, 0(0). https://doi.org/10.1177/14614448211059117.

Tomura, M. (2009). A Prostitute's Lived Experiences of Stigma. *Journal of Phenomenological Psychology*, 40 (1), 51–84.

Tremblay, F. (2021). Labouring in the Sex Industry: A Conversation with Sex Workers on Consent and Exploitation. *Social Sciences*, 10(3), 86.

Van der Meulen, E. (2012). When Sex is Work: Organizing for Labour Rights and Protections. *Labour / Le Travail*, 69, 147–167.

Van der Meulen, E., Durisin, E. M., & Love., V (2013) *Selling Sex: Experience, Advocacy, and Research on Sex Work in Canada*. Vancouver, Toronto: UBC Press.

Vanwesenbeeck I. (2001). Another Decade of Social Scientific Work on Sex Work: A Review of Research 1990–2000. *Annual Review of Sex Research*, 12 (1), 242–289.

Weatherall, A., & Priestley, A. (2001). A Feminist Discourse Analysis of Sex 'Work'. *Feminism & Psychology*, 11(3), 323–340.

Wedum, E. K. (2014). Ho is a Ho is a Ho: Prostitution, Feminism and the Nevada Brothel System. *Law School Student Scholarship* (Paper 602), 1–34.

West, R. (2008). Sex, Law and Consent. *Georgetown Law Faculty Working Papers*.

PART V

Legal and Political Representations of Consent

17

'SHE SEEMED TO BE HAVING FUN'

Construing Consent in the Sex Game Gone Wrong

Alexandra Fanghanel

Over the past 20 years there has been a proliferation of cases tried in court in which women (usually) have died or been injured by men (nearly always) as part of a so-called sex game which has gone wrong. The phenomenon of the sex game gone wrong is not in itself new but increasing prevalence of these cases is indicative of a social-cultural evolution within the criminal justice landscape. This evolution marks the emergence of, or increased acceptance of, the possibility that sexual violence might be consented to within these 'sex games'. Even though consent to sexual violence which is more than transient or trifling is impossible in law, as confirmed by *R v Brown* [1993] UKHL 19, [1994] 1 AC 212 and s. 71 of the Domestic Abuse Act 2021, the increase in cases where this defence is raised indicates that consent to sexual violence continues to play a part in socio-legal praxis and imaginary. The phenomenon of the sex game which has gone wrong, or consensual rough sex, intersects with bondage and sadomasochistic practices in that these centralise the possibility that some elements of sexual violence might be consented to, notwithstanding the legal impossibility of this. This chapter interrogates how consent is figured in cases of sex games that have gone wrong. In order to do this, I will outline some of the complexities of consent within sadomasochistic encounters. Despite these complexities, consent is intrinsic to sadomasochistic encounters and it is an intrinsic component in these cases. I then establish how research into consent in these cases was conducted before detailing and analysing three cases where consent to rough sex is claimed in court. The chapter concludes by highlighting rape myths that run through contemporary constructions of consent in these cases.

Construing Consent

What distinguishes sadomasochism from acts of sexual aggression or unwanted violence, is the role of consent in the encounter (Weinberg et al., 1984; Newmahr,

DOI: 10.4324/9781003358756-23

2011; Weiss, 2011, Pitagora, 2013). Within sadomasochistic sexual practice, not only is consent of central importance, but discussion about consent, how it emerges, and its nuances, abound. Consent emerges in a number of ways. It emerges through an active practice of negotiating consent – what people say they want – what people will agree to within the time-bound context of a scene or of 'play', and at an intersubjective level – the unspoken iterations of consent –what people really want, how far they really want to go, including whether they actually want their consent to be violated (see Williams et al., 2014). Though consent discussions are at the forefront of sadomasochistic practice – indeed, consent practices could be said to be intrinsic to the practice of building a sadomasochistic community – the practicalities of consent are complex (Fanghanel, 2020). Part of the pleasure of sadomasochistic sexual practice is in the risk-taking that is also inherent to it (Newmahr, 2011). This interplay with risk as pleasure may emerge in the practices that sadomasochists participate in – beating, branding, sensory stimulation, humiliation or other forms of power play – which all in themselves carry an element of risk to the self, whether physically or psychically, and also in the pushing of the boundaries of consent itself.

For some practitioners of sadomasochistic sex, pushing up against the boundaries of what has been agreed to is part of the pleasure of sadomasochism. To engage in this sexual practice is, in any iteration of it, to put one's body, and one's sense of self under pressure that would not usually be encountered in sexual practice that does not comprise sadomasochistic elements. Challenging the self in this way is one of the appealing elements of sadomasochistic practice, as a form of auto-poesies, or creation of the self (Fanghanel, 2020). The pushing of boundaries around consent can plunge questions of consent into a grey area where acts which have not been agreed to may happen but that happening has, in itself, been agreed to. How do practitioners of sadomasochism then know where the lines of consent lie over their play? Partially through practice and by acquiring knowledge and experience of sadomasochism and its specific culture and community norms. In part, this is also acquired through the interplay between risk and trust; an interplay which is heightened through intimacy, verbal and non-verbal communication, and connectedness: 'knowing' what people want to do, how far they want to go. Forging – and normalising – consent as an ethical praxis, as something that practitioners actively attend to and do, is ongoing work within sadomasochistic contexts (Fanghanel, 2020: 282). Consent work is work that is inexact, it can be tacit, and it can go wrong, but in some form, it is a presence and not an absence, simple acquiescence, or passive event.

How do these consent complexities help us to understand the phenomenon of the sex game gone wrong? In these cases, we encounter women who have been killed by men during sex as part of what is claimed is a consensual sexual encounter which had forceful, violent elements to it. The increase in the proliferation of cases coming to trial where consent is mobilised as a defence to explain injury or death demonstrates that something that looks like consent is operationalised, or certainly is operationalisable in court. In order to excavate what is going on in such cases, it is important to examine what this consent looks like and how it emerges. As demonstrated above, and elsewhere in sadoma-sochistic cases where consent is at stake, it can be hard to identify what consent looks like and where it emerges. But though it is hard, and sometimes it is ambiguous even to those who participate in sadomasochism themselves, there are shadows or spectres of consent which can show us how consent might have emerged. What I want to do here is explore how defendants who claim that certain sex acts or sex games were consensual evidence that consent. What does consent look like in the sex game gone wrong?

Considering Consent

In 2020–1, I acquired the transcripts of 10 cases in which a defence of consent is raised in an incident where a sex game had gone wrong. To identify cases of interest, I used the LexisNexis and Westlaw databases to search for cases using the key words 'sex game', 'rough sex', 'sadomasochism', 'SM' and 'BDSM'. Though these databases cover several jurisdictions, I limited my search to cases tried under English and Welsh law. The limitation of using these databases for this type of research is that they only list cases that have been sent to the Court of Appeal or beyond. For this to happen, a Crown Court needs to have found a defendant guilty of a crime. As such, it does not capture cases where defendants are found not guilty, or where cases do not, for whatever reason, go to appeal. During this project, I also noted that when examining issues of consent, sexual violence and BDSM, the Court of Appeal transcripts are less useful than those of the Crown Courts which are more explicit on the points of each case.

To mitigate this, I also conducted searches of media reporting of 'sex game gone wrong' and 'rough sex gone wrong' also using the LexisNexis news database. Here, the criteria for inclusion were cases where women were complainants or victims, and men were defendants. From this search it became clear that men as well as women die or are injured in a sex game gone wrong or as part of con-sensual BDSM, but that the defendants are nearly always men. Media searches enabled me to identify cases where a defendant was found not guilty, or otherwise was not captured by legal database searches. It also allowed me to triangulate information on the cases found through database searches for analysis. Of course, this misses cases which are not reported in the press. I supplemented my searches with data from the action group We Can't Consent to This, although unlike this group, I limited my search to cases that take place in England and Wales.

Once cases had been identified and the judge's summing up or sentencing remarks acquired, I conducted a thematic and discourse analysis of the text. In doing this, I coded specific areas where consent was mentioned either directly using the word 'consent' or cognate terms 'she said yes', 'it was at her request', for instance. Occasionally very little discussion of how consent was established appeared in the transcripts beyond merely stating that a certain act had been consensual. To enrich my analysis here, I examined the elements around the statement of consent in order to excavate more information about *how* consent was established, and how parties to the sexual practice *knew* that it had been established. By looking at these elements, a picture of what consent looks like in these cases begins to emerge. I analyse three of these cases here. I chose these cases to present here as though the cases have different outcomes, each case reveals similarities about how consent is construed within these contexts.

Case 1

This is the case of Marcus Coates who, in August 2011 strangled Jennie Banner to death in her flat. They had taken drugs and alcohol and had engaged in sexual activity together. We are told that 'she had many difficulties in her life and was a drug user and prostitute' (p.12). Coates was accused of tying a belt around Banner's neck and tightening it, fracturing her thyroid cartilage and killing her. He said that she had tightened the belt for her own sexual pleasure, and that he had nothing to do with her death; what she did, she did to herself as an act of auto-erotic asphyxiation or suicide. The prosecution claimed that he tightened the belt for his sexual gratification, that paraphilic practice was of no interest to her and that moreover, she hated to have anything, even jewellery, around her neck. He, on the other hand, had an established practice of tightening a collar around his former partner's neck as part of consensual foreplay (p.7). Though he had been charged with murder, he was found guilty of manslaughter.

Case 2

In February 2018, Richard Bailey met Charlotte Teeling just before she died. She had been out in Birmingham, UK until the early hours of the morning. It was a cold night. After the nightclub closed, she wandered around the city before meeting Bailey. Together they bought drugs and alcohol and went back to his apartment to consume these and to have rough sex. At her request, her choked her and slapped her. She died. He said it was an accident because he was surprised by someone knocking at his bedroom door. He didn't mean to kill her. He was found guilty of murder.

Case 3

In this case, Jason Gaskell, pleaded guilty to the manslaughter of Laure Huteson who died in February 2018:

> he's accepted that he deliberately held a knife to her neck during sexual intercourse. The knife passed through her skin and into the soft tissues of her neck, reaching a branch of the jugular vein and a branch of the carotid artery, and she died from the substantial blood loss caused in that way.
>
> (p.2)

Because Gaskell pleaded guilty the comments from this case are taken from sentencing remarks as opposed to the judge's summing up, as guilt does not need to be determined. The pair had met just a few hours before her death and had, according to the judge, enjoyed pleasurable and consensual sex at the home that Gaskell shared with two friends. In this case, the sexual encounter between Gaskell and Huteson was presented as consensual, and her death an unintended consequence of the knife play.

In each of these cases, consent to sex that is rough, that is kinky, or that is otherwise non-normative is presented as an explanation for how the women in these cases died. Though the claims that sex was consensual do not always work, what emerges is that something akin to consent is offered up as a potential mitigation for acts of violence which led to the deaths of women. How is this consent evidenced?

Coates

In Case 1, Coates's defence was that whatever happened to Banner was committed by her, herself as an act of suicide or a 'tragic accident' (p.8). They had a casual sexual relationship which also principally involved using drugs together. To evidence her consent to the strangulation, the defence explain that:

> He went round to Jennie's, she asked him to put a belt round her neck. He called her a weirdo in a laughable way. He put the belt round her neck and sat down. She said she'd tell him when to take the belt off, and just smiled at him. He sat down and when he looked at her she was going blue and he tried to get the belt off her neck.
>
> (p.8)

Affixing the belt to Banner's neck, we are told here, is at her behest. She asked him to do it. Even though he thought she was 'a weirdo' for wanting him to, he did put the belt around her neck. She smiles to him as she dies. Later another iteration of these events is presented:

> She had been a working girl, she asked him to put a belt round her neck, he said no. She then put a belt around her own neck. He noticed that she started to turn a funny colour, he attempted to get the belt off her neck but couldn't do so. He said he didn't have sex with her as he couldn't get an erection. He categorically stated he did not put the belt around her neck and that she put the belt around her own neck.
>
> (p.17)

She asks and then, following his refusal, now attaches the belt to her neck herself. This section of the summing up also aligns the encounter between Coates and Banner with deviant sexual practice. Even though, as we are told here, they did not have sex, it is explained that she was a 'working girl'. In the summing up, Banner is referred to as a 'prostitute', or 'known prostitute' four times throughout. Though her status as a sex worker does not directly infer consent, what it does is to discursively associate sexual deviancy in one context (sex work) with sexual deviancy in another (interest in erotic asphyxiation). A further detail that is notable in terms of this deviancy is in Coates's inability to get an erection. In his own words:

> When we first met, we tried to become fuck buddies but she didn't really do anything for me sexually ... We have had oral sex but she again couldn't get me hard.
>
> *(pp.19–20)*

Here, responsibility for not being 'able to get [him] hard' falls to Banner who does not 'really do anything' for him in terms of desirability. Deviant constructions of desire, heteronormative sexual practice and masculinity and femininity abound in these short phrases. Banner, not only a sex worker but also one who cannot excite the arousal of her companion, evinces a flawed heteronormative femininity that presents her as outside of normative conceptions of desirability. Cast as a 'weirdo' (p.8), a 'working girl' who 'didn't really do anything sexually' for the defendant, her apparent non-normative desire to have a belt tied around her neck becomes packaged within this deviancy:

> We both smoked crack. She also took heroin later. She invited me to put her belt around her neck as she told me she likes it kinky ... .
>
> *(p.17)*

And later:

> Reference is made to the belt she called her kinky belt: 'She then asked me to put the belt round her neck. I thought it was a joke and laughed, but I put it round her neck. It was already formed as a noose but none of the holes had been engaged by the metal prong. She herself then tightens the belt around her neck. I then put another rock on the pipe and she was still talking and said she would let me know when to release the belt. I smoked the rock and remember looking at her and she was smiling at me ... . Although Jennie talked about having rough sex, we never did it, and apart from the day in question, never used ropes or any other form of restraint.'
>
> *(p.20)*

These repeated images of a 'kinky' belt, 'liking it kinky', and talking about 'rough sex' as something that is laughable or weird, or not shared by the defendant furthers this impression that consent, if it exists, emerges because she is an outsider, or someone who has desires that he does not identify with. Throughout,

Banner is cast as the active agent; she asks for the belt, she either ties it herself or it is tied at her request, she smiles, she talks about having rough sex. Evidence of consent here is offered up in the form of direct requests but also in ancillary evidence around sexual practice, desire, and deviancy. Indeed, non-consent – which also tells us what consent looks like – is evidenced elsewhere by the prosecution:

> There were no sex toys or bondage equipment found in Jennie Banner's flat. Drugs paraphernalia were found, such as spoons to cook up drugs and syringes were also found.
>
> *(pp.17–18)*

We are also told that Banner had no interest in BDSM and asphyxiation, and she hated having her neck touched even by her mother. The lack of sex toys and lack of interest in paraphilia would seem to contest the likelihood that Coates's version of events took place. At the same time, what if there were sex toys in her flat? What if she was interested in some forms of non-normative sex? The presence of these would not infer consent to the practices that eventually unfolded, but that they are offered up in the negative – as proof that she did not consent to any asphyxiation – discursively suggests that this might have been the case. This observation rehearses rape myths about promiscuity. If Banner did have an interest in non-normative sex, the use of sex toys, or forms of bondage, would this have made it harder to believe that she did not consent to this asphyxiation?

Bailey

In this case, Bailey was found guilty of the murder of Teeling. As part of his defence, however, Bailey suggested that she had died as a result of an accident during consensual rough sex. The details of the consensual sadomasochistic encounter are detailed through the police interview undertaken with Bailey. A considerable amount of this was repeated in the judge's summing up of the case:

> Question: She asked you to be rougher?
> Answer: Yes.
> Question: Were those her exact words?
> Answer: Yeah, 'Do it harder. Fuck me harder,' this, that.
> Question: So, that's what I'm saying, so was that her? Tell me what her exact words was?
> Answer: They were that, they were that.
> Question: Tell me again.
> Answer: 'Fuck me harder. Pull my hair,' yeah, 'And choke me,' this. That I can, 'Choke me. Be rougher.'
> Question: Choke me?
> Answer: Yeah, but I didn't or I dunno. I dunno what happened.
> Question: What did you actually do when she was telling you that?

Answer: Pulled her hair a bit.

Question: And how did you pull her hair?

Answer: Not very hard. I was too – it was too, probably, too scared.

Question: What part of her hair did you pull? The side? The back?

Answer: I think so.

Question: Yeah, and apart from pulling her hair, how did she react when you were pulling her hair?

Answer: I don't know. Seemed to be enjoying herself anyway.

Question: What makes you say that?

Answer: I don't know, I don't know. She initiated it. She was enjoying it.

Question: Mm, and when she said about being rougher, what did you do as a result of that, other than pulling her hair?

Answer: I tried to go as she said.

(p.28)

In this extract Bailey posits that whatever he did to Teeling was at her request to 'be rougher' and to 'do it harder'. She asks to be choked and to have her hair pulled. When pressed by the interviewer about the choking, Bailey linguistically steps away from what he says: 'I dunno. I dunno what happened'. He pulls her hair 'a bit', and 'not very hard'. He 'tried to go as she said'. All of this casts Bailey as an unwilling participant in whatever Teeling was saying she wanted. Whereas he was 'scared', she 'seemed to be enjoying herself'. This imbalance of their desire for what they were participating in mirrors the imbalance of power in their interaction; she is submissive but willing, he is dominant but reluctant. This dynamic plays out in his accounts of engaging in similar practices with other women:

Question: You've mentioned that Charlotte seems to be the driving force of this. She's asking you to do these things. Have you ever done anything like that before with any other female?

Answer: Vaguely, but I was a bit scared. I met this girl and I was a bit scared, bit worried to what she was asking to do, and I actually asked her, 'Why have you not got a boyfriend cos you're every man's dream.' She says, 'Cos they run a mile, basically.' So, no, not really well, yeah.

Question: You've had experience before of another female asking you to do those things?

Answer: Worse this one female was asking to do, but I was just too scared to do anything like that.

Question: So, you've never choked a female in sexual intercourse before?

Answer: No, I don't remember. I don't remember. Vaguely, I remember what happened with this chick in Leicester, but I was scared.

Question: Have you ever been rough in terms of when you've been having sex with a female?

Answer: Yeah, I have a bit. A bit, but they've initiated it all, believe me.

(p.43)

Here, Bailey demonstrates that he has a history of unwillingly engaging – 'vaguely' – in rough sex with women but that on each occasion it scared him. In this extract of his police interview, Bailey expresses six times that he was scared of what women were asking him to do. Each time, he was only 'a bit' rough; each time it was they who initiated 'it all'.

The other noteworthy observation in this extract is the construction of the girls who were asking Bailey to do things that he found scary. He says she is 'every man's dream' for what she wanted to engage with as part of sexual practice, to which she responds that men 'run a mile' meaning that even as might be imagined to be 'a dream' she is also repulsive to men who might want to be romantically involved with her. She is not the victim in this case, and is only mentioned by Bailey in passing, but these observations work to cast women who engage willingly in this form of sexual practice – practice that scares Bailey – as flawed, difficult, and otherwise undesirable.

In these two extracts, Bailey attempts to demonstrate consent firstly though the requests made by willing women (so far, so consensual) but also through his reluctance and fear. How does he know that they like it? They seemed to be enjoying it. Consent is read off the body as part of the intersubjective encounter but this is also accompanied by considerable reluctance on his part. If there is consent to participate in this rough sex, it certainly does not seem to be on his part.

Gaskell

The case of Gaskell details the death of Huteson following some consensual knife play. As Gaskell pleaded guilty, what we have are the sentencing remarks as opposed to arguments about the facts of what unfolded. This means that the consensual nature of the sexual practice is not interrogated. Nonetheless, indicators of consent are alluded to through the judge's comments:

It's a sadness to report that she became a little distant from her parents. She had fallen into drug use herself and into what might be thought of by some as 'bad company', and she was a little vulnerable to the extent that she had an unhappy history of harming herself and being harmed by partners. She was a victim of domestic abuse.

(p.1)

As with Keeling and Bailey, Huteson met Gaskell on the same day that she died, so they did not have a pre-existing relationship. Huteson's background is explained by the judge perhaps as evidence of why, or how she found herself involved with Gaskell, engaging in a consensual act of sadomasochism. None of these facts – from the drug use, to the estrangement from her family, to her past victimisation – are offered as evidence of her consent (as, of course, they cannot be) but the offering up of these facts in the sentencing remarks works to paint a picture of the sort of person who might engage in this practice. Her background does not have any causal bearing on her death, yet in presenting it here, the judge's comments start to make this discursive link.

Consent was more explicitly considered in the context of Gaskell's history:

> QC: The defendant will accept that he has a practice, as it were, of taking risks during sexual intercourse, engaging in – in rough sex which—
>
> JUDGE: I mean, is the right – right way to label is, it's a form, this – the sort of activity that he indulges in – is a form of sadomasochist sex, I mean?
>
> QC: Well, there's an element of force used which—
>
> JUDGE: Yes.
>
> QC: – from which—
>
> JUDGE: It's consensual but it's – that's, I suppose, the appropriate label. [...] simply indulging in sadomasochistic sex doesn't necessarily involve a criminal act—
>
> QC: No.
>
> JUDGE : – but here, where you've got the knife involved, it's grossly dangerous.
>
> QC: Yes. It may be one of those hybrid-type cases. Holding a knife to somebody throat is – is an unlawful act potentially. But where she consents to that—
>
> JUDGE: Well, I think you can consent to that because you're not actually being physically hurt.
>
> *(pp.3–4)*

Consent to having a knife held against her throat is asserted and assumed on Huteson's behalf in this extract. We do not have any further evidence of Huteson's consent than these statements that the knife play was consensual. Unlike in the case of Coates or of Bailey where there appears to be a specific request for whatever sexual practice to take place, here we are not told how this knife play was negotiated or how consent was expressed and understood. Instead, because we are looking for signifiers of consent in these cases, we turn to different evidence which might suggest that practice was consensual:

> [the pathologist] found marks on Laura's neck consistent with rough sexual activity. There was no bleeding into the eyes or petechia of that type to suggest that it had been extreme force used around the neck, but there were marks on her neck consistent with rough sexual activity
>
> *(p.4)*

[the pathologist] said that [the knife] would have passed through the remaining tissue, once through the skin, with relative ease. There were no other injuries, no defence injuries, no other recent signs of serious trauma above and beyond those patchy bruises seen on Laura's neck.

(p.8)

Lack of evidence of defensive injuries or use of extreme force is offered as evidence and we are told elsewhere that 'the prosecution do not contend that what followed was not consensual sexual activity in his bedroom' (p.7). The lack of defensive injury partially evidences this; absence of struggle might be used to demonstrate consent, though it is not put to work in the service of this here, because consent is a priori always-already assumed in this case. Elsewhere we are told that the sounds coming from the bedroom and heard by the neighbours were 'consistent with sexual activity, no obvious sounds of distress' (p.7). Lack of distress and lack of injury are used to support claims that Gaskell and Huteson engaged in consensual sadomasochism:

QC: And the consensual element, which is apparent here, it's not reluctant consensual activity and it was straight consensual activity—
JUDGE: Yes.
QC: – presents other difficulties when one starts to consider the unlawful act aspect.
JUDGE: Yes. This was a knife used, in a sense, both ways; to present that degree of – of danger and, in a sense, you are dealing with circumstances, because consensual, within the privacy of somebody's own – own home. That does not make it lawful in the context of this case. That's not suggestion plainly. But it does present a difficulty which you would not ordinarily face but will have a significant impact so far as the final sentence passed.

(p.14)

The consensual aspect of the encounter is 'straight' and 'not reluctant' and will have a bearing on the sentence that Gaskell receives. The appeal to the privacy of a home as the rightful place in which such encounters are consensual bears attending to. The significance of the home as a place that is not rightfully the jurisdiction of the courts in which to intervene echoes the judgement in the Court of Appeal case of Wilson in 1996. That case concerned a married couple who enjoyed participating in consensual sadomasochism. On one occasion, as part of this play, Mrs Wilson asked her husband to brand his initials onto her buttocks. She presented to her doctor after the branding became infected and this was reported to the police. He was charged with assault occasioning actual bodily harm. His conviction was quashed at the Court of Appeal in part because it was held that 'consensual activity between husband and wife, in the privacy of the matrimonial home, was not a proper matter for criminal investigation, let alone prosecution' ([1996] 4 LRC 747 at 750). In part, this accounts for what appears to be the possibility for consent to emerge as a potential defence to sadomasochistic sex.

What Does This Consent Tell Us?

Scholars of sadomasochism have long campaigned for consent to function as a defence in encounters between sadomasochistic actors that are wanted by all parties, however that consent is negotiated, or emerges. As Haley (2014: 640) suggests, sexual expression and intimate relationships are a 'liberty right' meaning that people should have the right to lead intimate lives without interference from the state. It is certainly the case that in England and Wales much sadomasochism remains criminalisable, and that this sex negative, moralistic approach might have implications for social justice for people practising sadomasochism, which is, by virtue of the fact that it *is* sadomasochism, consensual. Anything other than consent (notwithstanding the complexity of consent (Weinberg et al., 1984)) is an offence against the person (Dunkley and Brotto, 2020). Maybe it is encouraging that courts appear to be shifting parameters to accommodate a certain acceptance that consent might be a possible defence. However, if we look at what consent looks like in each of the cases outlined here, we can see that the similarities between the ways that consent is construed are not unproblematic. In Cases 1 and 2 – that of Coates and Bailey – we are told that whatever happened to Banner and Keeling happened *at their request*. They were explicitly asking for it; for the belt to be tied around their neck, for it to be pulled, for the sex to be harder, to be choked. In each of these two cases, the men situate themselves as the unwilling and passive participants in a situation that the women are driving forward. The men are scared, or they find what they are being asked to do 'weird'. Just as the men are passive and the women active in the encounter so too are all the men dominant and the women submissive. This power dynamic certainly does exist in sadomasochistic relationships and encounters, but these are not usually accompanied by such explicit reticence on the parts of the dominant actors.

Moreover, alongside this active/submissive female and passive/dominant male dyad is the background context given about the women in each of these cases. All three – Banner, Keeling and Huteson – are painted by the court as troubled; drug addicted, estranged from their families, victims of intimate partner violence, sex workers. Living marginal lives and involved in subcultural or deviant practices does not act as a proxy of their consent but it is offered up as an explanation of how these women ended up in these circumstances. It is not a balanced, normatively successful woman who is engaged with these practices. It is a woman who is otherwise vulnerable. Casual sex, sex work, or drug use are never presented in these cases as practices that women would rightly choose for themselves, so the liaison that is made discursively here is that consent might be present here, because of the otherwise disadvantageous circumstances these women have found themselves in.

Additionally, pathological evidence is used in the case of Bailey and that of Gaskell to demonstrate that no defensive marks were found on the bodies of the women. Lack of struggle and no sounds of distress are used to allude to the consensual nature of the encounters.

It is interesting to note that in the case of Gaskell – the only case in which a guilty plea was entered – Huteson's consent is the least well excavated. We are simply told that she consented and that this was consensual sadomasochism that went wrong, and that is that. No evidence of, perhaps, her interest or engagement in sadomasochism as a subculture is offered, no evidence of her knowledge of the practice, or how they discussed what would happen, what might happen, and what the limits might be. Consent is taken as a given here without interrogating any element of what this consent might have looked like.

What we might also note is how far these evidences of consent – damaged women, who are rapacious in their desire for consensual violent sex with reluctant men, and who do not fight back – echo contemporary rape myths. The construct of sex-crazed woman who literally asks for it, and who has made bad choices with her life along the way, folds into contemporary neoliberal discourses about the ideal victim of rape; promiscuous, troubled, deviant. The lack of evidence of resistance or fighting back is also a well-rehearsed rape myth about what 'real' sexual violence looks like.

Conclusion

Though case law and statutes are clear that there is no defence of consent to a sadomasochistic encounter or rough sex, the rise in cases where such a defence is raised – no matter how transiently – demonstrates that at a discursive level, something like consent emerges in the socio-legal imaginary. Although consent defences do not always work in cases where men have killed women in sex (e.g. Bailey) in other instances, consent works either to add doubt to intention to kill (e.g. Coates) or to claim that what happened was an accident (e.g. Gaskell). This means that consent *does something* in these cases. And even where it does nothing, the potentiality that it might exist remains fertile.

This does not, however, signal a shift towards a more sex positive approach to engaging with these cases (Kaplan, 2014; Wodda and Panfil, 2020). Instead, where consent is evidenced, it is shrouded in rape myths that enshrine a rape culture that normalises gendered violence (Fanghanel, 2020). Evident in some of these cases (of which Gaskell is one) is also lack of curiosity about consent. Instead, we find courts merely stating that consent is present in a particular encounter.

Awareness about sadomasochism and consensual rough sex is increasingly penetrating the mainstream (Weiss, 2006; Tomazos et al., 2017). And yet, what is clear is that this awareness is only that of a rarefied version of sadomasochistic subculture which does not take account of the subculture in all of its complexity (Weiss, 2006; Wilkinson, 2009). This is not the move towards sadomasochistic acceptance that Pa (2001), Dunkley and Brotto (2020), and Haley (2014) posit might be possible. Rather, alongside a rarefied vision of sadomasochism, we also evince an under-developed conception of consent, how it emerges, and how encounters that might otherwise be figured as sadomasochistic, or as consensual rough sex, unfold.

Within criminological and socio-legal discourse more broadly, more nuanced understanding of consent, rough sex, BDSM and pleasure are needed, alongside continued awareness of rape culture which enables femicide that is dressed up as sadomasochism to emerge.

References

Dunkley, C. R., & Brotto, L. A. (2020). The role of consent in the context of BDSM. *Sexual Abuse*, *32*(6), 657–678.

Fanghanel, A. (2020). Asking for it: BDSM sexual practice and the trouble of consent. *Sexualities*, *23*(3), 269–286.

Haley, D. (2014). Bound by law: A roadmap for the practical legalization of BDSM. *Cardozo Journal of Law & Gender*, *21*, 631.

Kaplan, M. (2014). Sex-positive law. *New York University Law Review*, *89*, 89.

Newmahr, S. (2011). *Playing on the Edge: Sadomasochism, Risk, and Intimacy*. Indiana University Press.

Pa, M. (2001). Beyond the pleasure principle: The criminalization of consensual sadomasochistic sex. *Texas Journal of Women & Law*, *11*, 51.

Pitagora, D. (2013). Consent vs. coercion: BDSM interactions highlight a fine but immutable line. *The New School Psychology Bulletin*, *10*(1), 27–36.

Tomazos, K., O'Gorman, K., & MacLaren, A. C. (2017). From leisure to tourism: How BDSM demonstrates the transition of deviant pursuits to mainstream products. *Tourism Management*, *60*, 30–41.

Weinberg, M. S., Williams, C. J., & Moser, C. (1984). The social constituents of sadomasochism. *Social Problems*, *31*(4), 379–389.

Weiss, M. D. (2006). Mainstreaming kink: The politics of BDSM representation in US popular media. *Journal of Homosexuality*, *50*(2–3), 103–132.

Weiss, M. (2011). *Techniques of Pleasure: BDSM and the Circuits of Sexuality*. Duke University Press.

Wilkinson, E. (2009). Perverting visual pleasure: Representing sadomasochism. *Sexualities*, *12*(2), 181–198.

Williams, D. J., Thomas, J. N., Prior, E. E., & Christensen, M. C. (2014). From 'SSC' and 'RACK' to the '4Cs': Introducing a new framework for negotiating BDSM participation. *Electronic Journal of Human Sexuality*, *17*(5), 1–10.

Wodda, A., & Panfil, V. R. (2020). *Sex-positive Criminology*. Routledge.

18

TEACH US CONSENT

Digital Feminist Activism and the Limits of School-based Consent Pedagogies

Kellie Burns, Suzanne Egan, Hannah Hayes and Victoria Rawlings

In 2021 Chanel Contos, an Australian woman living and studying in London, posted an online poll that gauged her followers' experiences of sexual assault during or immediately after attending schools in Sydney. Following a substantial response, she then launched an e-petition, which precipitated a much larger movement called *Teach Us Consent*, calling for comprehensive consent education in schools. Contos' movement has received international media attention and has ignited dialogue within educational institutions, political chambers and the broader public discourse about how to reform school-based consent education.

This chapter critically analyses the mediation of the *Teach Us Consent* e-petition and subsequent campaign, examining discourses generated in and through the campaign itself and the media. We define mediation as inclusive of both the technological capacities and limitations of particular media and the ways in which consumers interact, moderate, negotiate and create in and through them (Brady et al., 2018; Mendes et al., 2019). The chapter begins by providing some background about *Teach Us Consent* and the public response to it. It then details research about sexual violence in the lives of young women and situates the movement within an expanding body of scholarly literature focused on the possibilities, limitations and ambiguities (Gill and Orgad, 2018) of digital feminist politics and grassroots organising via social media. Finally, the chapter contemplates what happens to consent when it is brought 'into the scene of pedagogy' (Gilbert, 2018), exploring some of the discursive and institutional shortfalls of trying to generate change in and through school curricula. Unlike social media, schools are bound by a broader 'culture of limitation' (Ferfolja and Ullman, 2020) that restricts the possibility of providing young people with relationships and sexualities education (including consent education) at school. The chapter proposes a rethinking of school-based consent

DOI: 10.4324/9781003358756-24

education that entails challenging adultcentric pedagogies and prioritising queer and intersectional analyses of gender and power.

Chanel Contos and the *Teach Us Consent* Campaign

The ramram poll that Chanel Contos posted in late February 2021 on her story (a time-limited, closed question that allowed a 'yes' or 'no' response), asked her followers: 'have you or has anyone close to you ever been sexually assaulted by someone who went to an all-boys school in Sydney?'. Within the 24-hour window, 204 people had responded 'yes'. A follow-up poll on Contos' Instagram story asked: 'If you went to an all-boys school in Sydney, do you think any of your friends has ever sexually assaulted someone?'. In this case, only 50 respondents replied 'yes'. Reading the responses to these two questions against each other, Contos later reflected that 'almost every girl knew someone who had experienced sexual assault or had themselves, but so few boys claimed to know anyone who'd ever been a victim or perpetrator' (Contos, 2021). We note that there has not been critical consideration of the gendered proportion of the story viewers (and poll respondents), and therefore no conclusions can be drawn about gendered comparative response rates or experiences. Nonetheless, this survey and the small pool of data it generated functioned as the discursive foundation for the *Teach us Consent* movement.

In the same week Contos built a website and launched an online petition, 'calling for more holistic sexual consent education, from an earlier age' (Contos, 2021). The petition provided a space for signatures and allowed individuals to share their experiences of sexual assault in the form of anonymised testimonials. Over the next several months, the website received over 45,000 signatures, and more than 6,500 testimonials, almost all from young women around Australia describing sexual assaults and harassment that they encountered while at school. Often, the testimonials named schools that the women had attended, or that their abusers had attended, but individuals were not identifiable by name (TeachUsConsent, 2021). While Contos had initiated a conversation about schools in Sydney, the influx of testimonials reflected that sexual assault on school-aged girls was a nation-wide phenomenon.

Contos described the precursor to her poll in mid-March in an article for *The Guardian*. She explained that at age 14 when she was in high school, she attended a party with friends. Partway through the evening they noticed that one girl from their group was no longer with them and went to find her. Here they encountered a terrible scene – they found their friend unconscious, topless, and with her pants pulled down, with a

> ...boy, pulling himself out. There was a commotion around the door, so someone rolled our topless friend off the bed, to save them the embarrassment of being exposed to everyone. Their limp body hit the floor as I

pushed the boy out of the room. He zipped up his pants, laughing, and telling us to calm down.

(Contos, 2021)

Contos (2021) explains that as she and her friends carried their incapacitated friend out of the party, they were referred to as 'cockblocks' and 'booed' out of the space by their peers – all privately schooled young men and women. This event was substantiated as the fundamental catalyst for her survey and subsequent campaigning in 2021. Reflecting on that night, Contos recalled that as they carried their friend home, she and her friends discussed 'the embarrassment of being told to leave', rather than the shock of their friend being sexually assaulted. Retrospectively, she claimed:

> we didn't know they had been sexually assaulted, because we didn't know what sexual assault was. Not a single person who witnessed it did. A group of people who were educated in supposedly one of the best school systems in the world.

(Contos, 2021)

Contos maintained that a lack of knowledge of sexual assault was a significant problem for her and her peers – that they could not recognise or articulate that what had taken place that night was sexual assault, and therefore, without the potential to name it as such, they had little potential for action.

While Contos' campaign and the debate that it precipitated commenced some years after this event, it occurred at a culturally significant moment in the Australian political landscape, when multiple women went public with claims of sexual abuse, garnering national and international media attention. In January 2021, just one month before Contos' Instagram poll, Grace Tame, a survivor of sexual abuse by a school teacher, was named Australian of the Year for her advocacy around the legal rights of sexual assault survivors to give public testimony. This is something that they were prevented from doing in the state of Tasmania, while their alleged abusers were not (Burnside, 2021), redressing the shame and silence disproportionately experienced by survivors. A month later, Brittany Higgins, an Australian Liberal Party staffer went public with allegations that in 2019 she had been raped by a male staffer in a Federal minister's office in Parliament House in Canberra. While the 'ACT Policing's Criminal Investigations – Sexual Assault and Child Abuse Team had first received a report about the matter in April 2019... the investigation remained open' (Grattan, 2021) until Higgins made a formal complaint in February 2021. Her allegations led to further revelations of staffers masturbating on the desks of female Members of Parliament, with photos taken and shared between some male staff. The government was implicated again that month, when it was revealed that another unidentified woman had died by suicide – her death linked to a historical allegation of sexual assault against the Attorney General,

Christian Porter (Karp, 2021). Despite strenuous denial of the claims, Porter stepped down from his position following intense public scrutiny (though he remained on the front bench in a different Ministerial portfolio and has so far avoided an independent review into the allegations) (Worthington, 2021). The public discourse generated around sexual assault and rape culture in early 2021 – a result of Tame's, Higgins' and Contos' collective public activism – has been referred to as 'Australia's MeToo moment' (Hill, 2021).

Sexual Assault in Australia

Mainstream media framed the response to Contos' petition and the stream of testimonials that followed as evidence of 'the depth of rape culture in Australia' (see for example Lai, 2021). Even in the context of the global COVID-19 pandemic, these events, to which Contos' e-petition and campaign contributed substantially, created sustained media discussion about rape culture in Australia and the failure of key institutions – including schools and the government – to adequately address it. Rape culture is defined as the pervasive social discourses and material structures that encourage male sexual aggression and condone violence against women.

Both the *Teach Us Consent* campaign and the media response to the campaign drew public and political attention yet again to the endemic rates of sexual violence in Australia and internationally, which have been evidenced time and again by large research studies. Perhaps though, something that set the Contos movement apart has been that it was initiated by young women and documented their experiences of sexual assault – especially in the schooling years, a time often depicted through tropes of naivety, innocence and purported safety. This departs from the periodic cycles in which, at least since the 1970s, activists have mobilised to bring the problem of sexual violence into public consciousness (Egan, 2020). The signatures and testimonies collected reinforce existing research about rates of sexual violence amongst young women. For example, the 2021 National Student Safety Survey (NSSS) funded by Universities Australia, which drew participants from across 38 Australian universities, found concerningly high numbers of university students overall (38.6%) had experienced sexual assault in their lifetime (Heywood et al., 2022). The study also highlighted the extent to which female students, transgender students, and non-binary students were disproportionately more likely than male students to have experienced sexual assault in their lifetime. Over 40% of female students and transgender students (41.8% and 42.9% respectively) and well over half (56.1%) of students identifying as non-binary or who identified as another gender had experienced sexual assault in their lifetime compared to just over 14% of male students (Heywood et al., 2022). Or put another way, the female and transgender students were almost three times more likely than male students to have experienced sexual assault in their lifetime, while non-binary students (and those who identified as another gender) were four times more likely than male students to have experienced sexual assault in their lifetime.

Similarly, some studies suggest that young women are disproportionately more likely to experience sexual assault compared to older women. For example, the last available Australia-wide prevalence study, the *Personal Safety Survey* (2016) found that over the preceding 12 months younger women were significantly more likely to have experienced sexual assault than older women. This was indicated by the 4.5 % of women aged 18 to 24 who had experienced sexual violence in the preceding 12 months compared to 0.6% of women aged 45 to 54 and 0.4% of women aged 55 and over (Australian Bureau of Statistics, 2021; Townsend et al., 2022).

Finally, it is important to note that while the *Teach Us Consent* campaign focused on young women's experiences of sexual assault during their school years, we have been unable to locate prevalence studies that include this age group. For example, participants in the studies we cited above are aged 18 years and over. The closest we have come to national data about adolescents is a national survey of secondary school students focusing on sexual health (Fisher et al., 2019). This survey included two questions about unwanted sexual experiences in the context of the much larger survey about sexual health. The first asked: 'Have you ever had sex when you did not want to?'. The follow up question gave participants a list of possible reasons and asked them to tick the relevant ones (i. e. partner wanted me to, fear, too drunk at the time, too high, friends wanted me to, other). The authors specifically state that the 'survey did not ask about forced or coerced sexual experiences nor did it attempt to assess lack of consent across unwanted sexual experiences' (Fisher et al., 2019). With that caveat in mind, it is nevertheless significant that over a quarter (28.4%) of the participants stated that they had had sex when they did not want to, with the most frequent reason given that their partner wanted them to. More males than females reported peer pressure, however there were consistencies between male and female students across remaining reasons (partner wanted me to, fear, too drunk at the time, too high, friends wanted me to). However it is important to highlight that similar to the sexual assault prevalence studies discussed above, significantly more female than male students reported having experienced unwanted sex – 36.8% of female students compared to 15.9% of male students.[1]

While the authors of this report are careful to distinguish coercive and forced sex from unwanted sex, feminist scholars have for some time queried such easy distinction (see for example, suggesting that once removed from the constraints of legal framing, women's experiences of unwanted versus coerced sex and rape are not so clear cut). Indeed Metz et al. (2021) have recently advanced this scholarship by suggesting that to better understand the practice of consent 'we need to research sex in the grey areas, analyzing the heterogendered power dynamics that undermine consent, normalize unjust sex, and mobilize rape' (p. 5). Against this backdrop, it is perhaps not surprising that Chanel Contos and her friends did not really understand – until some years later – that what had happened to their friend that night was sexual assault. Perhaps it also begins to 'make sense' – as Contos has also highlighted – that so few of the young men who completed her Instagram poll thought they had friends who would have sexually assaulted anyone.

Teach Us Consent and Digital Feminist Activism

The media response to Contos' survey and its evolution to the *Teach Us Consent* website was swift; within three weeks, 101 articles had been published on the testimonials in all major news outlets around Australia. This more than doubled in the two months that followed. Despite sexual violence and consent being a long-standing political issue for feminist activists and researchers, the sheer volume of signatures and horrifying testimonies shocked the nation and generated broad dialogue. As Contos herself comments: 'Consent education is not revolutionary … it really was the thousands of people who posted their testimony simultaneously that catapulted it into a priority for the government' (Brancatisano, 2022). Here she highlights that while the message and content of *Teach Us Consent* were certainly central to the national conversation that rapidly emerged, *the medium* from which the message was disseminated – Instagram – was also imperative to the campaign's effectiveness and to Contos becoming the face of consent activism in Australia and abroad (Contos has supported the start of an equivalent UK campaign, *Everyone's Invited*). Instagram is now commonly used by grassroots community activists because of its reach, with one billion monthly active users in June 2018 according to Statista (Djinis, 2021).

Digital social activism is now a commonly used term to describe the multiple ways in which activism is mediated across social media platforms such as Twitter, Facebook and Instagram/X. A growing body of feminist scholarship explores the complex and contradictory ways in which feminist politics have evolved in and through the use of digital and social media. Gill and Orgad (2018) describe the 'intensifying incorporation of social media into intimate lives', to capture the multitude of ways feminist culture and politics are shared, watched, listened to, tagged and commented on. Information, education, and 'calls to action' can be organised and shared at much faster rates and more widely than through traditional heritage or grassroots media. Young women in particular have taken to social media as a way of voicing feminist issues and challenging dominant, patriarchal structures, but also subverting institutional structures that position young women as unknowing, naive or non-citizens (Mendes et al., 2019).

Digital feminist activism has also enabled new ways of documenting and mediating issues of gender and power, including sexual assault. Successful online viral campaigns can provide new forms of critique around the naturalisation of everyday sexist culture to a broad audience. This was demonstrated as early as 2012 by the Everyday Sexism Project, a website collecting experiences of women from all corners of the globe. More recently the #MeToo movement sparked dialogue about gender, power and consent in the context of the workplace, and is often held up as a movement creating feminist solidarity across lines of class, race and sexuality (Gill and Orgad, 2018). Mendes et al. (2019) argue that sharing sexual assault experiences online with the use of hashtags can develop support and solidarity from people with a shared concern. They use the example of the hashtag #BeenRapedNeverReported which allows women to publicly state why they did not report their sexual assault, calling attention to rape culture, which is characterised by victim-blaming and the naturalising of violence.

Digital activism thus provides a point of connection and empowerment for victims, and given that sexual assault is an under-reported crime with profound impacts, this can be significant to the healing process. Disclosing sexual assault is often difficult because of the internalised shame commonly experienced by survivors coupled with the very real fear that they will be held to account for their behaviour, and their actions subject to scrutiny and condemnation rather than those of the perpetrator. While disclosure can aid in the recovery process, disclosing to an untrained or unsympathetic ear can have deleterious effects (Li et al., 2021). As such, the broad collective support of people with shared experiences challenges the individualising politics of sexual assault and violence prevention that tend to want to 'fix women' rather than the social structures that normalise violence and gendered power (Keller et al., 2018).

However, feminist digital activism, especially campaigns addressing the impacts of sexual assault, have been critiqued on several fronts. Some forms of violence (e.g. domestic violence) can be overlooked (Gill and Orgad, 2018), and likewise, issues of age and privilege are often unnoticed, prioritising the voices and experiences of younger women and/or women with the cultural capital to risk their image and career prospects by going public. There is also criticism that digital feminist movements are too often led by White ciswomen who embody what dominant culture deems 'respectable' forms of femininity and types of work, excluding, for example, the sexual violence experienced by sex workers. Li et al. (2021) raise the risk of survivors being re-victimised when social media campaigns attract misogynistic trolls who incite violence and victim-blaming. Contos herself received rape threats and misogynistic comments like 'you're too ugly to rape' (FitzSimons, 2022), which she points to as evidence of the normalisation of violence against women in online settings.

While there is some scholarship highlighting the solidarity created amongst women globally, issues of intersectionality are largely sidelined (Gill and Orgad, 2018). For example, #MeToo was first used in 2006 by sexual assault activist Tarana Burke on Myspace. Burke's initial purpose of was to provide a space of empathy, support and belief to empower young people who have been sexually assaulted, especially young women of colour. Likewise, understandings of sexual assault in campaigns like this one tend to centre around binarised gender framings at the exclusion of queer and non-binary sexual citizens. Gill and Orgad (2018) add that 'a significant part of the debate remains framed in terms of "bad apples" and "monsters" who did horrible things, not about the monstrous capitalist, patriarchal and sexist system that has produced, sustained and rewarded these "bad apples" over decades' (p. 1318). Likewise, #MeToo has become an umbrella term used to encompass all forms of activism against sexual violence, undermining the specificity of some of these movements, and minimising the progress achieved by this earlier activism (Hush, 2020). Finally, as Saraswati (2021) argues, the underlying structure of feminist social media campaigns is governed by neoliberal values (e.g. self-improvement, self-entre-preneurship, personal responsibility, sharing economy) which prioritise, what she calls, the 'neoliberal self(ie) gaze'–the production of the self on social media as a 'good neoliberal subject' who is appealing and inspiring.

With the opportunities, limitations and ambiguities of feminist digital acti-vism in mind, the aim of this chapter is not to determine whether Contos or the campaign she spearheaded have been effective or not. Instead, we trace the dis-courses mobilised in and through the movement and the media responses they have instigated. A unique focus of *Teach Us Consent* is that it has shifted public discussion of sexual assault and rape culture to *schools*, demanding reform to consent education, and into the lives of girls and young women. The final section which follows, considers the shortfalls of positioning schools as sites for social change. Schools are non-static, complex social institutions con-structed and constrained by the socio-political conditions that surround them at any given time (Welch et al., 2022). While *Teach Us Consent* has forced man-dated consent education and has been the impetus for some curriculum reform, translating these into effective pedagogy is by no means an easy or straightfor-ward process.

Activism to Pedagogical Failure?

In an interview with the *Australian Financial Times*, Contos said that when the e-petition and campaign were launched, she had three particular elite private schools in Sydney's affluent eastern suburbs in mind – the girls school she attended and two elite all-boys schools:

> When I started the petition, my intention was just to get [these schools] to teach consent. I never really thought it would go this far. If you had told me a year ago that I would have had a commitment from the government to mandate consent education in the federal curriculum I would have said, 'What the f—?'
>
> *(Murray, 2022)*

Through the evolution of the *Teach Us Consent* movement, Contos has argued that schools are the ideal location for consent education to occur. *The Teach Us Consent* website states that the testimonies are from: 'those who passionately believe that inadequate consent education *is reason for* their sexual abuse during or soon after school' (TeachUsConsent, 2021, emphasis added). The problem as identified by Contos is the failure of schools to deliver early or appropriate consent education to children and young people. She explains that on the brink of posting her initial poll on Instagram she lay awake with 'an overwhelming feeling of, "Well, maybe if that boy knew what consent was in sexual relationships...maybe he never would have done it in the first place"' (FitzSimons, 2022).

As part of the suite of federal government responses, it was announced on 17th February, 2022 that consent education will be mandatory for all Australian students from 2023 (Woodley et al., 2022). The government also committed a AUS $189 million package over five years directed by prevention and early intervention in family, domestic and sexual violence. $32 million of these funds were ear-marked for a consent campaign focusing on young people aged 12 and older and their parents (Brancatisano, 2022).

Ensuring consent education is implemented consistently and through appropriate pedagogies is a serious challenge for schools. If not taught well, the messages delivered could in fact reinforce rape culture and victim blaming, rather than help address it (Beres, 2020). Jen Gilbert (2018) argues that school-based sex education has now entered the 'age of consent' – with consent at the centre of debates in sex education across the Global North. The continual call for schools to 'repair the social harms that our other institutions have failed to redress', suggests that the simple inclusion of additional content will 'correct assaultive, coercive and exploitative sex with enthusiastic, voluntary and pleasurable relations' (Gilbert, 2018). In no way dismissing the importance of comprehensive consent education, Gilbert highlights the complexity of translating consent activism into the space of curricula, which often brings with it much 'conceptual baggage' (p. 269).

Hayes et al. (2022) address this conceptual baggage in their study of consent knowledge and attitudes at an all-boys school in NSW, Australia. They illustrate that even when schools are thoughtful in ensuring consent is taught across the secondary years, the pedagogies mobilised often reinforce hegemonic masculinity, failing to address the links between gender, power and sexual assault. Instead, schools may rely on discussing sexual assault and consent through legal framings that reinforce the criminality of sexual assault and in doing so, frame relationships as solely about responsibility and risk. Risk-aversion and harm minimisation approaches to consent education are grounded in crime prevention and public health approaches and therefore typically engage with risk avoidance discourses and fail to trouble gendered power (Carmody, 2014). Consent is positioned as a risky or dangerous element of sex, rather than as pleasurable or intimate.

In schools, consent education continues to be framed as difficult, sensitive and/or controversial classroom content. Ferfolja and Ullman (2020) use the term 'culture of limitation' to refer to the 'messy plethora of perspectives, beliefs and attitudes which come together at various points and contexts where they thwart the country's development towards becoming a progressive and equitable society' (p. 3). In Australia, dialogue around gender and sexuality in schools has long been constrained by a culture of limitation. Those opposed to or fearful of diversity (fuelled by undercurrents of colonialism, neoliberalism and neo-conservatism) engage in practices that marginalise gender and sexually diverse students and teachers (Ferfolja and Ullman, 2020). This has had implications for relationships and sexuality education (RSE) curricula. Throughout the twentieth century, morality approaches, underpinned by discourses of biological essentialism and abstinence-only-until marriage (AOUM), dominated RSE, privileging human reproduction within the context of heterosexual marriage (Jones, 2011). In response to the AIDS epidemic in the late 20th century, Australian states were provided with funding from health departments to address sexuality and HIV/AIDS prevention through the education system (Jones and Mitchell, 2014). This work provided an opportunity to shift away from more conservative, moralising approaches and towards a harm reduction approach (Jones, 2011). Despite the efforts of curricula designers, educators and researchers to challenge normative gender roles in sexualities education within the limits of this new approach, objections by politically and religiously conservative groups have continued to shape its delivery. Moral panics have widely impacted RSE delivery, most recently, in 2020 when conservative politician Hon. Mark Latham proposed the Education Legislation Amendment (Parental Rights) Bill, 2020, with the aim of upholding parental control of how gender and sexuality are discussed in schools (2020). The aims of this Bill echo Goldman's (2008) findings regarding parental resistance to sexuality education, which included discourses of parental rights and concerns about RSE encouraging sexual promiscuity and moral decline in society (Goldman, 2008). Objections to these troubling political discourses have been raised by teachers, parents, students and researchers as they operate as powerful impediments to comprehensive RSE. This has relevance for efforts to improve the delivery of consent education that includes critical engagement with issues of gender, power, sex and consent.

Conclusion

Teach Us Consent is an example of digital social media activism directed at curricular reform in Australian schools. The tremendous momentum created by this activism has catapulted the issue of school-based consent education into national conversation. This is undoubtedly an enormous accomplishment. However, some caution should be exercised around the cycle of curricular reform that places the onus on already stretched schooling systems to 'solve' complex social issues – in this case the alarmingly high rates of sexual assault and a pervasive rape culture. There is a risk that in the space of pedagogy, the campaign's political momentum will result in a consent education landscape not significantly different to the current one, with some teachers and schools covering this content comprehensively, and others covering it through a single lesson, or by using external programs that may reinforce that which the movement seeks to challenge. Despite revised curricula and/or policy, consent education, at least in some schools, may well still be framed by individualising discourses that fail to unpack sexual assault as a social problem produced and sustained by systems and structures that uphold gender inequalities.

While Contos routinely acknowledges the work of feminists who came before her, what she describes as the aims and focus of the newly mandated curricula is reflective of existing Australian curriculum resources developed over the past 30 years. Amanda Keddie (2021) provides an important critique of campaigns and mandates for curricula change like those incentivised by Contos:

> ...given my knowledge of the excellent curriculum and pedagogic resources and research conducted by fellow colleagues who have been attempting to address issues of gender injustice in schools for decades; from supporting teachers to problematise dominant gender norms (Martino & Pallotta Chiarolli, 2005) to providing them with comprehensive sexuality education curriculum (Ollis, 2014). Despite this excellent work, it seems to remain that whenever sexual misconduct is reported in the media, schools and, in particular, sex and sexuality education are called on to repair these social harms. Such calls seem to minimise the complexity of teaching about issues such as sexual consent as if a few lessons in affirmative consent would suffice in remedying coercive and exploitative sexual relations(Gilbert, 2018, p. 2).
>
> *(Keddie (2021, p. 504)*

Keddie calls attention to the cultural and pedagogical limitations governing the implementation of new topics like consent into school curricula, but also the tendency to make changes to curricula without addressing the broader gendered practices of schooling. This suggests that sexual assault happens simply because young people have not been taught about consent in the classroom. While *Teach Us Consent* is calling for more than this, for 'nuanced conversations' about power, toxic masculinity, rape culture, and they are arguing for the inclusion of LGBTIQ+ perspectives, this critical focus requires evidence-informed resources, professional development, and a broad socio-political climate that welcome complex discussions of gender and sexuality in schools, rather than sanctioning them.

School-based consent education could be more radically re-imagined by challenging the adult-centic priorities that have long underpinned the broad project of education, including how sex and sexuality are discussed at school and in the classroom. Teachers and parents tend to regulate when and how knowledge about gender, sexuality and sexual health is taught, infantilising and trivialising young people's sexual knowledge and undermining their agency as sexual citizens (Davies and Burns, 2022).

Additionally, consent education should resist risk frameworks that uphold individualising approaches that overlook the social norms and structures that underpin sexual assault and consent negotiations, and also fail to engage with sex as a pleasurable experience (for some people, but not all) (Hayes et al., 2022). Risk frameworks often prioritise cisgender relationships and overlook issues of intersectionality. Following Metz et al. (2021) we maintain that teaching young people about the 'grey areas' of sex and consent is critical to genuinely translating Contos' efforts into meaningful social change. Alongside this, and in challenging individualising pedagogies of consent, campaigns like *Teach Us Consent* are themselves useful pedagogical tools with which to critique gendered power and prioritise feminist perspectives. The political impact of this campaign also provides an opportunity to unpack some of the powerful and creative ways young people are producing and using digital and social media to re-imagine sexual citizenship and challenge discourses of danger, risk and youth apathy that dominate popular discussions of young people and digital technologies.

Note

1 While transgender and gender diverse students were part of the survey, the very small numbers (10) meant that statistical significance could not be reported. Further, while students where asked a demographic question about their sexual orientation, there was no breakdown of findings (including the questions about unwanted sexual experiences) based on sexual identity.

References

Australian Bureau of Statistics2021. *Sexual Violence – Victimisation*. ABS.

Beres, M. 2020. Perspectives of Rape-prevention Educators on the Role of Consent in Sexual Violence Prevention. *Sex Education*, 20(2), 227–238.

Brady, A., Burns, K. & Davies, C. 2018. *Mediating Sexual Citizenship: Neoliberal Subjectivities in Television Culture*. London: Routledge.

Brancatisano, E. 2022. Consent Education Has Reached an 'Important Milestone' in Australia. Here's What Experts Want to See Next. *SBS News*. Online.

Burnside, N. 2021. Sexual Assault Survivor and Advocate Grace Tame Named 2021 Australian of The Year. *ABC News*. Online.

Carmody, M. 2014. Sexual Violence Prevention Educator Training: Opportunities and Challenges. In: Henry, N. & Powell, A. (Eds.) *Preventing Sexual Violence: Interdisciplinary Approaches to Overcome Rape Culture*. Basingstoke: Palgrave Macmillan.

Contos, C. 2021. 'Do They Even Know They Did This To Us? Why I Launched the School Sexual Assault Petition. *The Guardian*. Online.

Davies, C. & Burns, K. 2022. HPV Vaccination Literacy in Sexualities Education. *Sex Education*, ahead-of-print, 1–9.

Djinis, E. 2021. Instagram's Become an Essential Tool for Activists. But it's a Double-Edged Sword. *Mashable*. Online.

Education Legislation Amendment (Parental Rights) Bill2020.

Egan, S. 2020. *Putting Feminism To Work: Theorising Sexual Violence, Trauma and Subjectivity*. Cham, Switzerland: Palgrave Macmillan.

Ferfolja, T. & Ullman, J. 2020. *Australia and a Culture of Limitation for Gender and Sexuality Diversity*. London: Routledge.

Fisher, C. M., Waling, A., Kerr, L., Bellamy, R., Ezer, P., Mikolajczak, G., Brown, G., Carman, M. & Lucke, J. 2019. *6th National Survey of Secondary Students and Sexual Health 2018*. Bundoora: Australian Research Centre in Sex, Health & Society, La Trobe University.

FitzSimons, P. 2022, August 21. What Chanel Contos uncovered about School-aged Sex Abuse, We All Need to Know. *The Sydney Morning Herald*. https://www.smh.com.au/national/what-chanel-contos-uncovered-about-school-age-sex-abuse-we-all-need-to-know-20220819-p5bb6x.html

Gilbert, J. 2018. Contesting Consent in Sex Education. *Sex Education*, 18, 268–279. https://doi.org/10.1080/14681811.2017.1393407.

Gill, R. & Orgad, S. 2018. The Shifting Terrain of Sex and Power: From the 'Sexualization of Culture' to #Metoo. *Sexualities*, 21, 1313–1324.

Goldman, J. D. G. 2008. Responding to Parental Objections to School Sexuality Education: A Selection of 12 Objections. *Sex Education*, 8, 415–438.

Grattan, M. 2021. Man to Face Court over Alleged Rape of Brittany Higgins. *The Conversation*. Online.

Hayes, H. M. R., Burns, K. & Egan, S. 2022. Becoming 'Good Men': Teaching Consent and Masculinity in A Single-Sex Boys' School. *Sex Education*, ahead-of-print, 1–14.

Heywood, W., Myers, P., Powell, A., Meikle, G. & Nguyen, D. 2022. *National Student Safety Survey: Report On The Prevalence of Sexual Harassment and Sexual Assault Among University Students in 2021*. Melbourne: The Social Research Centre.

Hill, J. 2021. Rights, Wrongs and Revolution: #Metoo Still Raging Against the Patriarchy. *Sydney Morning Herald*. Online.

Hush, A. 2020. What's in a Hashtag? Mapping the Disjunct Between Australian Campus Sexual Assault Activism and #Metoo. *Australian Feminist Studies*, 35, 293–309.

Jones, T. 2011. A Sexuality Education Discourses Framework: Conservative, Liberal, Critical, and Postmodern. *American Journal of Sexuality Education*, 6, 133–175.

Jones, T. & Mitchell, A. 2014. Young People and HIV Prevention in Australian Schools. *Aids Education and Prevention*, 26, 224–233.

Karp, P. 2021. NSW Police Never Started Investigating Christian Porter Rape Allegation, Internal Review Reveals. *The Guardian*. Online.

Keddie, A. 2021. Student Activism, Sexual Consent and Gender Justice: Enduring Difficulties and Tensions for Schools. *The Australian Educational Researcher*, 503–518.

Keller, J., Mendes, K. & Ringrose, J. 2018. Speaking 'Unspeakable Things': Documenting Digital Feminist Responses to Rape Culture. *Journal of Gender Studies*, 27, 22–36.

Lai, G. 2021. Chanel Contos' Consent Education Petition Lays Bare the Depth of Rape Culture in Australia. *Vogue*. Online.

Li, M., Turki, N., Izaguirre, C. R., Demahy, C., Thibodeaux, B. L. & Gage, T. 2021. Twitter as a Tool for Social Movement: An Analysis of Feminist Activism on Social Media Communities. *Journal of Community Psychology*, 49, 854–868.

Martino, W. & Pallotta-Chiarolli, M. 2005. *Being Normal Is the Only Way To Be*. Sydney: UNSW Press.

Mendes, K., Ringrose, J. & Keller, J. 2019. *Digital Feminist Activism: Girls and Women Fight Back Against Rape Culture*. New York, NY:Oxford University Press.

Metz, J., Myers, K. & S. Wallace, P. 2021. (Re)Mapping the Grey Area: How Sexual Violence is Normalized in Discussions with University Students. *Gender and Women's Studies*, 4.

Murray, L. 2022. Chanel Contos Intended to Get Only Three Schools to Teach Consent. *Australian Financial Review*. Online.

Ollis, D. 2014. *Building Respectful Relationships: Stepping out Against Gender-based Violence*. Melbourne: Victoria, Victorian Department of Education and Training.

Saraswati, L. A. 2021. *Pain Generation: Social Media, Feminst Activism and the Neolibral Selfie*. New York: New York University Press.

TeachUsConsent. 2021. *Testimonies* [Online]. Available: https://www.teachusconsent.com/testimonies/

Townsend, N., Loxton, D., Egan, N., Barnes, I., Byrnes, E. & Forder, P. 2022. *A Life Course Approach To Determining the Prevalence and Impact of Sexual Violence in Australia: Findings From the Australian Longitudinal Study On Women's Health*. ANROWS.

Welch, A., Bagnall, N., Burns, K., Cuervo, H., Foley, D., Groundwater-Smith, Harwood, V., Low, R., Mockler, N., Proctor, H., Rawlings, V., Stacey, M., Wilson, B. & Wood, J. 2022. *Education, Change and Society* (5th edn). Melbourne: Oxford University Press.

Woodley, G. N., Jacques, C., Jaunzems, K. & Green, L. 2022. Mandatory Consent Education is a Huge Win for Australia – But Consent is Just One Small Part of Navigating Relationship. *The Conversation*.

Worthington, B. 2021. Christian Porter Goes to the Backbench with his PM Aspirations in Tatters. *ABC News*. Online.

19

SEX WORK POLITICS AND CONSENT

The Consequences of Sexual Morality

Helen Rand and Jessica Simpson

This chapter studies the centrality of consent in feminist theory on sex work. We consider how these debates have migrated into inter/national policies seeking to eradicate sex markets resulting in the censoring of sex worker voices. Activists and allies have stressed the importance of understanding the nuances of consent and coercion within sex markets, yet consent is often framed as the line between sex that is accepted e.g., morally good, and sex that is unwanted e.g., illegal (Fanghanel et al., 2020). Through this moralising lens, sex workers are constructed as 'victims' and the concept of consent is disregarded in legal frameworks that seek to 'rescue' – primarily cis-women – from presumed coercive sexual labour. Under the guise of protecting women, this inherently colonial and Western approach not only allows countries to deny sex workers labour rights and migration protections but also perpetuates the violence that such laws ostensibly seek to eradicate and can even result in fatal outcomes.

The chapter starts by tracing the theoretical development of consent in sex work. Drawing on case studies from Asia, the Americas, Africa, and Europe, we then consider how consent is weaponised to propagate further anti-sex work ideology, policies, and laws globally that lead to the forcible detention and imprisonment of sex workers. We argue that when using consent to 'protect' women from sexual violence, we must centre and create space for marginalised voices to speak openly and freely about their experiences. However, as we discuss, the current paradox of the anti-trafficking juggernaut is that it has reduced women's opportunities to speak out, producing violent consequences. Focusing on sex workers' voices, perspectives and experiences, this chapter contributes to debates on how consent can be applied in more nuanced ways within legal frameworks reflecting the complexity and diversity of sex workers' contexts, motivations, and experiences.

DOI: 10.4324/9781003358756-25

Theorising Consent within Feminist Debates

From the mid-1970s onwards, Western feminism became deeply divided over the issue of sex work. Due to the heated and at times, violent response from either side, this period is commonly referred to as 'the sex wars'. Tensions and divisions remain today, and while we do not wish to reproduce often unhelpful polarised debates (which have been critically assessed elsewhere see Phipps, 2017; Walters, 2016), this chapter would be incomplete if we did not start with a historical reflection on how consent and coercion became integral to legal frameworks on sex work and trafficking for sexual exploitation, continuing to define many legal approaches around the world.

Labelled 'anti-sex work' radical feminists, scholars and activists such as Catherine MacKinnon (1989) and Andrea Dworkin (1981) categorised all sex work as violence against women, arguing that if sexual consent must be bought, it is not consent and is instead, paid rape. Within such arguments, women are deemed unable to give consent knowingly/willingly. Others such as Kathleen Barry, initially appear to acknowledge that women *can* consent to paid sex, however their consent is quickly disregarded as she argues 'when the human being is reduced to a body, objectified to sexually service another, *whether or not there is consent*, violation of the human being has taken place' (1995:23, emphasis added). Through this lens, the sex worker body becomes entirely passive, docile, and thus, powerless which, as we will discuss, is reflected in legal frameworks. Those who approach commercial sex as gendered violence and male oppression have been criticised for reproducing simplistic under-standings of consent, agency, and power. For example, Pilcher (2009) argues that while men do exercise power within the commercial sex industry, power is not a zero-sum game solely in the hands of men and denied from sex workers. Indeed, throughout this chapter, we provide examples of how sex workers resist male dominance at key moments.

In response to this dominance theory, a counter 'sex positive' movement emerged with scholars such as Gail Pheterson (1993) who challenged the pre-sumption that by virtue of their role, sex workers have no discretion over their work and that men have unconditional access to sex workers' bodies who have no choice but to have sex with 'everyone and anyone'. Instead, Pheterson lists the strategic use of consent by sex workers to maintain boundaries and control over their working conditions, for example, by refusing clients for being too drunk. Importantly, an individual's ability to refuse clients is not static nor equal among sex workers, nevertheless this argument does highlight the com-plexity of consent within sexual labour.

Sex workers' rights organisations actively challenged dominant narratives of sex work as 'violence against women', seeking to reframe sex work as 'work', and a job like any other (Jenness, 1993). The core tenets of the movement were that many women freely choose sex work; that sex work can be empowering (by charging men for what other women are expected to do for free); and that sex work should be respected as a legitimate form of labour. Some groups went as far as to claim there is no difference between work where a woman uses body parts such as her hands when typing and where she uses other body parts, such as her vagina, in sex work (Jenness, 1993; Pheterson, 1989). While the 'sex work is work' mantra remains politically important and prominent today, Weeks (2011) argues that the fight for recognition of sex work as work like any other leaves the inherent exploitation and coercion within *all* waged work unquestioned. The 'problem' with sex work then is work itself and the institution of paid labour under capitalism – shaped by other systems of oppression – meaning that consenting to sex work, or any other form of labour, becomes highly gendered, racialised and classed and produces global inequalities.

Both 'camps' within the so-called 'sex wars' have been criticised for creating a reductive anti/pro sex work binary relying on overly negative or positive accounts of sex work as either inherently violent *or* empowering. Scholars have since sought a reconciliation and to bridge the gap between the two extremes. For example, Ronald Weitzer (2013) argues that because sex workers are not a homogenous group, a 'polymorphous paradigm' is required to recognise *variation* within sex work. Through extensive research with sex workers, Julia O'Connell Davidson (2002) argues that either/or debates disallow the opportunity to support the rights of sex workers while at the same time being critical of the socio-economic inequalities that create market relations in general, and sex markets specifically. Similarly, Kate Hardy (2013) also champions a radical politics of sex work that allows for a 'multi-scalar analysis' to understand consent and coercion that considers not only the micro sex worker/client encounter but also the meso-labour relations and the macro social relations shaping the multiple forms of power/oppression at play.

Katie Cruz's (2018) work exemplifies the importance of accounting for such broader social forces *and* individual experiences. By mapping the work of migrant brothel and strip club workers in London, UK Cruz demonstrates how binary understandings of consent/coercion do not accurately reflect the realities of many sex workers. To counter radical feminist conceptualisations of all commercial sex as sexual slavery, sex worker activists clearly differentiate between 'voluntary' sex work and 'involuntary' trafficking for sexual exploitation arguing that the two should not be conflated. However, Cruz's research shows that by creating a consent/coercion binary and focusing only on the most extreme unfreedoms (e.g., physical violence and confinement), this over-estimates the 'freedom' enjoyed by sex workers, particularly migrant workers (e.g., freedom of movement, to change employers, to contest conditions). Broader macro forces that constrain the economic, legal, and political status of migrant sex workers allow 'employers' (e.g., owners/clients) to position workers as cheap and dependent labour which leaves them vulnerable to a host of 'unfree' labour practices as they are routinely disciplined and expelled without access to recourse. Thus, moving beyond the binary, Cruz aptly places sex workers – and all workers – on a continuum of un/free labour within capitalist relations of reproduction which are gendered, racialised and legal, and in doing so, demonstrates how 'consent' and 'coercion' are not mutually exclusive.

Focusing on sex work in the Caribbean, Kamala Kempadoo's (2001) research problematises dominant, Western conceptualisations of consent that do not account for the experiences of marginalised women of colour. Through a colonial lens, white Western women are positioned as autonomous agents while assigning all poor women of colour the role of oppressed victim, stripping them of subjectivity, agency, and voice. Kempadoo argues that power relations within sex markets are not simply (re)produced along the axis of gender but also ethnicity, race, nation, and class meaning that attention must be paid to the historical and contextual specificities that shape women's choices and opportunities for resistance. By ignoring differences between women and creating grand, universalised understandings of women's experience of consent, sex work and oppression, Kempadoo exposes the clear disregard of Third World, transnational and postcolonial feminist perspectives resulting in a limited definition of consent. Indeed, Mohanty's (2003) concept of 'oppositional agency' expands existing understandings of agency that fail to account for women's resistance to subjugation as also agentic. In a blog written by sex workers, Graceyswer (2020) explains their oppositional agency.

> it is important to make the distinction between 'I had no choice' and 'I had limited choices'…Consent, however, is about what happens and what I agree to. My limited choices may have led me to this decision, but it doesn't give anyone the right to mistreat me whilst I am here.

An empirical example of oppositional agency is found in Heidi Hoefinger's (2013) ethnographic work with Cambodian women working in the tourist bar scene. Hoefinger explores the complex decisions made by women sex workers in a post-conflict, postcolonial country with conservative gendered roles and expectations. In this context, the simple understanding of 'sex-for-cash prostitution' does not fully explain the experiences of many women who engage in long-term relationships with Western men as 'professional girlfriends', using their income to navigate a more financially secure future. It is not possible, nor should we, extract women's sexualities from the global political economy, however the reproduction of 'femininity' as (politically, physically, or emotionally) weak victims frames conversations in moral rather than legal or labour terms.

A wealth of research contests the imposed binary between coercion/consent, highlighting the complexity of human experience, the wide range of contexts and relations under which sex work is carried out, as well the role of broader social forces. Nevertheless, the 'sex wars' paradigm has continued to shape inter/national legislation regarding sex work and trafficking for sexual exploitation for the last twenty years. Importantly, both 'sides' of the debate have not had equal impact as 'pro-sex' feminism has had 'a negligible effect on policymaking' with 'anti-sex work' feminism (and conservative and Christian lobbies) creating the foundations of policy making on a global scale (Walters, 2016:7). The following section of this chapter outlines specific cases demonstrating how this binary continues to shape both legislation and thus, the lived realities of sex workers.

Consent within Inter/National Legal Frameworks

In 2000, in Palermo, Italy, the Coalition Against Trafficked Women (CATW) alongside other feminist and religious organisations lobbied the United Nations for the inclusion of Article 9 (5) in the Protocol on trafficking.[1] This sex work exceptionalism led to the inclusion that all states should '*discourage the demand* that fosters all forms of exploitation of persons, especially women and children, that leads to trafficking'. These groups argued that no woman could ever truly consent to selling sex thereby reducing all commercial sex to 'sex trafficking'.[2] In response, the Global Alliance Against Traffic in Women (GAATW) and other NGOs lobbied for the insertion of coercion, deceit, or force as a vital 'damage control' strategy (Wijers, 2021) to prevent the Protocol from conflating all prostitution with trafficking for sexual exploitation. Nevertheless, the UN Palermo Protocols laid the legal foundations that linked the cause of trafficking for sexual exploitation to the existence of sex markets; rather than the result of global capitalism, market relations, migration policies and neoliberal interests (Wijers, 2021; Bernstein, 2018; Kempadoo, 2001; O'Connell Davidson, 2002). This resulted in the expansion of anti-sex work policies globally which sought to 'discourage the demand' for trafficking for sexual exploitation by eradicating sex markets.

As we will discuss, this policy instrument has become significant in disseminating the existing trafficking discourse leading to violent and even fatal outcomes for sex workers globally (Bernstein, 2018:14). Since 2000, 178 countries have ratified the Protocol, meaning that most states have specific and detailed anti-trafficking policies (Gallagher and Pearson 2010) that are often interpreted as anti-sex work policies. National policies seeking to reduce sex markets are routinely interpreted as 'evidence' that such polices also reduce trafficking for sexual exploitation (Sandy, 2018; Gallagher, 2011; Agustín 2007).

The global/colonial dissemination of 'discouraging demand' for trafficking for sexual exploitation through eradicating sex markets started with the Bush administration (2001–2009). From 2003, recipients of United States funds were forced to sign a pledge that no US aid money could be used to 'promote, support, or advocate the legalization or practice of prostitution' (Trafficking Victims Protection Reauthorization Act, 2003). This meant recipients of US funding were prohibited from *any* activities seen to be supporting sex workers, including small but vital measures such as distributing condoms. This policy remained until 2013 for US organisations and is still in effect for foreign grant recipients. In the quest to 'save' women from the harms of trafficking for sexual exploitation, sex workers' consent and choice become inconsequential.

Following Palermo, the US government created the Annual Trafficking in Persons report which rates countries based on their efforts to tackle trafficking. The data used is collected by the US government whose methods have been questioned due to the lack of accounting for cultural differences, often leading to unfair financial penalisation of countries in the Global South who are seen as 'failing' (Agustín 2007; Sandy, 2018; Gallagher, 2011). One way that a country can demonstrate they are tackling trafficking is through the development of policies that aim to eradicate sex markets. Such stipulations created a zealous attempt by many poorly ranked and aid dependent countries to develop more punitive methods to ensure continued US funding (Echols, 2016; Sandy, 2018). By conflating anti-sex work policies with anti-trafficking policies, sex workers are reconstructed as victims unable to consent; creating what Laura Agustín (2007) has termed the 'rescue industry', a 'trafficking industrial complex' combining local, national, and international governments, feminist and faith-based activists, non-profit and for-profit organisations (Bernstein 2018:5).

India is often cited as a 'critical offender' in international rankings on trafficking putting pressure on the Indian state to respond 'appropriately' in order to receive financial aid. There is a long history of advancing legal measures to tackle labour exploitation and trafficking in India that predates the Protocol dating back to colonialism (see Kotiswaran, 2016 for a summary). Yet, as with the Palermo Protocols, legal efforts have become fused with 'sex work exceptionalism' (Kotiswaran, 2016) meaning that transactional sex has become the focal point of state intervention whilst ignoring labour exploitation and trafficking in other industries e.g., agriculture and construction. Through the Immoral Traffic (Prevention) Act (ITPA), the police have the power to remove 'persons' from prostitution and place them into 'rehabilitation homes'. Crucially, there is no requirement for the police to provide evidence that the person has been trafficked, nor do they require consent from sex workers to be removed from what many consider to be their place of work.

The detention of sex workers under the guise of rescuing victims of trafficking is not limited to India. In Malaysia it is the law to detain 'trafficking victims' (Gallagher & Pearson, 2010) and in Cambodia, the 2008 Law on Suppression of Human Trafficking and Sexual Exploitation made it legal to force women into rehabilitation centres. Thus, further criminalising sex workers who report anti-trafficking laws have made their daily lives worse (see Women's Network for Unity, a sex worker led organisation). As sex worker activist Seng Simouy states 'people in sex work have the right to be involved in formulating policies affecting their lives' (Simouy and Phal Niseiy, 2022). Instead, countries, particularly in Asia, become breeding grounds for Christian NGOs, feminist abolitionists, and capitalist philanthropists to advance their own moral crusade without consulting sex workers on how to tackle trafficking within sex markets. Many academics and activists have drawn attention to the violent consequences of the 'rescue industry' in Asia (Shih, 2017; Walters and Ramachandran, 2018; Dasgupta, 2019; Ramachandran, 2015, 2017).

In Europe, there has been a wave of 'end demand' policies that criminalise those who purchase sex. The first act to criminalise those who buy sex was the Prohibition of Purchase of Sexual Services Act [27] of 1999 in Sweden. Although the Act does not further criminalise those selling sexual services, consenting to selling sex is irrelevant in the broader pursuit of eradicating sex markets for 'the greater good of *all* women' and in achieving gender equality. Such policies are often labelled 'progressive' despite evidence that they reproduce rather than prevent violence against sex workers (Scoular & FitzGerald, 2021; Vuolajärvi, 2019; Levy, 2014). Even with this evidence, and despite countries having their own specific history and cultural context, the interaction of the Swedish Purchase of Sexual Services Act and the UN protocol has led many others to adopt similar polices (Jahnsen & Skilbrei, 2015). For example, sex purchase bans have since been adopted in Norway and Iceland (2009), Canada (2014), Northern Ireland (2015), France (2016), the Republic of Ireland (2017), Israel (2018). The Spanish government are currently debating proposals to criminalise buyers of sex as a means of eradicating sex markets.

Efforts to 'end demand' by eradicating sex markets are based on an overly simplistic logic that without sex markets, there will be no market to traffic people into, and that this will therefore end trafficking for sexual exploitation and sex work itself. This argument was proposed by Western feminists in the 1980s and despite no concrete evidence this logic remains prominent today. Indeed, there is also no concrete evidence to suggest that it is even possible to eradicate sex markets without firstly addressing problems of capitalism, colonialism, and patriarchy. For that reason, end demand policies and the raid and rescue paradigm has been rejected by Amnesty International (2016) and Human Rights Watch (2019). In the following section, we draw on the work of academics who have carried out careful ethnographies with sex work communities, and most importantly, on accounts from sex workers themselves to highlight the very real consequences of current anti-trafficking policies.

Disregarding Consent: Impact on Sex Workers

Amnesty International publicly supports the decriminalisation[3] of sex work following a report which evidenced the harm anti-trafficking and anti-sex work laws are causing sex workers globally (Amnesty International, 2016). Even though the same demand for decriminalisation has been made by sex workers, Amnesty's declaration was met with vocal resistance from governments, Christian organisations, the media, and well-intentioned 'feminist' celebrities, such as Lena Dunham and Meryl Streep (see Lee, 2015). Alison Phipps' (2017) analysis centrally locates the furore within the ongoing 'sex wars' paradigm. Through the oppression/empowerment binary, sex workers were positioned as either racialised 'victims' or as white, Western 'happy hookers' hiding the complexity of sex workers' consent, circumstance, and coercion. The 'sex wars' paradigm enabled those seeking to eradicate sex markets to argue that the voices of

Western sex workers were not representative meaning they could not speak on behalf of all sex workers. However, in silencing the sex workers who reject a straightforward victim status, Western anti-sex work feminists instead grant themselves the authority to determine what is 'best' for sex workers and the poor, racialised women they have labelled victims.

Given that anti-sex work and anti-trafficking policies directly impact sex workers lives, they should be an integral part of policy development. However, in reality, sex workers/sex worker organisations struggle to exist within debates and are routinely excluded. Such silencing allows countries to avoid any real consideration of labour or migrant protections for sex workers and leads to further criminalisation forming part of wider efforts to tackle social and moral issues with punitive responses. Indeed, Niina Vuolajärvi's (2019) careful ethnographic research in the Nordic region (Sweden, Norway, Finland) highlights the consequences of such punitive anti-trafficking policies specifically for migrants who sell sex. While nationals can access support including welfare and counselling helping them to leave sex work, migrant workers are excluded from services and financial support and are instead subject to detention, deportation, and evictions. Despite the seemingly good intentions of feminists, she describes the outcome as 'punitivist humanitarianism' or governing in the name of 'caring'.

The case of Yang Song who died in New York in 2017 after falling three stories while trying to flee from an undercover officer is evidence of the fatal impact anti-trafficking policies can have on those they ostensibly seek to 'protect'. Asian-owned massage businesses have been targeted by the New York Police Department and between 2012 and 2016, the number of Asian identified people arrested for prostitution-related offences increased by 2,700% (Stewart, 2022). Undercover officers solicit 'morally justified' sex acts as part of broader 'sting operations' to 'smash' international sex trafficking rings, however such encounters typically result in more harm for women – trafficked or not – who are vulnerable to arrest, deportation or in the case of Yang Song, death. Stewart (2022) argues that the vulnerability created by anti-trafficking policies is not an 'unintentional consequence' but rather, purposefully manufactured and shaped by a deep history of xenophobia, racism, and whorephobia. Indeed, we agree with Stewart (2022) that it is difficult to believe the real concern is in deterring trafficking for sexual exploitation when such stings routinely end in the deportation of immigrant women with no material shift or decrease in the prevalence of trafficking.

Research in South Africa conducted by GAATW with sex worker organisations SWEAT and Sisonke found that anti-trafficking measures create 'significant harm' to sex workers and exacerbate tensions between sex worker rights organisations, government officials and anti-trafficking organisations. Yingwana, Walker, and Etchart (2019) argue that consent cannot be so easily defined and identified as these policies and practices demand. Sex worker organisations on the other hand are well positioned to identify cases of sexual exploitation as rather than assuming all sex workers want/need to be rescued, they instead adopt a 'person-centred approach' and consider the nuances and complexities of individual circumstances.

Similarly, rather than focusing on one defining moment that identifies an individual as 'victim' or 'sex worker', Livia Valensise (2019), writing as a representative for the International Committee on the Rights of Sex workers in Europe (ICRSE), approaches consent as ambiguous. Valensise argues that an individual may give initial consent to sex work, but this does not mean they have consented to their working conditions and/or pay. Equally, an individual may be initially forced/tricked/coerced into sex markets, but this does not exclude the possibility that they consent to the work at a later stage. Thus, an individual's route into sex markets may not define their subsequent motivations and experiences.

These complexities are reflected in the biography of Nita-di (pseudonym), a sex worker living in Sonagachi, a notorious red-light district in Kolkata told by anthropologist Simanti Dasgupta (2019). Nita-di comes from a poor, rural family and was married to a man in his forties with suspected mental health issues when she was teenager. Despite both working as labourers, they had little money. One day, he took her to Kolkata and left her at Sonagachi explaining that here, she would not have to worry about money. She did not know where he was taking her but once in Sonagachi, the red-light district in Kolkata, she found herself poor, married to a man with mental health problems and so, with limited choices, she decided to sell sex. For 20 years she has worked in a brothel and considers it her home. When the police raid brothels, she runs away to avoid being forcibly detained in a rehabilitation home. Importantly, as she explains below, she does not want to be 'rescued'.

> Police oppression will not go away, so we will have to find ways to escape but then also find ways to return. This is my home, and this is the only place I could ever call home. It is only here I have some way to earn money to survive. I am not educated like you, so all I have is my gatar (body) to sell. But do I like it? Did I even want to get into line-er kaaj (sex work)? But here, at least I have been able to feed myself and take care of my daughter. So, this is all I know, like, you know, your home? And why don't the police just let us be in our homes? Who asked them to rescue us?
>
> *(Nita-di, quoted in Dasgupta, 2019:137)*

Sex Worker Resistance and Recommendations

Nita-di's example highlights individual resistance to the 'raid and rescue' operations in India and sex workers' power in managing their working lives, however more recently we have witnessed collective power and the persistence of sex worker-led groups, such as the National Network of Sex Workers India (NNSW) and allies, who have exposed and advocated to end police powers under the ITPA to forcibly detain women in 'rehabilitation homes'. Through legal cases lasting over a decade, the Supreme Court of India[4] has issued directives that put an end to forcing women into rescue homes and releasing those who are currently detained. The directives urge the police not to abuse sex workers and to instead treat them with dignity. Importantly, this legal decision centres sex worker agency and autonomy by recognising that sex workers can consent to selling sex, and the pivotal role sex workers can play in developing legislation to stop exploitation. While this is a positive step, the Supreme Court rulings are a stop gap until the Union of India develop legislation and it is yet to be seen how this legal intervention will manifest in sex workers' daily lives. Indeed, some weeks after the ruling, 80 sex workers escaped from a 'rehabilitation home' only to be forcibly returned (Walters and Raghavendra, 2022).

In response to the punitive and oppressive impact of anti-trafficking policies, more sex workers have organised to form advocacy groups such as ICRSE (Europe), GG (South Korea), X:Talk (Britain) among others, highlighting alternative methods of framing and enquiring into trafficking for sexual exploitation. For instance, in South Africa, SWEAT[5] and Sisonke[6] developed the Sex Work, Exploitation, and Migration/Mobility Model, and the Sex Work Opera[7] developed the Coercion—Migration—Sex Work (CO-MI-SE) Model. Key to these approaches is recognising specific convergences e.g., where migration meets sex work with no exploitation, where migration meets exploitation but no sex work, where sexual exploitation exists without migration and by identifying such specificities, this expands conversations about migration and the challenges that exist within sex work (Yingwana, Walker, and Etchart, 2019).

The Global Network of Sex Work Projects (NSWP), a network representing 314 sex worker-led organisations from over 100 countries, make clear recommendations that reflect our assessment of the current impact of anti-trafficking and anti-sex work policies. NSWP urge policy makers to end raid and rescue missions, to develop solutions to tackle trafficking and exploitation with sex workers, and to acknowledge different regional contexts. To quote sex worker activists P.G. Macioti and Giulia Garafalo Geymonat (2016:6) '"Sex workers" groups are clear on this point: all sex workers end up more vulnerable to exploitation, abuse, and coercion as a consequence of "anti-trafficking".'

Concluding Thoughts

Consent is often considered to be the line between sex that is accepted e.g., morally good, and sex that is unwanted e.g., illegal (Fanghanel et al., 2020). Through this moral lens, the sex carried out within sex work is constructed as unwanted/illegal and therefore becomes non-consensual. Within this logic, sex workers are both coerced victims and collateral damage in the broader fight against 'non-consensual' sex work through the eradication of sex markets. Importantly, while it may appear that consent, and sex workers' presumed coercion (e.g., their lack of consent), is at the core of debates on sex work and trafficking for sexual exploitation, on closer inspection, this chapter demonstrates how consent is in fact entirely disregarded within legal frameworks.

By tracing the theoretical development of consent in discussions on sex work, we can see the ongoing prevalence of dominance theory in shaping anti-sex work and anti-trafficking laws across the globe, which in many ways, aligns with religious and conservative ideology regarding sex work. Femininity is framed as (politically, physically, or emotionally) weak and through moral signalling, states can 'justify' punitive efforts to 'protect' women by 'rescuing victims' and forcibly 'rehabilitating bad women' who deny a straightforward victim status. This purposeful limiting of conversations in moral rather than legal or labour terms also enables countries to deny labour and migration rights and protections.

This chapter demonstrates how we cannot, nor should we, extract women's sexualities from the global political economy. Indeed, efforts to 'protect' trafficking victims, particularly racialised and poor women, as well as Western efforts to ensure countries in the Global South 'comply' with their aim of eradicating sex markets through financial manipulation and penalties, reflect and maintain the West's inherent colonial power. Western conceptualisations of consent within global debates not only narrowly define consent but attempt to universally apply the concept and in doing so, fail to account for the varied historical and cultural contexts that shape women's choices and opportunities. The examples we discuss highlight how differences between women must be considered and how consent and coercion are not mutually exclusive categories.

Given that there are no equivalent calls to 'end demand' or to eradicate any other industry where exploitation and trafficking are known to be commonplace, the overwhelming focus on sex markets and sex work exceptionalism not only eclipses experiences of trafficking and exploitation in other industries but exposes the centrality of morality and the drive to control gender, sexuality, borders, and movement on an international scale. For that reason, we question punitive legal frameworks seeking to eradicate sex markets in the name of tackling trafficking for sexual exploitation as such policies leave sex workers vulnerable to violence, arrest, deportation and even death which suggests the issue is not safety or protection.

At present, there is no concrete evidence to suggest that 'end demand' policies reduce rates of trafficking for sexual exploitation, nor is there concrete evidence that it is even possible to eradicate sex markets without firstly addressing problems of capitalism, colonialism, and patriarchy. For that reason, we – alongside Amnesty International (2016), Human Rights Watch (2019), academics who have carried out careful ethnographies with sex work communities, and most importantly, sex workers themselves – argue for the need to develop clear, evidence-based policies. Indeed, if the voices of sex workers – who are directly impacted – are not centred within policy debates and development, we question who then has the authority to speak in this context?

Notes

1 The three protocols – The UN Convention against Transnational Organized Crime; the Protocol against the Smuggling of Migrants by Land, Sea and Air (Smuggling Protocol);

and the Protocol against the Illicit Manufacturing and Trafficking in Firearms, Their Parts and Components and Ammunition (Firearms Protocol), are commonly known as the Palermo protocols, named after the Italian city, it was adopted in.

2 In many ways these claims can be linked back to campaigns in the 19th century of white feminists who sought to end 'White slavery' which resulted in legislation that monitored and restricted the migration of women (see Doezema, 2002 for a full discussion).

3 Decriminalisation refers to the end of all criminalisation of sex work and other forms of legal oppression in the first step to social justice for sex workers.

4 Budhadev Karmaskar versus Union of India, Supreme Court of India, 25 May 2022

5 Sex Worker Education and Advocacy Task Force (SWEAT) organise, advocate, and provide services for sex workers in South Africa employing sex workers in action and leadership.

6 Sisonke, South Africa's national sex worker movement.

7 The Sex Worker's Opera is a sex worker-led multimedia project, which presents over 100 stories from 18 countries across six continents on stage, in workshops with NGOs, and online. Retrieved 14 January 2019, http://www.sexworkersopera.com/about.

References

Agustín, L. M. (2007) *Sex at the Margins*. London: Zed Books.

Amnesty International (2016) Amnesty International Policy on State Obligations to Respect, Protect and Fulfil the Human Rights of Sex Workers. Available at https://www.amnesty.org/en/documents/pol30/4062/2016/en/ [Accessed 15 September 2022].

Barry, K. (1995) *The Prostitution of Sexuality: The Global Exploitation of Women*. New York: New York University Press.

Bernstein, E. (2018) *Brokered Subjects. Brokered Subjects*. Chicago: Chicago University Press.

Cruz, K. (2018) Beyond liberalism: Marxist feminism, migrant sex work, and labour unfreedom. *Feminist Legal Studies*, 26(1), 65–92.

Dasgupta, S. (2019) Of Raids and Returns: Sex Work Movement, Police Oppression, and the Politics of the Ordinary in Sonagachi, India. *Anti-Trafficking Review*, 12, 127–139.

Doezema, J. (2002) Who Gets to Choose? Coercion, Consent, and the UN Trafficking Protocol. *Gender and Development*, 10(1), 20–27.

Dworkin A. (1981) *Pornography: Men Possessing Women*. New York: Perigee.

Echols, A. (2016) Retrospective: Tangled up in Pleasure and Danger. *Signs*, 42(1), 11–22.

Fanghanel, A., Milne, E., Zampini, G., Banwell, S., Fiddler, M. (2020) *Sex and Crime*. London: Sage.

Gallagher, A. (2011) Improving the Effectiveness of the International Law of Human Trafficking: A Vision for the Future of the US Trafficking in Persons Reports. *Human Rights Review*, 12(3) pp. 381–400,

Gallagher, A. and Pearson, E. (2010) The High Cost of Freedom: A Legal and Policy Analysis of Shelter Detention for Victims of Trafficking. *Human Rights Quarterly*, 32, 73–114.

Graceyswer (2020) 'Consent and Choice in Survival Sex Work' *Streethooker.wordpress.com*. 4 August. Available at https://streethooker.wordpress.com/2020/08/04/consent-and-choice-in-survival-sex-work/ [Accessed 10 May 2023].

Hardy, K. (2013) Equal to Any Other, But Not the Same as Any Other. In C. Wolkowitz, T. Sanders, R. L. Cohen, & K. Hardy (Eds.), *Body/Sex/Work: Intimate, Embodied and Sexualized Labour*. Basingstoke: Palgrave Macmillan, pp. 43–58.

Hoefinger, H. (2013) *Sex, Love and Money in Cambodia*. Abingdon: Routledge.

Human Rights Watch (2019) Why Sex Work Should Be Decriminalized. Available at https://www.hrw.org/news/2019/08/07/why-sex-work-should-be-decriminalized [Accessed 9 September 2022].

Jahnsen, S. Ø., & Skilbrei, M. (2015) From Palermo to the Streets of Oslo: Pros and Cons of the Trafficking fFramework. *Anti-Trafficking Review*, 4.

Jenness, V. (1993) *Making it Work: The Prostitute's Rights Movement in Perspective.* New York: Aldine de Gruyter.

Kempadoo, K. (2001) Women of Color and the Global Sex Trade: Transnational Feminist Perspectives. *Meridians: Feminism, Race, Transnationalism*, 1(2), 28–51.

Kotiswaran P. (2016) Empty Gestures: A Critique of India's New Trafficking Bill. *Open Democracy*, 1–14. Available at https://www.opendemocracy.net/en/beyond-trafficking-and-slavery/empty-gestures-critique-of-india-s-new-trafficking-bill/ [Accessed 15 September 2022].

Lee, L. (2015) Actors Call on Amnesty to Reject Plans Backing Decriminalisation of Sex Trade. *The Guardian*, Available at https://www.theguardian.com/society/2015/jul/28/actors-streep-winslet-thompson-dunham-amnesty-decriminalisation-sex-trade [Accessed 24 September 2022].

Levy, J. (2014) *Criminalising the Purchase of Sex.* London: Routledge.

Macioti, P.G. & Garafalo Geymonat, G. (2016) Sex Workers Speak. Who Listens? *Open Democracy.*

MacKinnon, C. (1989) Sexuality, Pornography, and Method: 'Pleasure under Patriarchy'. *Ethics*, 99(2), 314–346.

Mohanty, C. (2003) *Feminism without Borders.* New York: Duke University Press.

O'Connell Davidson, J. (2002) The Rights and Wrongs of Prostitution. *Hypatia: A Journal of Feminist Philosophy*, 17(2), 84–98.

Pheterson, G. (1989) *A Vindication of the Rights of Whores.* Seal Press.

Pheterson, G. (1993) The Whore Stigma: Female Dishonor and Male Unworthiness. *Social Text*, 37, 39–64.

Phipps, A. (2017) Sex Wars Revisited: A Rhetorical Economy of Sex Industry Opposition. *Journal of International Women's Studies*, 18 (4).

Pilcher, K (2009) Empowering, Degrading or a 'Mutually Exploitative' Exchange for Women? *Journal of International Women's Studies*, 10 (3), 73–83.

Ramachandran, V. (2015) Rescued but not Released: The 'Protective Custody' of Sex Workers in India. *Open Democracy*. Available at https://www.opendemocracy.net/en/beyond-trafficking-and-slavery/rescued-but-not-released-protective-custody-of-sex-workers-in-i/ [Accessed 15/09/22].

Ramachandran, V. (2017) Critical Reflections on Raid and Rescue Operations in New Delhi. *Open Democracy*. 1–9. Available at https://www.opendemocracy.net/en/beyond-trafficking-and-slavery/critical-reflections-on-raid-and-rescue-operations-in-new-delhi/ [Accessed 29/09/22].

Sandy, L. (2018) Human Trafficking on the Global Periphery: A Terrible Spectacle. In K. Carrington (ed.). *The Palgrave Handbook of Criminology and the Global South*. London: Palgrave Macmillan.

Scoular, J., & FitzGerald, S. (2021) Why Decriminalise Prostitution? Because Law and Justice Aren't Always the Same. *International Journal for Crime, Justice and Social Democracy*, 10(4), 56–65.

Sex Worker's Opera (2019) http://www.sexworkersopera.com/about [Accessed 26/09/22].

Simouy, S. & Phal Niseiy, S. (2022) *The Struggle for Sex Worker Rights.* Available at https://cambodianess.com/article/the-struggle-for-sex-worker-rights [Accessed 15 September 2022].

Shih, E. (2017) Freedom Markets: Consumption and Commerce across Human-Trafficking Rescue in Thailand. *Positions: Asia Critique*, 25(4), 769–794.

Stewart, J. T. (2022) *Sex Work on Campus*, London: Routledge.

Valensise, L. (2019) What we Talk About When we Talk About Trafficking. *Open Democracy*. Available at https://www.opendemocracy.net/en/beyond-trafficking-and-slavery/what-we-talk-about-when-we-talk-about-trafficking/ [Accessed 29/9/2022].

Vuolajärvi, N. (2019) Governing in the Name of Caring—the Nordic Model of Prostitution and its Punitive Consequences for Migrants Who Sell Sex. *Sexuality Research and Social Policy*, 16(2), 151–165.

Walters, S. D. (2016) The Dangers of a Metaphor—Beyond the Battlefield in the Sex Wars. *Signs*, 42(1), 1–9.

Walters, K., & Ramachandran, V. (2018) A Recipe for Injustice: India's New Trafficking Bill Expands a Troubled Rescue, Rehabilitation, and Repatriation Framework. *Open Democracy*. https://www.opendemocracy.net/en/beyond-trafficking-and-slavery/recipe-for-injustice-india-s-new-trafficking-bil/.

Walters, K., & Raghavendra, M. (2022) India's Supreme Court Rules in Favour of Sex Workers, and Women Rise Up. *Open Democracy*. https://www.opendemocracy.net/en/beyond-trafficking-and-slavery/indias-supreme-court-rules-in-favour-of-sex-workers-sparking-riot/.

Weeks, K. (2011) *The Problem with Work: Feminism, Marxism, Antiwork Politics and Postwork Imaginaries*. Durham: Duke University Press.

Weitzer, R. (2013) Sex Trafficking and the Sex Industry: The Need for Evidence-Based Theory and Legislation. *Journal of Criminal Law and Criminology*, 101(4), 1337–1370.

Wijers, M. (2021) How We Got Here: The Story of the Palermo Protocol on Trafficking. *Open Democracy*. Available at https://www.opendemocracy.net/en/beyond-trafficking-and-slavery/how-we-got-here-story-palermo-protocol-trafficking/ [Accessed 09/09/22].

Women's Network for Unity (2022) Available at https://www.wnu.unitedsisterhood.org/ [Accessed 29 September 2022].

Yingwana, N, Walker, R and Etchart, A (2019) Sex Work, Migration, and Human Trafficking in South Africa: From Polarised Arguments to Potential Partnerships. *Anti-Trafficking Review*, 2, 74–90.

20

CROSSING BOUNDARIES AND CONSENT

Sex Offending and Criminalised Disabled Adults[1]

Chrissie Rogers

I bleed
I cannot bear to see the pain in your eyes
As you smile, a bit too brightly and tell me you're alright
But I can see your pain
And it slices to my core
The tears I cry I hide inside,
Not wanting to cause more.
I know you walk this path alone I cannot come with you.
I have my own.
I want to reach and hold you until the pain has gone.
But I stand back and it's hard to watch you walk away, alone.
My heartstrings stretch out to reach you, and snap like brittle glass,
crashing around my feet and stepping on the shards.
I bleed

(Elaine, Mother of a criminalised disabled son, Harry)[2]

Black Black Heart
Black black heart, blood red tears tumble – I am numb
Black black heart, my anger rages – I am numb.
I look through your eyes, into your soul.
I see me. I am here with you. I see you.
Recall yesterday? Do you? Your blood red beating heart.
Corners of my beating heart, I see it in you.
Fading light, broken, torn.
Black black heart, paralysed to mend.
Your pain is my pain.
I know you; I know this pain.
I am broken, I am whole.
You are broken, I will fix.
Black black heart, beat.

DOI: 10.4324/9781003358756-26

Beat. Beat. Beat.
Live.

(Mother of a victim of rape)[3]

Preface

I begin this chapter with these two poems written by women who have vicariously experienced sexual assault, as mothers. One mother, Elaine, has a son Harry, a criminalised disabled adult, who has been incarcerated for sexual assault, and the other has a daughter, *my daughter*, a disabled woman who has experienced rape and sexual assault. Harry told me in his interview 'she wanted me', that she consented to sex, yet the 15-year-old girl accused him of rape. My daughter told me she said no, yet did not know what to do after no. She did not consent. Elaine was heartbroken to see her son become criminalised as a young man, to want to take his own life, and to be charged of a sex crime and go to prison. She wrote the poem because of her desperate emotional pain, and to express herself. For me, I did not intend to write the poem, yet the events that occurred in 2022 led me to know more about sexual assault than I could have imagined.

To that point, my knowledge about this type of sexual assault and criminalised disabled men came from reading literature, listening to, and engaging with, participants in my research. Authenticity and positionality have always been key to how I tell stories, and for the purpose of this chapter, it is no different (e.g., Rogers 2019, 2021). Even though I started to reflect on my data, on my participants' lives and the writing of this chapter long before the horrific events of 2022, I am no longer the same person. My lens has shifted. What has not changed is my commitment to this research and the telling of criminalised disabled men's lives. Returning to the poems, they tell us that the impacts of sexual assault infect those who love the perpetrator and the victim respectively, and that the emotional responses, darkness, pain, and suffering occur, regardless. This chapter tells the story of what lies beneath these poems. Consent to sex is complex in these cases. No always means no, but we do need to understand what has gone wrong, to the point where disabled men spend a lifetime in and out of carceral enclosures, institutionalised, and with declining mental health.

Introduction

Challenges associated with sex and violence have been an area of peripheral interest to me for over 20 years. During my doctoral research, some mothers with disabled children spoke to me of their concerns over inappropriate sexualised behaviour and aggression on the part of their child. Tracy told me that when her son was eight or nine years old, he approached the babysitter and 'held a knife at her throat and said, "I'm going to fucking kill you"' (Rogers 2007: 75). She also told me about times when he behaved in violent and threatening ways towards her, and his siblings (ibid.: 154–155). Tracy went as far as to say, 'I hope that if he ends up in prison it's for theft or vandalism [and not] at the cost of somebody's life, through his rage, stupidity, or whatever' (Rogers, under review). In a similar way, Lynne, said about her son's behaviour, 'he was touching girls in assembly and erm, he didn't seem able to stop it, I mean he didn't rape anybody [...] he was saying sexual things to them' (Rogers 2007: 75). Later in the interview Lynne again said, 'I just did not know what to do, he was suspended for touching girls at school' (ibid.: 152). This subject matter was not one I pursued at the time. However, it was because of these maternal narratives, and other intimacy research (e.g., Rogers and Tuckwell 2016) that I began to follow up on disability and criminal pathways, and as a result this chapter draws upon the research funded by The Leverhulme Trust.

Considering sex crimes therefore, new criminal justice policies have emerged that are aimed directly at individuals who have been convicted of a sex offence (Lussier and Beauregard 2018). The carceral logics bound up in these policies are based on the notion that individuals are characterised by some fixed and stable predisposition to commit a sex offence. Along with public calls for tougher sentencing, a 'new penology' focusses on retribution and moral panic rather than rehabilitation. Criminal conviction can carry disadvantages long after release (Ben-Moshe 2020; Hamilton et al. 2021). From 2016, I carried out 43 in-depth life-story interviews and photo-elicitation[4] with criminalised disabled people, who have raped, sexually assaulted and/or carried out other crimes, mothers of offenders who fit within these categories, and professionals who work with them (Rogers 2018, 2020). For this chapter, the narratives in my study indicate that whilst unacceptable, underage sexual assault, violence, grooming, rape, and sexting, is carried out by someone who has misunderstood social and sexual cues. However early identification of complex difficulties had been noted yet left largely unchallenged. Furthermore, their experience of the criminal justice system has been experienced as frightening and harm inducing, yet on release, *with support*, no further sex crimes occurred. By exploring what happened as a precursor to these events and how then becoming embroiled in the criminal justice system is experienced, we can begin to understand sex offending trajectories in the context of consent, as well as prevent the incarceration of disabled people. This chapter first contextualises the area of disability, criminalisation, and sex offending, and then goes onto discuss narratives around sexual assault and rape.

Contextualising Criminalised Disabled Adults and Sex Offending

Stigmatised identities, social control, injustice, and the social/political gaze occur as persistent themes throughout much socio-political and criminological work (e.g., Foucault 1989, 1999; Ugelvik 2015), where emphasis on 'monstrous' humans are commonly surveyed, and yet carceral enclosures and court diversion are considered problematic (Steele 2017, 2020; Victor and Waldram 2015; Waldram 2009). Whilst sociological research is referred to in these texts, disability, particularly learning disability and/or autism, does not feature in the same way as classed, gendered and racialised injustices. Scholarship referring to intellectually disabled people, and autistic adults who have additional learning difficulties, especially those who have committed sexual offences, is often pathologising (Goddard 1915; Radzinowicz 1957; Sutherland 1950; Wootton 1959), situated within forensic psychology, and focuses on health, treatment, and assessment (e.g., Lievesley et al. 2018; Hocken et al. 2020), where arguably the criminalised disabled offender needs a cure, and is to be fixed. Considering disability, mental health and crime, during the eighteenth and into the nineteenth century, labels such as 'mad', 'bad', 'imbecile', 'lunatic', 'dull', 'cretin' 'idiot' and 'feebleminded', were all medically legitimate terms for those whose behaviour or ability was outside of the norms of society. Enlightenment philosophy promoted science, truth, reason and rationality, all of which have been persistently privileged (Jarrett 2020).

Scientism dominated knowledge production, which included medicine and health and the importance of 'the cure'. For example, concerning serious crime and disability, over a century ago Henry Herbert Goddard (1915: 102) asks the question 'what shall be done with these criminal imbeciles?' He goes on to say, 'Of all persons in the world, the criminal imbecile should be placed in custody under conditions that will forever make it impossible for him to repeat his offense'. Critical here is that Goddard suggests that those who have committed serious crimes due to anger or perverted rationality, could re-enter society: they could be treated or rehabilitated. Yet he rejects this could be the case for intellectually disabled people, saying that it would never be safe for them to live amongst others in society and besides, public others would want these criminalised disabled people to be 'committed to an institution for mental defectives, where they will be constantly guarded and prevented from doing injury' (ibid.: 103). By the middle of the twentieth century a study of sexual offences in England and Wales found 16% of offenders were said to be below average intelligence and some were 'borderline mental defectives including those who had attended special schools for backward children; and few were later certified and sent to institutions' (Radzinowicz 1957: 244). Their crimes were 'often the result of an inability to assess social relations properly, a lack of knowledge of sexual matters or an inadequate resistance to adverse influences' (ibid.).

In over 100 years, the terms for categorising disability and impairment might have changed, but how criminalised disabled people are treated, managed, administered before and/or after a diagnosis is still deeply problematic (Ben-Moshe 2020; Steele 2020). Especially if we deem locked wards, secure units, and imprisonment for public protection (IPP) sentences all part of processing criminalised disabled men and women (Edgar et al. 2020; Fish 2018). Reflecting upon this disability context, sex offenders generally are considered as 'the rigid, unchangeable pariah in such a system, depicted as being gripped by a nature or biology that is completely depraved and thus, intolerable' and always a threat (Spencer 2009: 219). So much so, the dangerous sex offender is not only perceived as monstrous, but as a 'ghostly being; a roving, lurking, nearly omnipresent individual that is difficult to locate or contain' (Werth 2022: 3). Once returned to the community, the dangerous sex offender is imagined as certain to strike again and as Robert Werth (2022: 3) suggests his research participants, parole personnel, 'blur the boundaries between happening and not happening' as they have a feeling, a sense that something, an event has occurred, leaving the dangerous sex offender always at risk of reincarceration for even the most minor misdemeanour. The disabled adult who has carried out a sex offence is placed in an illusory waiting room, seemingly unable to control urges, and therefore likely to strike again, inevitably to return to a carceral enclosure.

Similarly, Jill Peay (2016: 138) proposes, a lack of rationality, or volitional control feeds perceived dangerousness of disabled offenders, perhaps making them

> both less culpable and more amenable to therapeutic or rehabilitative endeavours, drawing on our humanitarian instincts. These two contrasting images – of threat and illness – constantly shift the shape of the disordered offender, evoking changing emotional response in us, and making 'them' ungraspable or unknowable to a system that aspires to work with presumed certainties.

Notably, disabled people, particularly those who have additional learning disabilities, have been locked away, incarcerated, and institutionalised throughout history. Furthermore, there has been very little political movement to do anything about this, largely based on these concerns over the unknowable, ungraspable, uncertainties that besiege them.

People who are disabled *and* break the law, markedly those who commit a sex offence, often find themselves embroiled in a never-ending criminal justice process, as well as experience moral exile from communities, families, and friends (Hamilton et al. 2021). They are incarcerated, sometimes on (in the UK) imprisonment for public protection (IPPs) for years, making them further institutionalised and therefore far less able to lead a meaningful life on release (Edgar et al. 2020; Ben-Moshe 2020). Liat Ben-Moshe (2020) connects deinstitutionalisation and prison abolition in a genealogical mapping of carceral logics and enclosures. Arguably, for abolitionist scholars, incarceration is against humanity, and no longer ought the trope the 'dangerous few' justify the existence of prisons, secure hospitals, residential schools and group homes.

It is indeed suggested that prisons are full of the 'Mad, Bad and Sad' (Weare 2017). This being the case, at least two thirds of prisoners should not be in prison. Notably, prison abolitionists suggest much of criminal justice reform focusses on the '"Non, non, nons" (nonviolent, nonserious, and nonsexual offences)' (Ben-Moshe 2020: 123). Despite this, those who are defined as having disabling conditions such as mental ill-health or are neurodiverse can often end up in more secure and punitive enclosures, and/or are highly medicated, due to either behaviour that is considered as, or is challenging and disruptive, or assumed vulnerability, theirs, and others (Ben-Moshe 2020; Ben-Moshe et al. 2014). Caitlin Gormley (2017: 66) states for disabled offenders, 'imprisonment creates new forms of disablism, [as] systematic marginalisation, routinised forms of oppression and exclusion places them at higher risk of being manipulated, victimised, and disadvantaged throughout the social fabric of prison'; even more so than their non-disabled peers.

When it comes to rape and sexual assault, it involves two (or more) people, at least an alleged victim, and an alleged offender, who may or may not be known to each other. Often when known to each other it is not to discover if an act occurred, but 'rather to determine whether the alleged victim consented or not' (Deslauriers-Varin et al. 2018: 300). In stranger rape cases, it is more often about gathering 'information that facilitates the identification of the alleged offender' (ibid.). Adding further complexity, such as intellectual disability and/or mental ill-health, for example, Jill Peay (2016) suggests courts of law and criminal justice struggle with this awkward fit, due to the intersection between disability and offending, thwarting matters concerned with consent and understanding. Below, I go on to discuss some of these matters.

Narratives of Sex Offending

For participants in my research, struggling with relationships, including sexual consent is complicated. Negotiating rules and regulations as well as understanding consequences of their actions, however, can be life changing for all involved. For example, some criminalised disabled participants talk of 'friends', but misinterpret what friendship, intimacy and sexual norms entail. In the narratives below, we recognise much of this with Ellis, Hugh and Harry.[5] Ellis for example, was accused of sexual assault twice. He told me after the second offence, 'I was arrested again, taken down to the police station, and all my clothes were taken to forensics, and stuff like that and apparently I raped her in the park'. For us here, it is not about whether the rape happened, but that Ellis seemed to narrate a lack of ownership over this accusation in a matter-of-fact way. He said, '*apparently* I raped her', implying that he did not believe it happened at all, or that he did not consider this attack to be a sex crime? He seemed unsure, and therefore consent does not even come into play here, for him as a relationship norm.

This is a multifarious situation, however having complex needs does not absolve anyone from a crime committed, but it does mean the need to understand with care (Rogers 2016). As care is not 'a type of secondary moral question, or the work of the least well off in society. Care is a central concern of human life. It is time that we began to change our political and social institutions to reflect this truth' (Tronto 1993:180). The narratives from life stories told in this chapter, are their 'truth'. The unimaginable life changing events for any victim is important, but I am discussing sex offending in relation to consent, from the accused men, mothers of perpetrators of a sex crime, and professionals who work with them.

Like Ellis above, Hugh was also accused of sexual assault, when he was 19, and a few years later of rape. Hugh said his victim 'gave me the wrong signal' and 'I thought that she quite liked me'. He went on to say, 'they believed her, they would not believe me, so I got arrested for something like, er sexual, yeah yeah, sexual harassment and I think I'm o- I'm on the sex offenders list as well'. I asked Hugh if this woman was a girlfriend, and he said, 'er w-well, I thought, I thought that, I thought that she was [...] I'm not meant to sorta like be anywhere near her'. Ellis and Hugh said they did not commit a sex crime. They suggest that if they did have sex, it was consensual. Yet Ellis and Hugh were placed on the sex offender's register impacting on their interaction with the community, their life chances, and their mental health (Hamilton et al. 2021), as both talked about extreme forms of self-harm. Ellis told me he took an overdose, but clarified that with, 'I didn't wanna end my life, I just wanted to end the pain' and Hugh said, 'I tried to k-kill myself'.

Reflecting further on what sex and intimacy involves, when it comes to consent, Harry's story of sexual assault goes beyond the accusation. He told me that he had met a young woman, and they did get intimate. He revealed 'I began to push the [sexual] boundaries, and I thought nowt about it, two weeks later, I've got the coppers at my door'. He was so shocked as he had not considered his behaviour to be anything other than consensual sex and said,

> I can remember sitting in the cell and I overheard, and they were like 'oh it's for the rape of a 15-year-old' and I was just like, whoosh, they've got the wrong bloke here, [...] and all these questions ganning round in my head and obviously they fucking put us in a cell for 8 hours before I got interviewed, so I told them everything [...] well I obviously didn't rape her.

Harry was sentenced to three years for this offence and went to an adult prison. Even though Harry admitted to having, according to him, consensual sex with this woman, she was under 16. He was therefore charged with having sex with a minor. Like Ellis and Hugh, Harry too has attempted to take his own life.

These narratives confront us, because they involve a sex crime (alleged or otherwise) as the perpetrator is judged or imagined as the most monstrous of humans (Werth 2022). Furthermore, when it comes to intellectual disability or irrational behaviour, the possibility of reason (or lack of) and therefore affect (Van Gelder 2013) can lend itself to the justification of medical intervention and indeterminate sentences for public protection (IPP). Furthermore, despite the abolition of IPPs in 2012, 'their legacy lives on' and 'concerns have now emerged about the high recall rates, with the number of IPP offenders being recalled to prison' (Trebilcock and Weston 2020: 89). This is confirmed with the narratives heard about in my research as well as Werth's (2022) data about how criminal justice professionals imagine criminal activity occurs even if there is little evidence to prove this is the case.

We have heard a little about what has occurred in terms of consent to sex (or lack of), criminalisation, and mental health for Ellis, Hugh, and Harry. But what happens before all of this; before a disabled person is criminalised? Perhaps we can gain some understanding by listening to mothers of criminalised disabled adults and professionals who work with them. Below, are examples from mothers whose sons were criminalised for sex offending. Significantly, from a young age support was requested by Elaine and Sorcha, yet very little was forthcoming. Elaine told me that Harry (Elaine is his mother), who we heard from above, was previously accused of sexual assault at the age of 11, but nothing came of it. Elaine continued, 'Harry's teacher said, "we'll send him for counselling", but I knew he hadn't done it, but thought, oh aye, if it does the job'. Elaine went on to talk about when Harry was a young teenager, he was always in trouble, and was suspended from school and told me 'I had to really fight. They weren't listening to me, to the help he needed. He ended up going to the one-to-one unit'. Elaine spoke of how Harry's violence escalated and said, 'he'd smash the place up, get violent [...] he was suicidal, he tried to commit suicide, I didn't know what I'd come home to'. Harry and Elaine were in a cycle of violence that started from a young age. Furthermore, Harry's behaviour towards women did result in him having a custodial sentence for sexual assault despite Elaine speaking to the teachers, the school administrators and social care staff, years before.

In a similar way, and reflecting upon early years, Sorcha, told me about how her son dealt with his emotions. Her son who is autistic and has been through the criminal justice system and incarcerated for 'grooming' young teenage girls says about him when he was 10 years old, he had this 'cage in the back of his head'. She said, 'in the cage there's a monster, and for 90% of the time it's locked up and can't get out'. Sorcha said her son was so terrified of it, that when the monster comes out, 'he goes in the cage, and shuts himself in and the monster takes over. He's described this to me. Yeah, and it's how I made more sense of it'. Sorcha went on to talk about what happened after her son's 'monster' had finished. She said: 'it calms down, they swap places again. [...] Once he's processed it, then he's like "I shouldn't have done that mum, I know I shouldn't have done that."' Although Sorcha and her son were evidently experiencing challenges from a young age, she suggested because her son was violent, predominantly towards girls, he was 'made out to be the demon child of the school' and had several school exclusions in the mid-2000s as a 10-year-old boy.

The situation with Sorcha's son was such that he was charged with grooming when he was in his late teens. He sent 'dick pics' to a small group of 13-year-old girls, who according to him were his 'friends'. The transcripts of the text messages, Sorcha told me, said such things as 'I love you; I want to be with you', and other more sexualised narratives. Read out in court, in the cold light of day, these seem wholly in keeping with how someone grooming might lure a victim in. Yet it is not uncommon for disabled adults, especially those with a learning disability to talk of love, especially if you like someone and they seem to like you. Equally it is not unusual for disabled adults to misunderstand social or sexual cues or have little perception about chronological age (Vinter and Dillon 2020). Arguably, if consent and intimacy work was carried out with these young men and if these mothers were listened to, the sex crimes might have been reduced, if not avoided. Moreover, there would be fewer victims of rape and sexual assault.

The rules around who does what with whom can seem blurred and confusing for disabled adults, as described by Kip, who works with men who have been through the CJS and been charged with sexual offences. Kip recollected about one man, 'he started to share about the love of his life and about how he'd had an amazing time with her, but his mum had insisted that erm, they didn't see each other anymore'. Kip went on to tell me that this man said, '"that's the trouble, you know, mums and daughters", and I was like "ah, she was your sister, I get it" [...] I'd been listening to him tell me about the love of his life and it was his sister!' Kip was talking about a criminalised disabled man, who did not, at the point of their first interaction, quite understand why he was criminalised.

Notably, Kip goes on to talk about what comes before these offences, as he is attempts to enable healthy relationships and integration into the community. However once incarcerated, whether in prison, or some other carceral enclosure, it is perhaps unrealistic to undo the grave impacts of institutionalisation from a young age (Ben-Moshe 2020) evidenced below, as Kip speaks about another man,

> We talked to him a lot about relationships, and kind of what comes after 'hello'. No one actually ever bothers to sit down and talk to people that have, have been segregated. [...] They've spent all their time in, you know, special school and then special college.

What is evident here is that if someone has been institutionalised or excluded, from a young age, for example, in 'special education', pupil referral units or residential settings, and then becomes incarcerated in a secure hospital or prison as an adult, living 'in the community' is threatening, especially if deinstitutionalisation is predicated by a lack of care (Tronto 1993) According to Kip, these men can learn to be in the community, to understand what consent means, but institutionalisation has had a hugely negative impact upon learning social and sexual norms. Ben-Moshe (2020: 79) says, 'In segregated settings like group homes and sheltered workshops, all life's activities, including eating, hygiene, sexuality and intimacy, are policed and surveilled constantly'. She goes on to say that those who work with disabled people in these environments 'become authorised to regulate sexual behaviours, even if no behaviours are present' (ibid.; see also Werth 2022).

However Kip, reflecting further on the criminalised disabled men who live supported in the community said,

> I always say to them 'you're not special, just quite unfortunately you haven't had those same experiences and now you're a 20-year-old man playing catch up'. So you're, you're still going through your 13, 14-year-old adolescence but actually as a 20-year-old man that's pretty scary to watch.

Similarly, Malcom a retired prison inspectorate talking about misunderstandings, institutionalisation and learning difficulties, sums up,

> I mean one guy had about eight different warnings, he had quite significant learning difficulties and he would touch women inappropriately, grope them and so on in public. I mean one guy I work with now, he looks strange, dribbles, and when you talk to him, he'll test out if he can give you a cuddle. He'll tell you about a girlfriend who he's only met once, and he's been arrested a number of times.

Malcolm is confirming what we have heard above, about friendships and intimacy confusion, as well as perhaps a lack of social and sexual awareness.

Jean-Louis Van Gelder (2013: 749), in his research about criminal decision-making talks of emotional competence or lack thereof, suggesting many individuals struggle to adaptively deal with their problems. His description of such has resonance with the narratives above, but also in the following examples, as the

> hot, affective, impulsive or heuristic, mode – is fast, requires little or no cognitive effort, employs heuristic judgements, and has a low threshold for processing incoming information. The opposite holds for the other – cool, cognitive, rule-based, systematic – mode of processing, which is associated with effortful, systematic judgements and decisions based on extensive thinking

> (ibid.: 751–752).

For example, I have heard from criminalised disabled men who have told me they raped or sexually assaulted a woman or child, seemingly without thoughts of repercussions, at least for the victim (see also, Courtney et al. 2006). As Vincent recalled what happened when he was in his 'friends' bedroom, in the group home. He told me, 'I borrowed a CD off her, and I listened to it, and I took it back to her bedroom, and she put me in an awkward position. She said, "if you leave the bedroom, I'll tell the staff you raped me, and if you stay, I'll tell the staff you raped me", so I raped her anyway'. As a result of this sexual assault, Vincent told me he was remanded in custody, but said 'they didn't think prison was suitable for me, so they sent me to a locked home, as I was 16'. It was from there that Vincent was moved around from one carceral enclosure to another. I asked Vincent if he had raped anyone before, and he said 'nope'. He told me that he knew rape was forced, non-consensual sex and said that he 'was honest with em (the police) but at the time they didn't know anything about learning disability people'. Notably, Van Gelder's (2013) hot and cold impulses, does not really work for my participants narratives, as Vincent's actions seem cold and measured, yet too, impulsive and in the moment. Arguably it is both.

Likewise, Warren seems evidently impulsive as he told me he

> committed a serious offence, it got me, got me arrested and stuff, got me remanded into prisons, you know, indecent assault, er a 25-year-old female, indecent assault, yeah, but it was that, it was that serious that they, I probably did get done for rape, but in my eyes, in my head, it was indecent assault. [...] I was on the street, in the – the open. Daytime, you know. I saw this lady, she was walking her dog, that's what she was doing. She walked up this grass verge off a main road. [...] I was com- coming up. I seen her cutting off, and then I cut off, and then it happened you know. She got dragged to gr-ground, and er I was touching her private parts and stuff, and i-i-it's it just, it's, it weren't like I, you know, it's jus – it's just weird, it really is.

Somewhat like Ellis above, Warren distances himself from the event, by saying '*she* got dragged', but went on to say, 'I was touching her'. I asked how did this incident get reported? And he said, 'she went to the police. I didn't beat her up, but the police were in the area within, within a matter of no time, then I got caught, yeah'. I asked if he confessed and Warren replied,

> yeah yeah [...] they put me straight on remand, remanded to er, that was the first time yeah, remand centre. I was there quite a long time [...] and then I was, I was taken, I was sort of sentenced to this hospital, to go to this hospital into er, an adolescent unit as I must have been 17. I got to a certain age, they had to release me from that, you know so I ended up, I was, I were classed as homeless cause I had nowhere to go.

Warren carried out a serious offence, as a 17-year-old, was incarcerated in a secure hospital adolescent unit, then he seemed to drop of any care and support with nowhere to live on release as an adult.

The fact that Warren was left to his own devices, with nowhere to live and no support, is significant, as we understand families and relationships are important factor in desistence (Farmer 2017; Hamilton et al. 2021; Saunders 2020). This lack of care and support post release had terrible impacts on other victims as Warren told me about further offending.

> It was on a kid this time, it was a sexual assault, more or less, yeah, same, more or less yeah, same. They said, they did they said, the victim says that

she saw me riding a mountain bike, you know, they were, these were in a park, a local park it happened, it was sunny like it is now. [...] There was two of 'em yeah two, two girls, yeah, the other one run off! [...] probably about same age, 10? The police come the next day, [...] he took a swing at me, you know, he hit me, like and he hit my head that hard that I fell over the other side of my bed, yeah he hit me yeah like, it was a DCI, he just whacked me in my face.

Although seemingly spontaneous, Warren was matter of fact about relaying this memory to me, displaying a combination of hot *and* cold impulses (van Gelder 2013), as he went on to tell me that he was sentenced to six years. For some of that time he was in the young offender's institution, but then went onto an adult prison. He told me he was 'frightened in the adult prison', and that he was 'refused parole because I didn't have no fixed abode to come out to'. So, this time, Warren was not given parole, due to having nowhere to live (Hamilton et al. 2021), but rather than this focus, perhaps we might want to consider what support, what care practices need to be in place to enable reintegration into the community on release, rather than waiting for a sentence to end? It seems, building and maintaining relationships, including families and friendships is critical for remaining out of prison and in the community, but that also public others free themselves from the fear of the 'dangerous few' (Ben-Moshe 2020, Farmer 2017, Hamilton et al. 2021, Saunders 2020).

Concluding Remarks

For criminalised disabled men who have sexually offended, the ongoing and long-term consequences are significant. These consequences include exclusion, stigmatisation, surveillance, and registration (Hamilton et al. 2021; Rolfe and Tewksbury 2018; Rolfe et al. 2016). As Hamilton and colleagues (2021) have found, collateral consequences for sex offenders are two-fold, as formal consequences include policy and legal requirements, for example, registration, fixed abode and so on, but informal consequences around social control are attempting to limit community participation and are often implemented by friends, family, employers, local community members, 'out of self-protection or a desire to distance themselves from the "deviant" individual' (Hamilton et al. 2021: 2; cf. Uggen and Stewart 2014; Rolfe and Tewksbury 2018). Formal consequences are often operationalised via legal procedures, and include additional punishment, yet significantly in the aftermath of punishment it is likely consequences fall into the informal category and are often unintended and long lasting (Hamilton et al. 2021), such as homelessness, discrimination, loss, harassment, abuse, mental ill health, and relationship challenges (c.f. Rolfe and Tewksbury 2018). As James Waldram suggests, for sexual offenders 'moral exile remains as they face a hostile community' (2009: 225). Furthermore, maintaining relationships is critical for remaining out of prison and in the community (Farmer 2017; Saunders 2020).

The narratives here indicate that whilst unacceptable, underage sex, violence, grooming, rape, sexting is carried out by someone who has misunderstood social and sexual cues, although not exclusively. Therefore, understanding consent in this context is complex. For my participants negotiating rules and regulations as well as understanding consequences of their actions because of their disabling condition, is challenging. For example, as we have heard, several offender participants struggled with what 'being a friend' means, to the detriment of their route through the criminal justice process. To come back to the poems that opened the chapter, this research cannot necessarily help those who are already a victim of sexual assault and their families, carers and support networks, but it can impact on the early identification of problems that occur around friendships, intimacy, sex and violence moving forward. The poems are a reminder that whilst we need to talk about criminalised disabled adults, it is always in context. Intimate relationships are often surveyed in the public sphere when sexual activity is experienced or understood as problematic, dangerous or risky and consent is absent or unknowable. Some adults might always need additional support, as with some participants in my research; but that does not mean they ought to be in carceral enclosures, indefinitely.

Notes

1 An extended version of this paper is in Rogers (under review), '"I'll tell the staff you raped me", "so I raped her anyway"': Sex offending and criminalised disabled adults', *International Journal of Disability and Social Justice*. To note, it does not include poems or the personal narrative.
2 I interviewed Harry in 2016 when he was 22. He had been in prison for arson and a sex offence. I interviewed Elaine (his mother) on the same day and again carried out follow up interviews with her. Harry is back in prison at the time of writing this. He has diagnoses of attention deficit, and other mental health challenges, and attended a 'special education' school and a pupil referral unit.
3 My adult learning disabled daughter, 35 at the time, was raped twice and sexually assaulted once, over a period of three weeks in 2022, in public toilets. The perpetrator is an autistic man over 10 years younger. The police interviewed her while I was present. No retelling of her story ever changed. We did not pursue a criminal investigation based on her wishes, and in support of her mental health. My daughter fully consents to the inclusion of this narrative; indeed, currently she says she would like to tell her own story at some point as difficult as that might be. That will always remain up to her.
4 Kate Herrity and colleagues (2021: xxiv) suggest, 'our language and disciplines have been constructed through very particular conceptions of the world in which the sensory has been relegated to an amorphous, intangible, and unmeasurable realm. But we do not experience the world singularly'.
5 To understand more about these men, I have written pen portraits elsewhere (Rogers, under review).

References

Ben-Moshe, L. (2020), *Decarcerating Disability: Deinstitutionalization and Prison Abolition*. Minneapolis: University of Minnesota Press.

Ben-Moshe, L., Chapman, C., and Carey, A. (2014) *Disability Incarcerated: Imprisonment and Disability in the United States and Canada*. New York: Palgrave Macmillan.

Courtney, J., Rose, J.and Mason, O.(2006)The Offence Process of Sex Offenders with Intellectual Disabilities: A Qualitative Study. *Sexual Abuse*, 18(2), 169–191.

Deslauriers-Varin, N., Bennell, C. and Bergeron, A. (2018) Criminal Investigation of Sexual Offences. In P. Lussier and E. Beauregard (eds.), *Sexual Offending: A Criminological Perspective*. Abingdon: Routledge.

Edgar, K., Harris, M., and Webster, R. (2020) *No Life, no Freedom, no Future: The Experiences of Prisoners Recalled under the Sentence of Imprisonment for Public Protection*. Prison Reform Trust.

Farmer, M. (2017) *The Importance of Strengthening Prisoners' Family Ties to Prevent Reoffending and Reduce Intergeneration Crime*. London: Ministry of Justice.

Fish, R. (2018) *A Feminist Ethnography of Secure Wards for Women with Learning Disabilities: Locked Away*. Abingdon, Routledge.

Foucault, M. (1989) *Madness and Civilisation: A History of Insanity in the Age of Reason*. London: Routledge.

Foucault, M. (1991) *Discipline and Punish: The Birth of the Prison*. London: Penguin.

Goddard, H. H. (1915) *The Criminal Imbecile: An Analysis of Three Remarkable Murder Cases*. New York: Macmillan Company.

Gormley, C. (2017) An Extended Social Relational Approach to Learning Disability Incarcerated. In D. Moran and A.K. Schliehe (eds.) *Carceral Spatiality*. Houndmills: Palgrave Macmillan, pp. 43–74.

Hamilton, E., Sanchez, D. and Ferrara, M. L. (2021) Measuring Collateral Consequences Among Individuals Registered for a Sexual Offense: Development of the Sexual Offender Collateral Consequences Measure. *Sexual Abuse*, 1–33.

Herrity, L., Schmidt, B.E. and Warr, J. (eds.) (2021) *Sensory Penalities: Exploring the Senses in Spaces of Punishment and Social Control*. United Kingdom: Emerald Publishing.

Hocken, K., Lievesley, R., Winder, B., et al. (eds.) (2020) *Sexual Crime and Intellectual Functioning*. Switzerland: Palgrave Macmillan.

Jarrett, S. (2020) *Those They Called Idiots: The Idea of the Disabled Mind from 1700 to the Present Day*. London: Reaktion Books.

Lievesley, R., Hocken, K., Elliot, H. et al. (eds.) (2018) *Sexual Crime and Prevention*. Switzerland: Palgrave Macmillan.

Lussier, P. and Beauregard, E. (eds.) (2018) *Sexual Offending: A Criminological Perspective*. Abingdon: Routledge.

Peay, J. (2016) An Awkward Fit: Offenders with Mental Disabilities in a System of Criminal Justice. In M. Bosworth, C. Hoyle, and L. Zedner (eds.) *Changing Contours of Criminal Justice*. Oxford: Oxford University Press.

Radzinowicz, L. (1957) *Sexual Offences: A Report of the Cambridge Department of Criminal Justice*. London: Macmillan and Co.

Rolfe, S. M. and Tewksbury, R. (2018) Criminal Justice Policies: The Intended and Unintended Consequences of Monitoring Individuals Convicted of Sex Crimes. In P. Lussier and E. Beauregard (eds.) *Sexual Offending: A Criminological Perspective*. London: Routledge.

Rolfe, S. M., Tewksbury, R. and Schroeder, R. (2016) Homeless Shelters' Policies on Sex Offenders: Is This Another Collateral Consequence? *International Journal of Offender Therapy and Comparative Criminology*, 61(16), 1833–1849.

Rogers, C. (2007) *Parenting and Inclusive Education: Discovering Difference, Experiencing Difficulty*. Houndmills: Palgrave.

Rogers, C. (2018) Life Stories, Criminal Justice and Caring Research. In G. Noblit (Ed.) *Oxford Research Encyclopaedia of Education*. New York: Oxford University Press.

Rogers. C. (2019) Just Mothers: Criminal Justice, Care Ethics and 'Disabled' Offenders. *Disability and Society*. https://doi.org/10.1080/09687599.2019.1655711.

Rogers, C. (2020) Necessary Connections: 'Feelings Photographs' in Criminal Justice Research and Doing Visual Methods. *Methodological Innovations*. https://doi.org/10.1177%2F2059799120925255.

Rogers, C. (2021) Mothering, Disability and Care: Beyond the Prison Wall. In J. Herring and B. Clough (eds). *Disability, Care and Family Law*. London: Routledge.

Rogers, C. (under review) Rape and Sexual Assault: The Criminalised Disabled Sex Offender. *International Journal of Disability and Social Justice*.

Rogers, C., and Tuckwell, S. (2016) Co-constructed Research and Intellectual Disability: An Exploration of Friendship, Intimacy and Being Human. *Sexualities*, 19(5–6), 623–640.

Saunders, L. (2020) The Transition from Prison to the Community of People Convicted of Sexual Offences: Policy and Practice Recommendations. *Prison Service Journal*, 251, 11–18.

Spencer, D. (2009) Sex Offender as *Homo Sacer*. *Punishment and Society*, 11(2), 219–240.

Steele, L. (2017) Disabling Forensic Mental Health Detention: The Carcerality of the Disabled Body. *Punishment and Society*, 19(3), 327–347.

Steele, L. (2020) *Disability, Criminal Justice and Law: Reconsidering Court Diversion*. Abingdon: Routledge.

Sutherland, E. H. (1950) The Sexual Psychopath Laws. *Journal of Criminal Law and Criminology*, 40(5), 543–554.

Tronto, J (1993) *Moral Boundaries: A Political Argument for an Ethic of Care*. Abingdon, Routledge.

Ugelvik, T. (2015) The Rapist and the Proper Criminal: The Exclusion of Immoral Others as Narrative Work on the Self. In L. Presser and S. Sandberg (eds.) *Narrative Criminology: Understanding Stories of Crime*. New York: New York University Press.

Uggen, C.and Stewart, R.(2014)Piling On: Collateral Consequences and Community Supervision. *Minnesota Law Review*, 99, 1871–1912.

Van Gelder, J.L. (2013) Beyond Rational Choice: The Hot/Cool Perspective of Criminal Decision Making. *Psychology, Crime & Law*, 19(9), 745–763.

Victor, J. and Waldram, J. (2015) Moral Habilitation and the New Normal: Sexual Offender Narratives of Posttreatment Community Integration. In L. Presser and S. Sandberg (eds.) *Narrative Criminology: Understanding Stories of Crime*. New York: New York University Press.

Vinter, L.P. and Dillon, G. (2020) Autism and Sexual Crime. In K. Hocken, R. Lievesley, B. Winder et al. (eds.) *Sexual Crime and Intellectual Functioning*. Switzerland: Palgrave Macmillan, 89–112.

Waldram, J. (2009) 'It's just you and Satan, hanging out at a pre-school': Notions of Evil and Rehabilitation of Sexual Offenders. *Anthropology and Humanism*, 34(2), 219–234.

Weare, S. (2017) Bad, Mad or Sad? Legal Language, Narratives, and Identity Constructions of Women Who Kill their Children in England and Wales. *International Journal of Semiotic Law*, 30, 201–222.

Werth, R. (2022) More than Monsters: Penal Imaginaries and the Specter of the Dangerous Sex Offender. *Punishment and Society*, 1–21.

Wootton, B. (1959) *Social Science and Social Pathology*. London: George Allen and Unwin Ltd.

21

WHOSE CONSENT?

Donor Conception, Anonymity and Rights

Róisín Ryan-Flood

Since 2005, donor conceived people in the UK have been able to access contact information about their donor once they turn eighteen. This applies only to those conceived after April 2005. For the first time, this new generation has the option of finding out about their biological origins in adulthood, whereas previously all sperm, egg and embryo donation was permanently anonymous. However, for donor conceived people who were born before this 2005 legislation, social media and genetic testing nonetheless have provided them with the opportunity to uncover their donor's identity. Similarly, some donor conceived people (or their parents) are able to use the same means to discover the donor's identity prior to the child turning eighteen. This can happen for example when genetic testing reveals a close relative, who may then be able to provide information about who the donor could be. Alternatively, the social parents may contact other families who have conceived via donation on social media such as private facebook groups and share their donor number or other identifying information so that children can meet with their genetic half siblings. This has become such a commonplace event that some clinics now refuse to divulge the donor's number from the clinic database and others ask patients to sign a form promising not to attempt to trace the donor via social media or allow their potential child to use ancestry or DNA websites.

It is often the case that assisted reproduction presents complex new scenarios that legal, medical, ethical and social regulators struggle to keep pace with (Ryan-Flood & Gunnarsson-Payne, 2018). In recent years, discussions of gamete and embryo donation and wellbeing have focused on the rights of donor conceived people to know their genetic origins. These issues are complex, and unlike in the case of adoption, a donor conceived person is raised by parents where one may be a genetic parent – for example a heterosexual couple who conceive via egg donation and the male partner's sperm – and one may be the

DOI: 10.4324/9781003358756-27

gestational, birthgiving mother. There are many different configurations of families within donor conception, including lesbian and gay parents, solo parents and so on. The emphasis on 'right to knowledge' of their genetic origins has also taken into account the rights of donors, who are not identifiable retrospectively prior to the law changing. Current donors are aware that they are signing up to identity release disclosure when any offspring turn eighteen.

Contemporary technologies challenge the privacy traditionally associated with donation by providing social parents and their offspring the possibility of identifying donors prior to identity release, or for those conceived prior to the identity release law change. This presents numerous practical, ethical and legal issues for consideration: what are the rights of donor conceived people? What ethical considerations are involved when parents investigate who their child's donor is, or who the genetic half siblings are, while they are still in childhood? What are the rights of donors? Previous research has often focused on the connections that donor conception gives rise to, and the effects on constructions of kinship within this new family formation. This chapter will explore the challenge to anonymity in donor conception presented by these technologies and the implications for consent in a donor conception context.

Donor Conception and Anonymity

The prevailing research on donor conception families has primarily focused on understandings of kinship (e.g. Ryan-Flood, 2009), identity (Nordqvist, 2012; Nordqvist & Smart, 2014), and the wellbeing of offspring (Pennings, 2017). In recent years, the importance of access to genetic origins has played a significant part in wider debates about donor conception. Such discussions often cite the rights of adopted people to learn the identities of their birth parents. There is a strong emphasis in the wider literature on the importance of donor conceived people having access to knowledge of their genetic origins. The arguments for this fall into several categories: an analogy with adopted people and their need to know their origins; the right to knowledge of genetic origins for wellbeing in both identity and private life (which also falls into the category of human rights); and health/medical information.

Chestney (2001) explores the analogy of adoption for donor conception. She argues that although the positions of birth parents and adoptive parents in an adoption situation are different to those of gamete donors and recipient parents in donor conception, the experiences of adopted people and donor conceived people have more similarities in that they may experience a longing to know their genetic origins. Chestney ultimately argues that donor identifying information should be provided to offspring, but only for future offspring so that donors will be aware of this before donating. This is because 'extending such a right may more significantly interfere with parental and procreative liberties' if applied retrospectively (2001: 391). She also notes that the 'private nature' of assisted reproduction as compared to adoption is meaningful here and points out that confidentiality in assisted reproduction is regulated by private contract. Finally, she suggests that the law should be guided by 'the best interests of the child', which in her view affirms openness here.

This reflects a broader international trend towards openness in the best interests of the (future) child. In 2014, the state of Victoria in Australia went further and retrospectively opened its gamete (egg and sperm) records retrospectively. This new legislation gave donor conceived adults *and* donors the right to apply for each other's identifying information, which was released to them if the subject of the application consented (Kelly et al., 2018). Interestingly, Kelly et al. (2019) found that some anonymous donors in their research expressed a desire for information about their offspring. They argue that future research should explore the emotional needs of donors further and point out that the perspectives of donors may change over time – from a preference for anonymity to openness to disclosure.

Correia et al. (2021: 70) point out that

> defenders of anonymity stress that the desire to understand the genetic origins of offspring following the use of ART techniques using donors may conflict with other interests, such as maintaining peace and stability within the family in which they are currently integrated in addition to preserving privacy rights of those who have donated genetic material.

This particular approach to the right to anonymity can be criticised for a traditional construction of the family and its dismissal of the meaningfulness of knowledge of genetic origins for many donor conceived people.

Ravitsky (2014: 36) argues in favour of donor identity disclosure as a human right. He claims that it is possible to be 'wronged, without being harmed'. Thus, while there is some variation among donor conceived people about their personal reaction to the circumstances of their conception, even those who do not feel harmed by any secrecy surrounding it, may still be wronged by being denied access to knowledge of their genetic origins. This perspective again emphasises the rights of donor conceived people to have access to the donors' identity.

However, there is also considerable international variation in policies around anonymity, including in countries that otherwise share many legal similarities, such as within the European Union for example. So despite the growing tendency to remove anonymity, cross national differences remain. There are many critics of the approach that emphasises the right to knowledge of donor identity as a human right. Ravelingien & Pennings (2013) point out that the right to know one's genetic origin would potentially apply not only to donor conceived people but also to all people with misattributed paternity. In order to apply this, they suggest – somewhat humorously – that this would require paternity tests to be administered to ALL children at birth. They also argue that in 'open-identity donation policies [...] disclosure of the conception circumstances is [...] a moral right, but donor conceived offspring are granted a legal right to information about their donor' (Ravelingien & Pennings, 2013: W7). In other words, recipient parents cannot be compelled to inform their children that they are donor conceived, unless for example this information is recorded on their birth certificate – which is a proposal recommended by some rights advocates.

Some authors also argue strongly in favour of retaining anonymity. This literature suggests that the importance of knowledge of genetic origins (for donor conceived people, not adopted people) is not consistent. They suggest that lifestyle is more significant than medical history for wellbeing for example and people typically retain the lifestyle they grow up in rather than make changes based on genetic history. Thus, Melo-Martín (2014) deconstructs the argument for donor identity disclosure on the basis of the human rights of donor conceived people. She argues that their interests are not adversely affected by lack of access to one's genetic origins. In her view, there is no clear empirical evidence that donor-conceived individuals suffer harm and even if they did, this does not provide sufficient justification to form the basis of a right to knowledge of the donors' identity. In her view:

> The interest that rights proponents want to protect is not an interest in developing a healthy identity but an interest in developing a particular kind of identity, one that conforms to culturally dominant narratives. But, of course, it is not at all obvious that we ought to satisfy one's interest in a particular identity.
>
> *(Melo-Martín, 2014: 33)*

She is critical of the idea that knowledge of one's genetic origins is necessary for a healthy self identity, arguing that this perspective reinforces problematic ideas about genetic essentialism and 'might also encourage problematic beliefs about the superiority of biological families' (Melo-Martín, 2014: 34). Similarly, Turkmendag (2012) argues that: 'By basing its assumptions on an adoption analogy, United Kingdom law ascribes a social meaning to the genetic relatedness between gamete donors and the offspring' (Turkmendag, 2012: 58).

Despite these different perspectives in the bioethics literature and international variation in legislation and policy, increasingly many countries are moving towards openness and donor identity disclosure in relation to donor conception. This is often due to the rights advocacy carried out by donor conceived adults, who have a strong social media presence and engage with policy. In the research presented in this chapter, interviews were carried out with people affected by tracing donors or donor relatives through 'unofficial' channels, such as direct-to-consumer genetic testing, or social media.

Methodology

The project was a qualitative study using in-depth interviews. Twenty-two individuals who self-identify as being affected by donor identity disclosure through either genetic testing or social media, were recruited to take part in individual interviews exploring their experiences. Recruitment took place via donor conception organisation networks and social media. Participants identified across three key groups: donors (n=7); recipient parents (n=6); and donor conceived people (n=13). Four participants identified across more than one category – for example a donor conceived woman who was also a recipient parent. The interviews covered a range of topics in relation to donor conception, including the experience of searching for a donor and post donor identification contact. Interviews were analysed using a narrative analysis approach to explore personal subjective experiences related to emergent themes.

Late Discovery of Donor Conception Status

Many of the donor conceived people interviewed, only found out about their method of conception when they signed up to a DNA testing site, such as ancestry.co.uk. The realisation that one of their parents was not a genetic parent, typically came as a huge shock. They described this experience as leading to a questioning of their identity and creating a need to find out who the donor was. For example, Jeffrey, a donor conceived man who found out via genetic testing in his early thirties, describes this experience:

> 'They [parents] sat me down and told me, it's like, "well, if you were to do a DNA test, [...] you wouldn't be on there either because you're both donor conceived". And it was, it's a monumental shock. I think I can divide my life up into all the time up until that moment and then everything, all the time since then. And the past four years have been this extraordinary journey of me trying to rebuild a sense of identity. I kind of didn't know who half of me was at that point. You have such a sense of how nature and nurture works from who your mum and dad are – I'm that person plus that person. That's the mathematics of me. And suddenly, none of that... I was missing half of the equation.'
>
> *(Jeffrey, DCP who traced donor and donor siblings via DNA testing)*

Through DNA testing, Jeffrey also made contact with seven donor half-siblings. They formed a WhatsApp chat group and meet every few months. Ultimately, he made the decision to try to find his donor. For those conceived before 2005, the donor's identity was not available and DNA testing offered the only way of finding out who the donor was. Jeffrey was able to do this by extensive research using both the ancestry website and social media. Although the closest relative to his donor who had signed up to ancestry was a third cousin, Jeffrey was able to narrow down the possibilities as he knew that it was someone who had been a medical student in London during the early 1980s. He describes the painstaking research it took to find the donor's identity in this way:

'That work has an element to it where you feel a bit voyeuristic. [...] It's not like you're kind of Sherlock Holmes solving a mystery, it's more like you're a slightly creepy sort of internet stalker. And that's a real thing to grapple with [...] and especially when you're dealing with the kind of living branches of this tree, these are real people out there in the world and you're poking around for their, I don't know, their place of birth, because that might give you a clue to this bit of the family tree, or you're dipping your toes into these really kind of unpleasant things. You know, the internet is full of these anonymous people who are kind of going through all your details and looking for my biological father turned me into one of those people a bit. And I kind of resent it. I resent having to become... feeling like I have to become this voyeuristic person prying into other people's information, other people's lives.'

(Jeffrey, DCP who traced donor and donor siblings via DNA testing)

In the excerpt above, Jeffrey expresses a sense of being demeaned by having to trace donors in this way. He felt strongly that he had both a need for and a right to this information about his genetic background but was also conscious that the donor had been given assurances of anonymity, which were now being undermined. This is a difficult scenario for those who were born prior to the current legislation that provides the donor's identity when the donor conceived person turns eighteen. Donor conceived people in this situation are forced to consider their own needs and possible right to knowledge, in relation to the donor's preference for and expectation of anonymity.

Tracing Donors or Donor Siblings Before the Age of Eighteen

A significant finding of the research was that even where donor identity disclosure at eighteen existed, some donors or donor siblings were traced earlier in the life of the donor conceived person. For example, some recipient parents felt that it was in the best interests of their child to be in contact with half siblings by the same donor earlier in life, as this would make any meeting with them less awkward. Many of these parents were members of social media support and information groups that advocated for openness about donor conception and meetings between donor siblings. Being exposed to these ideas through these groups, opened them to both the possibility of tracing their child's genetic half-siblings and made them more inclined to do so:

'So I'm part of lots and lots of different online forums. Some are a bit overwhelming, some not, some are so incredibly useful. And all the donor conceived adults that I have heard on podcasts and in interviews have said that they wished that their parents had started looking for their donor siblings earlier. And some clinics and some sperm banks seem to facilitate recipient parents, if they both agree, them getting in contact. Which for me is the safest and the most logical way of doing it, but not all of them do it and the [sperm bank] don't. [...] So I was trying to unpick what [...] is the best for my son. So in April last year, after being awake all night worrying about it, I'd joined the Facebook group that was specifically for the [sperm bank]. [...] And then suddenly in the autumn last year, I got a match. And again, it was, I felt like it was absolutely the most, like a life changing moment that you couldn't go back on, that suddenly I had found my son's half brother.'

(Jane, recipient parent via sperm donor)

Another recipient parent, Maria, describes being in contact with the mother of her son's donor sibling, who lives in a different country:

'She's shared an enormous amount of personal information with me. So [...] we've talked quite a lot about personal, about ourselves as well, which is quite nice [...]. And she shared quite a lot about her son. And we chat regularly [...] she did say to me that she wants to teach her son English and [...] so improve hers and teach her son English so that he could communicate with my son when he's a bit older, which I thought was really lovely. And it was that looking forward... Because it is so strange forming a relationship with somebody who you have no, you just have no idea who they are, but you share something really, really precious with them.'

(Maria, recipient parent via sperm donor)

Both of these recipient parents viewed finding their child's donor siblings as a major step that was initially daunting to take. They put a lot of thought into whether this was the right decision and researched stories from donor conceived people about this. Ultimately, they felt that it was in the best interests of their child to make these connections. Social media facilitated this. This is a growing trend. Some clinics recognise this and have taken the step of not providing fertility patients with the donor clinic number, or by requiring them to sign a form indicating that they will not try to trace the donor or siblings in this way. Yet much work needs to be done to indicate whether keeping siblings apart is in fact in anyone's best interests. If parents are open to it, then perhaps this contact could be facilitated. A key issue however is that if parents make this decision, then they are taking that choice away from children – whether to make contact or not.

A sperm donor who participated in the study, Gerald, donated some years ago at a time when he had no children of his own. Subsequently he became both a stepfather and a parent with his now wife. He was not signed up to ancestry, but a cousin of his father reached out to him because she matched with someone on the site and struggled to figure out how she might be related. Gerald was shocked to discover that the match was a donor conceived child who was nine at the time:

My dad's cousin contacted me in 2020. She was on Ancestry. And she said to me[...] "there's somebody on here. I don't know who it is." [...] And at the time it didn't register with me. You know, I said, I don't know who that is. To be honest with you, I thought it was maybe a sibling. I could have a half sibling with my dad. [...] But then my dad tested and I uploaded his stuff onto Ancestry. And I noticed this match and it had a match as a close relative, first cousin, but I could tell by the centimorgans it was too high. [...] And then I just thought, I wonder if it's a donor child. And I looked, I put it on the DNA painter and it said, you know, 75% chance of grandparent or grandchild. [...]. So [...] it came back as yeah, the child was donor conceived. [...] It was obviously, the mother was shocked. [...] the child that always known she was donor conceived, but she'd expressed an interest in knowing the donor and any siblings. So then she got tested in 2020. So she was only nine then.

R: So her mom uploaded her DNA?

G: Yeah. Which I didn't think was possible.

(Gerald, sperm donor)

Although Gerald had signed up for donor identity disclosure and was open to contact with offspring when they turned eighteen, it had not occurred to him that he might be traced when they were much younger. He wanted to behave ethically and respond appropriately but was unsure as there was no practical guidance available around this unique scenario. He agreed with the child's mother to email with the child to respond to any questions she might have.

R: And what has that correspondence been like?

G: Strange. It is strange for me. It must be strange for her as well. You know, I've sent her pictures. She's got pictures of me. She's got pictures of her siblings. She sent me pictures of her as well. Yeah. So obviously she's an 11-year-old girl, isn't she? You know, she wants to tell me about her pets and stuff like that and what she's doing at school. But then she also wants to know things about me. And, you know, I was a very big runner one time. I used to do lots of races and marathons and stuff like that. So, you know, she knows all about that. And she says, "well, I've not got that." You know, "I didn't get that gene." You know, and she's like asking me things, you know. What am I like? And, you know, some things that she's good at. Am I like that? What do I like? And, you know, some sort of things. She wants to know about her siblings as well.

(Gerald, sperm donor)

Although he was committed to doing the right thing, the lack of advice available surrounding the scenario caused him some concern. It also created complexities in his own life. In accordance with the discourse of openness that now dominates donor conception in the UK, he told his stepchildren and children about their donor sibling so that this would not come as a shock to them or create difficulties later. However, he struggled to explain this relationship to his children:

'You know, because even my son the other day, I was talking to him about the donor child. And I said that she's your sister. You know, he said, "No, she's not". So I said, well, no, she is, you know. And then he said, "Yeah, but you're not related to her dad". So I said, well, yeah, I'm a bio [father]. And he said, "Well, what? You married her mother?" [laughs] But I feel that I want to just keep talking to them. And then it just becomes a normal thing to them. Oh, we know we've got. Yeah. And they've seen a picture of her as well of the donor child [...] And when I got with [stepson's] mother, he was only very young. He was only 15 months old. So [...] I'm the only dad that's ever been. [...] I think it's hard for him. You know, as well, because he said to me, "Oh, well, does that make her my step-sister?" You think, oh, my God, you know, it's so complicated.'

(Gerald, sperm donor)

These experiences highlight the growing need for greater recognition of the realities of donor conception in the era of direct to consumer genetic testing and social media. The dramatic social policy shift from emphasis on secrecy and anonymity to openness is framed as in a child's best interests. However, it fails to take account of both retrospective tracing of those who donated prior to 2005 and early tracing of donors before children turn eighteen.

Conclusion – Challenging Consent?

This research illustrates that it is no longer possible to guarantee anonymity for donors. Direct to consumer genetic testing has transformed the landscape of donor conception. Although many countries now advocate openness in relation to donor identity from a rights-based perspective, this typically only applies when the donor has agreed to this. However, the principle of anonymity can now be contravened via DNA testing without the donor's consent. Even in countries where donor conceived people are able to access the donor's identity at the age of eighteen, donors can be traced when recipient parents upload their child's DNA to a genetic testing site. More commonly, recipient parents are finding their children's donor siblings and creating connections in the absence of a legal framework that facilitates this prior to the child reaching adulthood. This raises important questions about consent. Are donors' right to privacy being violated? Do the rights of donor conceived people to knowledge of their genetic origins trump donors' rights in this scenario? Are donor conceived children whose recipient parents trace either their donor siblings or their donors on their behalf being unwittingly opened up to connections that they may prefer not to have if left to decide for themselves, in ways that compromise their consent? This research illustrates that when these decisions are made, they are not done lightly and that respective parties do consider different perspectives. In fact, participants typically agonised over the best way forward and were very sensitive to the complexities for all involved. So what does this reveal about consent? Firstly, consent may change and transform over time. A donor who agrees to anonymity or later disclosure of identity may be open to contact. Recipient parents may find that they are open to creating connections between donor siblings that they assumed or initially preferred would be kept separate. Donor conceived people may be open to early contact. Of course, the opposite for all of these may be true too. Secondly, it is only through listening to the experiences and perspectives of these different interested parties that ethically informed laws, policies and practices can be created. This inevitably means grappling with complex scenarios that may require one person's consent – such as a donor conceived person's preference for knowledge of their genetic origins – to supercede another's, such as the donor who wishes to retain anonymity. Legislation is only one means of recognising these complexities. Finally, contemporary technologies have already profoundly altered the context of donor conception and the possibilities – consensual or otherwise – within which these connections occur.

References

Chestney, E. S. (2001). The right to know one's genetic origin: Can, should, or must a state that extends this right to adoptees extend an analogous right to children conceived with donor gametes. *Texas Law Review*, 80, 365.

Correia, M., Rego, G., & Nunes, R. (2021). The right to be forgotten versus the right to disclosure of gamete donors' ID: Ethical and legal considerations. *Acta Bioethica*, 27 (1), 69–78.

Kelly, F., Dempsey, D., & Authority, R. T. (2018). *The History of Donor Conception Records in Victoria*. A report prepared for the Victorian Assisted Reproductive Treatment Authority. VARTA, Melbourne.

Kelly, F., Dempsey, D., Power, J., Bourne, K., Hammarberg, K., & Johnson, L. (2019). From stranger to family or something in between: Donor linking in an era of retrospective access to anonymous sperm donor records in Victoria, Australia. *International Journal of Law, Policy and the Family*, 33(3), 277–297.

Melo-Martín, I. D. (2014). The ethics of anonymous gamete donation: Is there a right to know one's genetic origins?. *Hastings Center Report*, 44(2), 28–35.

Nordqvist, P. (2012). Origins and originators: Lesbian couples negotiating parental identities and sperm donor conception. *Culture, Health & Sexuality*, 14 (3), 297–311.

Nordqvist, P., & Smart, C. (2014). *Relative Strangers: Family Life, Genes and Donor Conception*. Springer.

Pennings, G. (2017). Disclosure of donor conception, age of disclosure and the well-being of donor offspring. *Human Reproduction*, 32(5), 969–973.

Ravelingien, A. & Pennings, G. (2013) On the right to know and the use of double standards: Response to open peer commentaries on "The right to know your genetic parents: From open identity gamete donation to routine paternity testing", *The American Journal of Bioethics*, 13(5), W6–W8.

Ravitsky, V. (2014). Autonomous choice and the right to know one's genetic origins. *Hastings Center Report*, 44(2), 36–37.

Ryan-Flood, R. (2009) *Lesbian Motherhood: Gender, Families and Sexual Citizenship*. Basingstoke: Palgrave.

Ryan-Flood, R. & Gunnarsson-Payne, J. (eds) (2018) *Transnationalising Reproduction: Third Party Conception in a Globalised World*. London: Routledge.

Turkmendag, I. (2012). The donor-conceived child's 'right to personal identity': The public debate on donor anonymity in the United Kingdom. *Journal of Law and Society*, 39(1), 58–75.

INDEX